Human Resources 12/13
Twenty-First Edition

EDITOR

Fred H. Maidment
Western Connecticut State University

Dr. Fred Maidment is professor of management at Western Connecticut State University in Danbury, Connecticut. He received his bachelor's degree from New York University and his master's degree from the Bernard M. Baruch College of the City University of New York. In 1983 Dr. Maidment received his doctorate from the University of South Carolina. In addition, he did post-doctoral work at the Warrington College of Business of the University of Florida where he was a Resident Scholar. He resides in Connecticut with his wife.

Connect
Learn
Succeed™

Connect
Learn
Succeed™

ANNUAL EDITIONS: HUMAN RESOURCES, TWENTY-FIRST EDITION

Published by McGraw-Hill, a business unit of The McGraw-Hill Companies, Inc., 1221 Avenue of the Americas, New York, NY 10020. Copyright © 2013 by The McGraw-Hill Companies, Inc. All rights reserved. Printed in the United States of America. Previous editions © 2012, 2011, 2010, and 2009. No part of this publication may be reproduced or distributed in any form or by any means, or stored in a database or retrieval system, without the prior written consent of The McGraw-Hill Companies, Inc., including, but not limited to, in any network or other electronic storage or transmission, or broadcast for distance learning.

Some ancillaries, including electronic and print components, may not be available to customers outside the United States.

This book is printed on acid-fee paper.

Annual Editions® is a registered trademark of The McGraw-Hill Companies, Inc.

Annual Editions is published by the **Contemporary Learning Series** group within the McGraw-Hill Higher Education division.

1 2 3 4 5 6 7 8 9 0 QDB/QDB 1 0 9 8 7 6 5 4 3 2

ISBN: 978-0-07-352871-7
MHID: 0-07-352871-4
ISSN: 1092-6577 (print)
ISSN: 2159-1008 (online)

Managing Editor: *Larry Loeppke*
Developmental Editor II: *Dave Welsh*
Permissions Coordinator: *Rita Hingtgen*
Senior Marketing Communications Specialist: *Mary Klein*
Senior Project Manager: *Joyce Watters*
Design Coordinator: *Margarite Reynolds*
Cover Designer: *Studio Montage, St. Louis, Missouri*
Buyer: *Susan K. Culbertson*
Media Project Manager: *Sridevi Palani*

Compositor: Laserwords Private Limited
Cover Image Credits: Mash/Getty Images (inset); Tetra Images/Corbis (background)

Editors/Academic Advisory Board

Members of the Academic Advisory Board are instrumental in the final selection of articles for each edition of ANNUAL EDITIONS. Their review of articles for content, level, and appropriateness provides critical direction to the editors and staff. We think that you will find their careful consideration well reflected in this volume.

ANNUAL EDITIONS: Human Resources 12/13
21st Edition

EDITOR

Fred H. Maidment
Western Connecticut State University

Preface

In publishing ANNUAL EDITIONS we recognize the enormous role played by the magazines, newspapers, and journals of the public press in providing current, first-rate educational information in a broad spectrum of interest areas. Many of these articles are appropriate for students, researchers, and professionals seeking accurate, current material to help bridge the gap between principles and theories and the real world. These articles, however, become more useful for study when those of lasting value are carefully collected, organized, indexed, and reproduced in a low-cost format, which provides easy and permanent access when the material is needed. That is the role played by ANNUAL EDITIONS.

The environment for human resource management is constantly changing. The events of September 11, 2001, as well as the current economic recession, are providing human resource professionals with challenges unmatched in recent memory. This challenging environment is one that is likely to be with human resource managers for a long time to come as the economy and the world are likely to remain in a continuing and accelerating pace of change. HR professionals will be in the front lines of those addressing these changes because they will be involved in dealing with the problems and opportunities presented by this rapidly changing environment. Meeting those challenges will be the task human resource managers will face in the future, and this task will play a key factor in the success of any organization.

Management must respond to these forces in many ways, not the least of which is the effort to keep current with the various developments in the field. The 40 articles that have been chosen for *Annual Editions: Human Resources 12/13* reflect an outstanding cross-section of the current topics in the field. This volume addresses the various components of HRM (human resource management) from compensation, training, and discipline to international implications for the worker and the employer. Articles have been chosen from leading business magazines such as *Bloomberg Business Week,* and journals such as *Training and Development, HR Magazine,* and *The Journal of Business Ethics* to provide a wide sampling of the latest thinking in the field of human resources.

Annual Editions: Human Resources 12/13 contains a number of features designed to be useful for people interested in human resource management. These features include a Table of Contents with short descriptions that summarize each article, including bold italicized key ideas and a Topic Guide to locate articles on specific subjects. The volume is organized into seven units each dealing with specific interrelated topics in human resources. Every unit begins with an overview that provides background information for the articles in the section. This will enable the reader to place the selection in the context of the larger issues concerning human resources. Important topics are emphasized and key points that address major themes are presented. Appropriate websites are also provided to the reader for further study and exploration, as well as a new feature: discussion questions after each article to help the student in reading and understanding the material. In addition, there is a list of websites for the student to explore for additional information and instruction.

This is the twenty-first edition of *Annual Editions: Human Resources.* It is hoped that many more will follow, addressing these important issues. We believe that the collection is the most complete and useful compilation of current material available to the human resource management student. We would like to have your response to the volume, for we are interested in your opinions and recommendations. Any book can be improved, and we need your help to continue to improve *Annual Editions: Human Resources.*

Fred H. Maidment
Editor

The Annual Editions Series

VOLUMES AVAILABLE

Adolescent Psychology
Aging
American Foreign Policy
American Government
Anthropology
Archaeology
Assessment and Evaluation
Business Ethics
Child Growth and Development
Comparative Politics
Criminal Justice
Developing World
Drugs, Society, and Behavior
Dying, Death, and Bereavement
Early Childhood Education
Economics
Educating Children with Exceptionalities
Education
Educational Psychology
Entrepreneurship
Environment
The Family
Gender
Geography
Global Issues
Health
Homeland Security

Human Development
Human Resources
Human Sexualities
International Business
Management
Marketing
Mass Media
Microbiology
Multicultural Education
Nursing
Nutrition
Physical Anthropology
Psychology
Race and Ethnic Relations
Social Problems
Sociology
State and Local Government
Sustainability
Technologies, Social Media, and Society
United States History, Volume 1
United States History, Volume 2
Urban Society
Violence and Terrorism
Western Civilization, Volume 1
World History, Volume 1
World History, Volume 2
World Politics

Contents

UNIT 1
Human Resource Management in Perspective

Unit Overview   xx

Part A. Human Resource Management in Perspective

The concepts in bold italics are developed in the article. For further expansion, please refer to the Topic Guide.

UNIT 2
Meeting Human Resource Requirements

The concepts in bold italics are developed in the article. For further expansion, please refer to the Topic Guide.

UNIT 3
Creating a Productive Work Environment

UNIT 4
Developing Effective Human Resources

The concepts in bold italics are developed in the article. For further expansion, please refer to the Topic Guide.

UNIT 5
Implementing Compensation, Benefits, and Workplace Safety

The concepts in bold italics are developed in the article. For further expansion, please refer to the Topic Guide.

UNIT 6
Fostering Employee/Management Relationships

The concepts in bold italics are developed in the article. For further expansion, please refer to the Topic Guide.

UNIT 7
International Human Resource Management

The concepts in bold italics are developed in the article. For further expansion, please refer to the Topic Guide.

The concepts in bold italics are developed in the article. For further expansion, please refer to the Topic Guide.

Correlation Guide

The *Annual Editions* series provides students with convenient, inexpensive access to current, carefully selected articles from the public press. **Annual Editions: Human Resources 12/13** is an easy-to-use reader that presents articles on important topics such as *employee hiring, retention, and compensation, labor unions, outsourcing,* and many more. For more information on *Annual Editions* and other *McGraw-Hill Contemporary Learning Series* titles, visit www.mhhe.**com/cls.**

This convenient guide matches the units in **Annual Editions: Human Resources 12/13** with the corresponding chapters in four of our best-selling McGraw-Hill Human Resource textbooks by Noe et al., Bernardin, Cascio, and Ivancevich/Konopaske.

Annual Editions: Human Resources 12/13	Human Resource Management, 8/e by Noe et al.	Human Resource Management, 6/e by Bernardin	Managing Human Resources: Productivity, Quality of Work Life, Profits, 9/e by Cascio	Human Resource Management, 12/e by Ivancevich/ Konopaske
Unit 1: Human Resource Management in Perspective	**Chapter 1:** Human Resource Management: Gaining a Competitive Advantage **Chapter 2:** Strategic Human Resource Management	**Chapter 1:** Strategic Human Resource Management in a Changing Environment	**Chapter 1:** Human Resources in a Globally Competitive Business Environment **Chapter 2:** The Financial Impact of Human Resource Management Activities	**Chapter 1:** Human Resource Management **Chapter 2:** A Strategic Management Approach to Human Resource Management
Unit 2: Meeting Human Resource Requirements	**Chapter 5:** Human Resource Planning and Recruitment **Chapter 6:** Selection and Placement	**Chapter 3:** The Legal Environment of HRM: Equal Employment Opportunity **Chapter 4:** Work Analysis and Design **Chapter 5:** Human Resource Planning and Recruitment	**Chapter 5:** Planning for People **Chapter 6:** Recruiting **Chapter 7:** Staffing	**Chapter 5:** Human Resource Planning **Chapter 6:** Job Analysis and Design **Chapter 7:** Recruitment **Chapter 8:** Selecting Effective Employees
Unit 3: Creating a Productive Work Environment	**Chapter 7:** Training **Chapter 8:** Performance Management **Chapter 9:** Employee Development	**Chapter 4:** Work Analysis and Design **Chapter 7:** Performance Management and Appraisal **Chapter 8:** Training and Development **Chapter 9:** Career Development	**Chapter 8:** Workplace Training **Chapter 9:** Performance Management **Chapter 10:** Managing Careers **Chapter 11:** Pay and Incentive Systems	**Chapter 9:** Performance Evaluation and Management **Chapter 13:** Training and Development **Chapter 14:** Career Planning and Development
Unit 4: Developing Effective Human Resources	**Chapter 7:** Training **Chapter 8:** Performance Management **Chapter 9:** Employee Development	**Chapter 6:** Personnel Selection **Chapter 7:** Performance Management and Appraisal **Chapter 8:** Training and Development **Chapter 9:** Career Development	**Chapter 8:** Workplace Training **Chapter 9:** Performance Management **Chapter 10:** Managing Careers	**Chapter 9:** Performance Evaluation and Management **Chapter 13:** Training and Development **Chapter 14:** Career Planning and Development
Unit 5: Implementing Compensation, Benefits, and Workplace Safety	**Chapter 11:** Pay Structure Decisions **Chapter 12:** Recognizing Employee Contributions with Pay **Chapter 13:** Employee Benefits	**Chapter 3:** The Legal Environment of HRM: Equal Employment Opportunity **Chapter 10:** Compensation: Base Pay and Fringe Benefits **Chapter 11:** Rewarding Performance	**Chapter 11:** Pay and Incentive Systems **Chapter 12:** Indirect Compensation: Employee Benefit Plans **Chapter 15:** Safety, Health, and Employee Assistance Programs	**Chapter 10:** Compensation: An Overview **Chapter 11:** Compensation: Methods and Policies **Chapter 12:** Employee Benefits and Services **Chapter 17:** Promoting Safety and Health
Unit 6: Fostering Employee/ Management Relationships	**Chapter 14:** Collective Bargaining and Labor Relations	**Chapter 7:** Performance Management and Appraisal	**Chapter 9:** Performance Management **Chapter 14:** Procedural Justice and Ethics in Employee Relations	**Chapter 9:** Performance Evaluation and Management **Chapter 15:** Labor Relations and Collective Bargaining
Unit 7: International Human Resource Management	**Chapter 15:** Managing Human Resources Globally	**Chapter 2:** The Role of Globalization in HR Policy and Practice	**Chapter 1:** Human Resources in a Globally Competitive Business Environment **Chapter 16:** International Dimensions of Human Resource Management	**Chapter 4:** Global Human Resource Management

Topic Guide

This topic guide suggests how the selections in this book relate to the subjects covered in your course. You may want to use the topics listed on these pages to search the Web more easily.

On the following pages a number of websites Have been gathered specifically for this book. They are arranged to reflect the units of this Annual Editions reader. You can link to these sites by going to www.mhhe.com/cls

All the articles that relate to each topic are listed below the bold-faced term.

Americans with Disabilities Act

6. HR Plays Pivotal Role in Adapting Policies to ADA Amendments Act Rules
7. Is Everyone Disabled under The ADA? An Analysis of the Recent Amendments and Guidance for Employers

Benefits

1. Are You a Leader or a Laggard?: HR's Role in Creating a Sustainability Culture
2. Building Sustainable Organizations: The Human Factor
21. Bonus and Incentive Compensation Awards—Navigating Section 409A, $1 Million Limit, and Golden Parachute Rules
23. The Politics of Executive Pay
26. Demystifying Health Reform Legislation
27. Making Benefits Matter
28. Ways to Phase Retirement
32. Sharing Work— and Unemployment Benefits
37. Trends Facing Tomorrow's World: Forces in the Natural and Institutional World
38. Offshored Headquarters
39. Multiple Choice

Blue-collar jobs

15. Rewarding Outstanding Performance: Don't Break the Bank
17. Your Co-Worker, Your Teacher: Collaborative Technology Speeds Peer-Peer Learning
19. The Broken Psychological Contract: Job Insecurity and Coping
20. Where Have All the High-Paying Jobs Gone?
22. Opening Keynote: Rethinking Pay for Performance
24. Putting the Hurt On
25. Workplace Bullying Threatens Employers
31. The Expanding Role of Temporary Help Services from 1990 to 2008
32. Sharing Work—and Unemployment Benefits
35. Global Outsourcing
37. Trends Shaping Tomorrow's World: Forces in the Natural and Institutional Environment
40. Business Is Booming

Business ethics

2. Building Sustainable Organizations: The Human Factor
3. The Leadership Challenges Facing HR: Top CHROs Share Learnings and Advice on What's Next
6. HR Plays Pivotal Role in Adapting Policies to ADA Amendments Act Rules
7. Is Everyone Disabled under the ADA? An Analysis of the Recent Amendments and Guidance for Employers
8. The "Equal Opportunity Harasser": The Slow Demise of a Strange Concept
12. Playing IT Big Brother: When Is Employee Monitoring Warranted?
18. Strategic Organizational Diversity: A Model?
19. The Broken Psychological Contract: Job Insecurity and Coping
20. Where Have All the High-Paying Jobs Gone?
21. Bonus and Incentive Compensation Awards—Navigating Section 409A, $1 Million Limit, and Golden Parachute Rules
22. Opening Keynote: Rethinking Pay for Performance
23. The Politics of Executive Pay
25. Workplace Bullying Threatens Employers
29 Finding and Fixing Corporate Misconduct

30. Harassment Goes Viral—What Can HR Do to Prevent It?
33. Fighting the Good Fight
34. Strategic Human Resource Management as Ethical Stewardship
35. Global Outsourcing
40. Business is Booming

Communication

1. Are You a Leader or a Laggard?: HR's Role Creating a Sustainability Culture
2. Building Sustainable Organizations: The Human Factor
3. The Leadership Challenges Facing HR: Top CHROs Share Learnings and Advice on What's Next
5. Engaged Employees = High-Performing Organizations
6. HR Plays Pivotal Role in Adapting Policies to ADA Amendments Act Rules
12. Playing IT Big Brother: When Is Employee Monitoring Warranted?
13. Make Your HR Portal a Destination Location
16. Employers Use Facebook Too, for Hiring
17. Your Co-Worker, Your Teacher: Collaborative Technology Speeds Peer-Peer Learning
19. The Broken Psychological Contract: Job Insecurity and Coping
25. Workplace Bullying Threatens Employers
29. Finding and Fixing Corporate Misconduct
30. Harassment Goes Viral—What Can HR Do to Prevent It?
33. Fighting the Good Fight
34. Strategic Human Resource Management as Ethical Stewardship
38. Offshored Headquarters
39. Multiple Choice
40. Business Is Booming

Corporate strategy and human resources

1. Are You a Leader or a Laggard?: HR's Role Creating a Sustainability Culture.
2. Building Sustainable Organizations: The Human Factor
3. The Leadership Challenges Facing HR: Top CHROs Share Learnings and Advice on What's Next
4. Grooming the Next Generation
5. Engaged Employees = High-Performing Organizations
10. Internships and Federal Law: Are Interns Employees?
11. Hiring Right
16. Employers Use Facebook Too, for Hiring
18. Strategic Organizational Diversity: A Model?
19. The Broken Psychological Contract: Job Insecurity and Coping
20. Where Have All the High-Paying Jobs Gone?
22. Opening Keynote: Rethinking Pay for Performance
24. Putting the Hurt On
25. Workplace Bullying Threatens Employers
26. Demystifying Health Reform Legislation
27. Making Benefits Matter
28. Ways to Phase Retirement
29. Finding and Fixing Corporate Misconduct
30. Harassment Goes Viral—What Can HR Do to Prevent It?
31. The Expanding Role of Temporary Help Services from 1990 to 2008
34. Strategic Human Resource Management as Ethical Stewardship

Internet References

The following Internet sites have been selected to support the articles found in this reader. These sites were available at the time of publication. However, because websites often change their structure and content, the information listed may no longer be available. We invite you to visit www.mhhe.com/cls for easy access to these sites.

Annual Editions: Human Resources 12/13

General Sources

Accountantsworld.com
www.accountantsworld.com

An online site dedicated to the field of accounting. Also included in the site are links to financial resources, including business, careers, e-commerce, insurance, and human resources.

American Psychological Association
www.apa.org

This site contains important information on workplace topics including revitalization of business and restructuring.

Bureau of Labor Statistics
http://stats.bls.gov

The home page of the Bureau of Labor Statistics (BLS), an agency of the U.S. Department of Labor, offers sections that include Economy at a Glance, Keyword Searches, Surveys and Programs, other statistical sites, and much more.

HRM Guide
www.hrmguide.com

This is a resources for a selection of articles on human resource management for the student.

National Bureau of Economic Research Home Page
www.nber.org

The National Bureau of Economic Research does specialized research on every aspect of economics. These projects include, but are not limited to, pricing, labor studies, economics of aging, and productivity.

Society for Human Resource Management (SHRM)
www.shrm.org

SHRM is the world's largest association devoted to human resource management. Its mission is to serve the needs of HR professionals by providing essential and comprehensive resources. At this site, you'll find updates on methods, laws, and events as well as career information.

United States Department of Labor
www.dol.gov

This site provides a wealth of information on a number of labor-management issues. It has statutory as well as regulatory information and more.

United States Small Business Administration
www.sba.gov

The Small Business Administration encourages the establishment and development of small businesses through subsidized loans, business advice, and other forms of assistance.

UNIT 1: Human Resource Management in Perspective

About.com
http://humanresources.about.com

This site provides information regarding employment, management, and success at work.

Human Resources. Com
http://humanresources.com

This is one of the premier sites for job seekers.

National Human Resources Association
http://humanresources.org

The National Human Resources Association (NHRA) is focused on advancing the development and leadership of human resource professionals.

School of Labor and Industrial Relations Hot Links
www.lir.msu.edu

This site is home of one of the world's leading master's degrees in human resources and labor relations. This portal takes you on a virtual tour that describes Michigan State University's graduate curricula and student activities, their lifelong professional education and development programming, their faculty and research, and their alumni relations.

What Is Human Resources?
www.wisegeek.com/what-is-human-resources.htm

This site defines what is human resources and is an excellent site for HR professionals.

UNIT 2: Meeting Human Resource Requirements

Job Recruiting
www.jobrecruiting.com

Excellent site for job searches.

TechAmerica
www.itaa.org

TechAmerica "is a leading voice for the U.S. technology industry worldwide." Their companies "serve as drivers of economic growth and job creation."

UNIT 3: Creating a Productive Work Environment

Blackbaud: Work Environment
www.answers.com/Q/What_is_work_environment

Provides various answers to the question "What is a work environment?"

Creating a Positive, Productive and Successful Work Environment
www.the-success-factor.com/successful_work_environment.htm

Shirley Scott helps people to understand how their thoughts can be examined to better their lives.

Creating a Positive Work Environment
www.mommd.com/positiveworkenvironment.shtml

This site, which is tied to the medical side of employment, gives advice on how to better function in the workplace.

Internet References

Leadership
http://management.about.com/od/leadership/Leadership.htm

This site has a number of articles about becoming a better manager/leader.

UNIT 4: Developing Effective Human Resources

Diversity.com
www.diversity.com

This site "provides best in class recruitment advertising and diversity branding." It also touts itself as "America's most trusted source for recruiting job seekers from diverse ethnic cultures, life styles, life stages, creative persuasions, abilities, religious affiliations and gender."

DiversityInc.com
www.diversityinc.com

DiversityInc is the leading source of information on diversity management. They are a consultancy and publish two web sites, www.DiversityInc.com and www.DiversityIncBestPractices.com, as well as a magazine, published five times a year. They also produce events, which average more than 600 attendees from 200 companies and have featured more than 20 CEOs of major corporations.

Laid-off and Left-out
www.unemployedworkers.org/sites/unemployedworkers/index.php

This grassroots online campaign and informational portal created in 2003 serves jobless workers.

Training Magazine
www.trainingmag.com

This is a professional development magazine that advocates training and workforce development as a business tool.

UNIT 5: Implementing Compensation, Benefits, and Workplace Safety

Benefi tsLink: The National Employee Benefits Website
www.benefitslink.com/index.php

This site's purpose is to support the people who administer, give compliance advice about, design, make policy for, or otherwise are concerned with, employee benefit plans in the United States sponsored by either private or governmental employers.

CNN Money Retirement
www.money.cnn.com/retirement

This site is an excellent source for information on investing.

Executive Pay
www.salary.com/compensation/executive_pay.asp

This site provides information on all things that impact those at executive levels.

Job Stress
http://www.workhealth.org/

This site assembles information about job strain and stress.

UNIT 6: Fostering Employee/Management Relationships

Business Corporate Ethics
www.washingtonpost.com/wp-dyn/business/specials/corporateethics

This site provides timely news updates relating to the business world, including articles on ethics in business.

Corporate Governance
www.corpgov.net

CorpGov.net facilitates the ability of institutional and individual shareowners to better govern corporations, enhancing both corporate accountability and the creation of wealth.

Employee Relations
www.opm.gov/er

This site provides guidance and information on such issues as discipline, misconduct, performance problems, and dispute resolution.

SmartPros Legal & Ethics
http://corporate.smartpros.com/ethics/index.html

This site "is an industry leader in the field of accredited professional education and corporate training."

UNIT 7: International Human Resource Management

Global Trade Information Services
www.gtis.com/english

Corporations, governments, and associations in more than 50 countries use this site's trade data systems to develop an enhanced understanding of global trade information.

Global Trade Watch
www.citizen.org/trade

"Public Citizen's Global Trade Watch seeks to ensure that in this era of globalization, all Americans can enjoy economic security, a clean environment, safe food, medicines and products, access to quality affordable services such as health care and the exercise of democratic decision-making in matters that affect them and their communities."

Global Trading
http://globaltrading.com

This site provides trading-related sites.

Offshoring May Slow Impending US Economic Recovery
http://gbr.pepperdine.edu/093/offshoring1.html

Link to an excellent article on offshoring.

Trade: Outsourcing Job
www.cfr.org/publication/7749/trade.html

This Council on Foreign Relations site provides a variety of information on the subject of job outsourcing.

UNIT 1

Human Resource Management in Perspective

Unit Selections

Learning Outcomes

After reading this Unit, you will be able to:

- Understand the role of Human Resources in the changing, hyper-competitive economy.

- Appreciate the role of Human Resources in building competitive organizations.

- Appreciate the role of Human Resources in developing strategy for corporations.

- Comprehend the loss of skills faced by employers with the impending retirement of the baby boomer generation.

- Understand the importance of the Americans with Disabilities Act and its recent amendments.

- Deal with sexual harassment and be able to protect the organization from lawsuits.

Student Website

www.mhhe.com/cls

Internet References

About.com
http://humanresources.about.com

Human Resources. Com
http://humanresources.com

National Human Resources Association
http://humanresources.org

School of Labor and Industrial Relations Hot Links
www.lir.msu.edu

What is Human Resources
www.wisegeek.com/what-is-human-resources.htm

The only constant is change. Industrial society is dynamic, a great engine that has brought about many of the most significant changes in the history of the human race. Since the start of the Industrial Revolution in England, about 240 years ago, industrialized society has transformed Western civilization in a multitude of ways. Many great inventions of the last 200 years have significantly altered the way people live and the way they see the world.

At the time of the Declaration of Independence, the 13 colonies were an overwhelmingly agricultural society that clung to the Atlantic coast of North America. At the beginning of the twenty-first century, the United States is a continental nation with the world's largest industrial base and perhaps the smallest percentage of farmers of any major industrialized country. These changes did not happen overnight, but were both the result and the cause of the technological innovations of the Industrial Revolution. The technological marvels of today, such as television, radio, computers, airplanes, and automobiles did not exist until after the Industrial Revolution, and a disproportionate number of them did not exist until after 1900.

Along with technological changes have come changes in the ways people earn their living. When Thomas Jefferson authored the Declaration of Independence in 1776, he envisioned a nation of small, independent farmers, but that is not what developed. Factories, mass production, and economies of scale have been the watchwords of industrial development. Industrial development changed not only the economy, but also society. Most Americans are no longer independent farmers, but are, for the most part, wage earners, who make their living by working for someone else.

Changes in the American labor force include the increase in women and minorities working next to white males. The nature of most jobs has changed from those directly associated with production to those providing services in the white-collar economy. Many other changes are developing in the economy and society that will be reflected in the workforce. For the first time since the early days of the republic, international trade represents a significant part of the American economy, having increased greatly in the past 30 years. The economic reality is that the American worker competes not only with other workers in the United States, but also with workers in Europe and Asia.

The society, the economy, and the workforce have changed. Americans today live in a much different world than they did 200 years ago. It is a highly diverse, heterogeneous world, full of paradox. When people think of American industry, they tend to think of giant-sized companies like IBM and General Electric, but in fact, most people work for small firms. The relative importance of the Fortune 500 companies in terms of employment in the economy has been declining both in real and percentage terms. Today, economic growth is with small organizations. Change has brought about not only a different society, but a more complex one. Numerous rules and regulations must be followed that did not exist 200 years ago. The human element in any organization has been critical to its success, and knowing what the human resource needs of the organization are going to be one, five, or even 10 years into the future is a key element for continuing success.

Individual decisions have also changed. In the first part of the twentieth century, it was common for a worker to spend his or her

entire life with one organization, doing one particular job. Now the worker can expect to do many different jobs, probably with a number of different organizations in different industries. Mergers, technological change, and economic fluctuations all put a premium on individual adaptability in a changing work environment for individual economic survival.

The changes in industrial society often come at a faster rate than most people are willing to either accept or adapt to. Many old customs and prejudices have been retained from prior times, and while progress has been made with regard to certain groups—no American employer today would dare to end an employment notice with the letters "NINA" (No Irish Need Apply), as was common at one time—for other groups, the progress has been slow at best. Women now represent over half of American workers but they are paid only about 70% of what men earn, and sexual harassment still represents a problem for both men and women, as discussed in "The 'Equal Opportunity Harasser': The Slow Demise of a Strange Concept."

African Americans and other minorities have been discriminated against for centuries in American society, to the point where the federal government has been forced to step in and legislate equal opportunity, both on and off the job. People with disabilities have also sought protection, and those protections have recently been enhanced as seen in "HR Plays a Pivotal Role in Adapting Policies to ADA Amendment Act Rules" and "Is Everyone Disabled Under the ADA? An Analysis of the Recent Amendments and Guidance for Employers."

The clash of differing cultures seems ever more pronounced in our society. America has traditionally viewed itself as a *melting pot,* but it is clear that certain groups have historically "melted" more easily than others, a situation that is reflected in the workplace. This is uniquely reflected today because, for the first time, there are four generations working side by side in the workplace, This is something new to industrial America. The prior experience has always been one of attempting to blend workers from different cultures and backgrounds. While this has not been easy, it is something with which industry is familiar. Attempting to deal with the needs, wants, perceptions, desires, and attitudes of four different generations on top of the historic problems of dealing with workers from different ethnic and cultural backgrounds makes the problem more complex.

Human resource management plays an important role in industrial America. Business leaders recognize the value of their employees to the future of their organizations. Increasingly, competition in world markets is becoming based on the skills and abilities of people, not machines. Indeed, among major competitors, virtually everyone has essentially the same equipment.

The difference is often what the people in the organization do with the equipment. Knowledge workers have become the ones in demand that will provide the competitive advantage for organizations in this new environment as discussed in "Grooming the Next Generation." One of the more interesting aspects of this is the role of the baby boomer generation. On one hand, these workers are being ushered out the door by some organizations looking to decrease their costs by replacing them with younger, usually less expensive workers. On the other hand, some organizations are looking to try to find ways to encourage these workers to stay on because they have a wealth of knowledge that will be walking out the door when they retire. Finally, the baby boomers themselves are split between those who want to retire, those who can retire, those who cannot afford to retire, and those who do not want to retire, none of which are mutually exclusive.

The American society and economy, as well as the very life of the average American worker, are different from what they were 200 or even 100 years ago, and both the workers and the organizations that employ them must respond to those changes.

Are You a Leader or a Laggard?

HR's Role in Creating a Sustainability Culture

Human Resources Management (HRM)—function, practices and systems—may be missing the next source of real competitive advantage. Leading and facilitating sustainability initiatives and creating a sustainability culture are the critical tasks confronting human resources professionals now. HRM, particularly in the specific practices impacting recruiting, hiring, training, compensation, knowledge management and development, holds tremendous opportunity to shape the firm's sustainability agenda.

ROBERT SROUFE, JAY LIEBOWITZ, AND NAGARAJ SIVASUBRAMANIAM

We find an immediate need for understanding the possibilities of transformation to a sustainable organization, and the range and type of actionable practices suitable for HRM and HR professionals. A small number of firms, including industry leaders like Nike and Starbucks, have recognized the emerging paradigm of sustainability and have taken steps to make sustainability a central component of their strategy (Epstein, 2008). Despite the increasing clamor for more sustainable business practices from multiple stakeholders, many firms are reluctant to move quickly, due possibly to a lack of understanding of policies and actions leading to sustainability.

We are concerned that HR professionals may be missing an opportunity to develop and capture unique resources and competencies that customers will value and the competition will find difficult to imitate. Instead, they find themselves waiting to see what emerges, as firms transition out of an emphasis on compliance and pollution prevention activities to those in which social and environmental impacts will be the basis of strategic opportunities and competitive advantage.

Our Investigation

We focus on two primary questions: (1) How do firms organize and manage themselves to promote and integrate new sustainability initiatives, and (2) How do HR practices influence a firm's ability to integrate and collaborate on a myriad of emerging sustainability-focused business practices? Our analysis of both quantitative and qualitative data helped us to:

- uncover three distinct types of firms integrating sustainability activities into the work place;
- identify three primary obstacles to implementing sustainability initiatives;

- develop strategies for overcoming these obstacles to implementation; and
- propose a stairway to sustainable opportunities for HR to take a leadership role.

Sustainable practices are those that go beyond process improvement and waste reduction (typically found in the operational approaches of the past), and focus on developing innovative social and environmental practices that promote collaborative efforts across functions, create unique social capital and build long-term economic value for the firm. A dominant theory in the literature, the resource-based view of the firm, stipulates that companies can gain sustainable competitive advantages if they are built on and supported by organization-level competencies (Barney, 1991). These competencies reflect unique combinations of resources that are rare, non-substitutable, difficult to imitate and valuable to customers (Barney and Wright, 1998). Organizations integrating organizational-level competencies within sustainability activities are predicted to have highly motivated and engaged employees who can focus their efforts on the reduction of materials and energy by several orders of magnitude, the development of new, innovative "green" products or services and new business models that they can design to have a strategic impact on sustainability (Epstein, 2008).

So what can HRM professionals do to increase the opportunities that await them in the new, "green collar" economy? An organization's culture and entrenched business practices, and the strategic importance given to human resources may be critical determinants of building a sustainable organization. Every day, managers are charged with developing new, "sustainability" focused programs and strategies in a way that will most benefit the firm. Yet, researchers and practitioners have few examples of what has been tried that focus on HR elements such as organizational design, recruiting, training and management practices; and several questions still remain unanswered.

After conducting an HR-focused forum on sustainability sponsored by the local chapter of the Human Resource Planning Society[1], and through the collection of survey data, we are able to highlight the importance of the HR function and offer an explanation for why some firms adopt certain sustainability practices and others do not. There is a significant opportunity to build upon an emerging paradigm of sustainable development and explore how the HR function can play a strategic role to help lead the efforts to build a sustainability culture.

Study Design

We designed and conducted a Web-based survey of executives of firms located in western Pennsylvania, eastern Ohio and northern West Virginia. The survey, sponsored by the local chapter of the Human Resource Planning Society, was designed to identify the extent to which firms had implemented various sustainability initiatives, and the role of the human resource function in creating and implementing these sustainability initiatives. Based on an extensive review of literature, we pooled many initiatives that had been identified as examples of environmental and social dimensions of sustainability. We rewrote the items to avoid redundancy and ensure clarity, and pre-tested them with a group of academics and practitioners. The Web-based survey, administered during October and November 2008 resulted in 76 complete responses. The sample consisted primarily of HR professionals (49 percent) along with operations (14 percent), sales and marketing (13 percent) and senior management (8 percent). Three-fourths of our respondents had nine or more years of experience in their field. Both small and large firms were represented in our sample. The firms represented a variety of industry sectors including manufacturing, healthcare, retail and services.

We identified six sustainability dimensions based on a factor analysis of responses to 21 items that measured whether the respondent firm implemented particular sustainability initiatives. These ranged from employee-related efforts, such as promoting ethics and integrity and encouraging community volunteer programs, to environmental protection initiatives such as conserving electricity and pollution reduction/prevention. We computed the dimension score by adding the responses to the initiatives that comprise each dimension. We then classified the 76 firms based on their score on the six dimensions spanning social (employee orientation and volunteerism) and environmental (conserving materials, environmental protection, employee conservation and sustainability measurement) sustainability initiatives. We identified three distinct groups of firms using cluster analysis; we labeled them *Leaders, People-focused* and *Laggards*. We conducted further analyses to validate the cluster membership, as well as examine the presence of any systematic differences across these three clusters of firms (additional details on the statistical procedures are provided in the sidebar).

Key Findings

Our analysis revealed four conclusions:

1. Firms differed significantly in the extent to which they had implemented sustainability initiatives. Those firms simultaneously integrating social and environmental sustainability initiatives were considered *Leaders*. Next, *People-focused* firms focused on social initiatives to a greater extent than environmental initiatives. Finally, *Laggard* firms had not implemented, to any significant extent, either the social or the environmental sustainability initiatives.
2. *Leader* firms saw a significant role for HR in facilitating and leading the sustainability efforts within their organizations.
3. *Leader* firms utilized a range of human resource systems to reinforce their firm's people practices and environmental practices to build a sustainability culture.
4. *People-focused* firms utilized a range of human resource systems to implement their firm's people practices to a greater extent than their environmental practices.

Sustainability Dimensions and Diffusion of Sustainability Practices

The six sustainability dimensions and the 15 specific sustainability practices that comprise them are summarized in Table 1. We also examined the extent to which the responding firms adopted or diffused these practices. The firms more widely adopted employee wellness, safety and ethics-related initiatives than environmental initiatives. For instance, 75 percent of the responding firms implemented employee health and wellness programs and promoted ethics and integrity as an integral part of their organizational culture. In contrast, fewer than 12 percent of the firms indicated that they conduct life cycle analysis of new products or calculated the carbon footprint of their companies. We captured the patterns of these differences in the adoption of sustainability initiatives using cluster analysis, and have summarized the results.

Leaders, People-focused and Laggards

A cluster analysis of the sustainability initiatives across the six dimensions revealed three distinct groups of firms that were most similar to each other within a group, and least similar across groups. We examined the profile of each group and labeled them as *Leaders, People-focused* and *Laggards* based on the extent to which they implemented social and environmental sustainability practices. Characteristics of these three clusters are summarized graphically in Figure 1.

We validated our classification by looking at two indicators. Firms that we classified as *leaders* and *people-focused* were significantly more likely to have a sustainability policy than firms classified as laggards (50 percent, 35 percent and 7 percent respectively, x^2 significant). We also examined whether the three clusters differed in their responses (using a three-point scale) to the question: *To what extent is your organization developing a sustainability culture/work environment?* Again *leaders and people-focused* firms were engaged in developing such a

Table 1   Sustainability Dimensions[1]

	Sustainability Dimension	Sustainability Business Practices[2]
SOCIAL	1. Employee Orientation	• Value diversity & inclusion • Promote ethics & integrity • Encourage innovation & risk-taking
	2. Employee Volunteerism	• Support community volunteer programs on company time • Encourage biking to work & taking mass-transit
ENVIRONMENTAL	3. Employee Conservation	• Promote conservation at home • Encourage telecommuting
	4. Environmental Protection	• Address climate change • Conserve electricity • Reduce pollution
	5. Conserving Materials	• Develop "green" products & services • Purchase recycled products
	6. Sustainability Measurement	• Establish an internal sustainability team • Conduct life-cycle analysis of new products • Calculate the carbon footprint of the company

[1] We did not include an economic dimension, as corporate financial performance is an outcome of social and environmental practices and not a strategic initiative in and of itself.

[2] The dimensions were identified using factor analysis; an index was constructed for each dimension by summing up the Yes/No (1/0) responses to the set of practices that comprised each dimension.

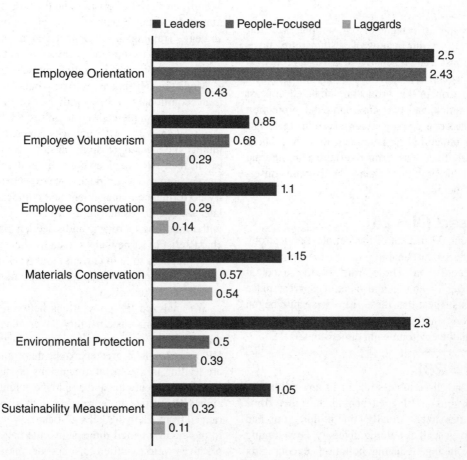

Score for each dimension was computed by summing up the Yes/No (1/0) responses to the set of initiatives that comprise each dimension (see Table 1 for information on specific practices).

Figure 1   Characteristics of leaders, people-focused and laggards

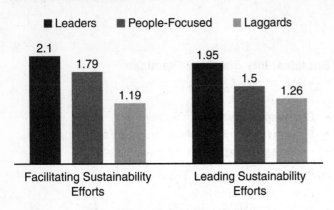

Response Scale: 1 – To a little extent;
2 – To a moderate extent; 3 – To a great extent

Figure 2   Role of HR in sustainability efforts

culture to a greater degree than laggards (2.20, 1.82 and 1.25 respectively, p < .001). While *leaders* and *people-focused* firms were not significantly different in either having a sustainability policy or developing a sustainability culture, their extent of adoption of many of the environmental initiatives was significantly different. These results confirm the existence of three groups of firms.

Leaders (N = 20)

These firms, comprising 26 percent of our sample, were far ahead of others on all six dimensions of sustainability practice, and were the most comprehensive in their approach to implementing both social and environmental sustainability initiatives. A typical firm in this group implemented at least two employee orientation and two environmental protection initiatives, and at least one employee conservation, materials conservation and sustainability measurement initiative. These firms were more likely than other firms to establish an internal sustainability team, address climate change or promote conservation at employees' homes.

People-focused (N = 28)

This group, comprising 37 percent of the sample, had a strong showing on two of the six sustainability dimensions: employee orientation and volunteerism. These firms clearly excel at becoming an employer of choice and creating a great place to work. Our results suggest that these firms have just begun implementing environmental initiatives, and are significantly behind the leaders on the environmental dimensions.

Laggards (N = 28)

This group showed no discernible strength in any of the six sustainability dimensions and lagged behind the other firms on five of the six dimensions. Virtually none in this group had implemented initiatives such as valuing diversity, encouraging innovation and risk taking, reducing pollution, encouraging telecommuting, promoting conservation at employees' homes, establishing an internal sustainability team or conducting life cycle analysis of new products.

The Role of HR in Sustainability

To gauge the level of involvement of the HR function in implementing sustainability initiatives, we asked the respondents to rate the extent to which the HR function either facilitated or led their sustainability efforts. Results of our analysis are summarized in Figure 2. As expected, *leaders* and *people-focused* firms were significantly different from *laggards* in the facilitating role played by the HR function. However, when it came to the HR function leading the sustainability effort, *leaders* were significantly different from both *people-focused* and *laggard* firms. Our results suggest that a leading role for the HR function can be crucial for firms implementing the full-range of sustainability initiatives. HR possesses an array of tools that can help to change an organization's culture (e.g., employee selection, training and reward systems).

We examined the extent to which specific HR practices were changed to support developing a sustainability culture within an organization. The results are summarized in Figure 3. In general, *leaders* and *people-focused* firms had modified their HR practices to a significantly greater extent than *laggard* firms, and ANOVA tests confirmed this. This was most apparent for recruiting, employee selection and new employee orientation—practices that enable organizations to change their culture, one hire at a time. This strategy of changing these practices first also might be prudent given the dual benefits of attracting an applicant pool with different characteristics and the possibility of encountering minimal resistance within the organization to implement new strategy. Training, development and mentoring practices also were modified to support sustainability initiatives, though not to the same extent as the recruiting and selection practices.

Modifying HR practices to help build a sustainability culture is an evolutionary process, with the firms we observed at different stages of implementing their sustainability strategies. Our results suggest that HR practices targeted at the external community, i.e., potential applicants, were modified to a greater extent than HR practices governing internal stakeholders, i.e., current employees. Logically, we expect HR managers to modify performance management and compensation practices at a later date. Our results imply a natural progression beginning with modifying recruiting and selection practices to impact the characteristics of new hires, then to alter training and development practices to help current employees develop new competencies, and finally changing the way employee performance is measured and rewarded.

We analyzed the correlations between the eight HR practices and the six sustainability dimensions. As expected, firms that are doing more sustainability practices also changed their HR practices to a greater extent than other firms. Firms that are leading in the social dimensions of sustainability practices (employee orientation and employee volunteerism) modified all eight HR practices to a greater extent than others (correlations ranged from .28 to .48, all significant at p < .01). When it comes to the environmental dimensions, the pattern also is clear. HR practices were modified to support employee conservation and materials conservation, but not the other two environmental dimensions (environmental protection or sustainability measurement). For employee conservation, modifying HR practices

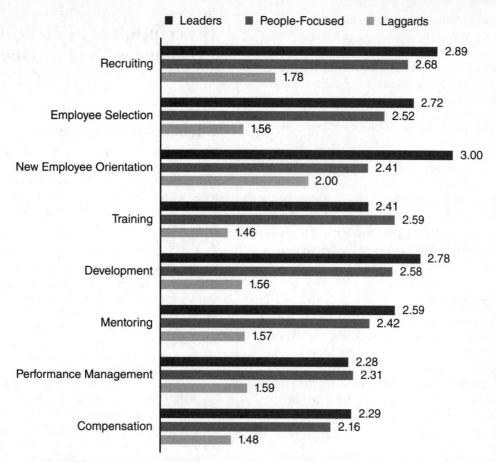

Response Scale: 1 - To a very little extent; 2 - To a little extent; 3 - To some extent
4 - To a significant extent; 5 - To a very great extent

Figure 3   Role of HR practices in sustainability efforts

related to recruitment, selection, orientation, training, development and performance management have the greatest impact, with correlations ranging from .21 to .31. Firms that implemented materials conservation initiatives to a greater extent also significantly altered HR practices, especially with regard to training and development.

In summary, our results suggest that *leaders* differed significantly from *people-focused* and *laggard* firms in the extent to which they implemented different sustainability initiatives. The human resource function played a critical role in these firms in leading and facilitating their sustainability efforts. *Leaders* and *people-focused* firms modified their HR practices to a greater extent than *laggards* to support their sustainability agenda. These changes in HR practices also are aligned with certain sustainability initiatives: supporting our argument that HR practices play a strategic role in implementing specific sustainability initiatives and creating a sustainability organizational culture.

Obstacles on the Pathway to Sustainability

Despite a growing consensus that firms can "do well by doing good" and considerable empirical evidence confirming a positive relationship between a firm's social and environmental

performance and financial performance (Orlitzky, Schmidt & Rynes, 2003), our results suggest a lack of widespread adoption of sustainability initiatives. Either there is no acceptance of the basic premise, despite evidence to the contrary, or the task of building a sustainability culture may be considerably more challenging and complex.

We asked the respondents what challenges and obstacles they encounter in creating a sustainability culture. We reviewed these open-ended responses for common themes and how frequently they occurred across the three distinct types of firms. Our research suggests three possible reasons for why firms either have not undertaken any sustainability initiatives or continued building on their early efforts to become a sustainable organization. These were (1) lack of commitment and buy-in from both management and employees, (2) lack of resources, and (3) cultural and institutional resistance to change. We also found systematic differences in the obstacles identified by *laggards* versus *leaders*.

Lack of Commitment and Buy-in

As we expected, this was a primary obstacle among *laggards* and an important issue for *people-focused* firms who felt there was widespread "apathy," and "lack of interest from top management" regarding environmental issues. This was not the case for *leader* firms. Without top management support and employee buy-in, it is very difficult to generate the momentum needed to implement any new sustainability initiatives (Wirtenberg, Harmon, Russell & Fairfield, 2007). One respondent stated the difficulty of building a sustainability culture without senior management commitment as follows:

> I work for XYZ Co. and they just don't care about sustainability . . .

We also heard other comments such as "lack of understanding and endorsement at the top of the organization" and the need for "changing the mindset of middle managers," reinforcing our conclusion that the lack of commitment and buy-in is a major obstacle. These comments suggest that it might be due to lack of awareness of sustainability issues or the fear of dealing with change.

Lack of Resources

This was a critical issue for *people-focused* firms and an important issue among *leaders* as well. Only two *laggard* firms identified lack of resources as an obstacle to creating a sustainability culture. Resources were broadly defined to include financial, human and knowledge resources. A respondent from a *people-focused* firm captured the need for specialized knowledge to create support and buy-in among employees:

> . . . having a hard time coming up with a clear definition of sustainability that can make sense and be motivating to employees

Another respondent expressed the difficulty of "getting employees to understand why we are pursuing this and understand the benefits rather than just comply," due to lack of knowledge or the resources to provide additional education/training to their employees. Respondents recognized that they are asked to do more with less resources and indicated that they "do the best they can" with limited resources.

Cultural and Institutional Resistance

This was a primary obstacle among *leader* firms. Even when there was commitment from the top—buy-in from employees and available resources, albeit limited, for sustainability initiatives—there remained cultural and institutional resistance to creating a sustainability culture. "Changing behavior and habits" is possibly the biggest and the most deep-seated hurdle. Comments such as the ones reproduced below confirm how hard it is to manage this cultural transformation effectively:

> . . . silos, business as usual, and established business metrics that do not yet reflect sustainability"

> . . . large company, so layers of politics and hierarchy"

This effort to change the culture and "educate employees of the alternatives" may "take more time upfront, but produce better, longer-lasting, successful outcomes."

Description of Statistical Procedures Used in This Study

Identification of Sustainability Dimensions

We asked respondents to indicate whether or not they had implemented 21 different sustainability initiatives. We subjected their Yes/No responses (coded 1/0) to these 21 questions to an exploratory factor analysis to identify the underlying dimensions. We next used the principal components extraction method with varimax rotation procedure to obtain six coherent factors. Questions that were not loading highly on one factor (factor loading less than .5) or were loading highly on more than one factor were eliminated from further analysis. Descriptions of the six factors, represented by 15 sustainability initiatives, are summarized in Table 1.

Because we used a Yes/No response for each of the initiatives, we computed the score for each dimension by adding the number of initiatives that the responding firm had implemented. For example, the first factor, *employee orientation,* comprises three specific initiatives: "Value diversity & inclusion"; "Promote ethics & integrity"; and "Encourage innovation & risk-taking." Hence the score for this factor ranged from 0 (had implemented none of the initiatives) to 3 (had implemented all three initiative). This dimension score was used in all further analyses.

Identification of Distinct Groups

Finally, we used the scores on the six sustainability dimensions to group firms into clusters. We used the K-means clustering procedure to identify groups of firms, and compared the group profiles for multiple solutions (2, 3, 4 & 5 cluster solutions). We also compared these results to cluster solutions derived from an alternative method of clustering procedure (2-step clustering). We sought to identify the smallest number of dusters that best explain the variance in the scores for the six dimensions. A three-cluster solution was identified as the best representation of the data based on analysis of variance results and the convergence with alternative methods. Based on the mean scores on the six sustainability dimensions, we labeled these three clusters of firms as *leaders, people-focused* and *laggards.*

Strategies for Dealing with the Obstacles

We also asked respondents to identify possible solutions to the obstacles and challenges they identified. A content analysis of the responses indicated significant differences among the three groups of firms. *Laggard* firms identified "education and communication" to improve awareness as the single best strategy to deal with the obstacles and challenges. *People-focused* firms wanted information and tools for building the "business case" for sustainability, and *leaders* unanimously pointed out the strategic benefit of sharing "best practices" in sustainability.

Education and Communication

Only respondents from *laggard* firms identified education and communication as the primary strategy for overcoming the obstacles, possibly due to their position. Suggestions for educating both management and employees ranged from "information posters" and ". . . radio, newspaper, billboards, etc. telling of the importance" to ". . . trained executive leadership on the models (of sustainability), otherwise you'll experience flavor of the month." For *laggard* organizations starting on the path to sustainability, education and communication of all employees is a first step to build a shared understanding of sustainability, generate interest and support for the initiatives, and lay the foundation for the sustainability culture.

Building the Business Case

Having identified lack of knowledge resources as primary obstacles for implementing sustainability initiatives, respondents from *people-focused* firms sought information and tools to make the business case. They wanted to convince other internal stakeholders of the benefits of such initiatives. Comments such as "(need) documentation of how it impacts profitability" and ". . . the benefits of functioning with greater efficiency, saving $ and resources" highlight the need for making the winning argument to other stakeholders, using language and metrics critical to their decision making.

Sharing Best Practices

Respondents from *leader* firms recognize the importance of collaboration both within and across firms, and seek the sharing of best practices to further their sustainability agenda. They commented on the need for sharing ". . . best practices for metrics that make sustainability everyone's responsibility" and "tips on how to create excitement within the organization." This is consistent with the observation by Wirtenberg, Harmon, Russell and Fairfield (2007) that some firms view sustainability not necessarily as a source of competitive advantage, but as an opportunity for holistic integration to build and be part of a sustainable ecosystem. After all, as one of their respondents indicated, it is not possible to be a sustainable company when the ecosystem, as a whole, is unsustainable. Seeking and sharing best practices is possibly one way of creating a sustainable ecosystem.

Stairway to Sustainability

Past research in both TQM (Blackburn & Rosen, 1993) and Environmental Management Systems (Daily & Huang, 2001) argued for the human resource function to play an active role in implementing these new systems. Blackburn and Rosen (1993), in their research of Baldrige Quality Award winners, found the HR function played a leading role in designing HRM policies and practices to create quality-oriented work cultures. Specifically, HR policies and practices helped communicate the importance of quality initiatives, empower employees to contribute to

the initiatives and design appropriate rewards and reinforcements to ingrain the total quality orientation into the firm's DNA.

Implementing a comprehensive sustainability strategy is no different a challenge than the TQM challenge of the 1980s and 1990s. Like TQM, sustainability is about managing change. We believe the HR function can and should play an active role in ensuring that change toward sustainability happens.

One of the biggest blunders in leading change toward sustainability is the failure to institutionalize sustainability within the firm (Doppelt, 2003). If the internal policies and practices are inconsistent with the needed sustainability culture, "the risks are high that old thinking and behavioral patterns will eventually rise up and overwhelm efforts to adopt more environmentally and socially responsible paths" (Doppelt, 2003, p. 36). We recommend an active and early role for HR to help create the systems and processes (for example, selection, training and reward systems) to reinforce the wide range of sustainability initiatives and institutionalize the change.

Our earlier observation that the adoption rates of different sustainability initiatives are not uniform across firms suggests that firms might not adopt a practice, either because of its relative difficulty or the need to follow a sequence for maximal effectiveness. Extending this logic, we suggest a definitive pathway to sustainability that incorporates three decision-making dimensions:

1. the need to maintain a strategic sequence to build on prior efforts,
2. the relative difficulty of adopting the initiative, and
3. the strategic pay-off over the long-term.

In a useful strategic sequence, the first step toward sustainability is to be employee-oriented-valuing employee diversity, ethics, risk taking and innovation. The strategic HRM literature provides convincing evidence of the benefits of starting here: engaged employees resulting in increased organizational identity and commitment leading to superior performance. A quick review of different rankings of "green companies," such as the recent list by *Newsweek*, reveals that the top companies are also among the most-admired companies and the 100-best companies to work for. Absent this "employee-first" philosophy, efforts to promote other sustainability initiatives are unlikely to gain traction, creating a lack of coherence in an organization's sustainability strategy. Makower and Pike (2008) coined the term "random acts of greenness" to identify firms that had no internal coherence or strategy when implementing "green" initiatives. This is primarily due to their weak foundation.

The strategic implementation sequence identified in our Stairway to Sustainability model is based on the assumption that successive stages of building a sustainability culture depend on the successful implementation of the previous steps. This provides coherence to the strategy and organizational readiness to implement the next initiative. If a well-thought-out strategic implementation sequence is not followed, the likely result is the "flavor of the month"—leading to the random acts of greenness mentioned previously. Our Stairway to Sustainability framework complements Wirtenberg, Harmon, Russell and Fairfield's (2007) work on the role of human resources in building a sustainable enterprise, by focusing on the "Foundation" and "Traction" stages of their Sustainability Pyramid.

As firms climb up the steps, the relative difficulty of implementing initiatives increases. The assessment of the degree of difficulty includes convincing the relevant stakeholders of the benefits of the focal initiative, as well as the resources required to implement it. Due to their higher adoption rates, there is abundant evidence of the positive effects of early stage initiatives, such as materials conservation (Esty & Winston, 2006). Yet evidence is scarce or the returns unclear as firms take on late-stage initiatives, like conducting life cycle analyses or measuring a firm's eco-footprint. The payback periods on these initiatives may be longer, and the time horizons for returns on investment might be more than the firm generally uses as hurdle rates for new projects. As a result, firms have to base decisions on the cultural and ethical rather than economic rationale.

The impact of a firm's sustainability strategy is indicated by the third dimension—strategic payoffs. As a firm moves up the stairway, there is a greater pay-off in making the firm sustainable. We have evidence of the performance implications of employee orientation and materials conservation; however, the linkages become weaker for other dimensions because of the excessive emphasis on measuring performance concurrently or at best, one or two years ahead. The benefits of the later initiatives are more strategic than financial, long-term than short-term, and as indicated above, the usual decision criteria may not be applicable.

Building a sustainability culture requires the sequential approach suggested here for two reasons. First, there is considerable evidence that the principle of "success breeds success" applies to individuals as well as organizations.

Building a sustainability culture requires the sequential approach suggested here for two reasons. First, there is considerable evidence that the principle of "success breeds success" applies to individuals as well as organizations. Early tangible wins from employee orientation and materials conservation efforts should increase the likelihood of creating a self-reinforcing, virtuous cycle that creates excitement and potency among stakeholders that changes can become sustainable. Second, successful early initiatives help build organizational capacity for taking on the more challenging late-stage initiatives, increasing the likelihood of both adoption and success.

Second, successful early initiatives help build organizational capacity for taking on the more challenging late-stage initiatives, increasing the likelihood of both adoption and success.

Implications for Managers

The first implication for executives creating a sustainability culture is that they need to start by creating HR policies and practices that embody becoming an employer-of-choice. Then, they should encourage their technical, scientific and environmental managers to work more closely with human resources to change the ways they handle recruiting, selection, orientation, training, development, performance management and compensation to reinforce sustainability as a core organizational value. They should begin their sustainability journey with initiatives on the lower steps of the stairway, and progress toward the highest level.

The three types of firms we identified will face very different sets of challenges to creating a sustainability culture. *Leader* firms already have climbed quite a few steps on the stairway to sustainability, and now have to deal with resource constraints to implement initiatives with less clear pay-offs, amid resistance from forces entrenched in the current system. HR managers in these firms are faced with leading deep change, and will benefit by collaborating with other leader firms to identify best practices. They also may benefit by aligning their performance management and reward systems with a comprehensive sustainability strategy. *People-focused* firms already have taken the first step of becoming an employer of choice and now should focus on building a business case for adopting a broader set of sustainability initiatives and implementing innovative practices to create buy-in and employee commitment. *Laggard* firms would do well to first focus on the social initiatives (i.e. becoming a great place to work) and then invest in education and training in sustainability so as to create awareness of sustainability issues and motivation.

Limitations

Our sample provides a glimpse into current HR practices drawn from a single geographic region. As such, it should be looked at as the tip of an iceberg. What was highlighted here as both obstacles and solutions may reflect the region's industrial history. Still, we strongly believe that the results provide valuable lessons for all managers. The amount and different kinds of sustainability initiatives and the challenges of implementing provide ample opportunity for further discovery and continued research.

Conclusions

Sustainability starts with a guiding philosophy or strategic vision of achieving profits through people, while minimizing one's impact on the planet. Human resource professionals have a very important role to play in developing and implementing sustainability strategies. The success of every sustainability initiative depends on the extent to which the firm's human capital is knowledgeable, engaged and committed to implementing new initiatives. Recognizing the need for a strategic rather than piecemeal approach to sustainability, the HR function can facilitate, if not lead, the sustainability effort by laying the groundwork, designing systems that help build a sustainability culture, and become the champion of the organization's transformation to sustainability.

Note

1. We are grateful to Peggy Fayfich and Michael Couch for their support of our research.

References

Barney, J.B. (1991). Firm resources and sustained competitive advantage. *Journal of Management, 17,* 99–120.

Barney, J.B., & Wright, P.M. (1998). On becoming a strategic partner: The role of human resources in gaining competitive advantage. *Human Resources Management, 37* (1), 31–46.

Blackburn, R., & Rosen, B. (1993). Total quality and human resources management: Lessons learned from Baldrige Award-winning companies. *Academy of Management Executive, 7* (3), 49–66.

Daily, B.F., & Huang, S. (2001). Achieving sustainability through attention to human resource factors in environmental management. *International Journal of Operations & Production Management, 21* (12), 1539–1552.

Doppelt, B. (2003). *Leading change toward sustainability: A change-management guide for business, government and civil society.* Sheffield, UK: Greenleaf Publishing Limited.

Epstein, M.J. (2008). *Making sustainability work: Best practices in managing and measuring corporate social, environmental and economic impacts.* San Francisco, CA: Berrett-Koehler Publishers.

Esty, D.C., & Winston, A.S. (2006). *Green to gold: How smart companies use environmental strategy to innovate, create value, and build competitive advantage.* New Haven, CT: Yale University Press.

Makower, J., & Pike, C. (2008). *Strategies for the green economy: Opportunities and challenges in the new world of business.* New York, NY: McGraw-Hill.

Orlitzky, M., Schmidt, F.L., & Rynes, S.L. (2003). Corporate social and financial performance: A meta-analysis. *Organization Studies,* 24, 403–441.

The Greenest Big Companies in America, (2009). *Newsweek,* Sept. 28, 34–52.

Wirtenberg, J., Harmon, J, Russell, W.G., & Fairfield, K.D. (2007). HR's role in building a sustainable enterprise: Insights from some of the world's best companies. *Human Resource Planning,* 30 (1), 10–20.

Critical Thinking

1. What is the importance of sustainability for corporations?

2. How can human capital participate in the effort to increase and maintain an organization's efforts in sustainability?

3. What role can human resource management play in this effort?

ROBERT SROUFE, (PhD, Michigan State University) is the Murrin Chair of Global Competitiveness in the Palumbo-Donahue Schools of Business at Duquesne University, Pittsburgh, PA. His research interests include environmental management systems, sustainable business practices, green supply chain management, performance measurement and human resource management. **JAY LIEBOWITZ,** SPHR (PhD, from the University of Tennessee, Knoxville) is an associate professor of Organizational Behavior & Human Resource Management in the Palumbo-Donahue Schools of Business at Duquesne University, Pittsburgh, PA. His research interests include the role of HR in sustainability, and new product development teams. **NAGARAJ SIVASUBRAMANIAM,** (PhD, Florida International University) is an associate professor of Leadership in the Palumbo-Donahue Schools of Business at Duquesne University, Pittsburgh, PA. His research focuses on measurement of sustainability orientation, climate protection strategies & models, and organizational impacts of individual and team leadership.

Building Sustainable Organizations: The Human Factor

Although most of the research and public pressure concerning sustainability has been focused on the effects of business and organizational activity on the physical environment, companies and their management practices profoundly affect the human and social environment as well. This article briefly reviews the literature on the direct and indirect effects of organizations and their decisions about people on human health and mortality. It then considers some possible explanations for why social sustainability has received relatively short shrift in management writing, and outlines a research agenda for investigating the links between social sustainability and organizational effectiveness as well as the role of ideology in understanding the relative neglect of the human factor in sustainability research.

JEFFREY PFEFFER

There is growing public and business interest in building sustainable organizations and increasing research and educational interest in the topic of organizational sustainability. The Academy of Management has a division called Organizations and the Natural Environment, and there are numerous journals and research papers concerned with ecological sustainability. There are growing numbers of higher education programs focused on sustainability and an Association for the Advancement of Sustainability in Higher Education (Fountain, 2010). Marcus and Fremeth (2009) noted that this enthusiasm for what they called "green management" came from people's expectations for how managers and the organizations they lead should conduct their business to protect the environment. As Ambec and Lanoie (2008, p. 46) noted, "firms are facing growing pressure to become greener."

As it is operationalized in the literature, sustainability is defined in part by an effort to conserve natural resources and avoid waste in operations. Conservation and the more efficient use of resources naturally lessen the burden of economic activity on the environment and helps to ensure that the activity can be sustained over time because the resources required will not be exhausted. Sustainability also appears to encompass activities that renew and recycle what it is used, once again with the goal of ensuring that the ecosystem that supports life and lifestyle can and will be preserved. Other aspects of sustainability include preserving what is—as in preserving threatened plant and animal species and, in cultural sustainability, preserving the values, arts, culture, and food of "communities threatened by globalization and modernization" (Navarro, 2010, p. 20). In the physical sciences, much of the research on sustainability has focused on the amount of stress an ecosystem can tolerate

as well as principles for restoring ecological balance. In management, research attention has focused on the possible links between profitability and sustainability as well as the factors that cause organizations to pursue different sustainability strategies (e.g., Ambec and Lanoie, 2008).

Although sustainability clearly could encompass a focus on human as well as physical resources—in fact, the Academy of Management division on the natural environment has as one of its foci "managing human resources for sustainability"—there is a much greater emphasis on the physical rather than the social environment[1] both in the research literature and in the actions and pronouncements of companies. To illustrate this point, a search of Google Scholar finds 20,800 entries for the term "ecological sustainability," 53,000 for "environmental sustainability," but just 12,900 for "social sustainability," and a paltry 569 for "human sustainability." And even a cursory review of the management literature shows that virtually all of the articles focused on sustainability are primarily concerned with the effects of organizations on the physical as contrasted with the social environment (e.g., Ambec & Lanoie, 2008; Bansal, 2002; Marcus & Fremeth, 2009). Even when there is concern with the social effects of organizational activities, these concerns are mostly directed to the consequences of economic development and resource exploitation for the viability of indigenous cultures (Bansal, 2002) rather than the consequences of management practices for every individual's health and well-being and the richness of social life as assessed by participation in civic activities (e.g., Putnam, 2000).

Environmental sustainability is important, and nothing in this paper should be taken to imply that this is not the case. Nonetheless, this emphasis on the natural environment raises an interesting research question: Why are polar bears, for instance, or even milk jugs more important than people, not only in terms of research attention, but also as a focus of company initiatives?

In 2008, Doug McMillon (Colvin, 2008), the CEO of Sam's Club, a division of Wal-Mart, expounded on the innovation in milk jugs and the fact that his company had introduced a new jug that was able to increase the shelf life of milk, reduce the cost between 10 and 20 cents, and eliminate more than 10,000 delivery trips, thereby conserving energy. In 2005, Lee Scott, Wal-Mart's CEO, made the first speech in the company's history broadcast to all of its associates. In that speech, also made available to Wal-Mart's 60,000 suppliers, Scott committed the company to the goals of being 100% supplied by renewable energy, creating zero waste, and selling products that sustain resources and the environment (Plambeck & Denend, 2007). Meanwhile, Wal-Mart paid its employees almost 15% less than other large retailers, and because of the lower pay, its employees made greater use of public health and welfare programs (Dube et al., 2007). In 2005, 46% of Wal-Mart employees' children were either uninsured or on Medicaid, a state program to provide medical care to low-income people (Rosenbloom & Barbaro, 2009). Compared to Costco, Wal-Mart offered fewer medical and other benefits, although these lower costs did not result in higher profits per employee (Cascio, 2006).

Wal-Mart's relative emphasis on the physical environment over its employees is far from unusual. British Petroleum, a company that touts its environmental credentials in its advertising and other presentations, was one of the first major oil companies to devote significant investment to alternative energy, and at one point wanted BP to also stand for "beyond petroleum." Apparently less concerned about its people, the company paid a record fine of $87 million for an explosion in its Texas City, Texas, refinery that killed 15 workers (Greenhouse, 2009). The fine penalized the company not for the explosion but also for numerous safety violations found during a subsequent investigation and a failure to correct those deficiencies even after the fatal explosion.

Even as businesses have appointed "eco-managers" (Hsu, 2010) to oversee company efforts to become more energy efficient and environmentally conscious, and even as companies track and publicly report carbon emissions from their activities (e.g., Kaufman, 2009), one would be hard-pressed to find similar efforts focused on employees. Just as there is concern for protecting natural resources, there could be a similar level of concern for protecting human resources. For example, there has been no groundswell of reporting on employee physical and mental health and wellness, even though that might be an interesting and informative indicator of what companies are doing about the sustainability of their people. This lack of concern is puzzling given that health-care costs, which as noted below are related in part to what companies do in the workplace, are an enormous problem in the United States and throughout the industrialized world.

In this paper, I want to first make the case for broadening our dependent variables in management research from a focus on profitability and other indicators of firm performance, such as shareholder return and productivity on the one hand and environmental sustainability practices and social responsibility on the other, to also include organizational effects on employee health and mortality. Being a socially responsible business ought to encompass the effect of management practices on employee physical and psychological well-being. Indeed, there is a large epidemiological and public health literature that suggests there may be important organizational effects on human health and life span. The available evidence suggests that there is a good likelihood of finding some interesting research results if we continue to expand our understanding of the connections between organizational practices and human well-being.

Then I want to open up the question as to why employee health has received relatively short shrift in discussions of organizational effects on the environment and the implications of such effects for sustainability. In so doing, I argue that an ideology of the primacy of markets (Davis, 2008) and shareholder interests and the associated idea that market outcomes are fair and just (Jost, et al., 2003), with sentient individuals making informed choices, may help explain the constrained focus of our research attention. The paper concludes with some implications for building a research focus on human sustainability.

Broadening Our Dependent Variables: Organizational Effects on Employee Mortality and Morbidity

In assessing and evaluating countries and other political units, measures of population health (e.g., infant mortality and life span) are frequently used as indicators of societal effectiveness and the level of country development. Cornia and Paniccia (2000) examined explanations for the dramatic increase in age-adjusted mortality, particularly for men, in Eastern and Central Europe during the 1980s and 1990s, taking these decreases in life span to be evidence of dysfunctional social conditions. Marmot and Bobak (2000) explored the "missing men of Russia"—the enormous increase in mortality and consequent reduction in average life span for men following the collapse of the Soviet Union, once again implying that the health of a society's people reflects at least to some degree the functioning of that society. Indeed, Marmot (2004, p. 247) explicitly argued that "health functions as a kind of social accountant. If health suffers, it tells us that human needs are not being met." Similarly, Gakidou, Murray, and Frenk (2000, p. 42) wrote that "health is an intrinsic component of well-being," and the economist Deaton (2003, p. 115) also noted that "health is a component of well-being."

What is true for countries or other political units is also true for organizations. The health status of the workforce is a particularly relevant indicator of human sustainability and well-being because there is evidence that many organizational decisions about how they reward and manage their employee have profound effects on human health and mortality. A few of the many ways company decisions affect the health and welfare of their people follow.

The Provision of Health Insurance

In the United States, in contrast to every other advanced industrialized country, access to health insurance—and, as a consequence, access to health care for working-age people who are not so poor as to be covered by increasingly limited social welfare programs—depends on whether or not one's employer voluntarily chooses to offer medical insurance as a benefit. Approximately half of the U.S. population today receives health insurance through an employer, and the evidence shows that the proportion of employers offering health insurance has declined while the amount employees pay for their coverage has increased. The Kaiser Family Foundation reported that between 1999 and 2009, worker contributions to health insurance premiums increased by 128%, while the proportion of companies offering health benefits fell from 66% to 60%.

These employer decisions about offering health insurance and the cost to employees, something that can also affect access, are consequential because there is a great deal of evidence showing that having health insurance affects health status. Levy and Meltzer (2001), reviewing the large literature on the connection between health insurance and health status, noted that hundreds of studies showed that the uninsured had worse health outcomes than people with access to insurance. Wilper et al. (2009) recently replicated the results of an earlier panel study (Franks, Clancy, & Gold, 1993) showing significantly higher mortality for people without health insurance. This result held when age, gender, income, education, race, smoking, alcohol use, exercise, body mass index, and initial physician-rated health were all statistically controlled. Based on their empirical results and population parameter estimates, Wilper and his colleagues estimated that there were more than 44,000 excess deaths per year in the United States because of lack of health insurance. Another study looking at the effects of health insurance on health used the fact that a random event, one's birthday, affects access to health insurance. At age 65, U.S. residents become eligible for Medicare, federally provided health insurance. Using this fact and data on health status, Card, Dobkin, and Maestas (2009) found that access to Medicare resulted in a 20% reduction in deaths for a severely ill patient group compared to similarly ill people who did not have access to Medicare because they had not yet turned 65.

Other studies show that people without health insurance are, not surprisingly, less likely to obtain various preventive screening tests for blood pressure and elevated cholesterol, Pap smears, and so forth (e.g., Potosky et al., 1998; Sudano & Baker, 2003). Such screening reduces mortality and morbidity through the early detection of harmful physical conditions (Sudano & Baker, 2003). Moreover, the data show that even short periods of not having health insurance substantially reduces the utilization of preventive services (Schoen & DesRoches, 2000; Sudano & Baker, 2003).

Having health insurance also affects people's economic well-being, because medical bills are a large contributor to personal bankruptcy. Himmelstein et al. (2005) studied a sample of personal bankruptcy filers in five federal courts. About half of the people filing for bankruptcy cited medical causes. "Medical debtors were 42 percent more likely than other debtors to experience lapses in coverage" (2005, p. W5-63). When employers decide to drop or curtail medical coverage, there are health and economic well-being consequences for their people.

In addition to providing, or not providing, health insurance, some employers have recently begun implementing health and wellness programs for their employees, which can also have important effects on health. Because most large employers are self-insured, any savings from better employee health and reduced medical expenditures flow directly to company profits. An evaluation of one such program at GlaxoSmithKline (Stave, Muchmore, & Gardner, 2003), covering more than 6,000 employees continuously employed from 1996 to 2000, reported an increased use of stress reduction techniques, more eating of fruits and vegetables, and an average cost savings of $613 per participant, largely because of reduced disability expenses.

The Effects of Layoffs

Employers decide on whether or not to have layoffs, how many people they will lay off, and who will get laid off. Budros (1997) has shown that layoffs are not just a consequence of economic conditions facing companies, a point made also by Cappelli (1999) in his discussion of the changing nature of the employment relationship. Budros found that layoffs are "contagious," in the sense that they spread through similarly situated and socially connected firms, which appear to model others' layoff behavior.

Research has shown that layoffs are very harmful to the physical and mental health of those laid off. There is consistence evidence that job loss is a significant predictor of reported symptoms of psychological disorders (Catalano, 1991). Being laid off increases the likelihood that an individual will engage in violent behavior by some 600% (Catalano, Novaco, & McConnell, 2002). One study reported that job displacement increased the death rate of those laid off by about 17% during the following 20 years, so that someone laid off at age 40 would be expected to live 1.5 fewer years than someone not laid off (Sullivan & von Wachter, 2007). A study of plant closings conducted in Sweden, a country with a relatively generous social safety net, nonetheless found that mortality risk increased 44% in the four years following job loss (Eliason & Storrie, 2009). A New Zealand study reported that unemployed 25-to-64-year-olds had more than twice the odds of committing suicide (Blakely, Collings, & Atkinson, 2003), which helps explain the cause of the increased mortality following layoffs. Another New Zealand study, based on an eight-year follow-up of workers from a meat processing plant that closed compared to a neighboring plant that remained open, found an increased risk of self-inflicted harm that resulted in hospitalization or death and also an increased risk of being hospitalized with a mental health diagnosis (Keefe et al., 2002). And downsizing is associated with negative changes in work behavior, increased smoking, less spousal support, and twice the rate of absence from work because of sickness (Kivimaki, Vahtera, Pentti, & Ferrie, 2000).

Work Hours and Work-Family Conflict

Employers determine the hours people work and when they work, subject to federal and state regulations and any union-bargained contracts. There has been an intensification of work, particularly in the United States (e.g., Rousseau, 2006). Americans work longer hours than workers in most European countries and now exceed the working hours of even Japanese (Yang et al., 2006). A report by the National Institute for Occupational Safety and Health (2004) summarized the extensive evidence on the harmful effects of long working hours and shift work on people's health-related behaviors as well as on-the-job injuries and employees' health status.

There is a reasonably extensive body of evidence connecting work hours to poor health outcomes. Some of this research focuses on hypertension. For instance, Yang et al. (2006), after summarizing studies showing the connection between hours worked and hypertension in Japan, reported their findings from analyzing the California Health Interview survey. They found that compared to people who worked less than 40 hours a week, those who worked more than 51 hours were 29% more likely to report having hypertension, even after statistically controlling for variables such as socioeconomic status, gender, age, diabetes, tobacco use, sedentary lifestyle, and body mass index.

Long work hours increase the likelihood that people will face a conflict between work and family responsibilities. Work-family conflict is a form of stress and has been found to influence health and health-related behaviors. Frone, Russell, and Barnes (1996), using two random samples of employed parents, found that work-family conflict was related to alcohol use, depression, and poor physical health. Moreover, work-family conflict is related to anxiety, substance abuse, and substance dependence (Frone, 2000). Depending on the type and degree of work-family conflict and the particular disorder being investigated, employees were between 2 and 30 times more likely to experience a significant mental health problem if they experienced work-family conflict compared to people who did not.

Work Stress and the Consequences of Job Design

Organizations design jobs, and job design has important psychological consequences—for instance, for motivation—as the large literature on job design attests (e.g., Hackman & Oldham, 1980). Job design also has important effects on people's physical well-being. One important dimension of job design is the amount of control people have over their work. High job demands that people cannot control, because they have little or no discretion over the pace and content of their work, coupled with work that is socially isolating, produce job stress. Marmot and colleagues have done extensive studies on the effects of job stress, emanating from an absence of control over one's work, on health outcomes ranging from metabolic syndrome (Chandola, Brunner, & Marmot, 2006) to cardiovascular disease and mortality (e.g., Marmot, 2004). Using both retrospective and prospective panel studies, Marmot reported large effects of job stress on mortality and morbidity.

Much of this research was stimulated by studies of the British civil service. These studies, called the Whitehall studies, showed that, controlling for numerous individual characteristics

such as family background, serum cholesterol levels, blood pressure, and so forth, it was nevertheless the case that the higher someone's rank in the bureaucracy, the lower that person's risk of cardiovascular disease and death from heart attack (e.g., Marmot et al., 1997).

Inequality

The Whitehall studies are just part of a larger literature showing the connection between inequalities in health outcomes and inequality in individual attributes ranging from income to education. Wildman (2003, p. 295) reviewed papers reporting substantial "income-related inequalities in health in a number of developed countries," noting that the United Kingdom and the United States were high-inequality countries. Marmot (2004) reported that virtually all diseases followed a status gradient and that gradients in both income and education were important in understanding differences in health. It is not just the case that people with more income, higher education, and better jobs are more likely to enjoy better health and live longer lives—although that is clearly the case (see Marmot, 2004, for a review of this research). Some argue that there is an effect of inequality, particularly income inequality, on the average health status of a population. Lynch et al. (2001) argued that income inequality in the United States in the 1990s caused as much loss of life as the combined mortality resulting from lung cancer, diabetes, motor vehicle crashes, homicide, and AIDS combined. Although the effect of inequality on average health outcomes remains a contested issue (e.g., Deaton, 2003), there is growing concern about inequality in health outcomes within societies and increasing research attention to the causes and consequences of a number of forms of health-relevant inequality.

The research and policy link to organization studies is clear: Many, although certainly not all, of the inequalities in social systems that result in inequalities in health are produced in and by organizations. Because most people work for organizations rather than being self-employed, income inequality is produced in part by decisions made by employers about how much wage dispersion to have, both within and across organizational levels, and who and what types of people will obtain higher and lower level positions and incomes (e.g., Baron & Bielby, 1980; Pfeffer and Langton, 1988). The organizations literature has a number of studies exploring the effects of wage dispersion on various outcomes ranging from satisfaction to indicators of organizational performance (e.g., Bloom, 1999; Cowherd & Levine, 1992; Pfeffer & Langton, 1993; Siegel & Hambrick, 2005). The importance of inequality for health suggests two important extensions to this line of research: first, including health outcomes as a dependent variable in studies of the consequences of wage dispersion, and second, renewing efforts to understand the factors that create greater or lesser inequalities in income, power, job responsibilities, time pressure, and other such dimensions inside organizations. If inequality is consequential for health, we need to better understand how that relationship operates inside organizations and what factors produce inequality in the first place.

The foregoing is only a partial review of a large epidemiological literature that potentially ties organizational decisions to health outcomes. There seems to be overwhelming evidence that organizational decisions about whether to offer health insurance and choices about layoffs, work hours, job design, and the degree of inequality created by wage structures have profound effects on employee physical and mental health and even people's life-spans. There are other aspects of the work environment that are also likely to be important and might productively be studied, including whether or not people have paid sick days, the amount of vacation they receive and take, and the emotional climate of the workplace, including whether or not there is bullying and verbal abuse. If we want to understand employee psychological and physical well-being and if we want to assess the effects of management decisions on people, health outcomes would seem to be one productive focus of research attention. That's because organizational effects on psychological well-being frequently manifest themselves in people's health status, as, for instance, in the effect of socioeconomic status on physical health as operating through its effect on negative emotions (Gallo & Matthews, 2003). Moreover, health-care costs are important both to companies and to society.

Why Does Human Well-Being Receive Relatively Short Shrift?

Given the profound effects of organizations and work arrangements on the psychological and physical well-being of the people who work in them and the growing interest in sustainability, it is interesting that the human dimension of sustainability remains largely in the background. In both social psychology and economics, there is increasing research attention to happiness as an important dependent variable in and of itself (e.g., Diener, Suh, Lucas, & Smith, 1999; Frey & Stutzer, 2002; Oswald, 1997; Ryff, 1989). And as already noted, health is considered an important indicator of well-being for both individuals and societies.

However, in the management literature, the focus on a somewhat related topic, job satisfaction has evolved over time to largely although not exclusively consider the connection between job satisfaction and turnover—which is costly to the firm—and also the relationship between job satisfaction or its conceptual cousin, employee engagement, and customer service and other dimensions of organizational performance. Although there is obviously a large and important literature on work-family conflict and its consequences, once again a focus of at least some significant fraction of this literature is on the consequences of such conflict for organizational well-being, as reflected in absenteeism, sickness, turnover, and job performance.

This is not to say there is no interest in social responsibility and people for their own sake, but in the management literature, such concerns are often, although not invariably, coupled with their connection to profits, costs, or productivity. This is scarcely the first time this point has been made. Walsh, Weber, and Margolis (2003, p. 859) have noted that while the Academy of Management was founded to deal with society's objectives and the public interest along with organizational economic performance, over time the field "has pursued society's economic objectives much more than it has its social ones." March and Sutton (1997, p. 698), in their critique of performance as a dependent variable, commented that organizational researchers lived in two worlds, one of which "demands and rewards speculations about how to improve performance."

Why some topics get attention and others don't, and how research questions are framed are themselves important topics for research and theoretical exploration. As Ferraro, Pfeffer, and Sutton (2005, 2009) have argued, theories matter, not just because theories influence the institutional arrangements, norms, and language of organizational management, but also because theories focus both research and public policy attention. Molotch and Boden (1985) described three faces of power. The first face is the ability to prevail in explicit conflicts over decisions. The second face of power concerns the capacity to set agendas—whether or not there will be any decisions over which to fight and what such decisions will entail. They defined the third face of power as "the struggle over the linguistic premises upon which the legitimacy of accounts will be judged" (Molotch & Boden, 1985, p. 273), and argued this aspect of power was the least visible and accountable and possibly therefore the most potent. In the present context, how we talk—or don't—about sustainability and what is considered legitimately included and excluded from such discussions affects what we study, how we study it, and by extension, what becomes included in public policy debates as well.

There are undoubtedly many reasons that the sustainability of the physical environment has received more emphasis than have people. One possibility is that the consequences of organizational actions on the physical environment are frequently much more visible and, therefore, salient. You can see the icebergs melting, polar bears stranded, forests cut down, and mountaintops reshaped by mining, and experience firsthand the dirty air and water that can come from company economic activities that impose externalities. Reduced life expectancy and poorer physical and mental health status are more hidden from view. Even the occasional and well-publicized act of employee or ex-employee violence has multiple causes and is often seen as aberrant behavior outside of the control and responsibility of the employer.

Another explanation for the relative attention to physical versus human sustainability is the differential actions taken to make sustainability salient. Organizations and groups focused on improving the physical environment have taken steps to increase the visibility of what companies do—reporting on carbon emissions and measures of environmental compliance, for instance, and trying to ensure that these reports generate news coverage. Partly as a result of this public attention, laws have been passed in numerous countries mandating environmental compliance to various standards and requiring assessments of environmental impact before certain forms of economic development can take place. These laws, at a minimum, ensure the availability of more data to assess physical environmental effects. And while between 1980 and 2006 there was a 62.3% increase in the number of U.S. federal staff dealing with the environment, during that same period there was a *decrease* of

34.5% in staff in agencies overseeing the workplace (Dudley & Warren, 2005). These changes in federal staffing oversight also provide some indication of shifting social priorities and alterations in the focus of public policy attention.

One lesson for those interested in human sustainability is that developing a consistent set of measures or indicators of the construct, gathering data on them, and publicizing such data might provide more impetus for focusing on the human sustainability implications of what organizations do. Another implication is that federal and state regulation and oversight matter—both for the substantive effect and as a signal of what society values.

Both environmental and social sustainability confront one issue: the belief that the sole goal of companies should be to maximize profits and the idea that "markets work well to reach optimal use of scarce resources" (Ambec & Lanoie, 2008, p. 45) so that markets should generally be left unimpeded. Davis (2008, 2009) has provided an account of the rise of shareholder (as contrasted with stakeholder) capitalism and the associated primacy of economic criteria in business and public decision making and has noted the growing importance of the market-like aspects of many domains of life, ranging from housing to employment. Because all forms of sustainability contravene both the idea of economic performance above all else and the inviolability of markets, much more research is needed to understand the waxing and waning of managerial ideas and ideology. A model for such an investigation is Barley and Kunda's (1992) exploration of the cycling of managerial discourse related to employee control between normative (cultural) and rational (economic) bases. The point is that ideas and ideology are themselves important topics of study and such an analysis is inextricably linked to variation in the interest in sustainability in any of its forms or manifestations.

In many respects, sustainability represents a set of values and beliefs. As such, it is an ideology. Unfortunately, as nicely documented by Jost (2006, p. 651), "the end of ideology was declared more than a generation ago by sociologists and political scientists." Jost, Nosek, and Gosling (2008) also detailed the resurgence of ideology as an explanatory construct in many branches of psychology and illustrated its explanatory usefulness. Ideology and belief may be even less frequent topics of study in management, with its emphasis on performance, efficiency, and rationality. However, as Tetlock (2000) demonstrated, political ideology can be empirically uncovered, dimensionalised, and, most important, used to explain how managers decide what course of action to take in realistic scenarios concerning topics ranging from correcting safety defects to corporate accountability. If we are to understand why human sustainability receives relatively short shrift, ideology, how and why it develops, and how it affects decisions will need to be a part of the research agenda.

Another factor that may explain the difference between environmental and human sustainability derives from the different actors in the two systems and the presumption of choice. Few would argue that trees "choose" to be cut down, that the air or water decides to be dirty, or that polar bears make decisions that result in the disappearance of food and habitat. Therefore, there is an implicit assumption that people must act on behalf of the environment, threatened species of plants and animals, and possibly even indigenous populations because these entities can't act on their own behalf. Employees, however, have choices, and exercise their choices in a labor market in which they compete for jobs and employers compete for talent. Presumably if they don't like the conditions of their jobs, including the degree of inequality, the amount of stress, or the absence of health insurance, employees can decide to work elsewhere. At the limit, if the conditions of work are really life-threatening, as the evidence shows, employees can choose unemployment over ill health and/or premature death.

Ideas about market outcomes being fair—even if they sometimes aren't (Blount, 2000)—the primacy of markets (Davis, 2008), and the fact that people are capable of making choices—even if such choices are constrained and socially influenced—lead naturally to a very different approach to human sustainability. Threatened plants and animals and the natural world need protection, but sentient humans making free choices in competitive markets can, and should, fend for themselves. This line of argument, coupled with the finding that profitable companies are believed to be more ethical than unprofitable ones (Jost et al., 2003)—as one way of justifying their profitability and as an example of the tendency to attribute good qualities to an entity that is successful—lead to greater reluctance to find human sustainability problematic and requiring intervention.

Although I have highlighted two factors—visibility of consequences and ideology—as helping to account for the relative emphasis on environmental as opposed to human sustainability, there are undoubtedly many other factors at work. The fundamental message is that we need to understand what subjects receive attention and why, as well as the beliefs and values that form the foundation for our theorizing—not just for the topic of sustainability but for many others, as well. The evidence suggests that these are important and underexplored issues.

What If We Took Human Sustainability Seriously? A Research Agenda

Throughout this article I have highlighted questions that could productively receive research attention. In this concluding section, I offer some additional suggestions that logically follow from the literature reviewed in this article.

As Ambec and Lanoie (2008) noted, one of the major issues addressed by research on environmental sustainability has been whether or not adopting sustainability practices imposes net costs on companies, thereby eroding their competitiveness, or whether the benefits of being "green" more than outweigh any costs incurred. Completely parallel questions and issues confront a focus on human sustainability. First, just as in the case of environmental pollution, companies that do not provide health insurance, lay people off, pay inadequate wages, and have work arrangements that stress and overwork their employees also impose externalities that others pay for even as they save on their own costs. That's because some portion of the extra costs of increased physical and psychological illness fall on the broader health system through, for instance, increased use of public health and emergency room facilities. Second, just as green companies enjoy reputational benefits that help in brand building and product differentiation, so, too, we might expect that companies with better records of human sustainability could enjoy benefits in attracting and retaining employees and also in building a reputation that could attract additional consumer demand. Therefore, whether or not it pays to be a company that offers a system high in human sustainability, and how the various costs and benefits balance and under what conditions, would be an important focus for research.

There are some data that suggest that human sustainability may pay off for companies. Each year the Great Place to Work Institute, in conjunction with *Fortune,* publishes a list of the best places to work. Most of those places are noted for their provision of good working conditions and benefits, including vacations, sick days, health insurance, training, and jobs that provide people autonomy and challenge. The Institute's Web site shows data indicating that companies on the list consistently outperform benchmark indices over varying periods of time, indicating that, at least as measured by stock market performance, it is good to be a great place to work. How and why these returns accrue remains to be explored in more detail. But it is quite likely that, just as in the case of environmental sustainability, human sustainability pays. Indeed, the literature on the positive effects of employee-centered management practices is extensive (e.g., Becker & Huselid, 1998). If so, that raises a third question: if it does pay to be green, whether "green" is assessed in environmental or human terms, or both, then why is it so difficult to get companies to adopt practices consistent with sustainability?

Another implication of the research cited may help to explain one of the paradoxes of the U.S. health-care system—why it costs so much even as it does not deliver measurable health benefits, as assessed by indicators ranging from infant mortality to life expectancy to survival rates for various serious illnesses, that are no better than in many other industrialized countries. Once again, there are undoubtedly many answers to this important question. But one possibility is this: If health status is affected by what happens to people on the job, the relatively poor health-care outcomes in the U.S. might result from a laissez faire labor market that leaves even the provision of paid sick days and paid vacation at the discretion of employers. In other words, differences in the distribution of working conditions across different countries (or, for that matter, other political units such as states or even industries) could possibly help account for differences in the differences in health outcomes. Because of differences in unionization rates (by industry and sector) and differences across states in both formal regulation of working conditions and the vigor with which such regulations are enforced, there is a great deal of natural variation in working conditions that research has shown to be relevant to health and mortality. Exploring whether those variations also account for variations in health-care outcomes and costs would be fruitful.

Wilper et al. (2009) estimated that there are more than 44,000 excess deaths in the United States annually because people lack health insurance. Some, although not all, of the absence of health insurance results from employer decisions. If one added to the portion of these deaths resulting from employer actions the mortality coming from layoffs, company-generated inequalities in income and control over work, and all the other factors briefly reviewed in this article, the resulting number would be both interesting and important. It might spark some serious effort to prevent deaths from employer decisions. There is already a great deal of employer and public policy focus on individual choices such as diet and exercise. Attention to the role of the employer in individual health status would round out the picture.

There is no reason why building sustainable companies should focus just on the physical and not the social environment. It is not just the natural world that is at risk from harmful business practices. We should care as much about people as we do about polar bears—or the environmental savings from using better milk jugs—and also understand the causes and consequences of how we focus our research and policy attention.

Note

1. In this paper I use the term social environment to include organizational effects on people and small groups. Just as physical sustainability considers the consequences of organizational activity for material, physical resources, social sustainability might consider how organizational activities affect people's physical and mental health and well-being—the stress of work practices on the human system—as well as effects of management practices such as work hours and behaviors that produce workplace stress on groups and group cohesion and also the richness of social life, as exemplified by participation in civic, voluntary, and community organizations.

References

Ambec, S., & Lanoie, P. (2008). Does it pay to be green? A systematic overview. *Academy of Management Perspectives, 22,* 45–62.

Bansal, P. (2002). The corporate challenges of sustainable development. *Academy of Management Executive, 16,* 122–131.

Barley, S. R., & Kunda, G. (1992). Design and devotion: Surges of rational and normative ideologies of control in managerial discourse. *Administrative Science Quarterly, 37,* 363–399.

Baron, J. N., & Bielby W. T. (1980). Bringing the firms back in: Stratification, segmentation, and the organization of work. *American Sociological Review, 45,* 737–765.

Becker, B. E., & Huselid, M. A. (1998). High performance systems and firm performance: A synthesis of research and managerial implications. *Research in Personnel and Human Resources Management, 16,* 53–101.

Blakely, T. A., Collings, S. C. D., & Atkinson, J. (2003). Unemployment and suicide: Evidence for a causal association? *Journal of Epidemiology and Community Health, 57,* 594–600.

Bloom, M. (1999). The performance effects of pay dispersion on individuals and organizations. *Academy of Management Journal, 42,* 25–40.

Blount, S. (2000). Whoever said that markets were fair? *Negotiation Journal,16,* 237–252.

Budros, A. (1997). The new capitalism and organizational rationality: The adoption of downsizing programs, 1979–1994. *Social Forces, 76,* 229–250.

Cappelli, P. (1999). *The New Deal at Work.* Boston: Harvard Business School Press.

Card, D., Dobkin, C., & Maestas, N. (2009). Does Medicare save lives? *Quarterly Journal of Economics, 124,* 597–636.

Cascio, W. F. (2006). The economic impact of employee behaviors on organizational performance. *California Management Review, 48,* 41–59.

Catalano, R. (1991). The health effects of economic insecurity. *American Journal of Public Health, 81,* 1148–1152.

Catalano, R., Novaco, R. W., & McConnell, W. (2002). Layoffs and violence revisited. *Aggressive Behavior, 28,* 233–247.

Chandola, T., Brunner, E., & Marmot. M. (2006). Chronic stress at work and the metabolic syndrome: Prospective study. *British Medical Journal, 332,* 521–525.

Colvin, G. (2008, October 16). How Sam's Club sees the future. *Fortune.* Retrieved February 15, 2010, from http://money.cnn.com/2008/10/15/news/companies/Wal-Marts_rising_star_colvin.fortune/index.htm.

Cornia, G. A., & Paniccia, R. (Eds.). (2000). *The mortality crisis in transitional economies.* Oxford, UK: Oxford University Press.

Cowherd, D. M., & Levine, D. I. (1992). Product quality and pay equity between lower-level employees and top management: An investigation of distributive justice theory. *Administrative Science Quarterly, 37,* 302–320.

Davis, G. F. (2008). The rise and fall of finance and the end of the society of organizations. *Academy of Management Perspectives, 23,* 27–44.

Davis, G. F. (2009). *Managed by the Markets: How Finance re-shaped America.* Oxford, UK: Oxford University Press.

Deaton, A. (2003). Health, inequality, and economic development. *Journal of Economic Literature, 41,* 113–158.

Diener, E., Suh, E. M., Lucas, R. E., & Smith, H. L. (1999). Subjective well-being: Three decades of progress. *Psychological Bulletin, 125,* 276–302.

Dube, A., Graham-Squire, D., Jacobs, K., & Luce, S. (2007). *Living Wage Policies and Wal-Mart: How a Higher Wage Standard Would Impact Wal-Mart Workers and Shoppers.* Berkeley, CA: U.C. Berkeley Center for Labor Research and Education.

Dudley, S., & Warren, M. (2005). *Upward trend in regulation continues: An analysis of the U.S. budget for fiscal years 2005 and 2006.* George Mason University, Mercatus Center, 2006 Annual Report, Regulators' Budget Report 27.

Eliason, M., & Storrie, D. (2009). Does job loss shorten life? *Journal of Human Resources, 44,* 277–302.

Ferraro, F., Pfeffer, J., & Sutton, R. I. (2005). Economic language and assumptions: How theories can become self-fulfilling. *Academy of Management Review, 30,* 8–24.

Ferraro, F., Pfeffer, J., & Sutton, R. I. (2009). How and why theories matter: A comment on Felin and Foss (2009). *Organization Science, 20,* 669–675.

Fountain, H. (2010, January 3). Urban environment: Sustainability comes of age. *New York Times,* Education Life, p. 20.

Franks, P., Clancy, C. M. & Gold, M. R. (1993). Health insurance and mortality: Evidence from a national cohort. *Journal of the American Medical Association, 270,* 737–741.

Frey, B. S., & Stutzer, A. (2002). What can economists learn from happiness research? *Journal of Economic Literature, 40,* 402–435.

Frone, M. R. (2000). Work-family conflict and employee psychiatric disorders: The national comorbidity survey. *Journal of Applied Psychology, 85(6),* 888–895.

Frone, M. R., Russell, M., & Barnes, G. M. (1996). Work-family conflict, gender, and health-related outcomes: A study of employed parents in two community samples. *Journal of Occupational Health Psychology, 1(1),* 57–69.

Gakidou, E. E., Murray, C. J. L., & Frenk, J. (2000). Defining and measuring health inequality: An approach based on the distribution of health expectancy. *Bulletin of the World Health Organization, 78,* 42–54.

Gallo, L. C., & Matthews, K. A. (2003). Understanding the association between socioeconomic status and physical health: Do negative emotions play a role? *Psychological Bulletin, 129,* 10–51.

Greenhouse, S. (2009 October 30). BP faces record fine for '05 refinery explosion. *New York Times,* p. B1.

Hackman, J. R., & Oldham, G. R. (1980). *Work redesign.* Reading, MA: Addison-Wesley.

Himmelstein, D. U., Warren, E., Thorne, D., & Woolhandler, S. (2005). MarketWatch: Illness and injury as contributor to bankruptcy. *Health Affairs-Web Exclusive,* W5-63–W5-73.

Hsu, T. (2010, January 2). Corporate eco-managers turning companies green. *San Francisco Chronicle,* p. D2.

Jost, J. T. (2006). The end of the end of ideology. *American Psychologist, 61,* 651–670.

Jost, J. T., Blount, S., Pfeffer, J., & Hunyady, G. (2003). Fair market ideology: Its cognitive-motivational underpinnings. *Research in Organizational Behavior, 25,* 53–91.

Jost, J. T., Nosek, B. A., & Gosling, S. D. (2008). Ideology: Its resurgence in social, personality, and political psychology. *Perspectives on Psychological Science, 3,* 126–136.

Kaufman, L. (2009, December 20). Coming clean about carbon: Industries disclose emissions to claim the high ground. *New York Times,* p. B1.

Keefe, V., Reid, P., Ormsby, C., Robson, B., Purdie, G., Baxter, J., & Ngati Kahungunu Iwi Imcorporated (2002). Serious health events following involuntary job loss in New Zealand meat processing workers. *International Journal of Epidemiology, 31,* 1155–1161.

Kivimaki, M., Vahtera, J., Pentti, J., & Ferris, J. E. (2000). Factors underlying the effect of organizational downsizing on health of employees: Longitudinal cohort study. *British Medical Journal, 320,* 971–975.

Levy, H., & Meltzer, D. (2001). *What do we really know about whether health insurance affects health?* (Working Paper No. 6). Ann Arbor, MI: University of Michigan, Economic Research Inititiative on the Uninsured.

Lynch, J., Davey-Smith, G., Hillemeier, M., Shaw, M., Raghunathan, T., & Kaplan, G. (2001). Income inequality, psychosocial environment and health: Comparisons across wealthy nations. *Lancet, 358,* 194–200.

March, J. G., & Sutton, R. I. (1997). Organizational performance as a dependent variable. *Organization Science, 8,* 698–706.

Marcus, A. A., & Fremeth, A. R. (2009). Green management matters regardless. *Academy of Management Perspectives, 23,* 17–26.

Marmot, M. (2004). *The Status Syndrome: How social standing affects our health and longevity.* London: Times Books.

Marmot, M., & Bobak, M. (2000). International comparators and poverty and health in Europe, *British Medical Journal, 321,* 1124–1128.

Marmot, M. G., Bosma, H., Hemingway, H., Brunner, E., & Stansfeld, S. (1997). Contribution of job control and other risk factors to social variations in coronary heart disease incidence. *Lancet, 350,* 235–239.

Molotch, H. I., & Boden, D. (1985). Talking social structure: Discourse, domination, and the Watergate hearings. *American Sociological Review, 50,* 273–288.

National Institute for Occupational Safety and Health (2004). *Overtime and extended work shifts: Recent findings on illnesses, injuries, and health behaviors* (Publication No. 2204-143, May). Washington, DC: Author.

Navarro, M. (2010, January 3). Sustainable cultures: A step beyond anthropology. *New York Times, Education Life,* p. 20.

Oswald, A. J. (1997). Happiness and economic performance. *The Economic Journal, 107,* 1815–1831.

Pfeffer, J., & Langton, N. (1988). Wage inequality and the organization of work: The case of academic departments. *Administrative Science Quarterly, 33,* 588–606.

Pfeffer, J., & Langton, N. (1993). The effect of wage dispersion on satisfaction, productivity, and working collaboratively: Evidence from college and university faculty. *Administrative Science Quarterly, 38,* 382–407.

Plambeck, E. L., & Denend, L. (2007). Wal-Mart's sustainability strategy. (Case No. OIT7-71). Stanford, CA: Stanford University, Graduate School of Business.

Potosky, A. L., Breen, N., Graubard, B. I., & Parsons, P. E. (1998). The association between health care coverage and the use of cancer screening tests: Results from the 1992 National Health Interview Survey. *Medical Care, 36,* 257–270.

Putunam, R. D. (2000). *Bowling alone: The collapse and revival of American Community.* New York: Simon and Schuster.

Rosenbloom, S., & Barbaro, M. (2009, January 25). Green-light specials, now at Wal-Mart. *New York Times,* p. BU1.

Rousseau, D. M. (2006). The shift in risk from employers to workers in the new employment relationship. In E. E. Lawler, III & J. O'Toole (eds.), *America at Work: Choices and Challenges* (pp. 153–172). New York: Palgrave Macmillan.

Ryff, C. D. (1989). Happiness is everything, or is it? Explorations on the meaning of psychological well-being. *Journal of Personality and Social Psychology, 57,* 1069–1081.

Schoen, C., & DesRoches, C. (2000). Uninsured and unstably insured: The importance of continuous insurance coverage. *Health Services Research, 35,* 187–206.

Siegel, P. A., & Hambrick, D. C. (2005). Pay disparities within top management groups: Evidence of harmful effects on performance of high-technology firms. *Organization Science, 16,* 259–274.

Stave, G. M., Muchmore, L. & Gardner, H. (2003). Quantifiable impact of the contract for health and wellness: Health behaviors, health care costs, disability, and workers' compensation. *Journal of Occupational and Environmental Medicine, 45,* 109–117.

Sudano, J. J., & Baker, D. W. (2003). Intermittent lack of health insurance coverage and use of preventive services. *American Journal of Public Health, 93,* 130–137.

Sullivan, D., & von Wachter, T. (2007). *Mortality, mass layoffs, and career outcomes: An analysis using administrative data* (Working Paper No. 13626). Cambridge, MA: National Bureau of Economic Research.

Tetlock, P. E. (2000). Cognitive biases and organizational correctives: Do both disease and cure depend on the politics of the beholder? *Administrative Science Quarterly, 46,* 293–326,

Walsh, J. P., Weber, K. & Margolis, J. D. (2003). Social issues and management: Our lost cause found. *Journal of Management, 29,* 859–881.

Wildman, J. (2003). Income related inequalities in mental health in Great Britain: Analysing the causes of health inequality over time. *Journal of Health Economics, 22,* 295–312.

Wilper, A., Woolhandler, S., Lasser, K. E., McCormick, D., Bor, D. H., & Himmelstein, D. U. (2009). Health insurance and mortality in US adults. *American Journal of Public Health, 99,* 2289–2295.

Yang, H., Schnall, P. L., Jauregui, M., Su, T., & Baker, D. (2006). Work hours and self-reported hypertension among working people in California. *Hypertension, 48,* 744–750.

Critical Thinking

1. What can organizations do to help "sustain" their employees?

2. Why have employees generally been ignored in the discussion of sustainability?

3. What can be done to remedy this situation?

JEFFREY PFEFFER (Pfeffer_Jeffrey@gsb.stanford.edu) is the Thomas D. Dee II Professor of Organizational Behavior at the Graduate School of Business, Stanford University.

Acknowledgement—I gratefully acknowledge the advice, encouragement, and inspiration of Nuria Chinchilla from IESE, who encouraged me to think about the issue of human sustainability in both societies and companies. The helpful comments of the editor and the reviewers substantially clarified the arguments.

The Leadership Challenges Facing HR

Top CHROs Share Learnings and Advice on What's Next

The Chief Human Resources Officer's job has never been more crucial, and, at the same time, more challenging. The severe economic downturn and slow recovery has impacted leader and employee engagement across industries and across the country. Frequent CEO succession, new financial regulations and ethics scandals, along with more active and engaged boards of directors, have added to the complexity that confronts HR leaders. And many of us still are locked into what seems the HR function's never-ending search for relevance and impact.

STEVE STECKLER

With this as context and leadership as the focus of this special issue, this is the right moment to engage in a rare and candid conversation with a small group of CHROs. We asked what they learned about having impact, being successful and about the serious challenges facing both HR leaders and the function.

You will recognize many of these leaders; they are well-known within our field, some reaching business media fame. They are from iconic brands and companies and have been acknowledged for their impact and for developing great business and human resources talent.

We specifically selected a group largely made-up of those who already have completed their careers as CHROs, although one or two said that they might be tempted to re-enter the arena. Most are currently consulting, teaching, writing or serving on boards. This created a singularly high level of candor and openness, including some raw self-reflection. We also included a relative newcomer to the role for her comparative perspective. Our interviews occurred during the final weeks of summer 2010.

The level of exchange exceeded our expectations. A small number of common themes emerged, including what was particularly difficult about being successful in the role, in what areas many of these leaders felt ill-prepared and what they learned about their leaders and the HR function. In addition, they shared a loud warning to current HR leaders about what may be next.

Steve Steckler: Mark Hurd's story at Hewlett Packard was just reported, so let's talk about ethics and the responsibility that human resources and HR leaders should have in company ethics. With so many scandals over the years in U.S. companies, what role does HR play?

Our CHRO Panel and Their Former Companies:

- **Dick Antoine;** Global Human Resources Officer at Procter & Gamble
- **Bill Conaty;** Senior Vice President of Human Resources, General Electric
- **Ursie Fairbairn;** Executive Vice President of Human Resources and Quality at American Express. Prior to that, she was senior vice president of human resources at Union Pacific
- **Libby Sartain;** Executive Vice President of Human Resources at Yahoo! Inc. Prior to that, she was vice president of people at Southwest Airlines
- **Dick Sibbernsen;** Executive Vice President of Human Resources for AT&T. Prior to that, he was chief human resources officer for BellSouth Corporation
- **Ian Ziskin;** Corporate Vice President of Human Resources and Chief Administrative Officer at Northrop Grumman Corporation. Prior to that he was executive vice president and chief human resources officer at Qwest Communications

Our current CHRO is **Kalen Holmes.** She is executive vice president of partner resources at Starbucks.

Ursie Fairbairn: Well, I think HR definitely has a role. I think that, to play that role successfully you have to have facts, you have to be connected and you need to be courageous. And sometimes that means you are placed in a very vulnerable

Recent Research on the CHRO Role

In 2009, the Cornell Center for Advanced Human Resources Studies (CAHRS) published the results of their first Chief Human Resources Officers Survey, "Strategies and Challenges of the Chief Human Resource Officer: Results of the First Annual Cornell/ CAHRS Survey of CHRO's." Our colleague Pat Wright led the study. Many of its conclusions mirror perfectly the comments of our interviewees.

The survey was sent to CHROs at U.S. Fortune 150 companies and to 10 additional CHROs at CAHRS partner companies. The study focused on a number of areas, including the different roles and responsibilities that CHROs considered to be the key parts of their jobs and how they allocated their time to different stakeholders and to these roles. The study found that there were seven distinct roles of the CHRO:

- Leader of the HR function (22% of time spent)
- Strategic adviser to the executive team (21% of time spent)
- Counselor/confidante/coach to the executive team (17% of time spent)
- Talent architect (17% of time spent)
- Liaison to the board of directors (10% of time spent)
- Workforce sensor (8% of time spent)
- Representative of the firm (5% of time spent)

Consider how closely these findings reflect what our CHRO panel said.

Moreoever, when the seven areas are combined based on total time spent with stakeholders, CHROs spend the majority of their time with their peers and the CEO.[1]

Here is a portion of the 2009 report:

"The results reveal that CHROs focus their attention in two general directions. They serve as business leaders who spend significant amounts of time with the CEO, the executive leadership team and the individuals making up the team, and the board of directors. They also devote considerable time with the HR leadership team and individuals who make up that team. In other words, they must be both business leaders and HR leaders."

"In addition, CHROs view their roles as strategic advisor, counselor/confidante/coach to the executive team, and talent architect as being the most important aspects of their job in terms of impact on the business, and the ones in which they spend significant amounts of time. In addition, while they spend the greatest amount of time as leaders of the HR function, they do not view that role as particularly high impact."

In 2010, the survey was expanded to the U.S. Fortune 200 and asked many of the same questions. Additionally, Wright and Mark Stewart, PhD also focused on the CHRO's relationship with the board of directors, along with identifying innovative practices that had been developed and implemented within their HR organizations. They found that the financial crisis that influenced 2009 survey responses had been replaced with a more optimistic view. They describe the move from "bunker" to "building."[2]

Wright and Stewart found that CHROs were now increasing their focus on retaining talent, building HR capability, spending more time with their HR leaders and addressing high potential talent.[3] CHROs were also giving more time to their role as HR leaders and as the talent strategist/architect.[4] For their CEOs, talent tops the agenda, and the lack of HR talent is one of the key obstacles to achieving the CEO's agenda for HR.[5]

Both the 2010 CHRO Survey Report and the Executive Summary of the 2009 CHRO Survey can be downloaded from: www.ilr.cornell.edu/cahrs/research.

---

[1]Wright, Patrick M. (2009). "Strategies and challenges of the chief human resource officer: Results of the first annual Cornell/CAHRS survey of CHRO's." 6.

[2]Wright, Patrick M. and Stewart, Mark. (2010). "From bunker to building: Results from the 2010 chief human resource officer survey Cornell center for advanced human resource studies (CAHRS)." 4.

[3]Wright, Patrick M. and Stewart, Mark. (2010). "From bunker to building: Results from the 2010 Chief human resource officer survey. Cornell center for advanced human resource studies (CAHRS)." 4.

[4]Wright, Patrick M. and Stewart, Mark. (2010). "From bunker to building: Results from the 2010 Chief human resource officer survey. Cornell center for advanced human resource studies (CAHRS)." 4.

[5]Wright, Patrick M. and Stewart, Mark. (2010). "From bunker to building: Results from the 2010 chief human resource officer survey. Cornell center for advanced human resource studies (CAHRS)." 4.

---

position whether that scandal is a business scandal or whether that scandal is a personal scandal.

Bill Conaty: I think that the best thing that HR can do and that the CEO can do is make integrity the all-encompassing value of the company. Sure, we all have got a list of values that are important that describe how you work and how you behave and what is expected of you, but integrity has got to be the centerpiece of the whole deal. I know in GE when it came to integrity violations, we said one strike and you're out. You weren't going to get a second chance.

Libby Sartain: I think that it is our job to monitor the behavior of our people and ensure that ethical behavior is a way of life in our organizations. My experience is that most of us take it seriously and we partner with our CEOs. As part of that partnership, we point out where there are issues that are concerning. HR can have a separate relationship with the board. If a situation cannot be resolved inside, is serious, or involves the CEO or a top executive, we must talk with the board when these things happen and recommend a course of action. I have known several CHROs that have had to go to the board and recommend that their bosses be fired over these situations.

Dick Antoine: HR is the guardian of the values of any company or organization. It's what we are uniquely charged with doing. We must protect those values and we must defend employees who have small voices and smaller jobs in organizations. And we do this through a combination of training and education and reinforcement of the values. We also do it by consistently enforcing discipline in cases where values are violated that normally will mean termination regardless of level in the organization.

Ian Ziskin: The short answer is yes, HR does play a role and should play a role going forward. HR contributes, perhaps most uniquely, by ensuring that there are mechanisms in place in the organization to make it safe for people to tell the truth, to surface things that are wrong and to surface things that are right for that matter. There should be tools that you use to solicit input and feedback and make it safe for people to tell you what is on their minds. I don't believe that HR has sole responsibility over that, but somebody has to be the advocate. I think the law department would say that it has a role to play and the finance organization would say that it has a role to play.

Steckler: Let's talk about what was most surprising to you when you first took the CHRO role?

Sartain: Well, I had two very different situations at the two companies where I was the head of HR. I had been at Southwest for seven years before I was promoted to become head of HR. In working for the same company, my biggest surprise was that as you reach a new level in the organization, there is sort of a new culture, a new set of unspoken norms and rules at that level. If you are not aware of that, you can make some mistakes. After a few years as head of HR, I was put on the executive committee, and at that point, I was the first HR person ever at the table. Even though I believed that I had been placed onto the executive committee because of what I had accomplished as the head of HR, I still had to earn my seat on the executive committee once I was there. At Yahoo, when I joined the company as head of HR, the company was so young that I had a lot of surprises. There was not any organized executive committee and no cadence about how decisions were made and no one really felt that was necessary. So we had to create an informal operating committee, and I worked with the COO to do that. Later, we had to establish formal decision rules so that we could get "stuff" done.

Dick Sibbernsen: For me, at both companies, the surprise was how each company you are at, has a different business model with different ways of making money. There were different ways that power was structured and decision rights created. It really brought home that there is not a prescription for success, but a range of solutions and that how you get the performance needed to achieve strategy is going to be different from company to company.

Fairbairn: Although I had held senior HR roles before at other companies, each time I became head of HR, first at Union Pacific and then at American Express, I was always surprised about the ability to influence and that the amount of opportunity to have an impact was so huge. There were so many ways that you could make a big difference, including helping leaders be more effective, helping the board select the right successor, helping to implement new technology, helping the leadership team be more effective.

Antoine: When I was named CHRO at Procter & Gamble, except for being a plant HR manager 20 years prior, my background was exclusively in operations rather than HR, so a lot of it was surprising and a learning experience. One specific area of surprise was that I was able to shape the role. It evolved from a narrower definition when I started, to a pretty broad role that included a significant role with the board of directors.

Conaty: Although, I spent my entire career with GE and moved up within the company, when I took the top HR role for all of corporate human resources for the entire company, the stakes became much higher. You are now dealing with the CEO of the corporation and you know at GE, a dozen or 15 different business units, versus working for just one singular business unit and one CEO. The job was much broader with stronger constituencies. You really learn whether you have the ability to see the bigger picture and really make a significant impact on a much larger stage.

Ziskin: For me, the most surprising thing was that sometimes what leaders said they wanted from HR, didn't really match their own behavior. I have had this experience twice, as head of HR for Qwest and then at Northrop Grumman. People seemed very clear at first about the things that they were looking for out of the HR function and out of the CHRO: Generally, the things that you typically hear, be a good business partner, lead change and invest in talent and help improve the performance of the business. But as I stepped into both jobs, I found that there was much greater resistance to actually making some of those things happen then you would imagine. It also meant that peers on the leadership team might also have to change, do things differently and be more receptive to the concepts that you were trying to sell as the new head of HR. This also included other people in HR, who were clamoring for more of a voice and for more of a seat at the table. They wanted to influence more things that they saw could be done differently and better, but even they were reluctant to change to achieve some of the things that they said they wanted.

Kalen Holmes: Compared to this group, I am a new CHRO. I have been in this role at Starbucks for just about a year. I spent a lot of time with Howard Schultz, our president, chairman and CEO and with others on the senior leadership team during the interview process. Through those discussions, it became apparent that Starbucks was entering a very exciting time as a company. The most surprising aspect for me entering this role is the pace at which we are entering our new evolution of growth; and, therefore, the immediate focus we are putting toward organizational capability and process to ensure we are readying the organization for this evolution.

Steckler: How did being in the role change your perspective about the company, leadership and HR?

Fairbairn: Several things come to mind: When you have more information, you are better able to prioritize and diagnose the issues. Sometimes you do all of your homework when you are not yet the head of human resources, but when you are inside, you understand it so much better and you, therefore, are more able to do your job superbly well. The second would be the importance of leadership. Leadership is so crucial in differentiating between the just average, the good, the very good and the excellent.

Ziskin: I agree. Great leadership does matter. Sometimes you might be able to convince yourself that any large, complicated organization can succeed despite itself and keep things chugging along irrespective of who is in charge. But at the same time, you know that who's in charge does make a difference in terms of the tone they set, the priorities on which they focus, the questions they ask and the people with whom they surround themselves. Great leadership has a multiplier effect that goes deeper down into the organization. I think that I learned a lot about the importance of quickly figuring out whether the leaders that you have are the ones who are going to take you to the next level. The role that HR has is in bringing that question up and then taking responsibility for doing something about it.

Sibbernsen: I believe that the main job of the CHRO is to set up the context in which the senior leaders can really do a deep dive and deep thinking about their people issues. Set the context, start the conversation and set up the going forward priorities. Identify five or six priorities, and then come up with the solutions. I would say that there are four categories that the CHRO is going to spend 75 percent of his or her time around: defining what the key organization implications of the business strategy are; facilitating a real deep discussion and deep thinking; the third bucket is then working up the solutions. Fourth is developing a project plan to go forward and to get these solutions into the operating system of the company. Delivery of all of this has to be linked to business outcomes. Did we lift revenue? Did we lift the productivity? Most companies are pretty good at strategy. The performance gap is execution. This is the sweet spot for the CHRO. What are the capabilities to perform this work? That is where I think the very value of an effective CHRO comes into play.

Conaty: When I took the top HR job at GE, I felt that I had become a true insider of the company. Literally and figuratively, you become a corporate insider from the standpoint of the technical, compensation and reporting rules. The other thing from an HR perspective, which I think is critical here, is that you become the HR face of GE, and people want to know who the face of GE is from an HR standpoint. You become part of the outside world with the HR Policy Association, later the National Academy of Human Resources. Your network expands.

Steckler: Do you think that the leader of HR should come from the HR function? What about coming from outside the function?

Sartain: A lot of people are threatened by someone from outside the function, I am not. If there is a solid leader in the business that the company wants to move into the position for a while, that can be a good situation. We can then feel good when that leader then acquires a much better understanding about what it takes to deliver HR and can go to their peers with that insight. At the same time, I have seen people come in and not know what they are doing and make big mistakes. The only way it can work is if they have very strong lieutenants in the HR function below them and they listen to those folks while helping them better serve the organization. I also think that it is great for an HR person to move into a business role and add value there.

Fairbairn: I think that it can be done, and there are certainly companies who have a history of that. I think that they generally go through a period where the HR function is at a disadvantage. On the other hand, I have learned that for every organizational situation, there are no absolutes. There can be a line person who can become a great head of HR, if they have the right mindset, the right learning, if they have the right team, if they listen and not only talk and if they have a leader who supports them. And here is a perfect parallel. Many companies believe in picking a CEO from inside, but if that hasn't worked then you have to go outside.

Antoine: Understanding my background, which was almost totally from operations, I will now give you the blanket statement. I think it's a really bad idea to put someone in charge of HR who doesn't know and understand HR. So putting me in charge of it was a really bad idea. It turned out some people would say it was a great idea, but I don't agree with that assessment. Unfortunately, there is a belief among many, I won't say the majority, but certainly a lot of CEOs and a lot of senior leaders of companies that anyone can do HR. And I think that's wrong, completely, absolutely wrong. HR has a technology and a methodology and skills around it just like finance does, or research and development or marketing or any other function. Would you have a CFO with no finance or accounting experience? Why would it be OK to have a CHRO without previous HR experience?

Steckler: What was most personally challenging for you about the role?

Conaty: I would say for me it was learning the HR role from the standpoint of dealing with the board of directors. That is the only HR job in the company where you have direct involvement with the GE Board of Directors, and as you might imagine the GE Board of Directors is a pretty star-studded group of rock stars.

Fairbairn: I agree. Working with the board was the most challenging part of the role. When you take on this role the first time, there are so many things that you need to understand and no HR person has done it all; if you had, you would be too old to then take on the CHRO role. You need to learn how to deal with the board in an effective way, recognizing that you have to balance between the board as the representative of the shareholder and your boss, the CEO, who is the leader of the organization. Once you have done it once, it gets easier.

Ziskin: Yes, it's in working with the board. Prior to taking on the CHRO role, you have much more limited exposure to and experience with the board then you really need to have to be effective in the role, and so there is really no great proxy for that. It is a shortcoming in how we develop and prepare our future HR leaders.

Antoine: Managing the boundary between senior leaders and the CEO. On the one hand, you are trying to help the senior leaders with advice and career perspective and on the other hand, you are trying to keep the CEO informed of critical concerns and development issues while protecting the confidences of the senior leaders that talk to you.

Steckler: So how do you better prepare HR leaders for working with the board?

Conaty: Look at what we have done with the National Academy of Human Resources. We have established the CHRO Academy where we spend a day and a half with newly minted VPs of HR. We spend a lot of time of talking about these kinds of issues, dealing with a board on succession, dealing with the board on strategy. I wish that I had had this before 1 took the SVP job at GE.

Steckler: What about other areas that were personally challenging about being in the CHRO role?

Sartain: The most challenging work is long-term strategic workforce planning. It was a little easier at Southwest because we had one business and we could plan our growth. We had to plan ahead to order the number of airplanes we needed in the future up to five years in advance. We didn't always know the cities we wanted to open that far in advance, but we had a long list of possibilities. With every plane ordered, we knew the number of workers we needed to add and HR could plan for staffing. The unknowns were what the economy and the competition would be doing in the future. At Yahoo, even though we knew that there were not enough software programmers in the United States to meet all of the needs that we had in software programming, it was difficult to plan ahead for the next tech center. We needed to open tech centers in other parts of the world, but we knew that we did not want to put a tech center where everyone else was putting one, and the competition didn't tell us where they were going. Yet, sometimes we would tend to focus more on the here and now or the next week, rather than three years from now. We were growing fast, so we didn't always have all of the planning tools we needed. I think that some of the bigger, more mature, companies were better at it than we were.

Ziskin: The other thing that was most personally challenging to me was being able to figure out who the people were within HR that I needed to invest in, to try to give them the tools that they needed to help me be part of the changes that I was attempting to bring about versus the people who were probably just good people, had good experience, but they are weren't really going to help me. You believe that if you give everyone enough information, enough feedback, enough rationale, enough support, they will eventually come around to join what you want them to be part of. But that doesn't always happen.

Steckler: What is so difficult about being successful in the CHRO role?

Holmes: In my view, HR leaders are not any less—or more—successful than other senior leaders. The CHRO plays multiple roles and you have to manage and prioritize your focus. First and foremost, you are the leader of a global function and you have to lead that global function, no one else will do it for you. So I think it is important to spend a lot of time developing your own function, putting the right attention and direction to it, along the way ensuring that you have the right talent, and the right kind of team around you to drive the business forward. At the same time, you have to be the senior generalist for the CEO and for the senior leaders.

Sartain: Everybody has a point of view about talent and about people. If you are the finance person or the head technologist or the chief counsel or whatever else, you don't have as many people who think they know as much as you do about what it is that you do. You really have to have an expertise that adds value beyond what everybody else thinks they know about it. And often, we are the people who have to say "no," or have to make the toughest decisions and that doesn't always make us the most popular leader in the room.

Fairbairn: Three things: One, there is so much to do. Two, the issues are really complex—they are not simple but inter-related, global, and they are complicated. Three, the issues are people issues and people issues that you deal with are never simple. So I think it is the complexity and then balancing the complexity of the issues with the appetite for solutions. It is a hard job, and it never ends, and that is another element. It just goes on and on.

Ziskin: I think that the things that make it most difficult are that the fact that you are in a role that is viewed by most people as a support, advisory and influence role. But you also have accountability for driving change, making unpopular decisions in some cases like we talked about earlier. You are making hard calls about how the business should be organized and who should be in key leadership roles. Not that you are making those decisions by yourself, but you are influencing certainly the CEO and others who have to make those decisions. You are trading on your own personal relationships with people and credibility, and they can choose to support you or not. And then you have to make decisions about how much you are willing to battle to fight for something that you believe is right and important but perhaps less important than other things.

Antoine: I think the difficulty is twofold. For people who are coming from operations or from the line, you have to get used to getting things done through influence with little formal authority. I think most people who come into the role struggle with it for that reason. All of a sudden you've got this incredibly broad portfolio, lots of responsibility, but little authority. The second thing that I found difficult and I think most people do, is the breadth of the role. It's from the mundane cost control to needing to be knowledgeable in all of the expert areas within HR like compensation or benefits or organization behavior, organization design and more. At the same time, you have your relationships with the C-suite team, other members of the senior management team, the senior HR team, the CEO and the board.

Conaty: I think that it is balancing that delicate tightrope walk of being a business partner at one end and an employee advocate on the other. I actually see some HR leaders become so ingrained and obsessed with becoming a business partner that they forget why they are at the table. They become so business- and analytically focused that they miss their role. Unless you can be both, you really are not going to be successful. So when I was in the CHRO role, I had to balance that and not be hesitant to be that employee advocate for all 350,000 people.

Sibbernsen: It goes back to getting the priorities right. That's number one. You have to avoid coming into an organization with a set of prescriptions and prescriptive solutions in your briefcase and start to find problems to solve. That is just the opposite of what is needed and what you should do. Build the priorities and then build up the relationships. Use power effectively and understand who has got the power and who doesn't. You have to use power constructively and establish key relationships.

> It goes back to getting the priorities right . . . Build the priorities and then build up the relationships. Use power effectively and understand who has got the power and who doesn't. You have to use power constructively and establish key relationships.

Steckler: I have seen top HR leaders try to elevate themselves almost a half-step or full step above their peers on the management team to get closer to the CEO because they believed that is part of their role. What do you think about that?

Fairbairn: I am in the school that you do not do that. It is not helpful to accomplishing your goals to put yourself ahead of your business colleagues as peers. You have a very special relationship with the CEO by the very nature of what you do. But you need to make your relationship really bring value to your colleagues and to your peers as well. And if you are seen as in the pocket of the CEO, or seeing yourself as one step closer to the CEO, I think that that has a possible detriment to your effectiveness overall.

Conaty: If the organization deems you to be in the CEO's pocket and that is how you carry yourself, you are dead. I can list a dozen CHROs who have been fired after enjoying an initial strong relationship with the CEO. I tell people who think that their role is to establish great rapport only with the CEO that will keep you alive for about a year. Then, something will hit you that you don't know where the hell it came from and it's your peer group and it's your subordinates that take you out.

Steckler: What are the most serious challenges facing the HR function in the future?

Holmes: The continued globalization of the world, specifically the growth of Asia Pacific and what that means to heads of HR in helping to ensure that the right talent, the right capability and the right processes are in place to become truly global. I think that there are very few companies today that are truly global, and it is going to become even more important as you look at the growth estimates for the next five to 10 years in Asia. The other challenge is the workforce demographic that is going to be entering the workforce over the next five to 10 years and their expectations of aligned real-time communication channels that flow both ways, as well as their ability to craft and shape their jobs. I think that the traditional hierarchical management structure is going to become even more challenged if we don't better understand how to organize, align, galvanize and energize the workforce that is about to join us.

Fairbairn: I think one of the challenges is having enough talented, motivated, experienced people ready to take on the top HR job. It's a combination of things. The job has grown, expectations are higher, and there are more companies that really want a strong contributing HR function, and we are not filling that pipeline effectively enough. To clarify, it's supply and demand. Most of us have done a good job at developing talent; it's when you assess the supply and you look at jobs that are open and for how long they remain open, there is just not enough of a pipeline. To have choice because the selection process is skills, experiences and chemistry and that means you need a larger supply of truly good successors, and I think we as a function are not doing enough of that.

Ziskin: I would pick a few. One is making sure that you have the right quality and quantity of leadership talent. Leadership depth is important because even the best companies increasingly are going to have a hard time holding onto people, and so you can't just have one solution for each job. You need to have more because it is equally likely that that good person is going to be courted by somebody else. The second challenge is around the reconciliation of performance with ethics. CEOs and other people who are moving into leadership positions are really under the microscope to show whatever performance they are going to show in much shorter periods of time. In that type of environment and the pressure that comes from budget cuts and the economic downturn and all of the other things that are going on out there in the world, even the most ethical people are going to be challenged. It is about creating an environment where you have a culture that is based on driving performance while at the same time you have a culture that highly values ethical behavior.

Sartain: We are all going to have to do more with less. I do not think that we are going to have all the resources we need at our disposal the way we might have in the past. So how do we continue to deliver the most important things without all the resources that we feel we need?

Sibbernsen: When I look back on it, I think that HR has got to do a better job of aggregating and analyzing the business intelligence around the workforce. When their line managers come and say, I have to remodel the structure, I have to consolidate these operations, I have to merge product lines—that is going to become more and more of a frequent item. And companies have to do it faster. Number two is that HR has got to be much better at quickly identifying the high-performing talent, the mission-critical talent. The third challenge would be that HR has got to do a better job of getting a common set of definitions around people investments and people processes. Get them better aligned, better understood and more user-friendly for line leaders.

Antoine: Making sure that HR is a good business partner. In a lot of organizations, we are in really good shape. In a lot of others, we are not. Until you fix that, these questions about a seat at the table, which drive me crazy, will continue. I think the ability to be flexible and adaptable is really critical because we are in a chaotic world, and look what's happened in the past year or two. That's what I worry about the most, because nothing stays the same for very long anymore.

Conaty: I believe that the biggest challenge for HR is the credibility of the organization itself. This is the time that HR leaders really need to step up and be counted. Because right now, I'm convinced that in most companies, employees are on the short end of the stick and that in these tough economic times where "take-aways" are the name of the game, you know you better have somebody that is in there plugging for employees and making sure that you don't overreach on the "take-aways." Employees do understand when you're in dire straits and you've got to take tough actions, but when the sun starts to come back out again, they expect you to react to that too. So I would say that these companies who have reinstated 401(k) matches, as an example, those companies are probably getting "high fives" from their employees saying, "Hey this company does care, they took it away from us but as things got better they gave it back." And then there are other companies where employees are saying, "Hey what gives, our earnings are up, everything is moving in the right direction but they don't seem to want to give us our perks back, and the reason they don't is because they know no one is going to leave anyway." Until things really get better in the economy, companies won't really feel the pinch of departures, but people who have been true blue and loyal over the years and have not answered the head hunters calls are now going to do so.

Steckler: Any other challenges facing HR?

Conaty: As mentioned before, one of the greatest challenges for HR going forward is the developing and growing our own future HR leaders. And my point there is that seldom, with few exceptions, do we develop our own HR leaders for major corporations. I did it at GE. I had four people who could do

my job when I left. Dick Antoine had a few people. Name me some other major corporations where that has happened. We all too often, are the biggest violators of succession. We talk and preach about CEO succession and developing internal candidates and the like and we are the shoemaker's children when it comes to HR. Still the majority of top HR slots go to somebody from outside the company.

Steckler: What was the toughest decision you made or action you had to take as head of HR?

Fairbairn: For me, I think those are always the individual people decisions when you have to deliver a tough message. A message that communicates that someone is not doing a good job, when you need to tell someone that we are all finished waiting for the good job to make itself apparent. I think that if those decisions at some point become no longer difficult, it may not be the right job for you anymore.

Sartain: Any decision that affects another's livelihood is a difficult one. For me, the toughest ones have been when there has been a reduction in force and you know not only do you have to help the whole company reduce, but you have to reduce your own team.

Ziskin: I agree. I have been involved several times in making decisions that somewhat dramatically reduced headcount to take cost out of the business in the name of survival or in the name of improved performance. No matter how many times I've done that, I always find that is the single most difficult decision; and I promised myself that if I ever stopped feeling badly about doing these things, I should probably get out of HR and do something else.

Sibbernsen: The hardest decisions, I agree, are those that involve letting people go, even if you do it for the right reason and you do it right. And you have to take care of the people that remain, too.

Antoine: I think one of the really tough aspects of our job is when you have to separate senior managers of the company for the violation of ethics or principles of the company. In the 10 years, I had fortunately only a few of those situations to deal with. Now I'm distinguishing between decision and action here. The decision was easy. At least in P&G, if you violate the ethics or the values of the company, you go. But then doing it, having to talk to those people, who were individuals that I knew as colleagues usually for many years, the action was really hard.

Holmes: I agree that, by far, the toughest decisions are when you have to let an employee go. Any time you are impacting someone's life it is a difficult situation. Therefore, it's important that all actions surrounding these situations are handled respectfully—for all involved.

Conaty: I had so many tough ones that it is hard to pick one out. But probably the toughest was when I was in the aircraft engines business and we had a major integrity issue in marketing. I don't want to talk about the specifics, but in the end we had to get rid of 23 high-level executives within the aircraft business. And I really put my job on the line arguing back and forth with the corporate office as to why we should discipline our people based on the role they played. You can imagine dealing with Jack Welch on that issue. He literally wanted everybody involved in any way to be let go. I disagreed and persevered, at that time when I didn't have a long relationship with Jack. I told him that that would be absolutely the wrong thing to do. I asked him to trust me to make sure that anybody that was really a violator receives the appropriate action. While if there were other people who were part of the organization but were not directly involved, I could mete out the discipline in an equitable way. And, quite honestly, that is how I ended up with the SVP job. Welch really loved the way I handled it, loved the way that I would fight back.

Steckler: Let's talk about the economy. With the economic "reset" and continued turbulence, what are the implications for HR leaders and their organizations?

Ziskin: Everybody who has gotten comfortable with the fact that retention is up and that their attrition is down, shouldn't get too comfortable. I believe that as the economy continues to improve, I think even happy people—those that are perfectly happy where they are—are going to be chased after by other companies. Also, we are going to have to pay attention to the people who want to stick around versus those who don't and segment the way that we treat talent, because companies aren't going to have the resources or the time to focus equally on everyone.

Antoine: I agree. I think a big challenge is how do you re-engage employees. Especially if you are one of the companies that had let a lot of people go and you cut back benefits, trimmed wages and so on. You have a lot of work to do to earn back the appropriate level of loyalty and commitment. If you had to have layoffs, but you did it in the right way, I would argue then I think it's easier. If employees saw you doing everything

you could to avoid what had to be done, and that that pain was shared equally all the way up to the top of the company, then I think it's a lot easier to get them back.

Fairbairn: I think that the implications for HR are probably similar to the implications to lots of organizations. But the adjectives that come to my mind are: flexibility, comfort with high velocity and resilience. You just need you need to be ready for every change and for creating change, for selling change and then realizing that you, too, have to change.

Steckler: I want to express my appreciation to each of you for participating in these interviews. Your level of openness and candor about the CHRO role, leadership overall and the future challenges facing HR, are all important contributions. Thank you!

Critical Thinking

1. What are the top leadership challenges facing human resource professionals?

2. What are some strategies that could be used to address those challenges?

3. How could these challenges be implemented?

STEVE STECKLER has held senior HR line and staff positions at WPP, Marriott International, TRW, Citibank and Ciba-Geigy. Most recently, he was director of HR Integration for Microsoft's Venture Integration team, responsible for integrating acquired companies and leaders. Steckler joined Microsoft as director of Strategic Talent Planning, managing a team focused on senior talent development and succession management. Steckler is an associate article editor of *People & Strategy* journal and is a member of HRPS's Board of Directors.

Reprinted with permission from *HRPS,* vol. 33, no. 4, December 2010. Published by HR People & Strategy, all rights reserved. www.hrps.org

Grooming the Next Generation

Sustain competitive advantage through succession planning and an early career development program.

KASTHURI V. HENRY, CTP

A viable succession plan for ensuring business continuity is crucial for a company to be able to sustain value for its stakeholders. To create a successful plan, the corporation must have a steady stream of resources that are valuable, rare, and not imitable. When the company belongs to the service industry, its most valuable resource is its intellectual capital, represented by its team of knowledge workers, so attracting, retaining, and developing the best minds to collaborate and deliver cutting-edge solutions to customers becomes the underpinning of the business. Aon Corporation built such a culture.

A major part of Aon's succession plan is the development of young talent to effectively contribute in the social exchange process and establish trust-based, business-to-business relationships that will nurture and grow the business. This pipeline of future knowledge workers comes from universities in the communities in which the company operates. Acquiring, retaining, and serving the client base necessitates a relationship-based approach to business development, so the social network and the ability to leverage relationships are required skills for doing business.

Motivation for the Plan

Aon provides risk management services, insurance and reinsurance brokerage, and human capital consulting through its 59,000 employees in more than 500 offices in more than 120 countries. The company grew through acquisitions. In the early 2000s, it integrated its various business segments and streamlined its operations to better deliver the customer value proposition. During this process, management made key observations about the organizational resources, customer base, and success factors necessary for an effective partnership between them. Here's a summary of the observations.

The existence of a generational gap in the workforce: Baby Boomers dominated the senior team, and there was no tangible game plan for when they retired. Also, 45% of the workforce was composed of Baby Boomers.

Growth and related needs: Business growth required additional knowledge workers. Since the business was specialized, recruiting needed to be strategized to guarantee long-term success.

Shift from male to female client contacts: The landscape of risk managers was changing in the United States. More women were entering the field of risk management at the customers' businesses, which resulted, for example, in a shift from clients wanting to do business over a game of golf to clients wanting to do business over a spa outing. Yet Aon's workforce continued to remain predominantly male.

Technological progress in the industry: Technology became all-pervasive, which started influencing how business was done as people were constantly connecting at all hours via mobile devices and social media as well as traditional means. Thus, a technology-savvy generation of knowledge workers became necessary to backfill the human resource pipeline.

Diversity: Aon had become increasingly conscious of the varied ideas and thought processes encompassed in a diverse workforce and made a targeted effort to build such a dynamic team.

These findings became the motivation for exploring equitable business solutions and culminated in Aon creating an Early Career Development Program (ECDP). The goal was to develop a scalable program that addressed the needs of the immediate future while remaining flexible to evolve as the dynamics of the business warranted. As the regional CFO based out of the corporate office, I was in a position to partner with the human resources team at Aon to develop the program and the model.

The Plan Model

The Early Career Development Program consisted of Rotational and Direct Development Programs that became a pipeline for future talent and business-unit long-term added value. The internship program was the feeder program, and the employee retention rate was 96% when entry into Aon was via this route.

Campus champions were identified from within the existing workforce to cultivate and nurture strategic partnerships with 15 national universities. The universities were selected based on the areas of specialization corresponding to the company's needs, which were risk management, consulting, human resources, accounting, and finance. Through these ongoing partnerships, the campus champions interacted with student organizations, faculty, and the administration to build brand awareness across the university community as well as identify potential talent. Based on campus interviews, the company selected third-year undergraduates to participate in its annual three-month summer internship program. The internship program was department-specific with performance goals and targeted deliverables identified. This way, Aon could evaluate the young talent in the context of day-to-day business performance and help the interns develop soft as well as technical skills that were necessary for a full-time career transition when they graduated. Both the intern and the manager had the opportunity to determine if a long-term engagement could be possible. At the end of their internship, the participants identified for a continued partnership were offered a permanent position as an associate through either the Rotational Development Program or Direct Development Program.

The associates embraced the idea of already having accepted a job offer when they returned to the university to complete their senior year. Aon embraced the internship program as its sustained recruiting pipeline and leveraged it to serve as the early career development initiative feeder program. This turned out to be a win-win partnership. But the ECDP associates weren't limited to the internship route. Recruiting from the national university partners and local university strategic partners filled the remaining talent pool opportunities. For example, if a strong candidate from a nonpartner university applied for the ECDP Direct Development Program, they were given fair consideration as a means for evaluating alternate partnership opportunities. When the candidates wanted to limit their engagement to the city of their university, the university was considered a local strategic partner. When the candidates were willing to relocate across the U.S., the university they came from was considered a national strategic partner. The local universities play a critical role in recruiting for offices outside big cities like Chicago (home of Aon Corporation world headquarters), New York, and Los Angeles.

It was clear as the program began rolling out that the associates preferred the Rotational Development Program because it gave them an opportunity to sample practical aspects of their field of education and training, but the managers preferred the Direct Development Program since it ensured that designated talent remained within the team. Associates in the Rotational Development Program needed to find a "permanent home" or job in the company when they completed their rotation, but those in the Direct Development Program already had a specific full-time role.

Here are the program criteria for selecting the associates:

- **Description of potential associate**
  - Undergraduate student of any major
  - Graduating in December of the previous year or May-June of the current year
  - A minimum 3.0 GPA
- **18-month program** (12-month development plan corresponding to the plan year and a new six-month development plan for the second year congruent with the new annual plan)
- **Seven tracks:** Aon Risk Services, Aon Consulting, Actuarial, Human Resources, Accounting & Finance, Strategy, and Aon Re (Aon Reinsurance Brokerage Service)
- **Established development plans for each track**
- **Ongoing performance management**

Table 1 shows the differences between the Rotational Development Program and Direct Development Program.

Implementation Plan

The ability to sustain the ECDP is contingent on a robust university-company partnership to keep the flow of talent into Aon and on Aon's ability to nurture the recruited talent and retain the brain trust. Naturally, the implementation cycle starts with an annual campus recruiting process. The recruiting interviews are two parts: oncampus screening interviews conducted by campus champion teams and a final interview at Aon with the Early Career Development Program participating managers. Interview sessions at Aon also give the potential associates the opportunity to experience the real work environment and the respective work groups. Associates selected for the program are brought in for an orientation before they begin

Table 1 Rotational Development Program and Direct Development Program

Rotational Development Program	Direct Development Program
Students are hired within one particular track in large offices (Chicago, New York, Los Angeles).	Students are hired within one particular track in offices across the country.
They rotate three times within 18 months, and the length of each rotation is defined by the track.	Students are hired into a single role and don't formally rotate.
Predetermined business rotations are selected prior to start date.	
Upon successful completion of the program, participants secure full-time placement.	

their assignments. The Chicago-based three-day orientation typically includes in-depth transition training by HR coupled with:

- Executive and business unit speakers,
- Program overview/expectations/development plans,
- Networking activities,
- Business etiquette, and
- Discussion about Aon's leadership model.

HR has an Early Career Development Program team dedicated to the talent management initiative. The team is headed by the vice president of HR for Americas, which assures executive sponsorship of the strategic efforts. The ECDP director, two HR managers, and an HR specialist work in unison with the campus champions and ECDP participating managers to make the plan come to life and stay focused. The onboarding process takes place at the local offices before the Chicago-based orientation, giving a two-week lead time for the various logistical steps to be coordinated.

After the first ECDP was complete, Aon conducted a survey to see how the participants felt about the program. The company found that training managers, work groups, and HR representatives are equally important for a successful program. The survey results also showed that associates have better experiences and more fulfilling programs if their managers are supportive and are engaged in the program. In addition, if the work groups and HR contacts were supportive of the associates, then the associates had an incrementally beneficial experience.

Transplanting students from universities into work groups won't automatically harness their potential talent. To bring about an effective transition, the talent has to be nurtured and developed as part of the ECDP curriculum, which encompasses core, track, and department curricula.

Core Curriculum:

This is made up of required common learning and development components for all associates. The curriculum aims at developing associates' soft skills in the areas of value-centric leadership; communication, including listening; decision making; team building; collaboration; critical thinking; basic finance; technology; and mentoring. This curriculum spans the first 12 months and culminates in a graduation presentation to the management team.

Track Curriculum:

This is track-specific to provide technical skills and expertise in effective utilization of track-specific processes and tools. Track-specific licenses are incorporated into this curriculum, and associates are required to earn the necessary professional credentials corresponding to their tracks. For example, an associate going through the risk management track is prepared for risk manager licensing, and an associate in the accounting and finance track is prepared for the Certified Public Accountant (CPA) credential. Since insurance is a regulated industry, risk managers are required to be licensed insurance brokers in the state in which they practice.

Department Curriculum:

This includes departmental knowledge necessary for associates to function effectively in their roles. For example, the accounting and finance track will train the associate on the processes around journal entries, monthly close, rolling 12-month forecasting, and monthly variance analysis along with teaching how the systems are used to perform the tasks.

The mentoring program, performance management, and peer discussions during networking sessions add to the program's success because they highlight the collaborative nature of the program and emphasize the common stake.

Progress Evaluation and Continuous Strategic Realignment

Program success is tracked and analyzed for university partnership performance, candidate work performance, track-based performance, associate satisfaction rate, manager satisfaction rate, financial impact, retention rate, and overall added value. The company also performs an ongoing SWOT (Strengths, Weaknesses, Opportunities, and Threats) analysis to directionally align the continuous progress with the dynamic business needs. This program evaluation survey is based on a 360-degree approach to identify what aspects of the program work and what aspects need improvement. Here are more results from the first program survey.

Areas of success:

- Manager/team training was highly appreciated.
- Work assignment experience was fulfilling to the associates.
- Sixty-nine percent of the associates indicated that their developmental goals were met.
- Eighty-eight percent of the associates said they had good working relationships with managers and work teams.
- There was a 91% rate of satisfaction with the availability of managers and the assignment team to aid in candidate development.

Areas of opportunity:

- Quantity of work could be higher.
- Associates can take on more challenging work.
- There should be more discussions between the manager and the associates about performance management and the process for establishing objectives or setting goals.

After the initial rollout and feedback, Aon made some changes to enhance the program. One such enhancement was that the roles and responsibility definitions establish functional clarity and streamlined coordination.

The program management role includes responsibilities such as setting program vision and strategy with business leaders, establishing consistent program definitions and timelines, collecting and reporting key deliverables and metrics, developing and clarifying program roles and responsibilities, recognizing key contributors to the program, and communicating about the program efforts.

The manager role includes ownership of the ultimate accountability for positive and meaningful early career professional experience. The manager works in partnership with the track champion, specifies and drives the development of assignment-related competencies, and carries out the performance development process. Providing continual feedback to associates, maintaining flexibility to support associates in completing all early career development plans, attending all manager training sessions, completing the required performance management training component, managing associates' day-today activities, and providing challenging assignments that create opportunities for continual growth are some additional aspects of the manager's role.

Champion roles are scattered across the country and represent all business lines. Champions act as business liaisons to the ECDP team and can take one of four forms, namely track champions, location champions, HR champions, and campus champions. Campus champions build the university partnership as well as establish working relationships with faculty, administrators, and student organizations. They have a campus presence and help establish brand awareness through various campus-based initiatives of the student organizations.

Another program modification was the alignment of the performance management plan with the Aon leadership model. Since the goal was to develop the talent pool, it made sense to instill the leadership values at the point of entry—or when the associates started with the company. The leadership model provides every employee with the fundamental tools to achieve the company's strategic imperatives and is grounded in its core value of acting with integrity across everything Aon does:

- Deliver distinctive customer value by leveraging relationships, client and industry knowledge, and the "Best of Aon," which means to bring the best cross-functional team to meet the complex client needs and to present the best possible solution, regardless of geography. In other words, a natural resource client in the Midwest will get the benefit of the Texas-based Aon Natural Resources Practice in order to provide distinctive solutions, such as risk management solutions, benefits solutions, etc.
- Develop unmatched talent and high-performing teams through continuous learning, honest feedback, rigorous development, and disciplined talent management.

- Build differentiated capability through innovation, proven solutions, and deep content expertise.
- Deliver business results with excellence and the best balance of investment and efficiency.
- Live Aon's values by always acting with integrity and by working every day in a way that positively impacts clients, colleagues, and communities.

Future Outlook

Recent events have led to a greater number of Direct Development Program associates than Rotational Development Program associates. Clients' need for an uninterrupted service relationship, managers' need for an uninterrupted resource pool, and economics have been the drivers for this shift. Rotational associates will continue working in the accounting and finance track, given the diverse skill set requirement of that professional track coupled with the fact that it doesn't require customer interfacing. Also, consulting, HR, and finance need more resources. Compared to 2007, associate roles at local offices outside major metropolitan areas have increased by 88%, and the 2009 program year saw a 48% increase over 2008 in actuarial roles.

The Early Career Development Program has opened the door for experienced employees to engage in a personally and professionally fulfilling endeavor—to leave their legacy through the development of the emerging generation of knowledge workers. The overall experience has allowed Aon to partner with national and local universities to develop future leaders. And the program has given students the chance to obtain corporate work experience in a career development program. The result of this collaborative long-term effort is a better, more powerful workforce and good community relationships.

Critical Thinking

1. What does it mean for the baby-boomers to be retiring?
2. How are companies dealing with the fact that many of their key personnel are leaving?
3. What are some of the steps that firms can take to get the best new employees?

KASTHURI V. HENRY, CTP, is the president of Kas Henry Inc, a consulting and training firm serving the corporate finance space. She is a visiting assistant professor at Southern Illinois University and an adjunct faculty member at North Park University (NPU) in Chicago. She is also a member of IMA's Northwest Suburban Chicago Chapter.

Engaged Employees = High-Performing Organizations

Disengaged employees have been found to be one of the biggest threats to successful businesses, whereas engagement—building a mutual commitment between employer and employee—results in just the opposite.

BOB KELLEHER

Many business leaders and chief financial officers have acknowledged the tough times driven by (the economy these past two years, while expressing relief that their employees are "hanging in there," as they note voluntary turnover numbers stand at record lows. But beware—these turnover metrics might change. There is a high probability the company's work environment may not sustain itself when economics improve.

The past two-plus years have taken their toll on many organizations. Training budgets have been slashed, wages frozen and promotions delayed as employees were asked to do more with less. With companies in survival mode, employees had no place to go so they stayed put. This lack of mobility, coupled with fear and insecurity, has resulted in historic low staff turnover in all industries.

Workforce experts are reporting that most companies reduced their voluntary turnover by two-thirds (a "normal" rate of turnover per year that was previously 15 percent is now 5 percent). However, contrary to statements in December 2010 by Federal Reserve Chairman Ben Bernanke on the television show *60 Minutes*—during which he predicted that the current high unemployment rate will remain for the next four years—significant activity is being observed in the job market.

At the same time, the recent economic travails have left many angry, disengaged employees who are now reenergized to start looking for a new opportunity—elsewhere. Employees are gaining confidence and looking for new jobs. This, in turn, should rejuvenate the job market, creating the necessary churn to jump-start the economy.

Signs of a Recovery

The Dow Jones Industrial Average had its best December in 20 years, as the market reached 11,700 and continued its upsurge through February to more than 12,000. There is growing optimism that the economic turnaround is solid. The Corporate Leadership Council reported in its *HR Quarterly News and Trends* (Q2 2010) that only 25 percent of employees are displaying high levels of "intent to stay."

And, as survey results reported in December by the Economic Intelligence Unit note, 84 percent of C-suite executives who responded to its survey said that "disengaged employees" are one of the biggest threats to their business.

Evidence is growing that significant job movement is anticipated this year, at which time many companies will unfortunately realize there is a price to pay after the era of layoffs, salary freezes and treating employees as disposable assets. On the other hand, there are many enlightened companies that have understood investing in employee retention and engagement is not analogous to light switches that can't just be turned on or off.

These companies had in place a strategy that could sustain the good times, as well as the not-so-good times. Smart companies understand that their human capital programs are like a dimmer switch—during financially challenging times, lower it slightly and during boom times, elevate slightly, while continuously communicating with employees the realities of the business challenges and successes.

The companies that solely focused on boosting short-term returns at the expense of human capital development will soon realize there was a price to pay.

Engagement and How to Get It

Employee engagement can be defined as "the unlocking of employee potential to drive high performance." According to a Gallup publication last year, *A Leading Indicator of Financial Performance*, companies with highly engaged employees have 3.9 times the earnings per share (EPS) growth rate of organizations with low engagement scores. It is this linkage between company performance and employee potential that will drive high performance with both employees and the business.

Companies need to focus efforts on building a mutual commitment between employee and employer, a commitment that is the foundation of employee engagement.

Only when this foundation is in place will companies experience the difference evident in a high-performing business—the discretionary effort of employees. Yet only six percent of employees are displaying high levels of discretionary effort, according to the Corporate Leadership Council report cited earlier.

But, it's not too late, as there are practices than can be instituted to help minimize disengagement and leverage engagement—the essential ingredient to building a sustainable high-performing work force.

1. **Link engagement efforts to high performance.** Employee engagement is not about employee satisfaction. The last thing you should want is a team of satisfied but underperforming employees. Employee satisfaction will be an outcome of a great culture, but it should not be the goal.

2. **Engagement starts at the top.** Most studies show that a strong engagement driver is the actions of senior leaders. Leaders must demonstrate support for an engaged culture by personally living their company's values. In today's recessionary times, leaders have large shadows, and employees are watching everything they do.

3. **Engage first line leaders.** The adage "employees join great companies, but quit bad managers" is true. Research shows the key driver of engagement is the relationship with one's direct manager. Studies indicate that if the line manager is disengaged, his or her employees are four times more likely to be disengaged themselves. Yet companies woefully under-invest in supervisory training.

4. **Focus on communication.** This is the cornerstone of engagement. Successful leaders recognize the power of a robust communication plan, one built on clarity, consistency and transparency. With today's technological advances, it's also an era of information overload. Communication experts say you need to repeat a message to your employees 13 times before they "hear" it. Learn how to leverage the various communication venues available (particularly social media) and how to adapt communications to reach vastly different generations in the workplace.

5. **Individualize Engagement.** Today's leaders must tailor their communication approaches, rewards and recognition programs, as well as training and development investments, to the unique motivational drivers of each employee. The Golden Rule of yesterday—"treat people the way you want to be treated"—no longer applies; the new mantra is "treat people the way *they* want to be treated."

Communication experts say you need to repeat a message to your employees 13 times before they "hear" it.

6. **Create a motivational culture.** Leaders cannot motivate employees long-term. They must create motivational cultures where employees can flourish. Leaders do need to understand the different intrinsic motivational drivers of their employees. Experts agree that a key engagement driver is showing empathy toward employees. Leaders are more apt to get the discretionary effort of their employees when they believe they are cared about as individuals.

7. **Create feedback mechanisms.** Companies need to ask employees what they think, and employee engagement surveys are a great tool to check an organization's pulse. Are your employees currently engaged? Are you capturing their discretionary effort? Recent research by the Corporate Leadership Council is staggering: only 5.9 percent of surveyed employees are giving their employers high levels of discretionary effort. That is startling. Are your employees highly engaged? How would you know? As we slowly recover from this deep recession, some enlightened companies are beginning to ask employees, "What do you think?"

8. **Reinforce and reward the right behaviors.** Employees are incredibly motivated by achievement, not money. Money can actually disengage if employees perceive unfairness. Because employers will get the behavior they measure, a blend of both quantitative and qualitative metrics is strongly suggested. To build a high-performing business that is true to its culture, leaders need to establish consequences for poor performance and behaviors inconsistent with the company's core values. Anything less will erode alignment with employees.

9. **Track and communicate progress.** It is surprising how few companies have balanced scorecards in place. Employees as well as management both want to work for a "winning" organization, and leaders need to reinforce "line of sight" by telling their staff where they're going, how they're performing and where they fit in. These are key alignment and engagement necessities.

10. **Hire and promote the right behaviors and traits to match the culture.** Often it's not an engagement issue, but a hiring issue—when companies hire individuals that possess the wrong behaviors and traits. To reinforce this message, consider a B.E.S.T profile of staff selection.

Although much emphasis is placed on one's educational background and skills (the E and S), people generally succeed or fail because of their behaviors and traits (the B and T).

Critical Thinking

1. What do you think employee turnover will be after the recession?
2. Do you think organizations are ready for it?
3. What steps can employers take, today, to keep employees from leaving in the future when the job market improves?
4. Do you think they will be successful?

BOB KELLEHER (www.BobKelleher.com) *is a speaker, consultant and author of* Louder than Words: 10 Practical Employee Engagement Steps That Drive Results. *He's founder and CEO of The Employee Engagement Group (*www.EmployeeEngagement.com*), a global consulting firm on employee engagement, workforce trends and leadership.*

HR Plays Pivotal Role in Adapting Policies to ADA Amendments Act Rules

For human resources practitioners, the Equal Employment Opportunity Commission's final regulations implementing the ADA Amendments Act signal the need to revise employee handbooks, update policies, and retrain managers on how to comply with a law that makes it easier for employees and job applicants to allege disability discrimination, management attorneys said in a series of interviews.

"Before, employers were rarely held accountable for the decisions they were making concerning injured or ill employees," Frank Alvarez, a partner in Jackson Lewis's White Plains, N.Y., office and national coordinator of the firm's Disability, Leave, and Health Management practice group, said.

"Few ADA cases ever progressed to the point where employers had to prove the judgments they made regarding employees' qualifications were correct. The ADAAA changes all of that," Alvares said.

When the final regulations take effect May 24, employers increasingly will have to "routinely" defend their decisions about individuals' qualifications, Alvarez said. A spotlight will be placed on any employment decision based in whole or in part on an individual's physical or mental ability, he added.

"One of the things I think is overwhelmingly important for HR is to not focus on the question of whether a particular individual has a disability, but to focus on the 'interactive process' and work on developing reasonable accommodations," Margaret Hart Edwards, a shareholder with Littler Mendelson in San Francisco, said. "This is the whole thrust of the ADAAA, and the EEOC regulations and interpretive guidance virtually hit the reader over the head with a mallet that this is what they want employers to do."

ADA Protections Expanded

The Americans with Disabilities Act was enacted in 1990. The ADA Amendments Act took effect Jan. 1, 2009, and made various significant changes to the definition of disability, EEOC noted in a recent fact sheet and separate questions-and-answers document.

"Among the purposes of the ADAAA is the reinstatement of a 'broad scope of protection' by expanding the definition of the term 'disability,'" EEOC said in its Q&A document. "Congress found that persons with many types of impairments—including epilepsy, diabetes, multiple sclerosis, major depression, and bipolar disorder—had been unable to bring ADA claims because they were found not to meet the ADA's definition of 'disability.'"

EEOC noted that the amended law also "explicitly rejected certain Supreme Court interpretations of the term 'disability' and a portion of the EEOC regulations that it found had inappropriately narrowed the definition of disability."

As part of this process, EEOC had to revise its ADA regulations to reflect amendments made by the ADAAA. Commission members approved the final regulations March 10, and they were published in the March 25 Federal Register (76 Fed. Reg. 16978).

EEOC noted that its final regulations, which apply in part to all private, and state and local government employees with 15 or more workers, make it easier for people seeking ADAAA protection to demonstrate they meet the definition of disability.

Nancy Zirkin, executive vice president of the Leadership Conference on Civil and Human Rights, a coalition of 200 national organizations, applauded EEOC's final regulations, saying in a written statement March 25 that they "fill a gaping hole in civil rights protections for people with disabilities."

"The overly narrow interpretation of what it means to have a disability has stood in the way of productive employment for millions of Americans," Zirkin said. "Many people with disabilities can now go to work with the confidence that they have the full protections entitled to them under the law."

Employers Facing Major Changes

For employers, the final regulations signal major changes on several fronts, lawyers said.

"The ADA hasn't really been on employers' radar screens like it was when it first came out," Robin Shea, a partner at Constangy Brooks & Smith in Winston-Salem, N.C., said.

"So first employers need to get familiar with it again, if they are not already, and make sure they fully understand their obligations regarding reasonable accommodations and engaging in the interactive process," among other issues, Shea said.

Edwards at Littler Mendelson said the idea of employers focusing on an interactive process to develop reasonable accommodations for employees or job applicants with disabilities has been a goal of the ADA since it first was enacted.

"But what happened was that in a lot of the litigation under the ADA in the ensuing almost 20 years, the focus on the defense efforts was on a threshold issue [involving] whether or not the individual had a disability," she said. "As a consequence, many employers . . . were spending a lot of energy looking at whether the individual's particular condition met the rather complicated definition of disability. And, of course, HR people got caught up in this, too."

Now, Edwards said, "HR has to be the thoughtful person on the team who's going to be looking at 'what is this job really about?' and 'are the functions listed truly job functions, or are they an actual means to an end?' "

Four Essential Steps

Connie Bertram, a partner with Cooley LLP and head of the firm's employment practice at its Washington, D.C., office, said employers should take four essential steps at this point:

- Review written policies and employee handbooks "to make sure that any definitions or provisions within the policy track the amended language within the regulation," she said.
- Revise or develop the company's accommodations policy and process and make sure the process is "routinized and independent," Bertram said. A department, an HR practitioner, or a third-party administrator should be designated to lead this process, she added. This is "for confidentiality reasons, but also because the more we get the managers involved in the accommodation process, the more likely it is that an employee will be able to claim discrimination or that he was perceived as disabled," Bertram said. Another key aspect of this process that should not be overlooked will involve employers requesting medical documentation from employees that substantiates "the disability, the need for accommodation, and the alternative accommodations that would allow the employee to perform the essential functions of the job," she said. Bertram said that given the expanded definition of disability under the new regulations, it is very important to treat the ADAAA certification process more like the Family and Medical Leave Act certification process. "Rather than expect the doctor to write a scratchy note describing the condition," she suggests that employers create a very specific form for them to complete where they could check off the condition that applies and list multiple alternative reasonable accommodations that would allow the employee to perform the essential functions of the position. When this form is returned to the employer, she said, the employer can then engage in the interactive process with the employee.
- Revise job descriptions to clearly identify the essential function of the job, including physical requirements of the position. "Employers are in a better position to take the position that an employee is not qualified or

that an accommodation is not reasonable if the essential job duties and requirements are identified in the job description and in postings for the position," Bertram said.
- Train HR practitioners and company managers about the ADAAA accommodations process. "For the managers it's very important that they know how to handle a request from an employee," Bertram said. "A typical problem I see is an employee makes an ADA request and the manager says, 'Oh, no problem,' and just orders the equipment." Instead, she said, such requests need to go to a designated person or department so they are treated consistently—and consistent with the ADA requirements. The second typical problem Bertram said she sees involves managers who react negatively to an accommodation request, such as a schedule change. Requests for a schedule change or other job modification for a medical reason should be treated as a request for an accommodation and handled by HR, she said.

Performing Functional Job Analysis

Alvarez also said one of the first steps for HR practitioners to undertake as a result of the final regulations should be to "ensure that their organizations have performed a functional job analysis for their positions." Make sure the functional job analysis is incorporated into job descriptions, and those descriptions identify the essential functions of jobs, he said.

"This is the cornerstone for conducting an interactive dialogue about reasonable accommodations, which will become increasingly important under the ADAAA," Alvarez said.

"Everything now will turn on the merits of employment decisions. Employers will have to show that their judgment was correct in whether people were qualified under the ADAAA," he said. "That requires an understanding of the essential functions of the job, and employers will be well served by having evidence of their judgment incorporated into job descriptions."

Alvarez said that historically employers would list the physical demands of a job in descriptions that stated, for example, an employee needed to be able to lift 50 pounds.

"But frequently employers would never connect that physical demand to the activities involved when lifting," Alvarez said. "Now, a functional job description would not just identify the ability to lift, it would also explain why they need to lift— 'so they can unload boxes from a truck and then place them on shelves in a warehouse,' " he said.

HR must educate managers, itself. Alvarez said HR should play a pivotal role in explaining to management who is responsible for what in the accommodations process. "They need to educate supervisors about the information that might trigger reasonable accommodation obligations," he said.

In addition, Alvarez said HR practitioners must become increasingly comfortable and knowledgeable with the procedures involved with obtaining and evaluating employee medical information relevant to determining whether employees are qualified under the ADA. "Too many companies are hesitant to communicate with medical professionals," he said. "However, failing to get medical input will lead to discrimination under the ADA."

Alvarez recommends that employers develop policies that communicate to employees that there might be a need for them to share medical information as part of the company's effort to explore reasonable accommodations.

"Set the expectation for employee cooperation for sharing medical information when it's necessary to make informed employment decisions," he said. "That step helps reduce the likelihood that employees will feel they are being singled out for discriminatory treatment when employers request medical information."

At the same time, Alvarez said, "HR needs to be sensitive to the fact that there cannot be a one-size-fits-all approach to requesting medical information." Requests should be narrowly tailored to address the specific job at issue, he said, and the precise job-related limitations of the applicant or employee.

"As a practical matter, what could be very valuable is for HR to identify recurring reasonable accommodation scenarios and develop a preliminary strategy for responding to those situations," Alvarez said. "Most companies can identify now what the most challenging accommodation scenarios might be at their organizations. They can then train managers and supervisors on the process they would follow when they confront those situations in the future."

Be aware of "changes in language." In a recent legal alert Edwards co-authored with Patrick Martin, a shareholder at Littler Mendelson's Miami office, the attorneys said HR practitioners, among other company leaders, should pay attention to "changes in language" when updating disability discrimination policies and reasonable accommodation processes to conform to the ADAAA and its rules.

For example, the Littler Mendelson alert noted that "major life activity is now defined under the rules to encompass not only those activities formerly included [in the ADA], but several more such as 'interacting with others.'"

Including this activity will pose an ongoing challenge for employers faced with claims that problematic worker conduct caused by mental disabilities is protected, the attorneys said.

Edwards and Martin also noted in the alert that the amended ADA added the operation of a major bodily function as a major life activity. In addition, they said, EEOC added to the statutory definitions "to include virtually every physiological function."

"Thus, major life activities now include the functioning of the immune, musculoskeletal, neurological, brain, genitourinary, circulatory, and reproductive systems, and all major organs," the alert noted.

"The EEOC makes it plain that the intention is to include virtually all physical and mental conditions, except those which have never been considered impairments," the Littler Mendelson alert said, citing a genetic predisposition to a disease and pregnancy, among others.

Edwards, among other attorneys, noted that EEOC declined to redefine "substantially limits" but instead developed nine "rules of construction" employers should follow to determine whether a disability substantially limits an individual in performing a major life activity.

The EEOC fact sheet noted: "The term 'substantially limits' requires a lower degree of functional limitation than the standard previously applied by the courts. An impairment does not need to prevent or severely or significantly restrict a major life activity to be considered 'substantially limiting.' Nonetheless, not every impairment will constitute a disability."

More "Regarded as" Claims?

"As required by the ADAAA, the regulations also make it easier for individuals to establish coverage under the 'regarded as' part of the definition of 'disability,'" EEOC said. Because of "court interpretations," EEOC said, it had become difficult for individuals to establish coverage under the "regarded as" prong.

To qualify for a reasonable accommodation, EEOC said, the regulations clarify that a person must be covered under the first prong, meaning he or she has an "actual disability" or the second prong, meaning there is a "record of disability."

"The regulations clarify that it is generally not necessary to proceed under the first or second prong if an individual is not challenging an employer's failure to provide a reasonable accommodation," the commission stated.

"What the EEOC has made clear is prong three basically drags in any situation where the employer makes a decision based on thinking that a person has a disability—even if that disability doesn't exist or there's no major life activity involved or impaired," Edwards said.

"As long as an employer regards a person as having a disability, that is a potential claim under prong three," she said. Because prong three was drawn so broadly, Edwards said, "HR needs to be extremely vigilant. This can come up in so many contexts."

Shea said the breadth of the "regarded as" provision surprised her. "Almost anything beyond a cold or flu will qualify as a disability under the expanded definition," she said.

Bertram predicted, "We are going to see more 'regarded as' claims."

EEOC already has reported an uptick in disability discrimination charges filed with the agency. Such charges climbed to 25,165 in fiscal 2010, up 23 percent from 21,451 charges the previous year, the agency reported.

Alvarez said the EEOC regulations confirm that virtually every time an adverse employment action is related to an employee's medical condition, he or she will have a viable "regarded as" claim.

"The threshold is so low that you can easily envision HR having to defend those decisions routinely," he said, "which means they must find ways to memorialize the legitimate, nondiscriminatory reasons for decisions affecting employees with injuries, illnesses, or other medical conditions."

To access EEOC's Fact Sheet and Q&A document on the final regulations implementing the ADAAA, respectively, go to www.eeoc.gov/laws/regulations/adaaa_fact_sheet.cfm and www.eeoc.gov/laws/regulations/ada_qa_final_rule.cfm.

Critical Thinking

1. How has the ADAAA changed the definition of a disability?
2. What does this mean for organizations?
3. How can HR help in administering this important program?
4. What are some of the consequences?

Is Everyone Disabled under the ADA? An Analysis of the Recent Amendments and Guidance for Employers

Under the Americans with Disabilities Act Amendments Act of 2008 (ADAAA), nearly everyone with any form of mental or physical disability is considered disabled. The focus now is on whether the employee can perform the essential functions of the job with or without a reasonable accommodation. The authors of this article advise employers to take strategic steps now to ensure compliance and minimize liability under the ADAAA.

A. Dean Bennett and Scott E. Randolph

On September 25, 2008, President George W. Bush signed into law the Americans with Disabilities Act Amendments of 2008 (the ADAAA). The ADAAA amended the Americans with Disabilities Act of 1990 (ADA) and became effective on January 1, 2009. Generally stated, the ADA prohibits discrimination or retaliation against a person with a disability by an employer. The ADAAA changed the landscape for employers by significantly broadening the statutory definition of "disability." Under the ADAAA, nearly everyone with any form of mental or physical impairment is considered disabled. The new, changing landscape poses obvious challenges for employers.[1] But these challenges are not insurmountable. Employers can minimize their exposure by implementing policy changes to ensure compliance with the latest developments under the ADA. These same policy changes might also make for a more efficient organization.

The Fundamentals of an Ada Claim

The ADA provides that a covered employer may not discriminate or retaliate against a qualified individual on the basis of a disability. A covered employer includes both private and government employers that employ 15 or more employees for each working day in each of 20 or more calendar weeks in the current or preceding calendar year.[2] A qualified individual includes any person with the skill, experience, or education to perform the essential functions of his or her job, with or without a reasonable accommodation from his or her employer.[3] An accommodation is a modification to the work environment that would allow an employee or prospective employee to perform a particular job. An individual is considered to have a disability for purposes of the ADA under three scenarios:

1. Where the individual in fact has a physical or mental impairment that meets certain conditions;
2. Where an individual has a "record of" having such an impairment; or
3. Where an employee is treated as or "regarded as" having an impairment whether or not the employee has an impairment.[4]

Revisiting the Past to Better Understand the Present

To understand the significance of the ADAAA on employers, it is important to understand the ADA as it existed prior to amendments. The original purpose of the ADA, enacted in 1990, was to protect the then-estimated 43 million Americans with some form of physical or mental disability.[5] In the decades following enactment, however, the United States Supreme Court narrowed the reach of the ADA through its interpretation of the meaning of disability. Some scholars suggest that Supreme Court cases narrowed the ADA to protect only about 13.5 million Americans.[6] In response, Congress passed the ADAAA to overturn a number of these cases, most notably *Sutton v. United Air Lines, Inc.,* and *Toyota Motor Manufacturing, Kentucky, Inc. v. Williams.*

Sutton v. United Air Lines

In *Sutton v. United Air Lines*,[7] near-sighted twin sisters with 20/20 corrected vision sued United Airlines because the company refused to hire them as commercial airline pilots. The company refused to hire the twins because they could not satisfy the company's uncorrected vision requirements. The United States Supreme Court affirmed dismissal of the disability discrimination claims because, considering the mitigative effect of eyeglasses, the twins were not disabled. Following this decision, lower courts from around the country extended this analysis and considered all kinds of mitigative measures in concluding that individuals were not disabled. This case gave employers attractive "coverage" arguments, meaning whether the individual was disabled and thus covered by the ADA.

Toyota Motor Manufacturing, Kentucky, Inc. v. Williams

In *Toyota Motor Manufacturing, Kentucky, Inc. v. Williams*,[8] the plaintiff suffered from carpal tunnel syndrome and was unable to perform certain tasks related to her job on the line of a Toyota plant. She requested an accommodation that would have altered her job duties to exclude the tasks that she was not able to perform. Toyota refused and she brought a lawsuit under the ADA. The United States Supreme Court concluded that she was not disabled because her impairment did not prevent or severely restrict an activity "of central importance to daily life." This gave employers other attractive "coverage" arguments.

The Old Battleground of the ADA Focused on "Disability"

In the 20 years since Congress passed the ADA, and thanks to the United States Supreme Court's treatment of the Act in *Sutton* and *Toyota,* one attractive argument for employers is that an individual did not have a "disability." Using that litigation strategy, employers could often prevail at summary judgment. For example, if mitigative measures corrected the impairment, the employee was not considered to be disabled under the ADA. Similarly, if the employee's impairment did not substantially limit a major life activity, the employee was not considered to be disabled under the ADA. And if the employer who regarded an employee as disabled did not consider the disability to be substantially limiting, the employee was not considered disabled under the ADA. Employers would often win summary judgment under any of these scenarios.

Mitigative Measures

Under the pre-amendment ADA as interpreted by *Sutton*, courts could properly consider mitigative measures when determining whether an impairment was a disability. For example, if an employee took medication, wore a prosthetic, or attended therapy, the employer could use these facts to argue that the employee was not disabled. Through the ADAAA, Congress changed the landscape and effectively told employers to view their employees as though they do not take medication, wear the prosthetic, or attend therapy when analyzing whether employees are disabled under the ADA.[9] One exception deals with eyeglasses and contact lenses. The ADAAA allows courts to consider the mitigative effect of eyeglasses or contact lenses in determining whether an employee is disabled.[10] Ironically, given this exception, the *Sutton* case that started the mitigative measure analysis would be decided the same way because United Airlines could still properly consider the mitigative impact of the plaintiffs' corrective lenses when determining whether they were entitled to accommodation under the ADA.

"Substantially Limits"

To be considered disabled under the ADA, a plaintiff must establish that he or she suffers from a physical or mental disability that substantially limits a major life activity. "Substantially limits" means that a person is "[u]nable to perform a major life activity that a person in the general population can perform" or is "significantly restricted" as to the manner or duration which a person can perform that activity compared with the rest of the population.[11] Because the pre-amendment ADA was "interpreted strictly to create a demanding standard for qualifying as a disabled,"[12] employers could successfully argue that although an employee's impairment somewhat limited the employee's activity, it did not "substantially limit" the activity, and therefore, the employee was not disabled. But under the ADAAA, Congress shifted the battlefield in favor of broad coverage. It directed that the question of whether an impairment "substantially limits" an activity should not demand extensive analysis.[13] Effectively, Congress wrote the "substantially limits" analysis out of the ADA when it passed the ADAAA. The US Equal Opportunity Commission (EEOC) is actively prosecuting cases under this expanded definition. Recently, the EEOC filed three new cases against employers who were alleged to have discriminated against qualified individuals with diabetes, cancer, and severe arthritis.[14] These cases are reflective of what is to come as the EEOC and the plaintiff's employment bar continues to prosecute claims under the expanded statutory definition of disability.

Major Life Activity

Under the pre-amendment ADA, the United States Supreme Court interpreted the term "major life activity" as an activity that is of "central importance to most people's daily lives."[15] Courts around the country often interpreted this to mean that a plaintiff must be substantially limited in an activity deemed by the courts to be "significant."[16] Activities that "lack central importance to daily lives" did not qualify.[17] And "working" was considered as a major life activity only if an impairment limited an employee in a broad range of jobs.[18] Employers could therefore successfully argue that although an employee was substantially limited in an activity, that activity was not a "major life activity." But under the ADAAA, Congress provided two non-exclusive lists of major life activities.[19] These lists are nearly all-inclusive. For example, Congress included working, thinking, concentrating, and communicating among the list of 18 "major life activities." Congress also stated that major life activities include operations of a major bodily function, and then listed every major system of the body. Thus, under the ADAAA, there is little room left for an employer to argue that an activity is not a "major life activity."

"Regarded As"

As identified above, one of the ways for an employee to establish a disability for purposes of the ADA is to prove that the employer treated that person as though that person were disabled, or regarded that person as being disabled. Under the pre-amendment ADA, an employee making a "regarded as" claim also had to prove that the employer perceived the disability to be substantially limiting of a major life activity.[20] But under the ADAAA, Congress made clear that an employee must prove only that the employer treated him or her as though he or she had a physical or mental impairment notwithstanding whether the employer perceived the limitation to be substantially limiting of a major life activity.[21] This amendment further narrowed opportunities for employers to prevail at summary judgment.

The Amendments Have Already Significantly Increased Claims against Employers

The ADAAA resulted in lower thresholds for bringing a claim and surviving summary judgment. The increase in charges of discrimination and litigation under the ADA since the effective date of the ADAAA has been dramatic.[22] In 2009, the EEOC received 93,277 charges of discrimination. Of that number, 21,451 were based on disability discrimination. In 2010, the EEOC estimates that it will receive 5,561 additional disability discrimination charges (a 26 percent increase from 2009). And in 2011, as awareness of the ADAAA grows, the EEOC estimates that it will receive an additional 9,020 disability discrimination charges, which is a 42 percent increase from 2009. With the increase in charges comes a correlative increase in litigation. For this reason, employers must assess what preventive measures and defenses remain to limit their liability under the ADA.

The New Battleground of the ADA Focuses on "Qualified Individual"

While Congress drastically expanded the scope of those who are considered to be disabled, it did not modify the way courts consider whether an employee is a "qualified individual." As a result, the new battleground centers around where an employee is a qualified individual. A "qualified individual" is an individual who: (1) with or without reasonable accommodation (2) can perform the essential functions of the position he or she holds or desires, and (3) has the requisite skill, experience, education, and other job-related requirements of the position.[23] It is essential for employers to be conversant with these terms and the related concepts to navigate effectively their obligations under the ADA.

Familiarity with Key Concepts Facilitates Compliance Under the ADA

Reasonable accommodations include modifications to the application process or the work environment that allow a qualified employee or applicant to perform the essential job functions or enjoy "equal benefits and privilege of employment

as are enjoyed by its other similarly situated employees without disabilities."[24] An accommodation is not reasonable if it poses an undue hardship on the employer. Undue hardship refers to whether the covered employer would incur "significant difficulty or expense" in implementing the requested accommodation.[25]

The employer must only provide reasonable accommodations for the "essential job functions." Essential job functions are the "fundamental" duties of a given position.[26] Essential job functions are distinguishable from "marginal job functions" which may include job duties that an employee performs but which are not necessary to employment. Whether an employer must accommodate a particular employee and the extent of that obligation is often resolved through what is known as the "interactive process." The interactive process is often described as a constructive dialogue between employer and employee about the employee's job-related limitations and any proposed accommodations that would allow the employee to perform the essential functions of the position. Each of these concepts plays an important role in an employer's effort to remain compliant and minimize liability under the ADAAA.

Implement Steps Now to Minimize Exposure Later

Employers should take action now to minimize their liability under the ADAAA and best position themselves in the event of a claim or charge of discrimination. These steps include:

- Regularly analyzing and updating job descriptions;
- Implementing a centralized decision-making process;
- Promptly engaging the interactive process; and
- Giving a proposed accommodation request a test run.

These proactive steps will not only have the effect of minimizing liability to the employer, but they will also likely result in increased efficiencies to the organization.

Analyze and Update Job Descriptions Regularly

Under the ADAAA, a critical issue remains whether an employee or prospective employee can perform the essential functions of the job to which he or she is assigned. It follows that employers must analyze and fully understand the essential job functions of each position within their organization. To accomplish that objective, employers without job descriptions should create them. And employers with job descriptions already in place should revisit them regularly to ensure that the written descriptions accurately capture the essential functions and exclude marginal functions for each position. The process of creating and updating job descriptions should be a collaborative one between the employer and its employees. If possible, employers should engage their employees in a dialogue about what the employees perceive to be the essential functions of their positions. Ultimately, the employer should seek to have employees sign off on their job descriptions. This approach minimizes the risk that an employee could later claim that he or she requires accommodation to perform an essential job function when the job function is only a marginal function.

This is not a one-time endeavor. Ideally, employers will regularly review existing job descriptions to ensure that the written job descriptions accurately reflect current essential job functions. At a minimum, this process should occur each time the employer engages in any structural or organizational changes. Often these events result in reallocation of work assignments and job functions. Failure to analyze and update all job descriptions during this period can result in exposure to even well-intentioned employers.

In addition to minimizing liability under the ADA for employers, the process of regular review and analysis of existing job descriptions can eliminate inefficiencies and redundancies that exist within the organization. Although this effort may not completely offset the costs associated with the anticipated increased exposure under the ADAAA for employers, regular review of job descriptions provides an opportunity for employers to remain efficient in the competitive marketplace.

Implement a Centralized Decision-Making Process

Employers can realize significant advantages by implementing a centralized decision-making process for handling all requests for accommodation under the ADA. This might be a single person within the organization or a subset of the human resources department depending on the size of the organization. In all cases, the process should be confidential so that employees feel free to share their medical information without risk of disclosure to persons without a legitimate need for access to the information.

The centralized decision-making process has many advantages for employers. First, an employer is entitled to consider the aggregate costs of a proposed accommodation when determining whether a particular accommodation is reasonable. It is much easier for an employer to calculate the true cost of an accommodation to the organization when a single person or department is responsible for handling all requests for accommodation. Additionally, the centralized process has the advantage of consistency between departments and decision-makers. An employer is poorly positioned in litigation if a manager in one department routinely approves a particular type of accommodation while a manager in a different department denies the same accommodation as being too costly or burdensome to the company. The employee requesting the accommodation in the other division is certain to discover the pattern of approval by other divisions and use that evidence to show feasibility of the proposed accommodation and the arbitrary decision-making by the employer.

Having a single department or person responsible for handling requests for accommodation has the additional advantage of reducing favoritism between employees or classes of employees. Employers should not, for example, provide costly accommodations for one class of employees, *e.g.,* executives, while refusing costly accommodations for another class of lower compensated workers. By providing an accommodation for an executive, and denying the same accommodation for a non-executive, an employer is exposing itself to unnecessary liability because it could be considered relevant evidence that the accommodation is reasonable.

Another advantage of a centralized process is that employers minimize exposure for claims for retaliation and discrimination where they can show that managers and supervisors were not even aware of a particular employee's disability, much less discriminated against him or her on that basis. In order to obtain this benefit, however, employers must take care to protect against improper dissemination of medical information to supervisors as well as other employees. Failure to safeguard this information can result in exposure under the ADA as well as liability under state and federal privacy laws.

Once an employer implements the centralized decision-making process, the employer should update employee handbooks and training materials. Where an employer implements a centralized decision-making process, but its handbook continues to read "contact your manager, supervisor, or the human resources department to request an accommodation," the benefits of the process are completely negated. Moreover, all managers and supervisors should receive regular training to ensure that all personnel understand how requests for accommodation are to be handled within the organization. Finally, employers should remind supervisors and managers to always base employment decisions on their employee's actual job performance and not on any perceived inability to perform the job duties based on a disability or perceived disability.

Promptly Engage the Interactive Process

The ADA does not expressly provide for how the interactive process should be handled. The regulations do, however, provide that "[t]he appropriate reasonable accommodation is best determined through a flexible, interactive process that involves both the employer and the qualified individual with the disability."[27] This should be an employer's focus upon receipt of a request for accommodation, because how the employer handles a request is a critical issue should the dispute proceed to litigation. Generally employees, not employers, must initiate the interactive process unless the need for accommodation is obvious to the employer.[28]

The interactive process contemplates a four-step process[29] that the employer should promptly and respectfully engage in good faith each time an employee makes a request for accommodation. The failure to respond to requests for accommodation in a timely manner can lead to claims of discrimination and potential liability.[30] Additionally, employers are currently facing claims for the failure to engage the interactive process.[31] To minimize this potential liability, employers should promptly undertake the following four steps:

First, upon receiving a request for accommodation, the employer must analyze the essential job functions of the position that are involved in the request for accommodation. With updated job descriptions, prepared with employee input, this should be a relatively simple task.

Second, the employer should consult with the employee to ascertain the specific job-related limitations and how the employee could overcome those limitations through a reasonable accommodation. Whenever possible, the employer should request that the employee or potential employee submit these job-related limitations in writing. It is appropriate for an employer to request a medical certification from the employee's or applicant's medical professional. By insisting that the employee or applicant provide this information in writing, the employer minimizes the potential for misunderstanding about the specific job-related limitations encountered by the employee. The documentation will also prove invaluable should litigation ensue, because it will allow the employer to demonstrate precisely what limitations the employee identified when requesting accommodation.

Third, the employer should identify potential accommodations and analyze the effectiveness of each alternative. This includes any modifications to the work environment that will enable the employee to perform all essential job functions and allow the employee to enjoy equal privileges of employment. When considering this issue, employers should consider whether any tax incentives may be available to defray some or all of the cost of the proposed accommodation.[32] Employers faced with a request for accommodation must analyze what steps can be taken to make existing facilities accessible. In some cases, this includes job restructuring, reassignment of the employee to a vacant position, and may include making readers available to the employee or applicant.

Finally, the employer should select the accommodation that the employer believes is most appropriate under the circumstances. In reaching this decision, the employer should take into account the employee's preferences whenever possible. Employers may properly consider whether the proposed accommodation poses an undue hardship on the organization. This includes an analysis of the cost of the proposed accommodation, the overall financial resources of the employer, the type of operation involved, and whether the accommodation poses a direct threat to other employees. This last step requires the employer to analyze the duration and nature of the threat as well as the likelihood and imminence of harm to others. An employer may properly reject an accommodation when it concludes that the risk of harm to others is too high.

Even if the process is unsuccessful, the employer should always conclude the interactive process with a defensible response to the last request by the employee. Any such response should be in writing and, if possible, signed by the employer and employee. If the employee refuses a particular accommodation, the employer should insist that the employee sign an acknowledgement to that effect. This allows the employer to demonstrate not only the particular job-related limitations identified by the employee but the accommodations proposed by the employer and the fact that they were rejected by the employee. These records are valuable evidence if an employee or applicant later contests the employer's decisions.

Give Accommodation Requests a Test Run

Even if an employer believes that an accommodation might be too expensive or pose too much of a burden in other respects, an employer should consider implementing the requested accommodation on a temporary basis. The advantage of implementing an accommodation on a temporary basis is that the proposed accommodation might turn out to be reasonable, and the employee can continue working for the employer. If,

however, the accommodation proves not to be workable for any number of reasons, the employer can later use that information to justify its decision to eliminate the accommodation and refuse similar requests for accommodation in the future relying on empirical data.

Conclusion: Take Steps Now to Avoid Liability Later

The ADAAA poses significant challenges for employers. Under the ADAAA, most employees are considered disabled. The battleground has shifted from whether an individual is disabled to whether that same person can perform the essential functions of his or her job, with or without reasonable accommodations. Employers should regularly create or review job descriptions for each position within their organization. Job descriptions should be updated where they are no longer consistent with the actual job functions performed by the employee. When faced with a request for accommodation, employers should promptly respond to the request for accommodation and document in writing each request by the employee and response by the employer. By implementing these steps, employers can minimize their liability under the ADA and realize some strategic efficiencies within their organizations.

Notes

1. The EEOC will soon issue new regulations interpreting the ADAAA. These proposed regulations reflect Congress's mandate in the ADAAA to expand the definition of disability and focus the emphasis on whether the disability can reasonably be accommodated by the employer. The EEOC's proposed rules are available at http://edocket.access.gpo .gov/2009/pdf/E9-22840.pdf (last visited Oct. 28, 2010).

2. *See* 42 U.S.C. § 12111(5)(A); 29 C.F.R. § 1630.2(e)(1).

3. *See* 42 U.S.C. § 12111(8); 29 C.F.R. § 1630.2(m).

4. *See* 42 U.S.C. § 12102(1)(A)-(C); 29 C.F.R. § 1630.2(g)(1)-(3).

5. *See* 42 U.S.C. § 12101(a) (2006) ("The Congress finds that-(1) some 43,000,000 Americans have one or more physical or mental disabilities, and this number is increasing as the population as a whole is growing older.").

6. Ruth Colker, "The Mythic 43 Million Americans with Disabilities," *Wm. & Mary L. Rev.,* 49:1 (2007).

7. 527 U.S. 471 (1999).

8. 534 U.S. 184 (2002).

9. *See* 42 U.S.C. § 12102(4)(E)(i)(I)-(IV).

10. *See* 42 U.S.C. § 12102(4)(E)(ii).

11. 29 C.F.R. § 1630.2(j).

12. *Toyota,* 534 U.S. at 197.

13. *See* 42 U.S.C. § 12102(4)(A)-(C).

14. "EEOC Files Trio of New Cases under Amended Americans with Disabilities Act," EEOC Press Release dated Sept. 9, 2010, available at www.eeoc.gov/eeoc/newsroom/release/9-9 -10a.cfm (last visited Oct. 28, 2010).

15. *Toyota,* 534 U.S. at 185.

16. *See, e.g.,* Adams v. Rice, 531 F.3d 936, 944 (D.C. Cir. 2008).

17. *Id.*

18. *See Sutton,* 527 U.S. at 492 ("To be substantially limited in the major life activity of working, then, one must be precluded from more than one type of job, a specialized job, or a particular job of choice.").

19. *See* 42 U.S.C. § 12102(2)(A)-(B).

20. *Sutton,* 527 U.S. at 489–490.

21. *See* 42 U.S.C. § 12102(3)(A).

22. *See* "EEOC, Fiscal Year 2011 Congressional Budget Justification" (Feb. 2010), www.eeoc.gov/eeoc /plan/2011budget.cfm (last visited Oct. 28, 2010).

23. *See* 42 U.S.C. § 12111(8); 29 C.F.R. § 1630.2(m).

24. 29 C.F.R. § 1630.2(o).

25. *See* 29 C.F.R. S 1630.2(p) (discussing relevant factors).

26. 29 C.F.R. § 1630.2(n).

27. 29 C.F.R. pt. 1630 App. § 1630.9.

28. *See* "Enforcement Guidance: Reasonable Accommodation and Undue Hardship Under the Americans With Disabilities Act," available at www.eeoc.gov/policy/docs/accommodation.html (last visited Oct, 28, 2010).

29. *See id.* (outlining process employers should follow).

30. Jodoin v. Baystate Health Sys., Inc., No. 08-40037-TSII, 2010 WI, 1257985, *18 (D. Mass. Mar. 29, 2010) (analyzing former employee's claim for disability discrimination arising out of, in part, delaying the interactive process by the employer) (slip copy).

31. Reese v. Barton Healthcare Sys., 693 F. Supp. 2d 1170, 1186 (E.D. Cal. 2010) ("Employers, who fail to engage in the interactive process in good faith, face liability for the remedies imposed by the statute if a reasonable accommodation would have been possible.") (quoting Humphrey v. Mem'l Hosps. Ass'n, 239 E3d 1128, 1137–1138 (9th Cir. 2001).

32. Resources relevant to this topic are available at www.business .gov/business-law/employment/hiring/people-with-disabilities .html (last visited Oct. 28, 2010). The Website contains links to information regarding tax incentives that exist to help employers and small businesses with the cost of complying with the ADA.

Critical Thinking

1. How has the ADA been expanded?

2. How can organizations respond to this expansion?

3. What are some of the Supreme Court decisions that were addressed by this law?

A. **Dean Bennett** is an attorney with Holland & Hart LLP, representing clients facing claims for retaliation, wrongful discharge, and charges of discrimination. **Scott E. Randolph**, also an attorney at the firm, represents employers through all stages of the litigation process, from preparing responses to administrative charges through final resolution. The authors may be contacted at adbennett@hollandhart .com and serandolph@hollandhart.com, respectively.

The "Equal Opportunity Harasser": The Slow Demise of a Strange Concept?

JOHN D. BIBLE

I. Introduction

It is well known that Title VII of the 1964 Civil Rights Act[1] prohibits covered employers from discriminating against an employee because of his or her sex and that sexual harassment is a form of sex discrimination. In 1998, the United States Supreme Court eliminated any doubt as to whether the act reaches only harassment committed by one sex against the other, holding that same-sex sexual harassment is illegal.[2] What is not commonly understood, however, is that Title VII may not be triggered if an employer does not target only male or female employees, but instead harasses both sexes. According to some courts, because the central issue in a Title VII sex discrimination case is whether members of one sex were exposed to disadvantageous employment conditions to which members of the other sex were not exposed,[3] the so-called "equal opportunity harasser"[4] who abuses both sexes is outside the scope of the act. The ironic result of this viewpoint is that it creates an incentive for harassers to be more abusive than they might otherwise be. If they verbally and/or physically mistreat one sex they risk running afoul of Title VII, but if they widen their net to include members of both sexes they may get off scot-free.

This article focuses on the equal opportunity harasser (EOH.) Part I summarizes the basic law of sexual harassment. In particular, it focuses on the interpretive conundrum in which courts find themselves due to Congress' failure to adequately define the meaning of the "because of sex" requirement. Part II discusses what courts and commentators have said about the viability of the EOH defense to employer liability for sexual harassment. As will be seen, although some courts have concluded that any harassment of both sexes, regardless of how quantitatively or qualitatively different it might be, precludes either sex from recovering under Title VII, there is a discernible trend in recent cases toward rejecting, or at least figuring out a way to circumvent, this defense.

Noting the absurdity of a rule that essentially holds that the more employees a supervisor or co-worker harasses, the less likely his employer will be held liable for that conduct, courts have examined plaintiffs' claims separately, espoused a broader meaning of the term "sex," bypassed discussion of the "because of sex" requirement altogether, or permitted claims to proceed where both sexes were harassed but to a different extent and/or in different ways.

II. The Law of Sexual Harassment

Title VII prohibits an employer from discriminating "against any individual with respect to his compensation, terms, conditions, or privileges of employment, because of such individual's race, color, religion, sex, or national origin."[5] Early on, the courts recognized two different forms of discrimination. Disparate treatment occurs if an employer intentionally discriminates against an employee because of his or her membership in a group specified in the act.[6] Disparate impact discrimination, in contrast, involves facially neutral employment practices that purport to apply evenhandedly to all employees and were not adopted with a discriminatory intent, but which still have significant adverse effects on a protected group.[7] The evidence in disparate impact cases usually focuses on statistical disparities, rather than specific incidents, and on competing explanations for those disparities.[8] The disparate impact doctrine seeks to remove employment obstacles that are not the result of any discriminatory animus *per se* but, in practice, operate to freeze out protected groups from job opportunities and are not justified by business necessity.[9]

Courts have recognized that sexual harassment is a form of sex discrimination and may take either of two forms: *quid pro quo* or hostile environment. The term *quid pro quo* does not appear in the text of Title VII; instead, it was introduced in an influential analysis of sex discrimination that was published in 1979[10] and gained currency after a federal appeals court adopted it in 1982.[11] *Quid pro quo* harassment conditions job benefits, such as pay increases and promotions, on sexual favors, and also involves adverse actions taken against people who reject sexual overtures. The hostile environment type of harassment was judicially sanctioned in 1986, when the Supreme Court endorsed Equal Employment Opportunity Commission guidelines that established that sexual harassment is actionable even if it involves no tangible economic loss. Under these guidelines, impermissible workplace conduct includes "unwelcome sexual advances, requests for sexual favors, and other verbal and physical conduct of a sexual nature."[12]

In 1999, the Court observed that the terms *quid pro quo* and hostile environment do not control in determining employer liability for harassment by a supervisor once a Title VII violation is found. Instead, the issue is whether a tangible employment action, such as firing or demotion, occurred. If so, the employer is strictly liable for the harassment; if not, the employer has a defense to liability if it can establish that it acted reasonably to prevent or correct any harassment and that the employee unreasonably failed to take advantage of available complaint mechanisms. The employer is liable for co-worker harassment if it negligently failed to discover or remedy the conduct. The *quid pro quo* and hostile environment constructs are, however, still relevant in answering the threshold question of whether Title VII was violated.[13]

The Court has made it clear that Title VII is not a general workplace civility code[14] and that a work environment is sufficiently hostile to be actionable only if it is "permeated with discriminatory intimidation, ridicule, and insult that is sufficiently severe or pervasive to alter the conditions of the victim's employment and create an abusive working environment."[15] To prevail, a hostile environment plaintiff must prove that the environment was both subjectively and objectively hostile. This means that she must subjectively perceive the harassment as sufficiently severe or pervasive to alter the conditions of her employment, and this subjective perception must be objectively reasonable.[16] The objective severity of harassment is judged from the perspective of a reasonable person in the plaintiff's position, taking into account all of the surrounding circumstances.[17]

The Court has also repeatedly stressed that Title VII is violated only if a harasser acts "because of" the victim's sex. A violation can occur even if the victim and actor are the same sex and regardless of whether the victim happens to be heterosexual, homosexual, or transsexual.[18] The ban on same-sex harassment applies, moreover, even if the harasser was not motivated by sexual desire, but instead (for example) bore an animus to the presence of one or the other sex in the workplace.[19] In the end,

however, Title VII is violated only if "members of one sex are exposed to disadvantageous terms or conditions of employment to which members of the other sex are not exposed."[20]

Deciding whether someone was harassed because of his or her sex has given courts fits. Indeed, the pages of the case reporters are filled with cases in which judges have wrestled with the issue of whether sex or some other reason, e.g. dislike of or a personal dispute with the victim, accounted for whatever abuse occurred. In many instances, the rulings seem inexplicable in that seemingly identical facts produced different outcomes.

The main reason for this confusion is that neither Congress nor the courts have clearly defined the meaning of the "because of sex" standard.[21] Thus, courts have continually had to grapple with the motive of the harasser and how much of the conduct must be sex-based to meet this standard. The result has been a mindboggling number of formulations of the "because of sex" causation standard. For example, in the 1989 case of *Price Waterhouse v. Hopkins,*[22] which involved a woman in an accounting firm whose bid to become a partner was turned down in part because she failed to conform to stereotypical notions of how women should act, the Supreme Court used over twenty such formulations, including "but-for cause," "significant factor," "discernable factor," "motivating part," and "substantial factor."[23] Each formulation, in turn, was left undefined, leaving room for wide-ranging interpretations of it. In the Civil Rights Act of 1991, Congress settled on the motivating factor standard, but it again failed to adequately define this term.[24]

The main reason for this confusion is that neither Congress nor the courts have clearly defined the meaning of the "because of sex" standard.

Another reason for the widely varying approaches to causation taken by the courts is the ambiguity inherent in the word "sex." Because Congress did not define this term when it enacted Title VII, a debate among scholars soon ensued. Two theories emerged. The biological view construes sex narrowly and recognizes only biological distinctions among people.[25] Supporters of this interpretation argue that it is logical because other Title VII classes—race, color, national origin—are, like biological sex, immutable physical characteristics. The gender-based view of sex is broader; under it, in addition to biological differences, sex includes personality attributes, socio-sexual roles, and behavioral expressions such as masculinity and femininity.[26] Its advocates assert that focusing only on biological differences ignores "culturally constructed dimensions" and fails to recognize that "biology and culture are all part of one piece" in the way society views men and women."[27]

The first courts to consider the meaning of sex adopted the biological view.[28] In their view, the sex discrimination prohibition was designed only to combat male-female inequities in the workplace, and this interpretation did not allow for consideration of the societal influences that distinguish the ways in which men and women are expected to act. In the 1980's, however, the biological view gradually lost out to the genderbased view. This trend culminated in the *Price Waterhouse* decision, in which the Court held that discrimination based on one's failure to conform to societal expectations regarding how members of his or her sex should act—the "gender stereotyping" theory of discrimination—is illegal under Title VII.[29]

After the Court held in *Oncale v. Sundowner Offshore Services, Inc.*[30] that same-sex sexual harassment also violates Title VII, plaintiffs in same-sex sexual harassment cases, which included homosexuals, transsexuals, and heterosexuals, began invoking the gender-stereotyping theory to obtain relief on the ground that they were abused because they acted too feminine (men) or too masculine (women). They took this approach to get around the fact that the act does not prohibit discrimination based on one's real or perceived sexual orientation.[31] The plaintiffs won when the court found that their failure to conform to gender norms accounted for the abuse they suffered,[32] but lost when the court ruled that the harassers acted because they knew or thought the victim was homosexual.[33] The reason for the varying results, it should be stressed, is that the courts could not agree on whether the plaintiff's contra-gender behavior, or his or her real or perceived sexual orientation, prompted the harassment. If, for example, co-workers of a male with a high-pitched voice and effeminate mannerisms, such as a "swishy" way of walking and a habit of flipping his wrists, taunted him with words such as "sweetheart," "doll," and "fag" and mocked his way of walking and talking, is that indicative of gender stereotyping, which is illegal sex discrimination, or an animus toward gays, which is not?[34]

Justice Scalia set forth an absolute standard under which recovery is precluded on proof of any harassment of workers of the sex opposite from the plaintiff's.

Aside from its same-sex sex discrimination holding, the 1998 *Oncale* decision set forth some important principles of sex discrimination law. In that case, a male oil rig worker endured sex-related acts and was threatened with rape by his all-male co-workers. After his complaints went unheeded, he quit and sued alleging sexual harassment. Speaking for a unanimous Court, Justice Scalia stressed that sexual harassment does not occur merely because the words or conduct at issue have sexual content or connotations. Instead, the issue is whether members of one sex are exposed to disadvantageous terms of employment to which members of the other sex are not exposed.[35] In the end, because the trial and appellate courts had held that no cause of action for same-sex sexual harassment exists, the Court remanded the case to the trial court to determine whether Oncale had indeed suffered discrimination because of his being male.

Justice Scalia cited three ways for a plaintiff to prove same-sex harassment based on sex. One could show that a harasser acted because of sexual desire, a route that requires evidence that the actor was homosexual, because it can then be logically inferred that the harasser would not have targeted the other sex. Sexual desire is not a *sine qua non* on a harassment claim, however, so one could also prove harassment of such a sex-specific and derogatory nature as to show that the harasser was motivated by hostility to the presence of that sex in the workplace. Finally, one could offer comparative evidence of how the harasser treated both sexes in a mixed-sex workplace to prove that his or her sex was singled out for abuse.[36]

As will be seen, some courts have concluded that, in stating that Title VII is violated only if one sex is exposed to disadvantageous terms of employment to which the other sex is not exposed, Justice Scalia set forth an absolute standard under which recovery is precluded on proof of *any* harassment of workers of the sex opposite from the plaintiff's. It is submitted, however, that the dicta offering examples of sex-based conduct do not purport to require those forms of evidence or to preclude plaintiffs from raising an inference of sex-based causation in other ways. Indeed, if under *Oncale* it is possible to find sexual harassment against a male in an all-male workplace, it must be possible to find sexual harassment without comparative evidence showing how the opposite sex was treated, since such evidence would not exist in that workplace. Also, if the evidentiary routes that Scalia discussed are the only ones, the gender-stereotyping theory would not be available to same-sex harassment plaintiffs, as it is a fourth route. As will also be seen, more courts are now reading *Oncale* in that less formalistic manner and therefore are, using a variety of approaches, allowing harassment plaintiffs to prevail even if the opposite sex was harassed as well.

III. Case Law Regarding the Equal Opportunity Harasser

A. Cases Endorsing EOH Concept

The first courts to consider sexual harassment visited on both sexes adhered to the narrow interpretation of sex that prevailed in the pre-*Price Waterhouse* era. Thus, they quickly found that the EOH does not violate Title VII. The EOH concept had its genesis in a footnote in *Barnes v. Costle,*[37] a 1977 decision by the U. S. Court of Appeals for the District of Columbia Circuit. There the court noted that demanding sexual favors from men and women is not sexual harassment because the conduct does not discriminate on the basis of sex. After *Barnes,* the Eleventh Circuit suggested in *Henson v. City of Dundee* that sexual implications directed toward men and women would equally offend both sexes and thus would fail under Title VII.[38]

Rabidue v. Osceola Refining Co.,[39] a 1986 Sixth Circuit ruling, shows how unreceptive courts in this era could be to sexual harassment claims. The plaintiff worked for seven years as the sole woman in management. In common areas she and other female employees were exposed daily to displays of nude women belonging to male workers. One poster showed a prone woman who had a golf ball on her breasts with a man standing over her, golf club in hand, yelling "Fore." In addition, a Supervisor Henry regularly spewed anti-female obscenity, referring to women as "whores," "cunt," "pussy," and "tits." Of the plaintiff, Henry remarked that "[a]ll that bitch needs is a good lay" and called her "fat ass."[40]

The panel majority concluded that the plaintiff could prevail only if she could prove that she had been subjected to unwelcome verbal and conduct and poster displays of a sexual nature that had unreasonably interfered with her work performance and created a hostile, intimidating, or offensive working environment that seriously affected her psychological well-being. Observing that Title VII was not designed to change the fact that some work environments involve rough humor and language, sexual jokes and conversations, and girlie magazines, and that society condones such things as written and pictorial erotica at newsstands, the court held that plaintiff had not shown that the conduct was so "startling" as to have seriously affected her or other workers' psyches. In dicta, the court observed that instances of complained-of sexual conduct that prove equally offensive to male and female workers would not support a Title VII claim because both sexes were accorded like treatment.[41]

Lack v. Wal-Mart Stores, Inc.[42] involved a suit against a supervisor, Bragg, who, among other things, told the plaintiff that he was probably "[f]ucking the cashier" and that "I need a small bag, and not the one between your legs, please." Displaying what he regarded as humor, Bragg also repeatedly used expressions such as "penis butter and jelly sandwiches," "spank me very much," and "oh my rod."[43] In its 2001 ruling, however, the Fourth Circuit ruled against Lack. Noting that *Oncale* held that under Title VII, regardless of the evidentiary route a plaintiff uses to prove his case, "he or she must always prove that the conduct at issue was not merely tinged with offensive sexual connotations, but actually constituted 'discrimina[tion] . . . because of sex,'" the court found that Lack had failed to prove that Bragg directed these comments at him because he was male.[44] It also rejected Lack's claim that Bragg had made sexual overtures to him, finding that, while Bragg taunted Lack with sexual gestures, he neither proposed sex nor initiated it, e.g. by touching Lack.[45] Finally, the court observed that Bragg was just as vulgar toward female employees as he was toward Lack. Although the court held that the females' complaints did not preclude Lack's claim as a matter of law, because under *Oncale* he could have offered direct comparative evidence of how the alleged harasser treated both sexes in the workplace, Lack had offered no such evidence. In the end, the court held, the aim of sexual harassment litigation is to deal with situations in which an employee is made the target of repeated, sexually charged and gender-based remarks; is threatened with sexual assault; or is subjected to unwelcome sexual contact," not to handle situations involving mere vulgar banter or offensive behavior such as occurred in this case.[46]

Holman v. State of Indiana,[47] a 2000 Seventh Circuit decision, solidified the EOH concept. A married couple alleged harassment by their male supervisor. Karen Holman claimed that the supervisor had stood too closely to her, asked her to sleep with him, touched her, and made sexist comments to her. Steven Holman asserted that the supervisor grabbed his head while asking for sexual favors, then retaliated against him for refusing to consent to the overtures. Emphasizing that the *Oncale* Court had stressed that the critical issue in a sex discrimination case is whether one sex was exposed to disadvantageous terms of employment to which the other sex was not exposed, the panel concluded that whether sex discrimination occurred must be decided on a gender-comparative basis. From this it logically followed that Title VII does not apply to the person who does not treat one sex better or worse than the other, but instead treats both sexes the same, albeit badly.[48]

B. Cases Rejecting the EOH Concept

There is, however, another, growing line of cases in which courts have refused to dismiss harassment charges based on the EOH concept. Whereas in the previous cases the courts, once having found that both sexes were harassed, declined to probe any further, the courts in the cases discussed below were willing to dig deeper and, using different approaches, permit harassment claims to proceed. The underlying premise of these cases is well summarized in Seventh Circuit Judge Posner's assertion in the 1996 case of *McDonnell v. Cisneros* that it "would be exceedingly perverse if a male worker could buy his supervisors and his company immunity from Title VII liability by taking care to harass sexually an occasional male worker, though his preferred targets were female."[49]

Some courts have gotten around the causation problem by directing attention away from the "because of sex" language. *Cisneros* is an example. The case involved an anonymous claim that a female Housing and Urban Development [HUD] employee was the "in-house sex slave" of her male boss, providing him with sexual favors in exchange for preferential treatment. In the ensuing investigation, the investigators told people that they believed the charge, and their methods caused even more lurid rumors, including claims of incest, to circulate; eventually the pair was ostracized in their workplace. They sued, alleging that they were sexually harassed by the hostile way in which the investigation was conducted. HUD defended on the ground that because the conduct was impartially directed at a male and a female, there was no discrimination because of sex.[50]

Speaking for the panel, Judge Posner dismissed this defense because it interpreted sex discrimination too literally. Noting that "unfounded allegations that a women worker is a 'whore,' a siren, carrying on with her coworkers, a Circe, 'sleeping her way to the top'" and so forth are capable of making a workplace unbearable for the woman verbally so harassed, and that because these allegations are based on the fact that she is a woman, they could constitute a form of sexual harassment. In addition, "by a further stretch of the concept a male supervisor for whom life is made unbearable by baseless accusations that he is extorting sexual favors from his subordinates" could also be thought a victim of sexual harassment. "Such accusations would be based on the fact that he was a man—that is, on the difference in sex between him and the persons he was accused of abiding."[51]

Similarly, in the 1997 decision in *Doe v. Belleville*,[52] the Seventh Circuit, commenting in dictum on a hypothetical bisexual harasser, suggested that courts espousing the EOH defense have wrongly taken the emphasis off the "factors we have regularly relied on [including] the content (physical and verbal) of the harassment, its gravity, its effect on the plaintiff, and its effect on the reasonable person."[53] In so doing, the court deflected attention from the causation requirement altogether and onto considerations it found to be more critical to the outcome.

> **A comparative-evidence approach asks not whether there was any harassment of the sex opposite from the plaintiff's, but whether one sex was harassed more, or in more gender-specific ways, than the other.**

Professor David Schwartz has advanced another means of getting around the equal opportunity employer defense. He advocates a revival of the "sex per se" rule, under which sexual conduct in the workplace is always "because of sex," without regard to the intent of the harasser. Such a rule, he argues, would "eliminate the 'bisexual harasser' problem for claims involving sexual conduct, since all sexual conduct is 'because of sex', regardless of whether it is directed at just women, or equally at women and men."[54]

Other courts have taken a comparative-evidence approach in these cases, although not the kind that Justice Scalia had in mind in *Oncale*. This approach asks not whether there was *any* harassment of the sex opposite from the plaintiff's, but whether one sex was harassed more, or in more gender-specific ways, than the other. Indeed, although some subtle variations in the comparative-evidence approach can be seen in the cases, it has emerged as the most popular judicial method of getting around the EOH defense to liability.

For example, in the 1993 case of *Kopp v. Samaritan Health System*[55] the Eighth Circuit focused on the difference in the harassment of male and female employees in concluding that a female had stated a viable sexual harassment claim sufficient to overcome summary judgment. She alleged that her supervisor had harassed roughly 10 female employees, but the employer countered that he had harassed four men as well. The court found that although the supervisor had treated both sexes harshly, he subjected more women to abuse than men, and his language toward women was more serious and frequent and sometimes resulted in physical contact. The court ruled that a fact finder could conclude that the defendant's conduct toward women was worse than his conduct toward men; therefore, there was disparate treatment of the sexes.[56]

In *Steiner v. Showboat Operating Co.*,[57] a 1994 Ninth Circuit decision, Steiner, a former blackjack dealer, alleged that Trenkle, a vice president, had repeatedly called her "dumb fucking broad" and "fucking cunt," among other things. After she complained to the state Equal Rights Commission, the company conducted an investigation which disclosed that Trenkle abused men and women. When Steiner was later fired, ostensibly due to performance shortcomings, and then sued alleging sexual harassment, Showboat defended on the grounds that Trenkle harassed everyone, male and female alike, and also that Steiner welcomed his behavior because she was "legendary for talking like a 'drunken sailor.'"[58]

The court rejected both defenses. Although the depositions of Showboat employees revealed that Trenkle was abusive to men, his abuse of women was different in that it relied on sexual epithets and offensive, explicit references to women's bodies and sexual conduct. Calling a man an "asshole," the court said, in no way relates to his gender, whereas referring to women by the terms noted above clearly does. The court also stated that Trenkle's harassment of women was not ameliorated by the fact that he referred to Asians as "UFO's—ugly fucking orientals"; on the contrary, that conduct likely exacerbated Showboat's woes by giving those employees a cause of action for racial harassment. Finally, the court stated that there was nothing in the record to suggest that Steiner welcomed Trenkle's abuse; indeed, if she did respond in kind it might have been because of the sexually abusive language to which he regularly subjected her.[59]

The same kinds of epithets and general comments regarding women were involved in *Williams v. General Motors Corp.,*[60] a 1999 Sixth Circuit ruling. In discussing the "because of sex" requirement, the court stressed that any unequal treatment of an employee that would not occur but for his or her sex may create a hostile work environment. Although the EOH issue was not involved in the case, this formulation of the causation requirement allows for the possibility that actionable harassment occurs when both sexes are harassed in sex-specific ways, but one sex is harassed a little and the other is harassed a lot, or only one is the target of sex-related comments. In such instances, the treatment of the sexes is "unequal." The court concluded that the myriad ways in which the plaintiff was ostracized when others were not, combined with the sex-specific epithets used, such as "slut" and "fucking women," created an inference, sufficient to survive summary judgment, that her sex motivated her co-workers' behavior.[61]

In *Smith v. First Union Bank,*[62] a 2000 Fourth Circuit decision, the plaintiff alleged that Scoggins, her male supervisor, subjected her to a barrage of threats and gender-based insults and made remarks reflecting his generally hostile view of women. Among other things, he commented that he would have preferred a male in Smith's team leader position because men are "natural leaders," that women should not be in management because they are too emotional to handle that role, and that a female employee who was upset about something needed "a good banging."[63] First Union defended by claiming that the fact that men and women complained about Scoggins' management style meant there was no sex-based discrimination. The court disagreed, replying that "[o]ne glance at the harassing remarks made by Scoggins to Smith . . . makes it clear that Scoggins singled her

out for harassment because of her gender. Explicit and derogatory references to women appear in virtually all of Scoggins' harassing remarks." Smith, therefore, had sufficiently alleged that Scoggins harassed her because of her gender.[64]

In *Brown v. Henderson,*[65] Issued by the Second Circuit in 2001, a female mail carrier claimed she was a victim of a campaign of sexual harassment instigated by co-workers who repeatedly taunted her because of her weight and relationship with a married male employee named Parrett. He was also subjected to teasing about his weight and his and Brown's alleged affair. Although the court concluded that the abuse of Brown stemmed from her participation in a heated union election, not her sex, it made several interesting observations. The court noted that it is unnecessary for a plaintiff to identify an employee who was treated more favorably than, and was similarly situated to, the plaintiff, except for being of the opposite sex. It also stated that the inquiry into whether ill treatment was sex-based "cannot be short-circuited by the mere fact that both men and women are involved [for] it may be the case that a co-worker or supervisor treats both men and women badly, but women worse." Here, insofar as the co-workers' conduct toward Parrett revealed their hostility toward Brown or was part of a campaign to isolate her from allies because of her sex, it could contribute to the creation of an actionably hostile work environment for her.[66]

> **The court noted that it is unnecessary for a plaintiff to identify an employee who was treated more favorably than, and was similarly situated to, the plaintiff, except for being of the opposite sex.**

Venezia v. Gottlieb Memorial Hospital, Inc.[67] is a 2005 Seventh Circuit decision that involved the mistreatment of a husband and wife by different people in the same workplace. One group of co-workers targeted Frank Venezia because he allegedly got his job through the sexual efforts of his wife, who became Director of Child Care. A different group launched a campaign of abuse against Leslie Venezia after she refused to fire a particular employee. The company argued that their sexual harassment claim should be dismissed based on *Holman,*[68] which also involved a husband and wife, because the claim asserted a cause of action against a single employer.[69]

The court disagreed. According to Judge Wood, *Holman* would control only if the idea of the EOH could be extended from the individual harasser to the overall entity. Such a step is unwarranted, however, because it would exclude the possibility of a lawsuit by a husband

and wife employed by the same large company, in which the wife reports to one supervisor, who discriminates against women, and the husband reports to a different person who discriminates against men. That the Venezias joined against a common defendant, where common issues of fact may include what kind of workplace harassment policy the employer had and how it was distributed to the employees, made no legal difference.[70]

> **Clearly, in the court's eyes, the phrase "disparately distributed" does not permit inquiry into the nature and/or extent of the treatment of both sexes, but instead means the mistreatment of only one sex.**

The court also discussed *Pasqua v. Metropolitan Life Ins. Co.,* 71 a 1996 ruling in which, anticipating *Oncale,* a Seventh Circuit panel observed that "[h]arassment that is inflicted without regard to gender, that is, where males and females in the same setting do not receive disparate treatment, is not actionable because the harassment is not based on sex." Relying on that principle, the *Pasqua* court found that workplace gossip based on a relationship between a male and female worker does not amount to sex discrimination.[72] Judge Wood observed, however, that *Pasqua,* like *Holman,* involved a male and a female in the same setting. This does not preclude vicarious liability for the employer with respect to two related employees who are in different settings, reporting to different supervisors, with different co-workers.[73]

The court then focused on the nature of the harassment that both plaintiffs experienced. Although Frank Venezia worked in a unisex environment, *Oncale* supported the view that he should be allowed to prove his claim that he was harassed because of his sex. Similarly, Leslie Venezia should have the chance to prove that her sex accounted for her treatment. Although further development of the case might reveal that some or all of the harassment was unrelated to her sex, or that it was not sufficiently severe or pervasive to be actionable, it was too soon to draw that conclusion. Judge Wood concluded by observing that unlike the plaintiffs in *Holman* and *Pasqua,* Leslie Venezia did allege some instances of harassment that were unique to her.[74]

A good place to end this discussion is with two decisions handed down one day apart in January, 2010, for they bring into sharp focus the different approaches that courts take in EOH cases. *Reine v. Honeywell International, Inc.*[75] is an unpublished Fifth Circuit decision that takes what may now be regarded as the minority position that any showing of harassment of both sexes automatically concludes the issue of whether actionable sexual harassment occurred. There the court turned down a sexual harassment claim filed by a woman who said that her supervisor, Gautreau, made several rude, offensive, and harsh remarks about her abilities and performance. She also put forward deposition testimony indicating that Gautreau demeaned African-American and white male co-workers as well. Without inquiring into the nature and extent of the abuse that Gautreau visited on the different groups, the court cursorily upheld the district court's grant of summary judgment for Honeywell, noting that "Title VII is not a shield against harsh treatment at the workplace; it protects only in instances of harshness disparately distributed."[76] Clearly, in the court's eyes, the phrase "disparately distributed" does not permit inquiry into the nature and/or extent of the treatment of both sexes, but instead means the mistreatment of only one sex.

By contrast, the Eleventh Circuit, sitting *en banc* in *Reeves v. C.H. Robinson Worldwide, Inc.,*[77] unanimously took a comparative-evidence approach in allowing the sexual harassment claim to proceed. During her tenure at C.H. Robinson, Reeves alleged that her co-workers incessantly used phrases like "fuck," "fucker," "asshole," and "fucking idiot"; referred to women as "bitch," "stupid bitch," "fucking whore," and "lazy fucking bitch"; and tormented Reeves and co-workers in other ways. Her complaints went unheeded, and she quit and sued claiming hostile environment sexual harassment. The district court dismissed the complaint on the ground that both sexes were afforded like treatment.[78]

The Court of Appeals reversed. Speaking for the court, Judge Marcus stated that, while sexual language and discussions that are truly indiscriminate do not constitute sexual harassment, a member of a group protected by Title VII cannot be forced to endure pervasive, derogatory conduct and references that are gender-specific, just because the workplace may be otherwise rife with generally indiscriminate vulgar conduct. Title VII does not "offer boorish employees a free pass to discriminate against their employees specifically on account of gender just because they have tolerated pervasive but indiscriminate profanity as well."[79]

> **Title VII does not "offer boorish employees a free pass to discriminate against their employees specifically on account of gender just because they have tolerated pervasive but indiscriminate profanity as well".**

Equally important, Judge Marcus went on, is the com-monsense rule that the context of offending words or conduct is essential to a Title VII analysis. If, for example, one were to shout, "Son-of-a-bitch! They lost that truck," no reference to gender would be involved. But if a male co-worker calls a female employee a "bitch," the term is gender-derogatory. Indeed, the terms "bitch" and "slut" are firmly rooted in gender and are more degrading to women than to men, and the use of these and similar terms in the workplace creates a hostile environment based on sex. Finally, the court observed that one may state a claim of hostile environment harassment based on sex even if the words are not directed specifically at him or her. It is enough to hear co-workers on a daily basis refer to female colleagues as "bitches," "whores," etc., to know that they view women negatively and in a humiliating and degrading way. The harasser "need not close the circle with reference to the plaintiff specifically: 'and you are a 'bitch,' too.'"[80]

IV. Conclusion

On the surface, Title VII sets forth a simple command: Employers shall not discriminate against (or harass) their employees because of their sex. In practice, however, deciding when words and conduct were directed at employees because of their sex can be a nightmare. One reason is that neither Congress nor the courts have clearly defined "sex." This has allowed for the development of competing theories as to whether the term should be read narrowly, as embracing only biological distinctions between men and women, or more broadly to include the features generally ascribed to the term "gender." Another reason is that the phrase "because of" is equally vague and susceptible to different meanings.

In the 1998 *Oncale* decision, the Supreme Court sought to bring clarity to this area of the law by saying that sex discrimination occurs when one sex is exposed to disadvantageous conditions of employment to which the other sex is not exposed. But the uncertainty lingers on. Did Justice Scalia mean that *only* one sex may have been exposed to such conditions? Did he intend that the three ways of proving a sex discrimination case that he discussed would be exclusive? How, in short, would he decide a case involving sexual harassment that was visited against both sexes but was qualitatively and/or quantitatively different in its impact on each one?

Courts applying the gender-stereotyping theory of sex discrimination in same-sex cases have had great difficulty in deciding whether the plaintiffs were mistreated because of their sex (failure to conform to gender norms) or their real or perceived sexual orientation.[81] They have been forced to carefully parse the words and conduct at issue to try to pin down the harasser's motive, and the result has been inconsistent outcomes. The same is true in the EOH cases. Some courts have taken the position that any harassment of both sexes precludes recovery by either one. They perceive nothing odd about the EOH concept, for they have stressed that abusive treatment in the workplace is not illegal *per se* but instead violates Title VII only if it is discriminatory, and they have used a rigid definition of that term. Other courts have taken a variety of approaches in concluding that the *Oncale* standard can be met even if both sexes were harassed. In their eyes, to preclude recovery in such cases, which could amount to saying "the more discrimination the merrier," would, to use Judge Posner's language, be "exceedingly perverse."

Reine v. Honeywell International, Inc. shows that the EOH concept is alive and well in some circuits. Increasingly, however, such cases are the exception and not the rule, for there has been a noticeable trend on the part of courts in recent years toward eschewing the formalistic approach to sex discrimination inherent in the term EOH and finding actionable harassment in cases in which both sexes were harassed. Although confusion in this area of the law will exist as long as Congress or the courts fail to precisely define the terms "because of" and "sex," it does seem clear that we are witnessing the slow demise of the EOH concept.

Notes

1. 42 U.S.C $2000e et *seq.* The act applies to employers who have at least 15 employees and are engaged in interstate commerce.
2. Oncale v. Sundowner Offshore Servs., Inc., 523 U.S. 75 (1998).
3. *Id.* at 80.
4. Barnes v. Costle, 561 F.2d 983, 990 n. 55 (D. C. Cir. 1977).
5. 42 U.S.C. $2000e-2(a)(l).
6. *Id.* See, e.g., Reeves v. C. H. Robinson Worldwide, Inc., 594 F.3d 798 (11th Cir. 2010) (en banc).
7. Griggs v. Duke Power Co., 401 U.S. 424, 429-30 (1971).
8. Watson v. Ft. Worth Bank & Trust, 487 U.S. 977, 986-87 (1988).
9. EEOC v. Joe's Stone Crab, Inc., 220 F.3d 1263, 1274 (11th Cir. 2000).
10. Catherine MacKinnon, *Sexual Harassment of Working Women: A Case of Sex Discrimination* (New Haven: Yale Univ. Press 1979).
11. Henson v. City of Dundee, 682 F.2d 897 (11th Cir. 1982).
12. 29 C.F.R. 1604.11 (1985).
13. See, e.g., Burlington Industries, Inc. v. Ellerth, 524 U.S. 742 (1999).
14. Oncale v. Sundowner Offshore Servs., Inc., 523 U.S. 75, 80 (1998).
15. Harris v. Forklift Systems, Inc., 510 U.S. 17, 21 (1993).
16. *Id.* at 21-22.
17. *Oncale* at 81.

18. See, e.g., Jon D. Bible., *Smith v. City of Salem: 'Sex-stereotyping' Becomes a Potent Way to Prove Same-Sex Sex Discrimination under Title VII,* 56 LAB. L.J. 47, 58; *Same-Sex Sexual Harassment: When Does A Harasser Act 'Because of Sex'?,* 53 LAB. L. J. 3-10.

19. *Id.* at 80-81.

20. *Id.* at 80.

21. Deborah Zalesne, *Lessons From Equal Opportunity Harasser Doctrine: Challenging Sex-Specific Appearance and Dress Codes,* 14 DUKE J. GENDER L. & POL'Y 535, 545. *See also* Bible, *supra* n. 18.

22. Price Waterhouse v. Hopkins, 490 U.S. 228 (1989).

23. See, e.g., Michael Katz, *The Fundamental Incoherence of Title VII: Making Sense of Causation in Disparate Treatment Law,* 94 GEO. L. J. 489, 491 n. 5. (2006) (listing the various formulations).

24. 42 U.S.C. $2000e-2.

25. Hilary S. Axam & Deborah Zalesne, *Simulated Sodomy and Other Forms of Heterosexual 'Horseplay': Same Sex Sexual Harassment, Workplace Gender Heirarchies, and the Myth of the Gender Monolity Before and After Oncale,* 11 YALE J. L & FEMINISM 155, 236 (1999)

26. *Id.*

27. Toni Lester, *Protecting the GenderNonconformist from the Gender Police—Why the Harassment of Gays and Other Gender Nonconformists is a Form of Sex Discrimination in Light of the Supreme Court's Decision in* Oncale v. Sundowner, 29 N. M. L. REV. 89, 98 (1999).

28. See, e.g., DeSantis v. Pac. Tel. & Teleg. Co., 608 F.2d 327 (9th Cir. 1979); Smith v. Liberty Mutual Ins. Co., 569 F.2d 325 (5th Cir. 1978).

29. Price Waterhouse v. Hopkins, 490 U.S. 228, 250 (1989) (plurality opinion); 258-61 (White, J. concurring); 272-73 (O'Connor, J. concurring) (accepting plurality's gender-stereotyping analysis).

30. Oncale v. Sundowner Offshore Servs., Inc., 523 U.S. 75 (1998).

31. It should be stressed that one's sexual orientation is not dispositive of the issue of whether he or she will exhibit contra-gender behavior. Thus, there are so-called "straight" men who act effeminately, and women who have masculine attributes, just as there are homosexuals who conform perfectly to expected gender norms.

32. See, e.g., Rene v. MGM Grand Hotel, Inc., 305 F.3d 1061 (9th Cir. 2002) (en banc); Nichols v. Azteca Rest. Enters., 256 F.3d 864 (9th Cir. 2001).

33. See, e.g., Dawson v. Bumble & Bumble, 398 F.3d 211 (2d Cir. 2005).

34. The en banc *Rene* decision, *supra* n. 32, is a classic example of the confusion that the "because of sex" requirement can produce in genderstereotyping cases. Although the court ruled 7-4 in favor of Rene, the eleven judges produced five opinions, with none commanding a majority of the court.

35. *Oncale,* 523 U.S. at 80.

36. *Id.* at 80.

37. Barnes v. Costle, 561 F.2d 983, 990 n. 55 (D. C. Cir. 1977).

38. Henson v. City of Dundee, 682 F.2d 897 (11th Cir. 1982).

39. Rabidue v. Osceola Refining Co., 805 F.2d 611 (6th Cir. 1986).

40. *Id.* at 624 (Keith, J. concurring in part and dissenting in part).

41. *Id.* at 620-22.

42. Lack v. Wal-Mart Stores. Inc., 240 F.3d 255 (4th Cir. 2001).

43. *Id.* at 258.

44. *Id.* at 260-61, quoting Oncale v. Sundowner Offshore Servs., Inc., 523 U.S. 75. 80-81 (1998).

45. *Id.* at 261.

46. *Id.* at 262.

47. Holman v. State of Indiana. 211 F.3d 399 (7th Cir. 2000).

48. *Id.* at 403, citing Oncale v. Sundowner Offshore Servs., Inc., 523 U.S. 75, 80 (1998).

49. McDonnell v. Cisneros, 84 F.3d 256, 260 (7th Cir. 1996).

50. *Id.* at 257-58, 260.

51. *Id.* at 259-60.

52. Doe v. Belleville, 19 F.3d 563 (7th Cir. 1997), vacated and remanded, 523 U.S. 1001 (1998).

53. *Id.* at 590.

54. David S. Schwartz, *When is Sex Because of Sex? The Causation Problem in Sexual Harassment Law,* 150 U. Pa. L. Rev. 1697, 1793 (2002).

55. Kopp v. Samaritan Health System, 13 F.3d 264 (8th Cir. 1993).

56. *Id.* at 269-70.

57. Steiner v. Showboat Operating Co., 25 F.3d 1459 (9th Cir. 1994).

58. *Id.* at 1462-63.

59. *Id.* at 1463-64.

60. Williams v. General Motors Corp., 187 F.3d 553 (6th Cir. 1999).

61. *Id.* at 565-66.

62. Smith v. First Union Bank, 202 F.3d 234 (4th Cir. 2000).

63. *Id.* at 238-39.

64. *Id.* at 242.

65. Brown v. Henderson, 257 F.3d 246 (2d Cir. 2001).

66. *Id.* at 253-55.

67. Venezia v. Gottlieb Memorial Hospital, Inc., 421 F.3d 468 (7th Cir. 2005).

68. *Supra,* n. 47 and related text.

69. *Holman,* 421 F.3d at 469-70.

70. *Id.* at 471.

71. Pasqua v. Metropolitan Life Ins. Co., 101 F.3d 514 (7th Cir. 1996).

72. *Id.* at 517.

73. Venezia v. Gottlieb Memorial Hospital, Inc., 421 F.3d 468, 471-72 (7th Cir. 2005).

74. *Id.* at 472-73.

75. Reine v. Honeywell International, Inc., 2010 WL 271352 (5th Cir. 2010) (unpublished decision).

76. *Id.* at *2, quoting Jackson v. City of Killeen, 654 F.2d 1181, 1186 (5th Cir. 1981).

77. Reeves v. C. H. Robinson Worldwide, Inc. 594 F.3d 798 (11th Cir. 2010) (en banc).

78. *Id.* at 804-06.

79. *Id.* at 809-10.

80. *Id.* at 810-13.

81. See, e.g., Jon D. Bible, *Disorder in the Courts: Proving Same-Sex Sex Discrimination in Title VII Cases Via "Gender Stereotyping,"* 31 EMP. REL. L. J. 42 (2006).

Critical Thinking

1. What is an "equal opportunity harasser"?
2. How has this defense been used in court?
3. How can companies prevent this?
4. What can an employee do about an "equal opportunity harasser"?

JOHN D. BIBLE is a a Professor at the College of Business Administration at Texas State University.

From *Labor Law Journal,* Summer 2010, pp. 84–95. Copyright © 2010 by John D. Bible. Reprinted by permission of the author.

UNIT 2

Meeting Human Resource Requirements

Unit Selections

Learning Outcomes

After reading this Unit, you will be able to:

- Understand the importance of staffing in the organization.

- Understand the importance of morale in the workforce.

- Have an appreciation for the current labor market and the attitude of workers in that market.

- Understand the position of employers when it come to security of IT operations at the place of business.

- Have an appreciation for the use of temporary workers in industry.

- Understand the importance of federal law when it comes to internships.

Student Website

www.mhhe.com/cls

Internet References

Job Recruiting
www.jobrecruiting.com
TechAmerica
www.itaa.org

Organizations, whether for profit or nonprofit, are more than collections of buildings, desks, and telephones. Organizations are made of people—people with their particular traits, habits, and idiosyncrasies that make them unique. Each individual has different needs and wants, and the employer and the worker must seek a reasonable compromise so that at least an adequate match may be found for both.

The importance of human resource planning is greater than ever and will probably be even more important in the future. As Thomas Peters and Robert Waterman have pointed out in their book, *In Search of Excellence:*

© Design Pics / Kristy-Anne Glubish

> Quality and service, then, were invariable hallmarks of excellent firms. To get them, of course, everyone's cooperation is required, not just the mighty labors of the top 200. The excellent companies require and demand extraordinary performance from the average man. Dana's former chairman, Rene McPherson, says that neither the few destructive laggards nor the handful of brilliant performers are the key. Instead, he urges attention to the care, feeding and unshackling of the average man. We labeled it "productivity through people." All companies pay it lip service. Few deliver.
>
> —Thomas Peters and Robert Waterman, *In Search of Excellence,* New York, Warner Books, 1987

In the future, organizations are going to have to pay more than just lip service to "productivity through people" if they want to survive and prosper. They will have to practice it by demonstrating an understanding of not only their clients' and customers' needs but also those of their employees. The only way they will be able to deliver the goods and services and achieve success is through those same employees. Companies are faced with the difficult task of finding the right people for the right jobs—a task that must be accomplished if the organization is going to have a future.

Organizations are trying to meet the needs of their employees by developing new and different approaches to workers' jobs. This means taking into account how society, the labor force, the family, and the nature of the jobs themselves have changed. Training and development will be key in meeting future human resource requirements. Employers will have to change the way they design their positions if they are to attract and keep good employees. They must consider how society has changed and will change in the future. Learning from experience that there are fewer young people and more middle-aged employees, as well as dual-career couples in the workforce, struggling to raise children, and dealing with aging parents, they will have to consider how the very nature of jobs has changed, especially from predominantly blue-collar to white-collar jobs, from "9 to 5" to "24/7." Meeting these problems will entail new and different approaches to how jobs are structured. Companies will have to learn to experience flex-time and other approaches to job design if they are to attract and keep valuable and productive employees. Human resource planning, selection, and recruitment will be more critical in the future. Companies will have to go to extraordinary lengths to attract and keep new employees. There is no mystery

about the reasons for this situation. America is aging, and there are fewer people in their late teens and early twenties to take the entry-level jobs that will be available in the future. Women, who for the past 20 years have been the major source of new employees, now represent over half the workforce. As a result, new groups must be found, whether they are retirees, high school students, workers moonlighting on a second job, minority group members. New ways of attracting that new talent must also be pursued in this new technological age as well as doing away with old ideas about employees who could fill the current openings as seen in "Beat the Overqualified Rap."

One thing is certain: The workforce is changing and organizations will need to unlock the potential of all their employees. Other means of recruitment will need to be employed in the future, and old ideas and prejudices will have to go by the boards in all post-industrialized societies. Organizations will be faced with the problem of building a better workforce, and some of these strategies are discussed in "Internships and Federal Law: Are Interns Employees?" and "The Disposable Worker." But this is no easy task.

Another aspect of human resource planning involves both the selection process and the termination process. The days of working for only one company and then retiring with a gold watch and a pension are over. People are going to change jobs, if not companies, more frequently in the future, and many of the tasks they will be doing in the next 10, 15, or 20 years do not even exist today because of technological change. Mid-life and mid-career changes are going to be far more common than they have been in the past, requiring people to change and adapt.

Human resource information systems offer important tools in managing human resources. The ability of computers to handle large amounts of data is now being applied to human resource management with very interesting results. These practices, applied to hiring and internal information management, promise much greater automation of human resources in the future as well as reduced costs. There are, however, concerns. Privacy, security, and confidentiality are all key issues for employees and employers. The unauthorized use of IT equipment by employees is of particular concern to employers as discussed in "Playing IT Big Brother: When Is Employee Monitoring Warranted?"

Meeting the human resource needs of any organization in the future is a difficult task. Assuming that the economy continues to grow at an acceptable rate after the recession, and the unemployment rate eventually goes down, the need for workers will continue to increase, but many of the traditional sources of supply for new workers will be either exhausted or in decline. Management must plan for this shortage and consider alternative sources of potential employees, especially in certain critical areas to the organization that might not be readily available. In turn, the individual employee must be ready to adapt quickly and efficiently to a changing environment. Job security is a thing of the past, and workers must remain flexible in order to cope with increased uncertainty.

Beat the Overqualified Rap

Finding a new job is extra challenging when you've been labeled overqualified. Here are 4 common concerns hiring managers have when a candidate's qualifications exceed the job requirements, and tips for overcoming them.

JULIE ANN SIMS

You've steadily worked your way up the career ladder, earning a greater salary and increased responsibilities over the years. Then, the unthinkable happens: You lose your job and find that the experience you've worked so hard to acquire isn't helping you in your search for work. In fact, it's causing many employers to turn you away, claiming that you're overqualified for the role.

That's the position Michael Sinanan found himself in last year when he was laid off from his position as an art director at a financial services firm in Vancouver, British Columbia. Career-driven Sinanan had worked as a high-level art director for a magazine before accepting the position with the financial services firm. Both jobs focused on print, and the long hours he put in left him very little time to acquire in-depth web skills. Given the sluggish economy and the emphasis on digital design within many organizations, Sinanan received a weak response to the high-level jobs he might typically be considered for, so he set his sights a little lower—to no avail. Instead of employers jumping at the chance to add someone of his caliber to their teams, they told him he was too experienced for the jobs he sought.

"I could see in their faces that they knew I would be pretty bored there," Sinanan says. "People also were saying, 'You're overqualified. We can't afford you.'"

Given the state of the job market, an increasing number of creatives are in the same position. Although they're willing to accept jobs at a lower level than they've held before, they find employers are reluctant to hire them, for fear that they'll be a flight risk once the economy picks up.

If you're one of the many people trying to beat the overqualified rap, the first step is to take a stroll in the employer's shoes. Following are some of the common concerns hiring managers have when presented with applicants whose qualifications exceed those needed for the position at hand, as well as tips for overcoming these objections:

You're Too Expensive

Budgets are lean within most organizations, and companies have less leeway than they used to when it comes to negotiating higher salaries. That's why a fancy résumé with previous positions that paid a pretty penny may give hiring managers pause. This was the objection Sinanan found himself up against with a potential employer who owned a small design studio. "He was concerned I wouldn't be interested in the position because it paid less than my previous job," Sinanan says. "However, the compensation was still quite good, and the role was a great fit for me."

For Sinanan, the lower pay was mitigated by the fact that the role offered a flexible schedule and more creative freedom than he had before. He also felt there was significant growth potential. Once Sinanan explained to the employer that compensation wasn't a concern, he was able to land an extended interview. The takeaway from this situation? Address an employer's concerns about pay head-on. Here are a few suggestions for doing so:

- Bring up the fact that you're more interested in the position itself than the pay and that you're flexible about salary.
- Discuss aspects of the job that are appealing to you and could compensate for a lower salary, such as creative freedom or flexible scheduling.
- If the position is in a different city, research average salaries and the cost of living in that area. If prices are lower in the new location, point out to the employer that you can maintain the same standard of living on a smaller salary.

Demonstrate enthusiasm about the company. Describe the things about the firm that you find most appealing, such as a good corporate culture, a start-up feel or the ability to develop fresh concepts.

You'll Get Bored and Leave

If you're accustomed to working on strategy and managing a design team, and the role you're applying for involves hands-on production work and no direct reports, employers may be concerned that you'll find the position humdrum and set your sights on something more challenging as soon as the job market picks up. Before an employer expresses this concern, it's wise to do a little soul-searching to see just how much of an issue this will be, says Julie Jansen, career coach and author of the career book "I Don't Know What I Want, But I Know It's Not This: A Step-by-Step Guide to Finding Gratifying Work."

"People's values and motivators change over time, and if the person will be satisfied doing a job he did 10 years ago, then it's absolutely a good idea to go for it," she says. "If, on the other hand, the person is taking any job because he needs one but has his eye on a more senior role as soon as he can find one, then it's not a good idea."

Those pursuing a certain job because they lack other options might want to consider project work until something more suitable comes along. If, however, a lower-level job truly appeals to you, you might be able to turn the tables in your favor by explaining what interests you about the role. Following are some tips that can help:

- Explain how much the job duties appeal to you. Perhaps they include tasks you've enjoyed the most throughout your career.
- Demonstrate enthusiasm about the company. Describe the things about the firm that you find most appealing, such as a good corporate culture, a start-up feel or the ability to develop fresh concepts.
- Emphasize that you can take the job and run with it. There will be no learning curve.
- When discussing your previous experience, focus on your former duties—rather than previous job titles—and how they're a match for the position.
- If you have a stable work history, discuss your longevity with previous employers to demonstrate loyalty.

You Seem Desperate

Underlying the concern that candidates will be underpaid and bored if they accept job offers for which they have excess qualifications is the idea that these professionals are desperate for a job, any job—an image that, unfortunately, detracts from any applicant's appeal. Although it's only natural to feel anxious and frustrated during an extended job search, it's important not to make those feelings apparent to hiring managers. Rich Stoddart, president of Leo Burnett, North America, says candidates who have a good story to tell and present themselves well have an edge, no matter their level of experience. "Show hunger, curiosity, passion and confidence." he advises. "Who are you? What makes you tick? What are you passionate about? What kind of things in your work bring you joy?"

Stoddart says the answers to these types of questions can help creative professionals craft a compelling story that grabs a potential employer's attention in a positive way. If the last year or so has left you battered and bruised, take a fresh look at yourself and come up with a new narrative—one that's uniquely you and helps define the skills, ideas and passion you bring to the table. Following are some ideas that can help:

- Re-examine how you present yourself in your application materials and in person from a personal branding perspective: What message does your brand convey? Does it highlight your key strengths and abilities?
- Are you putting out subtle signals that you're desperate or frustrated? If so, consider taking a break from your job search so you can recharge. Even a few days can put you in a better mindset.
- Develop anecdotes that demonstrate your passion for your work and the industry. These are useful stories to tell in cover letters and during job interviews.
- Be sure to take good care of yourself during your unemployment period, socializing with friends and getting plenty of exercise.

Re-examine how you present yourself in your application materials and in person from a personal branding perspective: What message does your brand convey? Does it highlight your key strengths and abilities?

You're Obsolete or Power-Hungry

Although the concerns above are the most common when it comes to overqualified candidates, occasionally an employer will have other, more negative ideas. If you've spent a good portion of your career with a single employer or working with more traditional media, for example, the hiring manager may fear that you're set in your ways or that your skills haven't kept pace with changes in the industry, A prospective employer may even worry that you'll soon set your sights on her job, especially if you've held a similar role in the past. Following are some tips that can help you overcome these obstacles:

- Avoid intimidating a less experienced hiring manager by emphasizing the teamwork involved with past successes, rather than your individual performance. Also, don't use phrases that can make you seem condescending, such as, "At my last job, we . . ." or "I would recommend that you . . ."
- To show that your skills are current, discuss any training or coursework that you've recently participated in, and how you've put these skills into action, even if it's been through volunteer work.
- Demonstrate that you're up to speed on current trends, not only within the industry as a whole, but as they pertain to the potential employer. Talk as specifically

as possible about how your skills could help the firm address its challenges.

Unfortunately, the overqualified label can be tough to shake. The best strategy is to proactively address an employer's concerns and try to convince the hiring manager that your creative experience and expertise are a benefit, not a disadvantage, "Don't forget that we're in the idea business, not the technology or widget business," Stoddart says. "People who can design and nurture big ideas are in short supply and are incredibly valuable."

Critical Thinking

1. How can being experienced be a bad thing?
2. What can experienced employees do to beat the "overqualified rap"?
3. Is overqualified sometimes a hidden way to discriminate based on age?

JULIE ANN SIMS is director of communications strategy for The Creative Group, a specialized staffing service placing creative professionals, and HOW's official career partner. www.creativegroup.com

Internships and Federal Law: Are Interns Employees?

The author explains that whether an intern or trainee is entitled to such things as minimum wage and overtime compensation will often depend upon whether the individual is receiving training without displacing other employees or providing any real benefit to the employer.

MATTHEW H. NELSON

Employers cannot avoid the requirements of federal law by simply labeling employees as "interns" or "trainees." As a general rule, those engaged in legitimate internships or training programs are not covered by federal employment law. But if the would-be intern or trainee is actually an employee by another name, an employment relationship exists, and the intern or trainee is entitled to all the benefits and protections of federal law, which include the rights to minimum wage, overtime, and a discrimination-free workplace.

The issue, then, is whether an employment relationship in fact exists; whether, despite the title, the would-be intern or trainee is actually an employee. Unfortunately, none of the primary federal employment laws, specifically the Fair Labor Standards Act (FLSA) and the antidiscrimination statutes, provides any meaningful guidance on the distinction between employees and interns or trainees. Thus, the question has been left to the Department of Labor (DOL) and the federal courts. And as is normally the case in such situations, the DOL and the courts have developed a highly fact-specific analysis, and even then, whether an employment relationship exists is not always clear. Instead, whether an intern or trainee is entitled to such things as minimum wage and overtime compensation will often depend upon whether the individual is receiving training without displacing other employees or providing any real benefit to the employer.

Internships and FLSA: Six Factors for Avoiding Liability

The primary issue employers face in this area, is whether an intern or trainee is entitled to minimum wage or even overtime compensation. The answer, of course, depends upon whether the individual is covered by FLSA. FLSA requires, among other things, that employers pay all employees at least the minimum wage. The difficulty is determining whether an intern or trainee is actually an employee.

FLSA's definitions are of little help. FLSA simply defines an employee as "any individual employed by an employer." An employer, in turn, is "any person acting directly or indirectly in the interest of an employer in relation to an employee." And to "employ," means only to "suffer or permit to work." That is, an employer is anyone who employs an employee, and an employee is anyone employed by an employer. Under a strict reading of these circular definitions, anyone who performs any work whatsoever, is likely an employee, and consequently entitled to minimum wage and overtime compensation.

The US Supreme Court, however, has long recognized that Congress did not intend FLSA to require that *all* individuals who work for an employer be paid minimum wage. In *Walling v. Portland Terminal Co.,* the Court found that, under certain circumstances, such as where individuals choose to work for their own advantage, an employer may provide training to unpaid volunteers, without violating FLSA.

Briefly, the issue in *Walling* was whether the employer, Portland Terminal Co., was required to pay its trainees minimum wage. At the time, Portland Terminal's policy required that any individual who sought employment as a brakeman, was first required to attend and complete a practical training course. The course typically lasted anywhere from seven to eight days, and all prospective employees were required to complete the course. Portland

Terminal would not consider any applicant who either refused to take or failed to complete the training course.

Once prospective brakemen completed the initial training course, they were then assigned to work on a yard crew. According to Portland Terminal, the purpose of this second assignment was so that the prospective employees could learn the necessary routines and activities through observation. Only after completing the course were the trainees finally put to work, and only then under very close scrutiny. The prospective employees were not compensated during this training period.

After an examination of the scope and purpose of the FLSA, the Supreme Court ultimately concluded that the trainees were not employees, at least for purposes of FLSA, during the training period. The Court noted that the trainees did not displace any regular employees, nor did Portland Terminal receive any immediate advantage from the trainees during the training period; indeed, the evidence indicated that the trainees actually hindered the company's productivity. Just as importantly, the trainees entered the arrangement without any expectation of compensation; they knew they would not be paid.

Accordingly, because the trainees were not employees, they were not entitled to the protections of FLSA, and Portland Terminal was within its rights to refuse to provide any compensation at all. The Court reasoned that although FLSA is an exceedingly broad statute, Congress could not have intended "to stamp all persons as employees who, without any express or implied compensation agreement, might work for their own advantage on the premises of another." Otherwise, as the Court analogized, "all students would be employees of the school or college they attended, and as such entitled to receive minimum wages."

Instead, the purpose of FLSA "was to insure that every person whose employment contemplated compensation should not be compelled to sell his services for less than the prescribed minimum wage." According to the Court, FLSA was not designed to prevent employers from providing free instruction, or to penalize them for doing so. Thus, where an individual "who, without promise or expectation of compensation, but solely for his personal purpose or pleasure," works on the premises of another, FLSA does not require that the individual receive minimum compensation.

Although the Supreme Court decided *Walling* in 1947, it has remained the seminal case in this area. Following the *Walling* decision, the Wage and Hour Division of the DOL devised a six-part test to guide its determination as to whether an employment relationship exists for purposes of FLSA. Specifically, the DOL considers whether:

1. The training, even though it includes actual operation of the facilities of the employer, is similar to that which would be given in a vocational school;
2. The training is for the benefit of the trainees;
3. The trainees do not displace regular employees, but work under close observation;
4. The employer that provides the training derives no immediate advantage from the activities of the trainees and on occasion its operations may actually be impeded;
5. The trainees are not necessarily entitled to a job at the completion of the training period; and
6. The employer and the trainees understand that the trainees are not entitled to wages for the time spent in training.

Unless all six factors are met, the DOL will find that an employment relationship exists. The agency has applied these six factors in several opinion letters. Most recently, on May 17, 2004, the DOL found that college students participating in a summer internship program may be covered by FLSA. According to the information provided by the potential employer, college students would be invited to participate in an internship, with the purpose of learning "marketing, promotion, and statistical analysis in a real world setting." The students could participate only if they simultaneously received college credit, and a faculty supervisor was responsible for consulting with the company regarding the performance of the student interns. The company, however, assumed the responsibility for direct supervision of the interns.

The would-be employer further explained that the internship was structured like a college marketing course, and the student interns would work flexible schedules of between seven and ten hours per week. Their duties would include wearing clothing embossed with the company's logo, and distributing stickers and flyers on campus. The interns would also be responsible for evaluating student responses to the promotional items, collecting data on the composition of the campus population and surrounding city, utilizing online chat rooms to track the effectiveness of certain Web sites, obtaining information on the most popular campus locations, surveying at least 50 people on campus, and ultimately compiling data to predict trends both locally and nationally.

Based on these facts, the DOL concluded that it could not definitively state that an employment relationship did not exist. That is, even under these facts, it was possible that the interns were employees under the six-part test, and thus entitled to compensation. The DOL found that the interns clearly satisfied the first criteria, as the training program was similar to what the interns would learn in school. Likewise, the second, fifth, and sixth factors were satisfied, since the program clearly inured to the benefit of the interns, the interns were not guaranteed jobs at the conclusion of the internship, and the interns neither received nor expected compensation.

But based upon the information provided by the company, the DOL could not determine whether the employer satisfied the third and fourth factors. Given the intern's duties it was at least possible that they displaced other employees (although, the DOL noted that this appeared unlikely), and that the company derived some immediate benefit from the intern's activities.

The federal courts, however, are less included to strictly follow the six-factor test. For example, the Fourth Circuit has repeatedly held "that the general test used to determine if an employee is entitled to the protections of the Act is whether the employee or the employer is the primary beneficiary of the trainees' labor."[1] Likewise, the Tenth Circuit adopted a "totality of the circumstances" test, under which the DOL's six factors provide helpful guidance, but are not dispositive.[2] And the Fifth Circuit, in *Donovan v. American Airlines, Inc.,*[3] cited the six-factor test with approval, but did not expressly adopt the test, nor require that all six factors be met in order to avoid an employment relationship under FLSA.

Internships and the Antidiscrimination Laws

A lesser, but nevertheless important consideration, is whether interns and trainees are entitled to the protections of the antidiscrimination statutes, including the Civil Rights Act, the Americans with Disabilities Act, and the Age Discrimination in Employment Act. Like FLSA, these antidiscrimination statutes generally apply to the employment relationship. And like FLSA, these statutes provide broad, if somewhat unhelpful, definitions of employment—each one defining an "employee" as simply "an individual employed by an employer."

The federal courts have traditionally applied common law agency principles to determine whether an employment relationship exists for purposes of federal antidiscrimination laws. Since the Supreme Court's decision in *Nationwide Mutual Insurance Co. v. Darden,*[4] courts have generally applied the following 13 factors to determine whether an employment relationship exists.

1. The hiring party's right to control the manner and means by which the product is accomplished;
2. The skill required by the hired party;
3. The source of instrumentalities and tools;
4. The location of the work;
5. The duration of the relationship between the parties;
6. The hiring party's right to assign additional projects;
7. The hired party's discretion over when and how long to work;
8. The method of payment;
9. The hired party's role in hiring the paying assistants;
10. Whether the work is part of the hiring party's regular business;
11. Whether the hiring party is in business;
12. The hired party's employee benefits; and
13. Tax treatment of the hired party's compensation.

As with the federal court's treatment of the six-factor test, no single element is dispositive. Instead, the courts once again look to the totality of the circumstances. Nonetheless, even a cursory glance shows that this test assumes that the putative employee was "hired" in the first place.

The second circuit addressed the application of this analysis to student interns in *O'Connor v. Davis.*[5] There, the issue was whether an unpaid student intern could bring suit under Title VII for sexual harassment. The employer argued that the intern was not an employee, and thus not covered by the antidiscrimination laws. The Second Circuit agreed, noting that the considerations articulated by the Supreme Court in *Darden,* assume an economic relationship; that the would-be employee was "hired" in the first place. And the Court reasoned that, absent some economic value in exchange for services, a "hire" had not occurred. That is, compensation is an essential element of employment. Importantly, other courts have found that benefits such as insurance may constitute compensation, and thus require an application of common law test.[6]

Thus, if an intern or trainee is not an employee under FLSA, then he or she is not entitled to minimum wage, or indeed any compensation. And if the intern or trainee is not compensated, then he or she is likely not an employee for purposes of the federal antidiscrimination laws. If, however, an intern or trainee is compensated, then the courts will apply the 13 factors set forth by the Supreme Court in *Darden* to determine whether an employment relationship exists. It is entirely possible that an individual may be an employee for purposes of FLSA, but not for purposes of the antidiscrimination laws.

Notes

1. Wirtz v. Wardlaw, 339 F. 2d, 785 (4th Cir. 1964), Isaacson v. Penn Community Services, Inc., 450 F.2d 1306 (4th Cir.1971), and McLaughlin v. Ensley, 877 F.2d 1207 (4th Cir.1989).

2. Reich v. Parker Fire Protection Dist., 992 F.2d 1023 (10th Cir. 1993).

3. 686 F.2d 267 (5th Cir. 1982)

4. 503 U.S. 318 (1992),

5. 126 F.3d 112 (2nd Cir. 1997).

6. Haavistola v. Community Fire Co., 6 F.3d 211, 221 (4th Cir. 1993).

Critical Thinking

1. What is the difference between an intern and an employee?

2. How has federal law changed the relationship between interns and possible employers?

3. What might be some of the consequences of these changes?

MATTHEW H. NELSON is a member of the Labor and Employment Department in Dinsmore & Shohl's Morgantown, West Virginia, office. He can be reached at matthew.nelson@dinslaw.com.

From *Employee Relations Law Journal,* vol. 36, no. 2, Autumn 2010, pp. 42–47. Copyright © 2010 by Wolters Kluwer Law & Business. Reprinted by permission.

Hiring Right

Recruiting the wrong person is costly. Follow this expert advice to make smart hiring decisions.

CAROLYN HEINZE

Running a successful equine practice presents its fair share of challenges but none quite so crucial as bringing in a new veterinarian. After all, the process of hiring is time-consuming and expensive, and can have either a positive or negative effect on the practice's business. Not only should potential recruits possess the skills required, they need to fit in with the culture of the practice. For owners and practice managers, this demands an investment of time in an effort that, for many, can be a daunting—and, at times, discouraging—task.

According to the Society for Human Resources Management, an association that supports HR professionals, you can determine the cost-per-hire for each associate or practitioner by adding together all the expenses required to recruit and then hire the individual, including travel, advertising and other costs. If you add up all the costs per hire of each associate, it can be quite a substantial sum of money, so making sure you hire the right person to begin with is key. When you hire the wrong person, it's even more costly: 100 to 150 percent of their annual salary, according to SHRM.

So how do you know if you're making the right hiring decision? According to Kurt A. Oster, practice management consultant at Oster Business Solutions in Sterling, Connecticut, practice owners can begin by envisioning an ideal candidate: What characteristics, exactly, are you seeking in a veterinarian? And, once you've established these criteria, Oster emphasizes that you should stick with those attributes, no matter what.

"What happens is, people say: 'I think I want somebody who can do this and this.' Then someone else who doesn't fit that mold will show up, but they're there, they're interviewing, they're interested, and they end up hired," he says. In many cases, veterinarians and practice managers aren't fond of the recruiting and interviewing process, leading them to make quick—and not always wise—decisions to get it all over with.

Articulating a list of attributes—both personal and professional—that you want in a candidate before you start looking is as important as job description. When you meet someone at a meeting, a conference or in another practice that you think would be a good fit in your operation, take note of his or her information and keep it on file. Then, when you're ready to hire, you'll have a starting list of potential candidates. Even if that individual isn't interested, he or she may know of someone else who would be a good fit.

David Grant, DVM, founder of Animal Care Technologies in Denton, Texas, advises that when seeking associates and practitioners, practices should cast their nets wide. "Recruiting doesn't necessarily mean geography; it also implies time," he says. "You want to be looking for people all the time—not in that reactionary, two-week window when most people do all of their resume-gathering, and then they make a quick decision,"

Depending on the practice's focus, market and location, the definition of the ideal practitioner or associate varies. In many cases, owners and practice managers are seeking to diversify in order to grow the business. Some practices, for example, may need someone specializing in lameness, while others may want to branch out into reproduction, necessitating a practitioner with these particular skills.

Refer to Their References

We've all heard it, but it merits stating once again: One of the biggest errors recruiters commit is being remiss when it comes to checking references. "Believe me, if you have a problem employee, you will spend a lot more time fixing mistakes than you will checking references," warns Kurt A. Oster, practice management consultant at Oster Business Solutions in Sterling, Connecticut.

Oster suggests that recruiters go above and beyond the references listed on the candidate's resume. "If you know a practice that they worked at before, or if you know the university they attended, contact somebody there and ask some questions," he says. He cites a case in his own business, where not long ago he hired a doctor who happened to have served on a committee on veterinary medicine. "I talked to some of the other people who were on the committee. They weren't people listed as references, but they were people who had contact and experience with them." It's often these individuals who will give you the most candid assessments on the candidate in question.

The Three Cs

Regardless of a practice's specific needs, when assessing a candidate, Grant believes in applying the "Three Cs": character, competence and confidence. The "character" element combines maturity, emotional I.Q. and good communication skills. "Competence" comprises hard skills, such as those associated with either general medicine or specialties, such as lameness or reproduction. "Confidence" is the trickiest—again, especially in relation to younger doctors. "What we find in young practitioners who lack experience is a lack of confidence," he says. "They haven't seen the diseases and conditions as much, so their diagnoses are oftentimes shadowed by a lack of confidence. That is almost impossible to hide from a client, so confidence is key."

Which, in a way, points back to "character," since good communication skills—and the confidence therein—are important in reassuring clients. "Good communication skills make a good veterinarian," Grant says. "Oftentimes, we are too quick to associate skills, training and advanced degrees [with competency], but having hired hundreds of veterinarians, I would take communications skills and bedside manner any day of the week." He adds that in equine veterinary medicine, clients tend to demand even more communication than in other areas of veterinary medicine. "Whatever it is, I find that they're going to be a more particular decision-maker when it comes to who is vetting the needs of their horses." Thus, an increased need for equine practitioners to be communicative.

Oster notes that while skills sets and personality are the primary factors in determining whether or not a candidate will be a good fit, "soft" items can often act as deal-breakers . . . and should be examined before both the practice and the candidate sign on the dotted line. "Scheduling is huge," he says. Do you require your practitioner to be on call? How is scheduling handled on weekends? Do your vets work five consecutive days, or are they scheduled for four long days, followed by four days off? "A lot of times, you start these relationships by looking at the hard criteria like skill sets and experience, and the relationship goes south because of things like disagreements over the schedule," he adds.

Beyond Veterinary Medicine

When assessing resumes, Oster advises owners and practice managers to look for any listed job experience that may have little to do with veterinary medicine—especially if you're hiring younger practitioners. "There is a tendency on the part of how they train younger veterinarians on putting together a resume. They tell them to only list their veterinary experience," he says. General job experience, however, often provides certain skills that are useful for veterinarians. "If I had two veterinarians that were equally trained, equally experienced, equally skilled, with equal personalities—everything was perfectly the same, only one flipped hamburgers at McDonald's and one didn't—that shows me that the person who flipped hamburgers for two years can get along with co-workers, they can follow a routine, they can show up on time, they have basic job and interpersonal skills and have demonstrated some responsibilities." A candidate in his or her late 20s who has either been in

school or only practiced veterinary medicine may not possess the work ethic or discipline your veterinary practice demands.

It seems like there are as many books out there on the art of interviewing as there are opinions on recruiting itself, but one thing for interviewers to remember is that their job is to listen more and talk less. "It goes back to the old saying: Two ears, one mouth," Oster says. "One should use that ratio when interviewing." He points out that problems arise when practice owners and managers who dislike the interviewing process use the job interview as a way to sell their practice to the candidate: This is the equipment we have on hand. These are the types of clients we service. These are the benefits we offer. "They spend the whole time selling the practice, and they never really find out what that candidate is about. During an interview, you want to learn about that candidate to see if they fit into your mix."

This is especially important in today's economy, where the market for jobs—even among veterinarians—has dwindled. "With student loan debt and everything else, a candidate will grab a job that is a less than an ideal fit thinking: Well, in six months or a year, if something better comes along, I will jump," Oster notes. "That doesn't help the owner of the practice."

Stephanie Keeble, operations manager at Campbellville, Ontario's McKee-Pownall Veterinary, explains that at McKee-Pownall Veterinary, interviewers apply behavior-based questioning, asking candidates to give examples of how they handled themselves in specific situations. "We find this more effective than questions like, 'In this situation, what would you do?'" she says. She adds that candidates must demonstrate open-mindedness and an emphasis on customer service. "Customer service is extremely important to us, so what's their experience with that? What's their viewpoint on treating customers?" A sense of humor and an acceptance of change are also important. "We've grown a lot over the last little while and the people who work for us have to be willing to go with the flow. If you can't stand change, then this is not the place for you." After the initial interview process, candidates undergo a "working interview," during which they spend several days working with associates and staff to determine if they will integrate well into the practice's culture.

Temp to Perm

Many companies hire temporary help as a way to fill gaps and as a way to "vet," as it were, potential employees. In fact, the temporary-to-permanent phenomenon is well ensconced in American business. According to the American Staffing Association, 59 percent of companies that use temporaries do so to find good, permanent employees.

So, one way to determine whether a practitioner or potential associate is a good fit with your practice is to enlist him or her in relief work. Grant notes that some of his company's most successful placements resulted out of such an arrangement. "I don't think you can replace the benefit of actually working with that person, even for an extended period of time if that's an option," he says. "It's kind of like a low-pressure date—they're not even thinking in terms of putting on their best face." In this scenario, both the temporary practitioner and permanent staff are more relaxed, giving both the opportunity to see each other for who they really are. "Whenever possible, hiring relief veterinarians as a way of looking for future associates or partners can be valuable," he explains.

Few successful relationships are born out of rapid-fire decisions, and this applies to hiring as well. Oster advises that owners and practice managers spend the necessary time to find the right candidate rather than settling for the wrong candidate and then trying to fix him or her. "I see so much heartache and people trying to fix things down the road," he says. "Not only is it your time and energy, but it also has an impact on your client base as well. You're better off short-staffed than with the wrong staff."

Critical Thinking

1. Why is it so important to hire the right people for the right job?
2. Does this also apply to professionals as well as blue-collar jobs?
3. What do you think happens when you don't hire the right person for the right job?

CAROLYN HEINZE is a freelance writer/editor.

From *EquiManagement*, published by Equine Network/Active Interest Media, Summer 2011, pp. 18–23. Copyright © 2011 by Active Interest Media. Reprinted by permission.

Playing IT Big Brother
When Is Employee Monitoring Warranted?

BRUCE GAIN

Instant messaging, YouTube videos, personal email accounts, and social networking sites represent an ever-burgeoning number of attention-grabbers that can prevent users from getting their work done. On a business level, time-wasting Internet use represents lost productivity and, ultimately, money lost.

Of more concern is the possibility that a user will use enterprise property to download viruses, transmit sensitive company information, or use enterprise property to break the law. A recent worst-case scenario involved Societe Generale, one of the largest banks in Europe, and its now-famous French rogue trader who, left virtually unchecked, allegedly lost the bank $7.1 billion.

What is an admin to do? The immediate reaction for many admins might be to invest in increasingly smarter employee monitoring technologies that facilitate tight surveillance and control to make sure employees are not using the enterprise's machines and network to do things they shouldn't. But how far should monitoring of small to midsized enterprises go? When does it cross the line between employee and company rights?

There are no black-and-white answers to these questions. The solution you adopt should take into account your enterprise's particular needs, user education, and ultimately a common-sense approach when it comes to employee monitoring.

Enterprises Jump on the Bandwagon

Whether it is in response to employees using online outlets such as instant messaging and consumer websites or just a more paranoid business climate, the use of employee monitoring is rapidly increasing. The technologies are also increasingly cheaper to implement.

"Surveillance is now routine business practice among American employers both large and small as the cost and ease of introducing [surveillance products] have dropped," says Jeremy Gruber, legal director for The National Workrights Institute.

Adam Schran, chief executive and founder of Ascentive (www .ascentive.com), which offers Internet monitoring software, says employee monitoring as well as blocking and filtering product sales have become a $300 million-a-year market. "There are more distractions out there," he says. "A few years ago, [potential customers] said it was like Big Brother. Now they are saying, 'Here is my credit card number.'"

100% Legal

Enterprises in the United States today also have much leeway when it comes to monitoring what their employees do at the workplace. There are few mandates or court decisions that prohibit enterprises from tracking employees' activities.

"Employees have few if any rights when it comes to electronic surveillance in the workplace," Gruber says. "Only two states, Connecticut and Delaware, even require that employers give notice of monitoring, let alone actually regulate the monitoring itself."

But just because tight surveillance is not illegal does not necessarily make it ethical—or something that IT will necessarily want to put into place, Gruber says. "While there are some legitimate threats that form the basis for surveillance, they are often exaggerated, and rarely is the surveillance tailored to meet the specific objective or balanced with employee privacy concerns," he notes. "Employees are working longer hours than they ever have before. It should be acceptable to allow for reasonable personal and private use of computers and other forms of electronic communication, but only a minority of employers allows for reasonable-use policies, and even then the surveillance continues uninterrupted."

On a practical level, the advantages of catching people who are not doing their work or are doing what they shouldn't might not outweigh the disadvantages of employees who resent being watched.

"You can lock down their systems and monitor them to the point that they cannot do anything except use company software," says Ira Herman, co-CEO of Logic IT Consulting (www. logicitc.com). "But a lot of times, employees will ask 'Why are you being mean and locking us down?'"

In situations where professionals are paid for results, some employees think that it is none of management's business if they take a break and use their work Internet connection for personal reasons, provided they get their work done. For users of this mindset, heavy-handed surveillance is especially prone to back-fire for employees who work in creative fields, Schran says. "If you work for a company that is too strict and you are a creative type, why would you want to stick around?" he asks.

One solution is to allow for employees to have a certain amount of privacy time when their Internet and computer use remain private.

"Some software can turn on private time features and turn off the monitoring so the employee can go on YouTube and email their kids and spouses," Schran says. "You can use it for an hour or 90 minutes a day. But it is the folks that are spending four to six hours a day on YouTube who are going to get caught anyway."

Middle Ground

The degree to which employees' computer and Internet use needs to be monitored varies from enterprise to enterprise. Strict surveillance of financial services industry personnel is often legally required, for example. But an administrator of a 700-user network for an airline components firm will not have the same concerns.

Indeed, network activity and PC usage need to be monitored to a certain extent for any enterprise. If employees are spending an inordinate amount of time watching streaming video content, for example, the network's bandwidth can surfer. In this case, using monitoring technology to determine whose personal use of the network is causing problems is warranted.

"The cost implications are things that come into my mind as what you have to watch for," notes Andras Cser, an analyst for Forrester Research. "You look at where your bandwidth goes to. If you start seeing activities that really are out of the normal and ordinary, then you start interfering."

One approach for SMEs might be to adopt a policy prohibiting downloads or installation of any kind of third-party software and access to certain kinds of websites. The guidelines might also allow for reasonable personal use of the network and computer equipment, such as for communicating with spouses or even taking a break from work to read an online newspaper. But employees should also be aware that usage might be watched to prevent problems from arising, such as when the monitoring system alerts you that someone is slowing down the network by regularly downloading large video files.

"There are two extremes when it comes to employee monitoring, and the answer is somewhere in between," Cser says.

Monitoring Tips

It is relatively easy to monitor and track practically everything users do on their machines and the network, but creating a working policy that addresses both employees' privacy concerns and the security needs of the enterprise requires some finesse. Following certain guidelines can help achieve the right balance between locking down users' PCs and giving them free rein to do whatever they want. Here are some things to keep in mind:

- It is crucial to educate users about what activity is prohibited and that any electronic communication they make with the enterprise's equipment is subject to monitoring.
- The degree to which your enterprise's employees need to be actively monitored varies depending on each user's position and business activity.
- Your legal department will likely tell you that most electronic surveillance is allowed, but that does not necessarily mean any and all means of monitoring is ethical (or good for employee morale).

Ultimately, your monitoring policy will have to take into account the specific needs of your enterprise and should evolve as the network's infrastructure, users, and applications change over time. The right approach is less about gaining control than it is about striking a balance between your users' privacy concerns and how to prevent employees from disrupting the network. Cser says, "As far as I am concerned, this is more about common sense and saving costs."

Critical Thinking

1. Do employers have the right to monitor the IT activity of their employees?

2. Should employers monitor the IT activity of their employees?

3. What actions should an employer take when they find an employee abusing his or her IT account?

4. Do employees have the right to expect IT privacy at work?

Acknowledgements—Reprinted with permission from Processor Magazine. To see more articles like this, visit www.processor.com.

Make Your HR Portal a Destination Location

Build a personal, user-friendly, dynamic site to create a go-to resource.

DAVE ZIELINSKI

When Kim Mann and her colleagues decided to upgrade their organization's human resource intranet in 2007, they had more than a few tweaks in mind: Team members wanted to change the way they communicated with employees. Mann, director of compensation, benefits and human resource information systems (HRIS) for Hershey Entertainment & Resorts in Hershey, Pa., knew the technology existed to revamp the intranet from a valued but largely one-dimensional repository of benefits and policy information into a dynamic, versatile and full-fledged portal.

The existing intranet had created important cost savings and reduced administrative burdens by moving paper-based employee handbooks, benefits enrollment and personal contact data online. But the site wasn't easy to tailor for the needs of Hershey's diverse employee segments, didn't have desired employee engagement features and didn't allow content to be easily updated without calling in information technology staff. In addition, Mann and her team too often had to communicate with 7,500 employees by phone or e-mail, when they suspected the portal could handle more of those duties.

So Mann turned to Enwisen Inc., a Novato, Calif.-based vendor, to help implement a hosted portal called My Path, short for "My Personal Access To Hershey." The portal has delivered on her team's vision of a customer-friendly site where transactions and communications are never more than two clicks away. The next-generation portal provides a single access point for revamped onboarding processes, employee engagement and wellness surveys, e-learning courses, and new communication tools. Hershey has used the portal to communicate information on the H1N1 influenza virus, for example, and to let employees know if they have to come to work during snowstorms. My Path gives employees 24-hour access from work or home. It also features "in context" decision support tools that help workers make benefits plan choices during enrollment periods.

Evolution of Portals

The evolution of Hershey's portal reflects a growing movement of human resource intranets away from "link farms"—designed primarily to reduce paper-based costs and promote self-service—toward more-personal, interactive and multidimensional sites. HR portals have been in existence for more than a decade, but experts say those that live up to their designers' goals remain in the minority. That's due in part to:

- Challenges that HR staff with limited technical knowledge face in updating portal content.
- The inability of employees to complete transactions because they lack seamless access to third-party vendors, such as 401(k) or health plan providers.
- Site designs that aren't intuitive or user-friendly.
- More dynamic portals, on the other hand, are characterized by systems that:
- Enable HR staff to create, manage or edit content with little help from information technology staff.
- Have identity management features that display portal content tailored to users' specific attributes, such as job categories, union status or benefits plans.
- Feature single sign-ons that grant employees access via the portal to content from third-party vendors without forcing them to type in additional passwords.

Employees in today's web-savvy workforce often compare corporate portals to popular sites they use outside the workplace, like Amazon.com or Yahoo.com. Such commercial sites offer the latest in personalization, engagement and search technologies. If your portal's features and functions don't measure up, experts say, don't expect employees to bless you with high ratings or stay on the site any longer than necessary.

There are a growing number of affordable options for making your portal more dynamic and valuable to employees. Some organizations turn to vendors' hosted services to avoid investing in hardware or on-premises software and to acquire new features and functions.

Costs vary depending on the feature sets and components offered by individual vendors and on functions sought by users. In addition to startup fees, organizations can expect to pay annual subscription fees ranging from $40,000 to more than $100,000,

Online Resources

For additional information about creating a dynamic HR portal, see the online version of this article at www.shrm.org/hrmagazine/0610Zielinski.

according to Michael Rudnick, national portal, intranet and collaboration leader for Towers Watson, an HR consulting firm based in New York. Mann, at Hershey, pays an annual subscription tab of $75,000 for her company's hosted portal.

This Time, It's Personal

Personalization has become a hallmark of many next-generation HR portals. Dynamic portals cater to users who have little patience for slogging through benefits or policy information that doesn't apply directly to them. At Hershey, for example, employees logging on to the portal see different information displayed on the screen depending on whether they are in the resort or entertainment groups or part of the corporate staff, as well as whether they are part of a collective bargaining group.

Personalization has distinct advantages for global organizations.

Personalization has distinct advantages for global organizations. For example, employees in Brazil or Belgium don't have to cut through the underbrush of benefits information meant for United States workers to find content they need, and local policies based on differing regulations or cultural practices can be addressed.

Online Decision Support

Another defining feature of dynamic portals is online decision support, tools designed to help employees compare benefits plan features, understand insurance coverage relating to specific events and estimate medical costs while enrolling via portals. These tools give workers a "consultant on their shoulder" while reducing the volume of e-mail and calls to HR staff members for help with benefits decisions.

When the state of Montana began looking for a portal platform to consolidate HR information for its 34 separate agencies, officials turned to Oracle's PeopleSoft 8.9 software solution. With thousands of seasonal workers such as snowplow drivers, parks and recreation staff, and firefighters being hired and furloughed en masse, the platform's self-service features have proved to be a lifesaver to workers in the state's personnel division, says Randy Morris, Montana's HRIS manager based in Helena.

Workers now can enroll in benefits plans on their own, make changes to their personal data, enter work hours on electronic time sheets or search for applicable HR policies based on their specific agencies. These features significantly reduced the one-on-one transactional duties once handled by HR staff.

But Morris also wanted to include decision support tools on the portal to aid state employees in making annual benefits choices. That feature is now integrated with the PeopleSoft platform, enabling employees to search for, compare and evaluate benefits plans that best meet their requirements, as well as estimate medical costs.

Owing to its features and user-friendliness, the portal has gone from receiving 300 hits per month in May 2007 to averaging 14,000 hits per month in early 2010, with many employees now logging on after work hours. Morris says the portal's self-service features have reduced his department's transactional costs by 38 percent in that period and freed up staff to spend more time on strategic initiatives such as talent management and workforce planning.

Seek Single Sign-On

Utilization rates and satisfaction rankings of many first-generation HR portals are often low because they lack single sign-ons to access third-party vendor content, such as 401(k) balances. Because content on HR web sites often is derived from independent rather than bundled sources, it's helpful for employees to be able to navigate to all of those areas seamlessly to complete transactions—without receiving multiple login prompts.

The benchmark for gauging a portal's third-party integration quality and navigational dexterity is, surprisingly, not colleagues' web sites but rather Amazon.com, the online seller of books, electronics and other products. The e-commerce company pioneered the use of "web services" technology that enables visitors to easily access a mishmash of content from third-party providers without ever traveling outside the site.

Whether searching for Amazon products or those provided by other manufacturers, the look, feel and navigation on the site remains constant. "You always see the Amazon interface [and] use the same navigation and check-out process even if you are buying a camera from a Canon web site," Rudnick says. "That's a good model for today's human resource portals."

Show, Don't Tell

As bandwidth capacity expands and executives gain insight into employees' communication preferences, video is playing a more prominent role on HR portals. When BB&T Corp., a banking company based in Winston-Salem, N.C., held its annual benefits enrollment in 2009, it posted on its portal a short instructional video covering key changes to benefits plans and enrollment processes.

"Our usability surveys found that employees weren't big fans of reading text documents," says Steve Reeder, senior vice president and benefits manager at BB&T. "We spend a lot of time in HR writing documentation about our benefits plans and enrollment processes, but we discovered our employees much prefer to watch a video and be told how enrollment works."

Reeder has stepped up the use of video clips on his portal—many are vendor-generated, and others are developed in-house—to educate employees about, for instance, recent landmark health care legislation, wellness issues and defining terminology in insurance plans.

Some HRIS managers say web-enabled video is replacing podcasting as the "new wave" communication medium of choice on many portal platforms.

Perpetual Beta

HR professionals with in-demand portals have learned that they have little time to rest on their laurels. Their advice: Don't assume the heavy lifting is over once planning and initial implementation are complete. Administrators of portals that have high employee utilization and satisfaction rankings tend to see their sites in perpetual beta mode.

"We initially fell into the trap of 'We built it, employees are using it, and there's not much more we need to do,'" Mann says. "We quickly discovered the downside of having outdated information on the portal. So, we created a system to keep it fresh and highly useful."

> **"Tomorrow's human resource portals are likely to be much more engaging."**

One person on Mann's staff dedicates half of her time to updating portal content, but keeping the site current and relevant requires all HR hands. Because Mann is most familiar with Hershey's benefits plans, she might spot something that needs modification. Yet HR managers in operations units "usually know when things change in the handbook before I do, so

we need their input and eyes on the portal, to To make sure the portal stays user-friendly, Man conducts a regular site "optimization," a type of usa that helps them ensure that the information Hershey e search for most frequently is easiest to find.

The Coming Wave

As HR portals continue to evolve, many experts say the next wave will feature social networking-type tools that encourage employees to share expertise, join communities of practice or connect in other ways. Some organizations already are using a feature of Microsoft's SharePoint portal software dubbed "My Site," which creates a Facebook-like version of employee directories. Employees use these personal sites to post contact information and to list areas of expertise, job skills and project experience, among other things.

"Tomorrow's human resource portals are likely to be much more engaging, two-way communication tools," Rudnick says. "Employees will become more active participants, whether it be choosing benefits plans, rating the quality of e-learning content on the portal, mentoring others on career planning or sharing lessons learned as subject matter experts."

Critical Thinking

1. How can IT technology help HR?
2. What are some of the uses of technology that HR can apply?
3. How successful have some of these applications been?
4. Do you think technological applications will be more common in the future?

DAVE ZIELINSKI is a freelance writer and editor based in Minneapolis.

...ng a Productive
...ork Environment

Unit Selections

Learning Outcomes

After reading this Unit, you will be able to:

- Understand the importance of rewards in motivating employees.

- Understand the importance of keeping rewards within budget.

- Understand the importance of making rewards appropriate.

- Comprehend the importance of communication in leadership.

- Appreciate the importance of making communications in business clear and consistent.

- Realize the impact that online communication can have on the present workplace climate as well as future employment endeavors.

Student Website

www.mhhe.com/cls

Internet References

Blackbaud: Work Environment
www.answers.com/Q/What_is_work_environment

Creating a Positive, Productive and Successful Work Environment
www.the-success-factor.com/successful_work_environment.htm

Creating a Positive Work Environment
www.mommd.com/positiveworkenvironment.shtml

Leadership
http://management.about.com/od/leadership/Leadership.htm

For years, management theorists have indicated that the basic functions of management are to plan, direct, organize, control, and staff organizations. Unfortunately, those five words only tell what the manager is to do. They do not tell the manager how to do it. Being a truly effective manager involves more than just those five tasks. It involves knowing what goals to set for the organization, pursuing those goals with more desire and determination than anyone else in the organization, communicating the goals once they have been established, and having other members of the organization adopt those goals as their own. Motivation is one of the easiest concepts to understand, yet one of the most difficult to implement. Often the difference between successful and mediocre organizations is that the usual 20 percent in successful organizations are motivated, and the other 80 percent are also motivated. They are excited about the company, about what they do for the company, and about the company's products or services. Effective organizations build upon past successes. All of the employees are performing at very high levels. If people feel good about themselves and good about their organization, then they are probably going to do a good job. Whether it is called morale, motivation, or enthusiasm, it still amounts to the same fragile concept—simple to understand, difficult to create and build, and very easy to destroy.

In order to maintain a motivated workforce for any task, it is necessary to establish an effective reward system. A truly motivated worker will respond much more effectively to a carrot than to a stick. Turned-on workers are having their needs met and are responding to the goals and objectives of the organization. They do an outstanding job because they want to, which results in an outstanding company.

Perhaps the single most important skill for any manager, or, for that matter, any human being, is the ability to communicate. People work on this skill throughout their education in courses such as English and speech. They attempt to improve communication through an array of methods and media, which range from the printed word, e-mail, and television, to rumors and simple conversation. Yet managers often do not do a very good job of communicating with their employees or their customers. This is very unfortunate, because ineffective communication can often negate all of the other successes that a firm has enjoyed. This is something that managers must strive for if they want to have people working together for a common goal. Managers, and the firms they represent, must honestly communicate their goals, as well as their instructions, to their employees. If the manager does not do so, the employees will be confused and even distrustful, because they will not understand the rationale behind their instructions. If the manager is successful in honestly communicating the company's goals, ideals, and culture to the employees, and is able to build the motivation and enthusiasm

that are necessary to successfully accomplish those goals, then he or she has become not just a manager, but a leader, and that is, indeed, rare.

Creating a positive work environment is not easy. Communicating with and motivating people, whether employees, volunteers, citizens, or Boy Scouts, is difficult to do. Effective managers realize that their employees are not just employees, but people too. They have lives, families, and interests outside of the work environment. A workplace that simply focuses on the workplace is not going to be a very pleasant place to work and that means that the employees are not going to enjoy working there or be particularly motivated. While there may be some who will say that the employees are not there to enjoy the work, but to do the work, people who are at least not miserable doing the job are likely to be doing a better job than those who are. An environment that focuses entirely on the work at hand, all the time, is likely to be a fairly dismal place to work and morale and motivation are likely to suffer.

In these times of social networking, it is incumbent upon job seekers to make sure that their postings don't jeopardize their future hiring prospects. This same warning can be applied to those who are presently employed and who post something unflattering about a coworker or manager.

Whenever anything is being accomplished, it is being done,
I have learned, by a monomaniac with a mission.

—Peter Drucker

The "Brain Drain": How to Get Talented Women to Stay

What happens when you don't get the promotion or title you've consistently been promised and deserved? You stop trying. And maybe you leave.

Jennifer Millman

Rosie Saez, now senior vice president and Leadership Practices Group director for Wachovia, got burned twice early in her banking career. The first time, it happened after a merger. Saez's manager was impressed with a selection process she helped develop and told her he would submit her name for a vice-president title.

A few months later, he came back to apologize. "We have Gus who's a black man and he's been working on some of this, so we're going to put him in first and we'll put you in next," recalls Saez.

There was another excuse the following quarter, when Saez's manager told her, "There was this white woman who was really upset and felt like she should be promoted."

"I thought, 'Why is it one or the other? Why can't it be both?'" she says. "By the time I got the VP title, it wasn't worth what it was supposed to be."

Saez didn't give up, but many women do. Even the most progressive companies, The 2007 DiversityInc Top 50 Companies for Diversity®, still struggle to promote women at levels equal to their representation in the talent pool. Many companies are paying attention to this, yet too many women in corporate America still feel excluded from important networks, have fewer role models, receive limited experience in line-management positions and face gender stereotypes.

"Women who don't feel like there is much progress in breaking the glass ceiling are more likely [than men] to reduce their aspirations," says Ellen Galinsky, president and cofounder of the Families and Work Institute.

That's not something companies can afford. The talent pool is drying up, and women make up most of it. Women have earned most of the associate's, bachelor's and master's degrees granted each year for the last two decades; by 2014, they will supersede men on the doctorate level, according to the National Center for Education Statistics.

"The women who advanced have had to change jobs. It's not that they weren't talented; they got locked into the perceptions in their former company," says Galinsky. "It's the meeting when a woman says something and nobody responds, and then the man says the same thing a few minutes later and everyone says, 'What a good idea!'"

Here, five talented women tell you in their own words why they've stayed in corporate America, or if they've left, what companies could have done to keep them.

Rosie Saez
Senior Vice President, Director, Leadership Practices Group, Wachovia, No. 11 in the Top 50.

I started out as a strong community activist. The first couple of years in a nonprofit allowed me to begin to understand that you can't change the world overnight, and that it takes patience, skill, learning how to influence, be more strategic.

When I moved into the banking industry, I was the one woman of color in the human-resources organization in a leadership position and all of the people that I supported in a staff function were white men, who led all the big functions.

There were times when I wasn't included. I'd hear things like, "What are you doing here? You don't belong in this meeting." **I could have** been a **victim,** but I just figured out ways to **develop one-on-one relationships** with a lot of them, show the **added value** that I could bring. With time, I didn't have to ask to be included; it was natural for them to say, "We need to make sure Rosie's at the table."

As a woman of color, I experience things and I step back and say, "Wow, did that just happen because I'm a woman of color?" I've learned to say, "Let me meet people where they are, give a little bit of grace, trust that the intent is really a good intent and be patient while people learn to change."

When you're beginning the work, you want things to happen quicker, faster. [Some people wonder] why you can't understand that what I'm trying to get you to do is really the right thing, and three years later you figure it out.

Through predecessor banks, I have spent 19 years here. Because I've performed and I've been willing to take risks, the company has always been willing to take risks with me.

You can lose a job, but you don't lose your skills. I do bring some skill sets that are transferable, so I don't question myself. I trust my gut a lot more than I used to. If I could've given my younger self some counsel, it would've been to learn early on that yes, I want to change the world, but I have to do it in a way where I model it so that as I leave these prints on people's lives, others can actually hear me and see me perform.

Sherry Nolan
Vice President of Diversity and Workplace Development, Pepsi Bottling Group, No. 2 in the Top 50.

I've had seven jobs in seven years. Women need to examine the landscape and take stretch assignments that put them in places where they're less comfortable, because there is a tendency sometimes to excel vertically. I had to put myself out there and say, "If I want to be a [chief people officer], what do I need to know?"

"I don't know that there are a lot of type A executives who aren't also type A mothers."

—Sherry Nolan, Pepsi Bottling Group

I took a cross-country relocation to California. I'm a **single mother.** I don't know that there are a lot of **type A executives** who aren't **also type A mothers.** I don't want to be a fantastic player for Pepsi and a lousy mom, so I try to do both. You have to have a strong sense of your resources at home. When I went to California, that was the most challenged because my network was changing. I had to excel in a new job and make sure my daughter was excelling as well.

Make decisions about career and family that feel like choices, not sacrifices. If you continue to make things feel like sacrifices, it's not sustainable. California was absolutely a choice, but it was a hard choice. I knew that in order for me to lead a function like I'm leading now, I needed to lead a regional business in the field. For me, the sacrifice would more have been not taking it and limiting my career growth.

We own it. Organizations can provide all the right tools like great leaders, clear career expectations, challenging work, autonomy, and those are all the reasons I stay, but you own it. This confidence comes from delivering, getting recognized and being willing to step out into something that's perhaps more challenging than you've had before.

You have to deliver results no matter what. We calculate every day [whether we are] winning or losing. You have to know that you're delivering on the organization's big bets.

May Snowden
Vice President, Operations/Consultant, Creative Wealth Alliance Former Vice President, Global Diversity, Starbucks.

I was raised by a very strong mother who taught me I was valued. She also helped me understand that it is my responsibility

not to feel devalued by others, because it's so easy. I had to fight with that constantly in my career because I was often the only black person in the role, and in many cases, the only woman.

I remember when I was promoted to a plant-manager job and then to a district position where I had all of outside telecommunications, which was a 98 percent-male organization. This little voice would just constantly chat at me about "You can't do this, you don't have the experience," and I constantly had to talk to myself and say, "You can do this; that's why they selected you for the job."

"There are some men who depend on women being sexist against women."

—May Snowden, Creative Wealth Alliance

There are some men who depend on women being sexist against women. You think a woman in a position can bring in other women, but they won't. You get a person of color in a position; a person of color could bring more people of color, but they won't. [There's] this concept of **expecting the individual** who is the **minority not** to **bring in others like them.** That's why women come in and they're not promoted; they don't have any support.

You have to have people that are willing to fight for you, to bring up your name when there are opportunities, to ensure that if issues come up, they're on your side.

Women of color sometimes call me in tears because they fear they're not heard and that people are threatened by them, which causes them to be in fear, and nothing positive comes about when there's fear. When women of color can embrace white women and white women can embrace all women of color, we can really be strong. We have so much power; we've got to take it, do something with it and hold people accountable.

Linda Denny
President and CEO, Women's Business Enterprise National Council (WBENC).

I was the fifth woman to be a managing partner for New York Life Insurance (one of DiversityInc's 25 Noteworthy Companies) and I continued up the ranks into the home office. About three years into that, Aetna (also one of the 25 Noteworthy Companies) came along and made me an offer I couldn't refuse. The section of Aetna that I worked for was sold to ING; then ING merged all 14 companies they had and that became a real challenge.

"I just thought, 'I'm killing myself here, and I don't think I want to kill myself."

—Linda Denny,
Women's Business Enterprise National Council

I had 45 days when I had hardly slept in my own bed, and they wanted me to move again . . . and I just thought, "I'm killing myself here, and I don't think I want to kill myself."

8 Tips for Advancing Women

1. Change the Mindset around Work/life

"People don't use work/family benefits because we find in our national studies that 39 percent of employees feel there's a penalty," says Galinsky. "If you ask bosses in a company whether there is a penalty, they'll say no; ask employees and they'll say yes, so where is the truth? It's probably somewhere in the middle but closer to the employees."

PricewaterhouseCoopers, No.12 in the Top 50, couldn't get people to take vacations or stop e-mailing, so they have closed offices down and shut off e-mail between Christmas and New Year's; they make time off a value. Deloitte, No. 19 in the Top 50, has a mass career-customization program that enables people to rethink careers as being linear with fixed schedules.

"The problem with the notion of off-ramps and on-ramps is that there is the ideal job and there are others," says Galinsky. "It's the industrial model of success where presence equals productivity. There is the ideal notion of how you do it, and an ideal way."

It's not the only way. "My manager asked me to run the entire region—15 teams in 15 states—and allowed me to do it out of Philadelphia. I had a sister who was dying at the time and my father who was very ill, and she was very conscious of the need for me to have some balance in my life," says Saez.

"She didn't have to worry about if I would get the work done because she knew I would; she didn't need for me to do it between 9 and 5," she adds.

2. Build Strategic Relationships

"In any Fortune 500 company, the alignment process that you have to go to be successful can be five to 20 people depending on who's in the zone," says Nolan. "I made sure I had relationships that would facilitate productivity for me. This notion about growing vertically in organizations can lead to lack of confidence."

"You become comfortable in one particular discipline, and then when you need to cross over, if you're not nimble because you haven't started thinking about those tactical relationships, you're probably not considered for a role because you don't have that dexterity," she explains. "If you don't have that dexterity, another counterpart—either male or female—will be chosen to get that work done."

3. Move Diagonally

"A lot of my jobs were lateral," says Snowden. "After spending 30 years in a company, you'd expect to have had senior-level or officer positions; I did not make officer until I left telecommunications and went to Eastman Kodak."

"I don't think young people will stay as long as I did in one industry without being promoted. The expectation is that if they're career-minded, they would be an officer," she adds. "People have to know when it's time to move, even though they may be happy and satisfied, because I was content. In being content, you stay wherever you are and leave it up to others to see your worth."

4. Communicate Candidly

"Communication at home is as important as it is at work," says Nolan. "You're driving a car with passengers in the back; you're not alone."

"Everybody needs to be able to put their thoughts aside and see the other person's position, but it's really hard when you're at a standoff because no one wants to give," adds Snowden. "I've been the first one to give, but after I give, the other person can. Then we can come up with a compromise that's going to be better than the [ideas] each of us had on our own."

5. Have a Game Plan

"You have to work right to left; know where you want to go and look for experiences that are going to round you out. If it's a book, does each chapter make sense?" says Nolan. "I've had great leadership. They're tactical about delivering me assignments and feedback that are progressive. I ask for it on a regular basis, but just when you hit the point and you're wondering what's next, something comes because you've been talking about what the next steps are for you."

6. Find a Mentor, Be a Mentor

"Every day that we are in leadership positions, particularly as women of color . . . we are leaving footprints in the lives of people," says Saez. "We've got so many people thinking, "How did she get there? If she can get there, I can get there."

7. Network Proactively

"You don't want to be a solo person. I've seen that happen to people, where they do good work and that's all they want to do. They go to work, keep their head down and they have no help," says Snowden. "Networking is so important; you just have to do it. Pick and choose what you're going to participate in and know why and network with different individuals."

8. Involve Women in Decision Making

"Have women involved in a visible way in setting goals for women, and then addressing the issues that they face in a visible way where there is real follow-through, not just lip service," says Galinsky. "IBM sets up a group of women to say what stands in the way of their success, what could we do to make it more successful at this company, both in your personal life as well as in your work life. What could we do to also attract people like you as customers or as clients?"

I burned out. I had spent all these years climbing the ladder, and I loved my career, but I was ready for something fresh and different. I took 10 months off and went to work for WBENC. Come April, I will have been here five years. I had thought I would go back to work for another corporation, but after all of my years of travel and having such a level of responsibility, I was just exhausted in every way you could be exhausted—mentally, physically, spiritually. I had to step back, regroup, find myself again, and look at what I wanted to achieve.

I don't mind demands and I don't mind pressure, but I was just ready to make a little more impact and have more control. I can tell you of so many [women who] left corporate careers and started their own business because they reached that point of **burnout** or felt like they were **never going to go where** they felt **they had the ability to go.**

The pipeline is full of women who are going to have the job experience and the capabilities of moving into those senior executive-level positions. When I was coming through, that pipeline just wasn't there. I just got to the point of saying, "I've had enough. I don't want to do this. I want to go have some life."

Louise Liang
Senior Vice President, Quality/Clinical Systems Support, Kaiser Foundation Health Plan and Hospitals, Kaiser Permanente, No. 27 on the Top 50.

One of my executive admins said that she had never had a woman boss and she didn't know whether that was going to work for her. I was startled because it never dawned on me, at least not for women. We worked well together and she realized that was just borne out of her experience of not having a woman boss or observing one. Several men over the years clearly had questions in their mind as my supervisory role began.

There's always a person who's just not going to be able to work that through. I haven't had any of them working for me. Most of the people I've encountered assess on merit. At the end of the day, it's **not about gender or race.** It's about whether you have the **capabilities** and you can develop a working relationship and guide and support people who work for you in a way that gets the work done. Be open-minded and willing to learn about how different systems work and what the levers are. Those can vary from company to company, different kinds of cultures or mechanisms. Having been successful in different places, you're able to identify the elements you can use to create change and drive an agenda.

Right after I completed my clinical training, I was hired by Henry Ford Hospital as the first pediatrician in a brandnew clinic. They made me chief of the department. I had no training to do it. Take the opportunities that present themselves. People either want to have experience or special training, but sometimes you just have to go with it.

That means there will be occasions when you'll stumble, but opportunities don't always come in exactly the size, shape and timing you'd prefer. It's only by trying things out that you find out what you might be really good at.

Critical Thinking

1. What are some of the things that are making women consider interrupting their careers?

2. What is it about society that makes these decisions so important for women?

3. What can organizations do to help women continue their careers?

Rewarding Outstanding Performance: Don't Break the Bank

Some of the most effective methods of rewarding outstanding performers involve little or no money.

ELIZABETH (BETSY) MURRAY AND ROBYN RUSIGNUOLO

In these challenging economic times, it may be tempting to focus solely on the bottom line, and to forget the importance of motivating your employees. After all, don't employee incentives cost money, and who has extra money to spend on-raises or bonuses? While money certainly is a contributing factor to employee happiness, it is not the only cause of employee satisfaction.

Employees who are happy are more productive than those who are dissatisfied. Therefore, it makes economic sense to encourage excellence. Moreover, if you can find ways to reward your outstanding performers and keep them motivated, you are more likely retain these top players—which in and of itself is a savings. Importantly, some of the most effective methods of rewarding outstanding performance involve little or no money. Create your own employee stimulus without breaking the bank.

Employees who are happy are more productive.

Praise, Recognition: Simple, Cost-Free and Effective

Praise and recognition are simple, cost-free and effective ways to reward individual employees, or even a group of deserving employees. Indeed, many studies show that thanking employees for outstanding work is one of the most effective ways to reward your staff. Employees who perform a job well should be told their work is recognized and appreciated.

Praise is most effective when the employee is told how his or her performance merited acknowledgement. Rather than a general "good job," provide some specific information (for example, "You did a good job handling that customer complaint. You politely listened to what he had to say, you apologized for and fixed the error and then thanked the customer for bringing the matter to your attention so you could resolve it. That goes far in creating customer loyalty.") Where possible, provide this feedback immediately, when it is fresh on everyone's mind.

Praise should be delivered in public (remember the adage, "praise in public; punish in private"). A public congratulations and a "thank you" makes the employee who performed well feel good about his or her work and motivates that individual to continue to work hard. It is also a lesson for the employee's co-workers. When they hear a peer being celebrated, they learn exactly what behavior the employer considers commendable.

In addition to informal praise, consider implementing a formal recognition program. An "Employee of the Month" or "Customer Service Star of the Month" award does not have to include a monetary component, or it can include a low cost financial gift. To make such a program successful, the criteria should be announced to employees. If an "Employee of the Month" is being selected, the winner may be the employee with the best overall performance, or one month the winner may be the employee with the best customer service and the next month the winner is the employee who most successfully up-sold your product or service. The award for being Employee or Customer Service Star of the Month could be as simple as a certificate, presented publically to the winner. Employees could also be given a small prize, such as movie passes or a DVD rental and popcorn.

Allow Top Performers to Set Their Schedule

Your best performers are probably also your most reliable employees. You can schedule them when and how often they are needed, and they will consistently arrive at work on time. In fact, these employees will change their personal schedules to meet your organization's needs. Nevertheless, all employees would appreciate the flexibility of being able to set their own schedule, or to have first choice of a preferred schedule. If your operations permit, consider rewarding a top performer with the ability to choose his or her schedule for a set period of time (for example, one or two weeks). This well-regarded employee may want to use his or her week to choose the prime shifts or to request time off from work. Either way, the employee will consider this to be a perk, and other employees will strive for the same reward. And from the employer's perspective, this flexibility should cost little or nothing to implement.

Reward Excellent Performance

Paying an employee when he or she is not at work is definitely a cost to the employer, but everyone enjoys having some time off, especially when they are paid for being away from work. If your employees currently do not have paid vacation or sick leave, a bonus day off is an excellent motivator. Even if employees do have paid time off, most would appreciate an extra paid day.

A bonus day off is an excellent motivator.

Discount Your Own Product or Service

Giving away or discounting your own product or service is not cost flee, but it could be cost effective. Even if your staff can currently obtain a discount on the product or service you sell, consider enhancing this benefit for your top performers. For example, if your franchise is a restaurant, employees may be allowed to eat a free or discounted meal immediately before or after their shift, as long as the meal is consumed on the premises. For a set number of shifts or for a set number of meals (not necessarily coinciding with a shift), allow deserving employees to take the meal home; or give such employees a free meal certificate and allow the employee to use the certificate him or herself, or give the certificate away to a friend or relative. If your franchise provides a service, reward outstanding performance by discounting your service; if you already provide a discount, provide a deeper discount, or allow the employee to choose a friend or relative who will receive the employee discount on a one-time basis.

Provide Training and Advancement Opportunities

Your most valuable employees should be rewarded with advancement opportunities. If formal promotions are not available, keep these employees engaged and interested in their work by cross-training them on different aspects of your operation. This investment of time will pay off in the long run. In this regard, as employees learn new skills, they become more valuable to your organization; they also feel more connected to the company, which results in enhanced loyalty. On a related note, choose your top performers to train new employees. The trainer will understand his or her efforts are being recognized, and the new employees will learn good habits and skills from a star player.

Time with Company Leaders Is Valued

Employees who have invested their hard work in the organization will view one-on-one time with a company leader as a bonus. This time can be a lunch or a cup of coffee, or just a brief private meeting in which the leader solicits feedback about the work environment, and answers the employee's work-related questions. Employees like to be "in the know" about company issues, and meetings such as this can tie valued employees to the organization.

Best Workers, Best Parking Space

If most of your employees drive to work and you exercise some control over your parking lot, celebrate your best employees by rotating access to the best parking space in your lot. Yes, customers should have parking spaces that provide the easiest access to your establishment, but most will enjoy meeting the employee who merited the great parking space. And the chosen employee will relish the recognition.

There are numerous cost-effective (and in some instances, cost-free) ways an employer can acknowledge its best employees. While difficult economic conditions may present challenges to increasing profits, you can easily—and inexpensively—increase workplace satisfaction and motivate your employees. Whether implementing a suggestion discussed above or designing your own employee incentive, you can celebrate your top performers without breaking the bank.

Critical Thinking

1. What are some of the ways that people can be rewarded for outstanding performance besides money?

2. Why would you want to keep cost under control?

3. How do you think people feel about getting nonmonetary rewards?

ELIZABETH (BETSY) MURRAY is chief legal officer and vice president of human resources and ROBYN RUSIGNUOLO is assistant senior counsel and human resources manager of Modern Business Associates. They can be reached at 888-622-6460 or *betsym@mbahro.com* and *robynr@mbahro.com*.

Employers Use Facebook Too, for Hiring

MARY OLENICZAK ET AL.

Introduction

Facebook started five years ago at Harvard and has grown into a worldwide social networking tool where users can connect to virtually anyone anytime on the web. Founded by Mark Zuckerberg in 2004, it was originally available to students at Harvard. Later Facebook opened up to students at other Ivy League universities and then to all colleges. When it was first launched, the Web site was www .thefacebook.com but changed in August 2005 with the new address www.facebook.com purchased for $200,000.

Facebook is a well popularized social networking site that has millions of users and is growing exponentially on a daily basis. Since it is known as a social site where people can communicate, many do not realize that potential employers are in fact searching these types of sites to view job candidates. In fact, a survey in October 2007 by Vault.com found that 44 percent of employers use social networking sites to examine the profiles of job candidates and 39 percent have looked up the profile of a current employee[7]. Facebook has a short history which has impacted our society greatly. The charts show interesting usage statistics, as well as demographic breakdowns.

Figure 1A shows the changing demographics of Facebook users. Within just one year the typical users, those in the range 18–24 years, have decreased in use, whereas all other groups have expanded. This shows a lot about where the future of Facebook is headed, which is toward older age groups who will most likely use the site for networking or other career-related uses.

The above figure shows just how quickly Facebook use is increasing. In just over two years the amount of users has increased from 10 million, to upwards of 140 million. That, combined with the results in Figure 1A, show that Facebook is a force that will not be slowing down anytime soon, and it will have an increased impact in the future. Since Facebook is such a powerful influence, we chose to look further in on the subject of employers using Facebook as an aid for hiring purposes. Through our supporting research, we will argue that employers should not use Facebook as part of the hiring process for reasons including invasion of privacy, current laws and inaccurate information or portrayal of information.

Students Opinions Why Employers Shouldn't Use Social Networking Sites:

Facebook—There are many reasons which make employer's use of Facebook dangerous to the employer. Possible violation of privacy laws, discrimination cases and wrongful firing cases may all be outcomes of Facebook use by

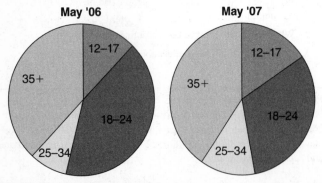

Figure 1A   Facebook Users by Age

www.techcrunch.com/2007/07/06/facebook-users-up-89-over-last-year-demo graphic-shift/

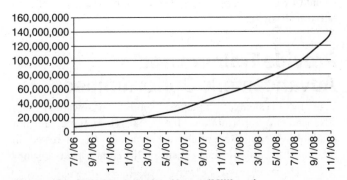

Figure 1B   Facebook Active Users (Millions)

www.insidefacebook.com/2008/12/16/facebook-now-growing-by-over-600000-users-a-day-and-new-engagement-stats/

employers, costing the company in the long run both in the financial sense and damage to the company's reputation.

First, many privacy laws enacted by the Federal Government make the practice of looking up possible employees by an employer a questionable action. There are eleven information privacy principles under section 14 of the Privacy Act of 1988. The interpretation of these laws will determine if the company can face reparations from the use of Facebook. The first principle references the manner and collection of personal information. The principle states: "Personal information shall not be collected by a collector for inclusion in a record or in a generally available publication unless:

(a) The information is collected for a purpose that is a lawful purpose directly related to a function or activity of the collector and
(b) The collection of the information is necessary for or directly related to that purpose (Information Privacy Principles)".

Facebook would fall under this principle as a generally available publication and the problem arises in the fact that the collection of the information that is available is not necessary or directly related to the purpose of hiring an employee. An employee could argue that the information available on Facebook includes activities and relationships the person holds outside of the work environment and has no connection to performance while on the job.

Principle two also refers to collection of information from a generally available publication. This principle states that when a person is collecting information about an individual, that individual is "generally aware of the purpose for which the information is being collected". Employees could argue that companies looking at their Facebook during the hiring process have had their privacy invaded because they were not informed that their Facebook profile would be investigated. The third principle references the solicitation of personal information in a general sense. This principle is the strongest argument made against employers using Facebook during hiring. It states: "Having regard to the purpose for which the information is collected:

(c) The information collected is relevant to that purpose and is up to date and complete and
(d) The collection of the information does not intrude to an unreasonable extent upon personal affairs of the individual concerned"[6].

The largest concern students have in regard to Facebook is that the information is not up to date and does not give a complete picture of who the person is. Facebook is a social network and cannot serve the purpose of showing how the individual will work. The second argument this principle brings up is that looking at an employee's Facebook does indeed intrude an unreasonable amount on the individual's personal affairs.

Many lawsuits have been brought against companies that have used Facebook when hiring, which is a financial motivation for other employers not to use Facebook. First there are employees that argue that using Facebook was part of discrimination, arguing that only the Facebook pages of minority workers were looked at, not those of every employee. This also applies for workers that are homosexual and the employer found out about it from Facebook. In discrimination lawsuits it may be hard for the employee to prove discrimination took place, but it is equally difficult for the employer to prove their innocence. Since providing information that proves the employee was not hired for a valid reason can be difficult, companies should not use Facebook as it gives the employee something to use against them in a lawsuit[8].

Other lawsuits involve the violation of Facebook's terms of service agreement by employers. Part of the agreement states that the user will not use the site for any commercial use. Employees that argue employers have used Facebook in making hiring decisions say that it is considered commercial use. A tactic that some employers have used includes posing as students or affiliates with an organization of which they do not belong in order to gain access to view a person's account. The service agreement states that users can not "impersonate any person or entity, or falsely state or otherwise misrepresent yourself or your affiliation with any person or entity"[8]. Employees can use misrepresentations of employers against the company in a lawsuit as well. Again while these situations may be hard to prove employers guilty, it is in the company's best interest to avoid them all together.

"Failure to hire" lawsuits are also expected to become more common for employers that use social networking sites as part of the hiring process. This again comes back to the discrimination case. While there are no formal guidelines stating how these sites can be used, employers are having issues when they look at the page and fail to go back to consult the employee about the content. If the employee is not consulted, they can argue that the information found on the site is the reason they were not hired, leading to a discrimination case that could include discrimination based on race, sexual orientation and political stance. Employers should avoid using these sites just as they have stopped asking for pictures along with applications, discrimination lawsuits will become too common and are difficult for the company to defend themselves against. In today's society, our personal freedoms are important assets. As Americans we always make sure that we have all our freedoms within our grasp and none are being held against us. But when does the new technology of fun personal profiles cross the lines of personal freedoms?

Equal employment opportunity laws affect specific types of employment discrimination. These laws deny discrimination on the basis of race, color, religion, sex, age, national origin, or disabilities/war veterans. (1) Most hiring laws cover making sure a person is not discriminated against in the hiring process or fired from the job because of these reasons. However, how do we (as applicants) know why it is we were not hired? Presently with the advancement in technology and personal viewing profiles online people can check on applicants and employees without even filing a background check. Because these new technologies such as Facebook and MySpace have come so fast and government is so slow, we have yet to see new laws actually being passed and enacted yet. Facebook is a place where students, workers and international friends find other people whom they already know, or have yet to meet personally. But with it becoming such a large network with millions of people displaying their personal profiles out there for anyone to see, is it really worth the stress? The positives of the website are people get to connect with friends from the past, make new friends in the future and make new connections in the business world and in everyday life. The negatives, however, are turning out to be just as extensive. Employers are finding these sites and using people's personal information against them.

When is this okay and when is this wrong? If someone is pictured on Facebook or MySpace doing something legal but what could be thought of as "irresponsible"? Should it be used against them in the hiring or firing instances? We believe it should not because it is also coming very close to some hiring laws that could get businesses into some trouble they are not willing to fight. Jackie Ford[4] sees four distinct reasons as to why employers should think twice before using Facebook as recourse for hiring. "Various studies suggest that upwards of 40% of employers have trolled Facebook and other social networking sites for information on potential hires—and that when they find negative information on these sites, more than 80% of the employers factor that information into their hiring decisions."[2] Four reasons for employers to "beware" are:

1. State and federal discrimination laws discourage "too much information." For example, say an applicant's Facebook page includes heartfelt descriptions of his ongoing battle with cancer.
2. The jury is still out on whether a Facebook search may be subject to limits on background checks. If you use a third party service to conduct certain types of background checks, the Fair Credit Reporting Act (FCRA) requires that you give prior notice of the check to the individual being investigated.
3. Some States prohibit denying a job to someone because of off-duty conduct that is not illegal.
4. Shockingly, not everything on Facebook is true. It is one thing to rely on information an applicant directly provides to you. It's another thing to rely on information posted by the applicant or others on a website. A Facebook page, like every other public forum, can be the voice of puffery, trickery and yes, fakery. In short: Browsers beware[4].

These are only some of the legal issues that companies could be facing with the use of Facebook in their hiring processes. Because most of these internet profile issues are so new to the job finding process, nobody really knows how to treat them, or go about correcting them. There are no specific laws or rules to abide by when it comes to Facebook and hiring. In Workforce Management.com, "Lawyers Warn Facebook a Risky Tool for Background Checks." Lawyers warn their clients to be careful in using Facebook to help make their decision to hire or not. "Observers say that without adequate policies in place, employers may be leaving themselves vulnerable to charges that they are using the data available on the Web sites to cull minorities, homosexuals and other applicants who are members of protected classes."[3] Imagine being an employer wanting to hire a very nice, smart 28 year old male who seemed to fit the job perfectly. But on his Facebook profile you see he is gay, although this may not be the only reason you decided not to hire him and could cost that particular employer hundreds of thousands of dollars[7].

Internet Savvy World

In today's Internet savvy world, an individual's Web presence has the potential to be scrutinized to the same extent as might his or her academic transcript and résumé. As of late, employers have turned to the Web site when considering applicant's qualifications. According to a 2007 CareerBuilder survey, 22% of employers use on line social profiles such as Facebook as a way to judge potential employees prior to their hiring. Facebook has become this generation's way of connecting and now it could become the new interview. Basically, there should be nothing on the social networking sites that you wouldn't want your parents to see. You want to project moral character.

Considering the rise in the amount of employers using Facebook in the hiring process, one would expect to see students and other potential employees more concerned about what they post on their Facebook. However, that is not the case. In an article posted CBS News, the issue of hiring using Facebook is discussed. When Tim DeMello, owner of the internet site Ziggs, was asked whether or not he used the internet when hiring, he replied. "Of course. Everybody does and employers are even finding ways to look at profiles that students think are private"[1]. This sort of invasion of privacy for the purpose of screening an employee students find ridiculous. The feel that an employer should not be able to, "find a way," to look at a profile that is listed as private. They should be hiring based on credentials and the resume that the potential employee brings to the company. These profiles are listed as private for a reason, they are only meant for friends to see. Though people work with other people and their employees, these are colleagues, not friends, If someone wants to keep something they post on their Facebook private, it should not be admissible as grounds for not hiring or for firing an employee. Suzanne Helbig, the marketing coordinator and career counselor at the University of California, Berkeley, feels that what these social networking sites like Facebook show may not reflect how well an individual can perform a job they are applying for. She also states that employers should, "keep in mind that personal Web profiles are best considered in context"[2].

European Union (EU) Lays out Operating Guidelines

In a move to address concerns about handling of users' personal information, the European Union regulators have laid out operating guidelines for Facebook, MySpace and other social networking Web sites to ensure they comply with the European Union privacy laws. The privacy issue is key for social networking companies. Regulators state that social network users are protected by the 27-nation EU's privacy laws which require web sites to warn users of privacy risks and limit the sites' ability to target advertising based on members' race, religion or other sensitive categories. Some say that the EU data privacy laws are more expans/stricter than the US laws.

Preventing Cyber Crime

Cyber Crime often comes in form of a friend updating his or her Facebook status with a link or friend messaging a link from a personal account. When these links are opened, users are often brought to fake websites that trick them into giving passwords and personal details. This is called 'phishing attack' or 'malware'. The ICCC (Internet Crime Complaint Center—a partnership between FBI, National White Collar Crime Center and Bureau of Justice Assistance) reported almost 3,200 cases of

account jacking since 2006. Security is a constant arms race. Malicious actors are constantly attacking the sites. Unfortunately, not every site is safe. It can be extremely difficult to tell legitimate from fraud. Attackers play on your 'trust' and 'loyalty' under the guise of being a 'friend'. Face to face is the safest encounter. But online isn't such a sure thing. Remember that the "employers" are always looking for what kind of character they are hiring. Resumes gives only half of the picture. Resumes indicates what qualifications you have but not what kind of person you are. While students may find employers' use of social networking sites "unfair or underhanded", employers are fully within their rights to discard an applicant based on information obtained from online profile. Recently there has been considerable attention given in media to instances of employers rejecting candidates or firing employees based on in information obtained from social networking sites such Facebook, Twitter, My Space. Here are some cases:

Case Woman Claiming Employer Used Facebook to Spy on Her and Hire Her

A Swiss woman who worked for National Suisse Company reported sick complaining that she had a migraine and need a dark room to recover. The company found out that she was well enough to go online/access a computer but not well enough to come to work. She confided to a friend whom she met recently on Facebook but the friend disappeared after she got fired. She believes that the company was monitoring her activity. At the firing interview her boss made note of a number of excerpts from her Facebook account. She claims that the company was monitoring her but the company denied it. If you are sick, you want 'rest" rather than go online.

Case of Dan Leone

Dan Leone, a young man, had the dream job of his life. He was happily employed by the Philadelphia Eagles football franchise and took his job seriously. However, a post he made on Facebook made all of that disappear. Leone has a neurological disorder that causes him discomfort and often gives him trouble standing. He started out his job with the Eagles as a worker at the guest services gate; however, after a few years of employment, he was promoted by the franchise to run the front gate of the stadium. He worked through pain and would often have to stretch and bend to relieve some of his discomfort from his job. He was a hard working employee who loved his job with his favorite team. He posted one angry message on his Facebook wall stating that he was unhappy with the team's decision and did not approve of the move. The Facebook post was up for two days and did not go unnoticed. Leone arrived to work on the third day and was called into his boss's office. Leone was informed that the team had found out about the post and had made the decision to let him go[2,3].

ABC News reported that they looked closely at the lives of two people. "Person A" as they called her, was a 36 year old publicist living in Silicon Valley, CA. She is a mother of three and has many clients and colleagues that use Facebook. She had a sorority sister from college join Facebook and post old pledge photos, which did not depict her in a good light. Even though "person A's" profile was blocked, her friend had the option of letting anyone see these pictures, including any business acquaintances the woman had. This is a case where pictures posted on Facebook did not portray the woman correctly and misrepresented her life, therefore employers and/or clients should not judge the woman based on what they see on Facebook[5].

Case of Miss New Jersey Amy Polumbo

A specific case that really drew public attention was when Miss New Jersey Amy Polumbo almost lost her crown after being blackmailed over pictures that were taken off of her Facebook profile. Polumbo had posted pictures of herself drinking at clubs and posing provocatively and they almost cost her Miss New Jersey. During an interview with the Today Show. Polumbo told Matt Lauer, "This was meant to be private". She continued to say that she would like to help spread the word that "nothing you post on the internet are private, even if it is in a privately accessed website." After she was crowned Miss New Jersey, someone went on to her Facebook account and printed off the pictures of her. They tried to demand money from her or they would show the pageant officials. Polumbo had a few pictures of herself posted on a social network site and when put in a false pretense changed the public's overall perception of her.

Conclusion and Recommendation

Services like Facebook, Twitter, MySpace enable users to post an overwhelming array of personal information on websites, creating a public record of things like one's Spring break photos, the video of a friend's birthday, smoking pot, drinking or trying Meth etc. having "fun", etc. You feel that these are "private/confidential pictures only available to friends" and employers have no right to look at these photos. You are mistaken. Anything you post on Web, one should have "lower expectation of privacy". Because what one posts on line is not as private as you think. For an employer to view photos on Facebook or My

Space does not constitute an invasion of privacy. Many students argue that it is not available to the public but only to my "Facebook and MySpace friends". But be careful.

Friends/Competitors/Employers have fairly simple ways of getting around your "reasonable expectation of privacy claims". Several Web browsers like Opera,' Mozilla Firefox, MySpace, and Facebook log-in information get saved or memorized and Opera, Mozilla Firefox, automatically offer this convenient service to users which of course allows easy access. We can recall several times when we have logged in and found some "mischievous friends" managed to post something under our names which we would never have posted online or on the Web for others to see. So we should watch the company that we keep and check our web posting from time-to-time. We recommend that you post "positive" things about you that will increase your "visibility" and make you a "good" candidate for future employers etc. You might lose some unneeded friends but gain an upper hand with the employers/future spouses.

Facebook profiles may not be a true, accurate portrayal of their personal lives and definitely not of their ability to work effectively. The information may not be current, nor correct in many situations, whether it is their own fault, or the work of friends posting information about them. But you as a candidate get only one chance to make the first impression. As the popular saying goes, "You never get a second chance to make a first impression." Image consultants note that "only seven percent (7%) of a person's first impression of you is based on what you say," which implies that ninety-three percent (93%) is based on your image. To compete today, it requires Webphotos, appearance, voice, wardrobe, communication skills, body language, attitude and etiquette, technical skills, knowledge and abilities.

Employers are always looking for what kind of character they are hiring. Resume gives only half of the picture. Resume indicates what qualifications you have but not what kind of person you are. While students may find employers use of social networking sites "unfair or underhanded", employers are fully within their rights to discard an applicant based on information obtained from online profile. The authors suggest "Internet rule of thumb" that one shouldn't post on Web anything that they wouldn't wish to see in a newspaper or public broadcast. Privacy settings are valuable tools, but not fool proof. Employers are not the only Facebook users who judge people based on their online profiles. There are many other people who form an opinion of you like your future roommate, spouse or outside public including authorities are forming an opinion about you based on the content of information that you have posted on line. They don't know how to differentiate the "real" you from your "Web" identity.

Employers should consider the whole person and cut employees some slack and remember that there were once young too and did some "stupid" things.

References

1. Clark Amy S., "Employers Look At Facebook, too". *CBS NEWS.* 6 June 2006, 22 March 2009, www.cbsnews.com /stories/2006/06/20/eveningnews/main1734920.shtml. (2009)

2. Cuesta Christina, "Students Love Social Networking Sites And So Do Employers", *FoxNews,* 31 Aug. 2006, 22 Mar. 2009. www.foxnews.com/story/0,2933,208l75,00.html. (2009)

3. "Football Fan's Dream Job Cut Short Over Facebook Post". *FoxNews.10* Mar. 2009, 11 Mar. 2009, www.foxnews.com /story/0,2933,508566,00.html. (2009)

4. Ford Jackie, "Why Employers should reconsider Facebook fishing". Market Watch, Feb II (2009)

5. Goodman Michelle, "Facebook: Job Hunters Over 30 Beware". *ABC News,* 04 Dec 2008, 10 Mar 2009, http://abcnews.go.com /Business/CareerManagement/story?id=6384818&page=1. (2009)

6. "Information Privacy Principles under the Privacy Act 1988." Tne Office of the Privacy Commissioner. 22 Mar. 2009. www .privacy.gov.au/publications/ipps.html. (2009)

7. "Lawyers Warn Facebook a Risky Tool for Background Checks," Workforce Management, 2009, Mar. 22, 2009. www .workforce.com/section/06/feature/25/45/83/254585.html. (2009)

8. Lenard George, "Employers Using Facebook for Background Checking, Part I," www.employmentblawg.com/2006/ employers-using-facebook-for-background-checking-part-i/. (2009)

9. United States Department of Labor, Hiring Issues: Equal Employment Opportunity (EEO), March 22 (2009).

(Received 7th November 2009, accepted 15th December 2009)

Critical Thinking

1. How much credence should employers put in the information they find on Facebook about a prospective employee?

2. Will you take safeguards to protect your posted information? What would you do?

UNIT 4

Developing Effective Human Resources

Unit Selections

Learning Outcomes

After reading this Unit, you will be able to:

- Understand the importance of training for the future of the organization.

- Appreciate why training and development is important to the career success of the employee.

- Understand how training should be used and how it should not be used.

- See how training is developing in the workplace.

- Understand the importance of diversity in the workplace.

- Understand how the issues of diversity and EEO are changing in the workplace and what that means for organizations and employees.

- Appreciate the use of diversity to accomplish the strategic goals of the organization.

- Understand the situation facing older workers in the economy when they have been laid off.

- Understand how the arrangement between the employee and the employer has changed in the past several years.

Student Website
www.mhhe.com/cls

Internet References

Diversity.com
    www.diversity.com
DiversityInc.com
    www.diversityinc.com
Laid-off and Left-out
    www.unemployedworkers.org/sites/unemployedworkers/index.php
Training Magazine
    www.trainingmag.com

Every organization needs to develop its employees. This is accomplished through a number of activities, including formal corporate training, career development, and performance appraisal. Just as the society and the economy will continue to change, so will the human resource needs of organizations. Individuals and their employers must work together to achieve the effective use of human resources. They must plan together to make the maximum use of their abilities so as to meet the challenge of the changing environment in which they live. American industry spends approximately the same amount of money each year on training and developing employees as is spent by all colleges and universities in the United States combined when the salaries of the participants are included in the equation. It also trains roughly the same number of people as there are students in traditional post-secondary education. Corporate programs are often very elaborate and can involve months or even years of training. In fact, corporate training and development programs have been recognized by academia for their quality and excellence. The American Council for Education has a program designed to evaluate and make recommendations concerning corporate and government training programs for college credit. Corporations themselves have entered into the business of granting degrees that are recognized by regional accrediting agencies. For example, McDonald's grants an associate's degree from "Hamburger U." General Motors Institute (now Kettering University) offers the oldest formalized corporate sponsored/related degree-granting program in the United States, awarding a bachelor's in industrial management; several companies offer MBAs in cooperation with a number of universities, and a PhD program in policy analysis is available from the Rand Corporation. Even the unions have started offering academic degree programs. American industry is in the business of educating and training employees, not only as a simple introduction and orientation to the corporation, but as a continual and constant enterprise. Lifelong learning is essential so that both firms and employees can meet the challenges of an increasingly competitive world. Meeting these challenges depends on knowledge, not on sweat, and relies on the ability to adapt to and adopt technological, social, and economic changes faster than competitors.

But, for training to be truly effective and beneficial for the organization, management must be able to set priorities that will be effective and appropriate for the firm. Corporations must also take advantage of the latest in instructional technology, recognizing the value of performance simulations, computer-based instruction, as well as other new techniques, and address the problems of employees who do not respond well to the new methods of instruction. But this does not mean that all training is successful. Much of training is wasted and needs to be restructured and redesigned.

There is an important difference between jobs and careers. Everyone who works, whether self-employed or employed by someone else, does a job. While a career, which is made up of a series of jobs and positions over an individual's working life, is more than that. It is a sense of direction, a purpose, and a knowledge of where one is going in one's professional life. Careers are shaped by individuals through the decisions

© Design Pics / Don Hammond

they make concerning their own lives, not by organizations. It is the individual who must ultimately take the responsibility for what happens in his or her career. Organizations offer opportunities for advancement, and they fund training and development based on their own self-interest, not solely on workers' interests. Accordingly, the employee must understand that the responsibility for career development ultimately rests with him- or herself. In today's world of short job tenure, people will frequently change jobs, and they must be prepared to do so at a moment's notice. Jobs are being lost, but they are also being created. Potential employees, especially those just starting their careers, need to consider this. They must continue to learn and remain competitive or become the kind of worker whose skills will be a commodity and as with all commodities, will be employed/purchased by the lowest bidder.

One of the ways that organizations can assist in the career development of their employees is to engage in appropriate and effective performance appraisals. This process benefits both the employee and the employer. From the employers' perspective, it allows the organization to fine-tune the performance of the individual and to take appropriate action when the performance does not meet an acceptable standard. From the employee's perspective, appraisal allows the individual to evaluate his or her situation in the organization. Appraisal will indicate, in formal ways, how the individual is viewed by the organization. It is, for the employee, an opportunity to gauge the future.

One of the pressing issues today is diversity. The American, and for that matter, the global workforce is made up of many different people with many different backgrounds. All of them have a wide degree of potential, none of which is based on race, creed, gender, or ethnic origin. It is very dangerous for any organization to ignore any potential labor pool whose talent can be used in a competitive environment, especially if that talent can be used competitively against the organization. Organizations that ignore diversity do so at their peril. The next Henry Ford, Bill Gates, or Warren Buffett could come from anywhere, and given today's world, it is far less likely to be a white male than 20 or 30 years ago. It is, in fact, far more likely to be a minority group member or a woman, but it could come from anywhere, and white males should not be overlooked. Organizations need a strategic plan to implement their diversity approach, based on sound business principles as proposed in "Strategic Organizational Diversity: A Model?"

In today's world, many employees find themselves without a job through no fault of their own. They have worked for decades and now, perhaps just a few years before they had planned to retire, find themselves out of work for the first time in their lives. These people are the victims of a double hit. The first is the current recession, and the second is the changing economy from a national to a global labor market. They have been caught in the transition, often too young to retire and too old to make it economically justifiable to retrain. How many of these workers are dealing with this dilemma is explored in "The Broken Psychological Contract: Job Insecurity and Coping." To ignore the development of the potential of the employees of any organization is to court disaster—not only for the organization, but for the employees. People who have stopped developing themselves are cheating themselves and their employers. Both will be vulnerable to changes brought on by increased competition, but the workers will be the ones who join the numbers of the unemployed.

Your Co-Worker, Your Teacher: Collaborative Technology Speeds Peer-Peer Learning

In today's fast-paced business world, workers need to be able to quickly swap knowledge without waiting for a structured training initiative. That doesn't mean traditional e-learning is dead, however.

ED FRAUENHEIM

The latest trend in corporate training technology can be summed up simply: Water Cooler 2.0.

Organizations are trying to encourage the kind of informal learning that has long come from sometimes chance encounters with colleagues and industry peers. These days, however, corporations are tapping into collaborative technologies such as blogs, wikis and pod casts to allow their workers to pick up crucial information whenever and wherever they need it.

That's not to say traditional training is dead. Thanks in part to the need to comply with a multitude of regulations, demand is growing for structured learning—whether it be instructor-led classes or online courses. That means healthy business for vendors of learning management software systems that track employee course work and certifications.

But some of those vendors are upgrading their products in ways that accommodate peer-to-peer learning. Essentially, the training field is realizing that the most valuable learning moments often occur when employees exercise their curiosity on the spot, says Jay Cross, a consultant and author of a new book, *Informal Learning: Rediscovering the Natural Pathways That Inspire Innovation and Performance.*

Cross says today's accelerating pace of business all but requires letting workers quickly swap their knowledge on topics like new products without waiting for a corporate training program from on high. The traditional

---

Informal Learning Tech

Some companies are using social networking technologies to promote the sharing of knowledge and expertise among their employees. Some of the tools being used are blogs, wikis and podcasts.

Blogs

Web logs, or blogs, are websites where someone can post content including messages and images. Readers can respond to postings in the form of a threaded discussion.

Wikis

These are websites that allow multiple users to author the same content. Like blogs, they can be kept within a company's internal computer system or located on the public Internet. Changes made to the site can be tracked.

Podcasts

These are audio or video files that can be downloaded onto portable digital media players, such as iPods.

---

approach to new-product training could take months to complete, given such elements as a needs analysis, a description of the product and the creation of an interactive CD-ROM for its sales force. It was too slow, he says.

"To keep employees current, information must be transferred in weeks or days or even hours, not in months," he says.

Rise of E-Learning

The first generation of e-learning, launched about a decade ago, is often regarded as a misguided experiment, where too much content was crammed online and many dollars were wasted. Several years ago, organizations sought to restore a balance by blending instructor-led activities with online activities. Today, blended learning is coming to mean mixing formal learning—which can include in-person instruction and e-learning—with informal employee epiphanies.

Those "Aha!" moments are much more likely with the advent of the new social networking technologies, says Colleen Carmean, director of research at the Applied Learning Technologies Institute at Arizona State University. Blogs, wikis and other content that remains online and is searchable mean that employees can tap into colleagues' knowledge no matter when the entries were made. And given the way search engines rank pages by their popularity, smart ideas can rise over time, she says.

"The strength of an organization can be based on how well complex information moves up" through the ranks, she says. "These new learning technologies can really allow us to do that."

In 2006, employers budgeted $55.8 billion for formal training in the U.S., according to research conducted by advisory firm Bersin & Associates for *Training* magazine. That figure was up 7 percent from 2005, the report said, thanks partly to a new focus on talent management and employee development to address "talent gaps in the global workforce." The percentage of online learning increased as well. The Bersin study found that online self-study and virtual classrooms accounted for 29 percent of formal training delivery in 2006, up from 23 percent in 2005.

E-learning is particularly prevalent for training done to comply with company or government regulations, such as worker safety courses and sexual harassment prevention tutorials. Fully 35 percent of mandatory or compliance training is conducted mostly or completely online, the Bersin study found.

Given the rise of e-learning, technology has become a vital part of training operations, according to the Bersin research. Learning technology and infrastructure ranked as the top priority among organizations surveyed, and 75 percent of organizations with more than 10,000 employees now have a learning management system.

Health insurance provider Health Net is in the process of implementing a learning management system from SumTotal Systems. Suzanne Rumsey, Health Net's director of workforce planning, says the system will help her 10,000-person company meet compliance requirements as well as make sure workers get credit for the many courses they take. Another reason Health Net signed up for the software is to signal that it is willing to invest in people. In an era where lifelong employment is no longer expected and retirement benefits have been declining, a sound employee development program can play a key role in keeping workers engaged with the business, Rumsey says. "Learning is sort of that untapped retention tool," she says.

The Right Balance

It's hard to quantify in dollar figures the growing interest in technologies for informal learning, because vendors for such products are scattered across multiple categories.

> **Companies typically have their priorities backward. "Only 20 percent [of learning] comes in the formal way. But what do we do? We spend a lot of money on the 20 percent."**
>
> —Claire Schooley, Forrester Research

Whatever the precise figure, it's probably not enough, says Claire Schooley, senior industry analyst with Forrester Research. She says companies typically have their priorities backward by focusing on structured courses as opposed to the sorts of educational experiences that happen on the job, just as an employee needs them. "Only 20 percent [of learning] comes in the formal way," Schooley says. "But what do we do? We spend a lot of money on the 20 percent."

Research company Quintiles Transnational is trying to strike the right balance in terms of learning methods. The 16,000-person company, which manages clinical trials on behalf of pharmaceutical firms, offers a range of in-person and electronic courses. Topics include project management and clinical practice training, and many of the classes are mandated by government regulation, says Tim Toterhi, Quintiles' director of learning and development strategy. To help keep track of all the structured training, Quintiles is installing a new learning management system.

But Quintiles chose the new software partly because it facilitates informal learning activities. Toterhi declined to name the vendor of the system but said it may eventually help with an experiment in podcasting. Quintiles wants to create audio tutorials on various topics that employees can download into portable devices and learn "on the fly," Toterhi says. A Quintiles sales representative about to meet with a client might get a podcast from a more seasoned sales official that contains insights into that particular company and tips for closing deals. "The walk from the car to the customer becomes a classroom of your own design," Toterhi says.

Consultant Cross says formal learning activities typically neglect an organization's veteran key contributors. "After you've got a basic grounding, you don't want courses. Courses are for novices," he says. "Advanced people need to fill in holes in their knowledge, not be dragged through what they already know."

New software products are making it ever easier for average employees to fashion multimedia demonstrations or mini-lessons. These include Microsoft's Power-Point, software firm Articulate's Presenter application and Adobe's Captivate 2 product, which is designed to help people create things including software demonstrations and interactive simulations.

Such products have reduced the time it takes to create tutorials by a factor of three or more in just the past few years, says Glenn Greenberg, e-learning specialist at utility company Southern Co. "These tools have become rapid e-learning development tools," he says. What's more, he says, they typically don't require great technical skill, allowing subject-matter experts throughout a company to generate learning content.

Variety of Tools

One vendor betting on informal learning is Proton-Media. The Lansdale, Pennsylvania-based software firm allows clients to establish a three-dimensional "virtual world" where employees interact and can pose questions. The system matches a person's need with other users logged on, relevant courses, and blogs and wikis. Clients, who include pharmaceutical giant Johnson & Johnson, also have noticed employees deciding to hold impromptu meetings in the virtual world, says ProtonMedia president Ron Burns. "It's as if we've extended the water cooler out over a large, distributed workforce," he says.

Other, much simpler collaboration technologies can be harnessed for informal learning. Web log software enables workers to create blogs in order to share their insights or expertise, while other employees can post comments in response. Wikis are websites that allow visitors to add or change information.

Also helpful for peer-to-peer exchanges are corporate search engines that scour the various types of data contained in a company's computer system. IBM and Yahoo recently announced a free product designed to find information stored within an organization and across the web.

Applications that establish intranet "portals" also can be effective. Microsoft's SharePoint software is a popular choice, says Jason Averbook, chief executive of consulting firm Knowledge Infusion. He says organizations often use SharePoint to let workers post content such as presentations. "We see it being used as a very, very significant content repository," he says.

Overall, Averbook notices corporations in a phase of assessing what they want workers to learn. In the wake of investing heavily in e-learning courses several years ago, firms want to make sure they are directing their training dollars wisely, he says. "There's a lot of money spent monitoring what your workforce needs, versus buying content," he says.

Just as companies are keen to tie their training efforts to their overall corporate strategies, niche vendors of learning management systems have been branching out to add other talent management tools to their lineup. The heavyweights of the HR software world, Oracle and SAP, already offer a broad set of applications in addition to learning management systems.

Tracking Learning

Vendors in the training tech arena are taking note of the informal learning trend. Oracle, for example, touts the way its learning products are inherently interactive and ready for employees to share ideas. "Collaborative tools have been a large part of Oracle's offerings from the beginning," says Gretchen Alarcon, Oracle vice president for human capital management product strategy. "For example, we provide built-in instant messaging capabilities, forums, chat, learner ratings and reviews."

Learning management software from SAP has similar features, including instant messaging, chat and document sharing. When it comes to informal learning, one of SAP's priorities is to make it easier for organizations to capture what employees do outside of structured courses. Lacking that information, companies are hamstrung in their ability to make smart talent decisions such as which employees are indispensable and who may be ready for advancement, says David Ludlow, the SAP vice president in charge of global product strategy for HR applications.

Among the tactics under review at SAP is looking at an employee's Microsoft Outlook calendar to see if any appointments amount to a "learning event." Meetings

Learning Vendors Branching out in Talent Management

The March of the learning management companies is under way.

Vendors that specialize in learning management software systems have been expanding in recent years into other fields of talent management, such as performance management. The idea is to offer customers more complete products, ones that can enhance the ways companies develop particular individuals and shape their overall workforce.

The most recent example of boundary pushing by learning management players came in November. Learning specialist SumTotal Systems said it acquired performance management software firm MindSolve Technologies. And it isn't done growing in terms of talent management, says Karen Hickey, senior director of marketing for SumTotal. "We will continue to fill out the functionality," she says.

SumTotal, which now offers products in the fields of learning, performance and compensation management, still lacks a recruiting product to encompass what many consider the four pillars of talent management. Talent management applications are among the fastest-growing categories of human resources software. Companies are buying these tools as they recognize the value generated by employees and focus on adapting to demographic changes on the horizon, such as the graying of the baby boomer generation.

Jason Averbook, CEO of consulting firm Knowledge Infusion, says corporations are seeing learning activities as directly tied to their efforts to prepare critical succession moves and plan what their workforce will look like in the future.

> **"Learning is playing a bigger role in the 'people chain' than it ever has before."**
>
> —Jason Averbook, Knowledge Infusion

"Learning is playing a bigger role in the 'people chain' than it ever has before," Averbook says, drawing an analogy between workforce planning and the supply-chain planning companies do to optimize the creation of products and services.

Learning management systems refer to software applications for keeping track of the courses employees take and certifications they earn. Major vendors also offer applications for creating online training content.

In addition to SumTotal, learning management vendors Plateau Technologies and Saba have broadened their product offerings. Each now offers performance management and succession management products.

These three vendors are competing in a crowded market for talent management applications overall. A number of companies, including Vurv Technology and Authoria, sell multiple talent management products but not learning management. HR tech's biggest players, Oracle and SAP, offer all four of the primary talent management products, in addition to HR information systems that track essential employee data.

Both giants tout the benefits of an integrated set of talent management products with ties back to the core HR system. SAP's learning management product may not have all the features that the smaller specialists have, concedes David Ludlow, the company's vice president in charge of global product strategy for HR applications. But Ludlow argues that buying SAP's array of talent management products makes more sense than going with multiple niche products, because all the SAP applications are based on a single set of data that makes for smooth integration between the tools and the core HR system. "I think that adds more value than a long list of features and functionality," he says.

His point is at the center of a long-standing debate between the big, comprehensive vendors and smaller specialists. But the companies that have historically focused on learning management are looking more like soup-to-nuts providers. Plateau, for example, hasn't ruled out moving into other talent management areas such as compensation and recruiting, says Ed Cohen, Plateau's chief technology officer. "It's something we've looked at," he says.

such as mentoring sessions would be recorded in their learning history, Ludlow says.

Learning management vendor Plateau Systems also aims to help companies track on-the-job learning moments. It recently launched iContent, which includes a web portal allowing companies to post content including traditional courses and internal presentations as well as link to external blogs or podcasts. When employees log on to the site, they can conduct searches and any information they access can be documented in a customer's learning management system. "It's Amazon.com-type functionality designed to work with a learning management system," says Ed Cohen, chief technology officer at Plateau.

SumTotal has discussed a software upgrade that would let organizations create wikis. Last year, it teamed tip with Google to let Google's corporate search product peer into SumTotal's learning management system to find such things as courses, class materials and presentations.

SumTotal also offers a portal where employees can post documents and carry out threaded discussions. And for several years, SumTotal's system has allowed employees to download audio broadcasts. This feature can be used by managers to deliver podcasts to employees, says Karen Hickey, senior director of marketing at SumTotal.

Challenges

Creating a vigorous and valuable climate of informal learning may not be easy. Employees themselves may hesitate to share their gems of wisdom because of the time it takes to do so and the risk they may be wrong, says Arizona State's Carmean. "The missing factor is how we get workers to shift into a cultural engagement with these tools," she says. "You have to do more than seek information; you have to contribute."

The contributions can pose their own challenges. Worker blogs can result in content that is offensive, embarrassing or highly sensitive—as a number of fired bloggers can attest.

Consultant Cross says corporate distrust of workers also can impede informal learning. "Top-down organizations are accustomed to controlling the flow of information and are not comfortable with learning that comes from the bottom up," he says.

But he and other proponents say smart companies will persevere to encourage unstructured education. According to Cross, the tactics can be as low-tech as the water cooler, version 1.0. A major Silicon Valley company once asked him for advice on how to generate more conversations among its knowledge workers. Cross recommended replacing a third of the cubicles at its headquarters with leather sofas and espresso machines.

"Informal learning will happen if you just get out of its way," he says.

Critical Thinking

1. How do you think on-the-job training works?
2. Where do you think it would be most appropriate?
3. Do you think it is successful?

ED FRAUENHEIM is a Workforce Management staff writer based in San Francisco. To comment, e-mail editors@tworkforce.com.

Strategic Organizational Diversity: A Model?

FREDERICK TESCH AND FREDERICK MAIDMENT

Using resources, especially human ones, effectively is a key issue facing organizations and their managers, especially the human resource management staffs. Diversity is about the human resources available to an organization, about recognizing and using the breadth and depth of differences in its employees' experiences, backgrounds, and capabilities, and about viewing these differences as assets to the organization (Watson & Kumar, 1992). A key assumption is that diversity in a population should produce a similar diversity in our labor markets and in turn in the workforces derived from those labor markets.

Organizations that pursue workforce diversity are more likely to be successful than ones that do not (Cox & Blake, 1991; Marquez, 2005). Human diversity can actually drive business growth (Robinson & Dechant, 1997). An organization that manages diversity well can, for example, understand its markets better, increase its creativity and innovation, and improve its problem solving, thereby reducing its exposure to risk and increasing its chances of higher returns on investment. Clearly, these effects make workforce diversity a goal worth pursuing.

The major problem encountered in pursuing diversity is the lack of agreement on a definition. A recent study by the Society for Human Resource Management found that "Almost three-quarters of the HR professionals who responded said their organizations had no official definition of diversity. Those who had a definition said it was very broad and included an extensive set of differences and similarities among individuals, such as race, gender, age, etc." (Hastings, 2008, 34). How are we to manage what we have yet to define conceptually or operationally?

Given the potential benefits of workforce diversity, discussion of possible theoretical linkages between diversity and organizational goals has been minimal. What paradigm could account for the range of positive effects? What ideas move diversity from a practical concept to a management principle? Most discussion has focused on the practical matters and applications. Pragmatically, diversity works. Research (Parkhe, 1999) shows that managing diversity well

gives organizations a competitive edge and reduces business risk. Given these robust, positive effects, we need not examine nor debate the mechanisms producing them. Do it; don't analyze it!

Unguided diversity, however, might lead an organization to a state of confusion and to actions not consistent with its strategic goals. Much diversity training appears to promote diversity for diversity's sake, often as a moral or ethical imperative. A stance of maximizing all types of human diversity as an end in itself might lead an organization to some dysfunctional thinking and actions. For example, would having recently hired someone from University X with a degree in Discipline Y prohibit hiring another such applicant? Hiring the second, similar applicant could be seen as promoting intellectual and academic homogeneity. Should an applicant be hired because her constellation of skills, knowledge, abilities, and background is unlike that of any other employee, even if her attributes have no relevance to the organization's goals?

Developing a Model for Diversity

Our thesis is that an organization's quest for diversity should be guided by the organization's goals and needs, not by a diffuse concept of diversity as the means to social responsibility or good citizenship.

There are two paths to building a theory. The first path is developing a model to explain the observed events, just as scientists build constructs to explain the phenomena they study (Kuhn, 1970). The second path, typically used by business disciplines, is borrowing a model or paradigm from another discipline and modifying it to the new phenomena. Ideas from economics, psychology, engineering, and mathematics abound in finance, marketing, and management. For example, in finance, portfolio analysis is a tool for managing stock purchases and sales, but marketing borrowed it to use in managing a portfolio of products (Hedley, 1977). Borrowing and using what works is characteristic of the business disciplines and of business people.

Following the second path, there is a theory of diversity in investments that can be applied to diversity in human resources. This application becomes especially clear when organizations view their employees not as an expense but rather as an asset—a view fundamental to human resources, as opposed to personnel, management. Employees, when viewed as an asset, are the equivalent of stocks in a portfolio.

Modigliani's Theory of Diversity in Investments

Franco Modigliani won the Nobel Prize in Economics for this theory of diversity in investments. He began by distinguishing between systematic and unsystematic risks. Systematic risk, also called market risk, is the risk that affects all securities. "Unsystematic risk is the risk that is unique to a company. It can be eliminated by diversifying the portfolio. Thus, systematic risk and unsystematic risk are referred to as non-diversifiable and diversifiable risk, respectively" (Fabozzi & Modigliani, 1992, pp. 154–55).

Building on this difference, he discusses how risk can be reduced or removed. "[U]nsystematic" risk . . . can be washed away by mixing the security with other securities in a diversified portfolio . . . Increasing diversification gradually tends to eliminate the unsystematic risk, leaving only systematic, i.e., market related risk. The remaining variability results from the fact that the return on every security depends to some degree on the overall performance of the market" (Fabozzi & Modigliani, 1992, p. 135).

There will always be some market (systematic) risk: such is the nature of capitalism where organizations compete with one another in the marketplace. Eliminating these risks requires a centrally planned or monopolistic economy.

The case of unsystematic risk is different since it is unique to a company and can be eliminated by diversifying the portfolio. Modigliani's point is that people can control the amount of risk they accept and that the risk can be eliminated if there is enough diversity. The goal is to maximize the long-term results while minimizing, if not eliminating, unsystematic risk. Individually risky stocks remain in the portfolio, but holding a variety of stocks in a variety of industries minimizes risk. Simply stated, "Don't put all your eggs in one basket."

Joe Watson, a diversity expert, captured the argument when he said "Think about diversity in terms of your stock portfolio. If someone came to you and said they were going to put everything you own in Southeast Asian bonds, that's probably not what you would want to do. People want a balanced portfolio with 10% in this and 20% in that because it's understood in business that over time that is what will give you the best possible outcome. Well, how is the workforce any different? It also needs to be diverse to give companies the best possible outcome" (Harris et al., 2008). The organization's goals and strategy should determine the specific securities/people (i.e., differences) in which it needs to invest and which it should ignore.

Human Resources à la Modigliani

Building a parallel from how investors view their stocks in a portfolio, managers should view employees as assets to be managed, not a cost to minimize. With this perspective, Modigliani's concept of diversity for investments becomes a model for human resources diversity. Diversifying an organization's workforce should reduce the unsystematic (non-market) risk unique to the organization's human resources. The greater the diversity, the lower the organization's controllable risk, and the greater the likelihood of higher financial return as a result of the efforts of the employees.

Diversity in an organization's human resources can, for example, reduce the possibility of groupthink (Janis, 1982), "A mode of thinking that people engage in when they are deeply involved in a cohesive [perhaps homogenous] group, when the members, striving for unanimity, override their motivation to realistically appraise alternative courses of action." Groupthink diminishes the group's capabilities to consider, thoroughly, all realistic courses of action. Groups of people with similar backgrounds, experiences, and educations are more likely to fall prey to groupthink than groups having diversity of those factors. Diversity, when properly managed, brings a richer, stronger set of individuals who should be more resistant to the groupthink trap when dealing with organizational issues.

A classic example of the lack of diversity as a tactical organizational weakness is the famous incident of General Motors introducing their "Chevrolet Nova" into the Latin American market (Schnitzier, 2005). In Spanish the phrase "No va!" translates to "No go!," a costly blunder in marketing to the Spanish speaking countries of Latin America. Had the groups involved in this decision at GM contained diversity that was representative of Latin America the episode could have been avoided.

Strategic diversity is not diversity for diversity's sake (i.e., simply maximizing all differences randomly), but is rather diversity aligned to the organization's goals, strategies, mission, and vision (Bonn, 2005). Strategic diversity encourages developing a pool of relevant diversity and not developing differences that are not strategically relevant. For example, an organization doing business in China should probably not hire people from Argentina to conduct its business in Hong Kong. Diversity makes business sense when it is done strategically, not when it is done simply for the sake of diversity or in the name of moral or philosophical agendas. Doing business in the United State of America requires a diverse workforce because it is such a diverse country. To operate in any other way would not only be illegal (e.g., EEO) but also illogical and detrimental to its long-term success.

Similarly, doing business in Norway requires a workforce reflecting the Norwegian stakeholders and having an understanding of Norwegian markets, practices, and laws.

The only sustainable competitive edge that can be unique to an organization is its workforce (Pfeffer, 1995). Most organizations have access to the same technology, transportation and communication systems, and financial markets. Managers exert little influence on their organization's external environments, but do have some control over internal ones. Diversifying the organization's human resources promotes controlling, minimizing, and perhaps even eliminating unsystematic (non-market) risk. This is the theoretical base for workforce diversity.

A strong corporate culture, one that embraces diversity, is one approach to reducing risks. When an organization's operations are scattered across distances, time zones, and cultures, a strong corporate culture is a significant element of the glue holding the pieces together. But no glue can overcome missing pieces. All the cultural variables surrounding the organization must be adequately represented within that organization. Recruiting, selecting, hiring, promoting, training, and compensating must all reflect the drive for diversity. Not doing so would leave the organization vulnerable in an increasingly competitive marketplace and subject to unsystematic risk. Managing diversity well brings the advantage of reduced unsystematic risk in a factor that is controllable and has the most potential for competitive advantage, that is, its human resources.

Human Resources Implications

The HR diversity model based on Modigliani's thinking supplies an additional base, a business justification, to the case for workforce diversity. Arguing for diversity based on legal compliance, ethical posture, or simple cost reduction cannot carry the day. HR executives and managers need the stronger theoretical position this model provides by eliminating or at least reducing unsystematic or non-market risk to the organization in the area of human resources. Let's look at some typical applications.

As organizations go global, those drawing only on their home countries to staff senior positions practice a form of discrimination that severely limits their long-term capabilities. As corporations, for example, become more globalized, their management staff must do the same in order to reduce the unsystematic risks (Bell & Harrison, 1996). One example would be the few non-USA nationals who lead or have led USA corporations (e.g., Ford Motor Company, NCR).

Diversity as a risk management strategy means that we must go beyond simply having people of diverse backgrounds in our organizations. It argues, as does EEO, that the strategy requires offering everyone the same opportunities for movement and advancement within the organization. No department, division, unit, or level can be permitted to be too homogenous, but its diversity must be structural, not random.

And that structural linkage should derive from and reflect the organization's strategic goals.

Workforce diversity promotes the achievement of excellence in human resources and the concurrent reduction of organizational risk leading to enhanced competitiveness and performance. Under these conditions of risk management the cream of the organization's human resources can perform exceptionally. The cream of the workforce that rises to the top is made of richer ingredients and is a better grade of cream (Ng & Tung, 1998).

Diversity's Challenge to Human Resource Management

In today's highly turbulent and hyper-competitive environments, organizations simply cannot afford to allow their competitors the competitive advantage of better workers, managers, and executives, that is, better human resources. To do so is to risk becoming second rate—or even becoming extinct (Collins, 2001; Olson & van Bever, 2008). HR professionals need to develop action plans that are strongly linked to the organization's goals and that guide their recruiting, succession planning, career development, and compensation activities. They must create workforces having diversity that is congruent with the organization's strategic goals and that promotes and ensures equitable treatment and opportunities for all employees.

References

Bell, M. P. & Harrison, D. A. (1996). Using intra-national diversity for international assignments: A model of bicultural competence and expatriate adjustment, *Human Resource Management Review,* Spring, 6(1), 47–74.

Bonn, I. (2005). Improving strategic thinking: A multilevel approach, *Leadership & Organizational Development Journal,* 25(5), 336–354.

Collins, J. (2001). *Good to Great: Why Some Companies Make the Leap—and Others Don't,* New York: Harper Business.

Cox, T. H. & Blake, S. (1991). Managing cultural diversity: Implications for organizational competitiveness, *Academy of Management Executive,* August, 5(3), 45–56.

Fabozzi, F. J., & Modigliani, F. (1991). *Capital Markets: Institutions and instruments,* Englewood Cliffs, NJ: Prentice Hall.

Harris, W., Drakes, S., Lott, A., & Barrett, L. (2008). The 40 best companies for diversity, *Black Enterprise,* 38(12), 94–112.

Hastings, R. (2008). SHRM diversity report a call to action: Majority of companies say they haven't defined diversity, *HRMagazine,* 53(4), April, 34.

Hedley, B. (1977). Strategy and the business portfolio, *Long Range Planning,* February.

Janis, I. (1982). *Groupthink: Psychological studies of policy decisions and fiascos,* Boston: Houghton-Mifflin.

Kuhn, T. (1970). *The structure of scientific revolutions,* Chicago: University of Chicago Press.

Marquez, J. (2005). SHRM survey shows diversity contributes to bottom line (Society for Human Resource Management) *Workforce*

Management, 84.12, November 7, 8. Retrieved February 26, 2007, from General Reverence Center Gold database.

Ng, E. S. & Tung, R. L. (1998). Ethno-cultural diversity and organizational effectiveness: A field study, *International Journal of Human Resource Management,* December, 9(6), 980–995.

Olson, M. S. & van Bever, D. (2008). *Stall Points: Most Companies Stop Growing—Yours Doesn't Have To,* New Haven, CT: Yale University Press.

Parkhe, A. (1999). Interfirm diversity, organizational learning, and longevity in global strategic alliances, *Journal of International Business Studies,* Winter, 22(4), 579–601.

Pfeffer, J. (1995). Producing sustainable competitive advantage through the effective management of people, *Academy of Management Executive,* February, 9(1), 55–72.

Robinson, G. & Dechant, K. (1997). Building a business case for diversity, *Academy of Management Executive,* August, 21–31.

Schnitzier, P. (2005). Translating success: Network of language experts key to Pangea Lingua's growth, *Indianapolis Business Journal,* 26(21), August 1, 3.

Watson W. E. & Kumar, K. (1992). Differences in decision-making regarding risk-taking: A comparison of culturally diverse and culturally homogeneous task groups, *Journal of Intercultural Relations,* 16(1), 53–65.

Critical Thinking

1. Why is diversity important to organizations?
2. What is happening to the legal rationale for diversity?
3. Why should diversity be implemented to achieve strategic goals?
4. How does diversity make organizations more competitive?
5. How can increased diversity reduce business risk?

FREDERICK TESCH, Western Connecticut State University, USA.
FREDERICK MAIDMENT, Western Connecticut State University, Connecticut, USA.

The Broken Psychological Contract: Job Insecurity and Coping

Courtney Keim and Amy Wilkinson

Introduction

Recently, many employees have lost their jobs or become fearful about losing the job they currently hold. Their fears may be well founded. During times of economic recession, the restructuring of organizations is prominent (Hartley et al. 1991, 3), which can result in severe organizational changes that include: the shifting of resources, movement of entire companies, elimination of certain jobs, and even company closures (Hartley et al. 1991, 4; Sverke and Hellgren 2002, 25). These factors have a direct effect on the labor market.

Based upon the information in Figure 1, unemployment rates began to rise in 2008, coinciding with the beginning of the Great Recession that began in December 2007 (Isidore 2008). Figure 1 also shows a significant jump in the unemployment rate of 3.5 percent in 2009, which indicates the severity and significant duration of the current crises. In fact, the economy has not been so damaged since the Great Depression, and most economists see no end to this recession in the near future, indicating unemployment rates will most likely increase or stay

elevated for some time (Isidore 2009). An elevated unemployment rate almost certainly affects the labor market in that both employees and employers are likely to have negative experiences during tough economic times. These negative reactions can compromise the delicate balance that exists between an employee's hard work and efforts and an employer's offerings of security and pay, which can be thought of as the "psychological contract" that exists between employees and employers in an organization. This article examines the psychological contract and the resulting consequences of the contract being broken (job insecurity) and offers suggestions for lowering workers' job insecurity, especially during times of organizational change.

The Psychological Contract

A psychological contract includes the expectations between the employee and employer above and beyond any formal contract, which incorporates the beliefs, values, and aspirations of both

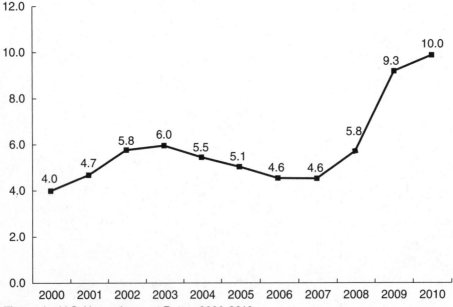

Figure 1 U.S. Unemployment Rates, 2000-2010
Source: Bureau of labor statistics

the employee and the employer (Smithson and Lewis 2000, 681). The psychological contract is based on the belief that "hard work, security and reciprocity are linked" (Smithson and Lewis 2000, 681). From an employee's perspective, the psychological contract guarantees job security, fair wages, benefits, and a sense of self-worth for doing a job well. The employer obtains and retains dedicated workers who perform their jobs well, are satisfied in their jobs, and are committed to the organization. The subjective and time-sensitive psychological contract varies in changing economies or social contexts (Smithson and Lewis 2000, 682). Therefore, an organization that has a strong and vibrant psychological contract with its employees may find that the contract needs to be renegotiated as the economy changes. Also, because of its subjectivity, employees may feel that the psychological contract with their employer is being threatened even when no real objective threat exists (e.g., organizational restructuring, merger with another company, etc.).

Balance is an important part of the psychological contract. An employee must feel that his or her efforts are balanced by what the organization offers (De Witte et al. 2008, 88). If the employee senses an imbalance, the employee feels the psychological contract is broken, which can lead to negative effects (De Witte et al. 2008, 88). These negative effects include but are not limited to an employee feeling insecure in his or her job, which is a topic that has received much attention in organizational research.

Job Insecurity

Job insecurity (the overall apprehension about the continuance of one's job) is a subjective phenomenon. Two workers in the same job in the same organization can experience different levels of job insecurity. Job insecurity can lead to negative effects on an employee's health and well-being. Studies have shown job insecurity being related to psychosomatic complaints, depression, nervousness, fear, sadness, and guilt, which are all considered to be manifestations of poor mental health (van Vuuren et al. 1991). Also, job insecurity has been shown to be related to critical job-related variables, including job performance, job satisfaction, trust, job involvement, organizational commitment, and turnover intentions (Cheng and Chan 2008; Sverke, Hellgren, and Näswall 2002; van Vuuren et al. 1991).

There have been numerous studies that have looked at the potential precursors to job insecurity. Research has shown that employees who work in temporary jobs, part-time jobs, or blue-collar positions, and who report a lack of communication within their organization or who work in an organization experiencing organizational changes are more likely to report high levels of job insecurity. Other precursors to job insecurity include a worker experiencing role ambiguity and/or role conflict. Role ambiguity occurs when an individual does not know his or her responsibilities and goals for the job (Sawyer 1992), while role conflict occurs when workers experience demands from various sources, resulting in increased uncertainty (Ameen et al. 1995). Workers experiencing role ambiguity or role conflict simply do not know what their obligations are to their employer. In these situations, workers may become anxious because they are unable to fulfill their psychological

contract with their employer, resulting in feeling insecure about their job (Ashford, Lee, and Bobko 1989, 806).

Many of these factors are beyond the control of organizations. An organization may not be able to turn every part-time worker into a full-time worker, make every temporary job permanent, convert every blue-collar job into a white-collar position, or be invincible to economic crises. But, these limitations do not mean organizations are powerless in their ability to stave off job insecurity in workers. In fact, organizational research offers suggestions for ways in which job insecurity in employees can be lowered.

Lowering Job Insecurity in Workers

Job insecurity may be lowered by strengthening the psychological contract with employees. The key to this strengthening is communication. Kinnunen and Natti (1994, 316) note that providing adequate information to employees can reduce job insecurity. Petzall, Parker, and Stoeberl (2000, 601) suggest that an open dialogue between employers and employees can help stave off the negative effects a recession brings by building trust. It is important for employers to communicate the fairness of organizational decisions and processes because "it is not necessarily what really happens but rather what the workers perceive as happening that will dictate their reactions to management's actions" (Petzall, Parker and Stoeberl 2000, 601, emphasis added). Since job insecurity is a subjective phenomenon, it is important for workers to perceive that the balance between their efforts and the offerings of the organization are set fairly.

Also, both role ambiguity and role conflict (which can both lead to increased levels of job insecurity) can be lessened by an increase in communication between employers and employees. Organizations should be sure that their workers have adequate amounts of information, including knowing what their jobs entail, understanding what is expected of them, and giving them the control they need to do their jobs, especially in ambiguous or transitional settings that occur all too often during times of economic uncertainty.

Increasing Organizational Communication

How can organizations increase communication with their employees, especially during times of economic uncertainty when changes inevitably occur? Lewis, Schmisseur, Stephens, and Weir (2006, 120) systematically analyzed bestselling books on communicating during organizational change and identified strategies and tactics employers can use to help increase the flow of information.

Lewis et al. offer general strategies for communicating and dealing with major changes in an organization (2006, 120–122). The first strategy involves emphasizing participation and empowerment by making workers feel they are part of the change process. Here, leadership in an organization should

General Strategies for Communication and Introduction of Change

General Strategies for Dealing with Major Change:

- Emphasize participation and empowerment
- Create a change culture
- Emphasize purpose and vision
- Emphasize communication

Specific Ways to Increase Communication:

- Ask for input
- Use informal networks
- Disseminate information
- Manage the style and content of communication
- Be motivational
- Formulate and follow a communication plan
- Create and communicate vision

Source: Laurie K. Lewis, Amy M. Schmisseur, Keri K. Stephens, and Kathleen E. Weir "Advice on Communicating During Organizational Change." *Journal of Business Communication* 43.2 (2006): 113–137.

encourage autonomy and ownership in their workforce. The authors also encourage the use of organizational culture as a tool to enable change, which can be achieved by creating an environment open to new ideas, sharing those ideas freely, and ensuring the workforce is prepared for potential changes. Also, Lewis et al. suggest emphasizing the purpose and vision of the organization and how the resulting changes are part of that vision, accomplished by having leadership consistently link organizational decisions to the overall purpose of the organization. Linking decisions to the overall organizational mission allows employees to understand the organization's direction and how they as employees help the organization meet its goals. Finally, the authors suggest emphasizing communication, which is vital to successful problem solving and organizational change (Lewis et al. 2006, 122). Communication can take many forms, including face-to-face meetings, questionnaires or surveys, or focus groups. It is important that leadership keep open lines of communication with employees at all levels.

The authors also identify specific strategies to emphasize and increase communication in an organization (Lewis et al. 2006, 123–128). The first strategy is to ask for input from workers, which includes listening to those who give their opinions, fostering an environment where workers feel open to voicing their opinions and concerns, and encouraging feedback from various perspectives. A second way to increase communication is to use the informal networks of key employees to disseminate information and deal with any resistance encountered. The

authors warn to not underestimate the importance of "front-line" supervisors, middle management, and other employees in getting information out to all employees. These leaders have informal networks and relationships that can help ensure information gets to those who need it.

Also, Lewis et al. suggest that companies disseminate information to all important members of their organization as soon as possible using as many methods as are plausible. The repetition of information can help ensure important information is seen as such. Information should be open and honest, even if it could be considered negative. The authors point out that "any information, even negative information, about change can help alleviate anxiety and reduce some negative reactions to change" (Lewis et al. 2006, 131). Organizations should also be sure to manage both the style and content of communication. The authors suggest the use of appropriate and clear language, specificity, and getting straight to the point. Also, being motivational, e.g., rewarding employees who support any changes to the organization, can help all employees embrace the change that is occurring and foster a positive organizational change culture.

The authors suggest formulating and following a communication plan. These plans vary in their intensity and design depending upon which strategy an organization follows, but the main point is to be organized and intentional in communicating with employees. And lastly, organizations should create and communicate their vision, where appropriate. If communicating with employees can best be described visually, then the organization should do so. But, be sure any visual communication is unambiguous, relevant, and simple. For example, an organization can use newsletters, posters, and stories to help employees understand the vision of the organization in the midst of significant change, as cited by Lewis et al. (2006, 128).

Conclusion

Clearly, job insecurity is abundant among the labor force today. As the economy struggles to recover and unemployment rates stay elevated, workers continue to feel insecure in the continuation of their employment. However, the amount of job insecurity an employee feels varies from person to person because job insecurity is a subjective phenomenon, the result of an imbalance in the psychological contract between employee and employer. Communication is the key to restoring balance and lowering job insecurity among workers, especially in times of change and uncertainty. Effective organizational communication should involve giving direction, promoting participation, emphasizing purpose and vision, and ensuring fairness within the organization. This article offers specific steps or strategies in effectively disseminating information in an organization, including asking for and using employee input, developing and following a plan of action, using employee networks, and rewarding those employees who embrace and utilize the information given. Increasing organizational communication effectively through these techniques will strengthen the psychological contract between employee and employer and most likely decrease job insecurity within the company. Thus, even during rough economic times, organizations can continue to reassure and engage their workforce and in return have motivated, dedicated, and productive employees.

References

Ameen, Elsie C., Cynthia Jackson, William R. Pasewark, and Jerry R. Strawser. "An Empirical Investigation of the Antecedents and Consequences of Job Insecurity on the Turnover Intentions of Academic Accountants." *Issues in Accounting Education* 10.1 (1995): 65–82.

Ashford, Susan J., Cynthia Lee, and Philip Bobko. 1989. "Content, Causes and Consequences of Job Insecurity: A Theory-based Measure and Substantive Test." *Academy of Management Journal* 22 (1989): 803–829.

Cheng, Grand H.L., and Darius K.-S. Chan. "Who Suffers More from Job Insecurity? A Meta-Analytic Review." *Applied Psychology: An International Review,* 57.2 (2008): 272–303.

De Witte, Hans, Magnus Sverke, Joris Van Ruysseveldt, Sjoerd Goslinga, Antonio Chirumbolo, Johnny Hellgren, and Katharina Näswall. "Job Insecurity, Union Support and Intentions to Resign Membership: A Psychological Contract Perspective." *European Journal of Industrial Relations* 14 (2008): 85–103.

Hartley, Jean, Dan Jacobson, Bert Klandermans, and Tinka van Vuuren. *Job Insecurity: Coping with Jobs at Risk.* Newbury Park, CA: Sage, 1991.

Isidore, Chris. 2008. "It's Official: Recession Since, Dec. '07." *CNNMoney.com,* December 1. http://money.cnn.com/2008/12/01/news/economy/recession/index.htm (accessed August 5, 2010.)

Isidore, Chris. 2009. "The Great Recession." *CNNMoney.com.* March 25. http://money.cnn.com/2009/03/25/news/economy/depression_comparisons/index.htm (accessed August 5, 2010).

King, James E. "White-Collar Reactions to Job Insecurity and the Role of the Psychological Contract: Implications for Human Resource Management." *Human Resource Management* 39.1 (2000): 79–92.

Kinnunen, Ulla, and Jouko Nätti. "Job Insecurity in Finland: Antecedents and Consequences" *European Work and Organizational Behavior* 4 (1994): 297–321.

Lewis, Laurie K., Amy M. Schmisseur, Keri K. Stephens, and Kathleen E. Weir. "Advice on Communicating During Organizational Change." *Journal of Business Communication* 43.2 (2006): 113–137.

Petzall, Barbara J., Gerald E. Parker, and Philipp A. Stoeberl. "Another Side to Downsizing: Survivors' Behavior and Self-affirmation." *Journal of Business and Psychology* 14 (2000): 593–603.

Sawyer, John E. 1992. "Goal and Process Clarity: Specification of Multiple Constructs of Role Ambiguity and a Structural Equation Model of Their Antecedents and Consequences" *Journal of Applied Psychology* 77(1992): 130–142.

Smithson, Janet, and Suzan Lewis. "Is Job Insecurity Changing the Psychological Contract?" *Personnel Review,* 29.6 (2000): 680–682.

Sverke, Magnus, and Johnny Hellgren. "The Nature of Job Insecurity: Understanding Employment Uncertainty on the Brink of a New Millennium." *Applied Psychology: An International Review* 51.1 (2002): 25.

Sverke, Magnus, Johnny Hellgren, and Katharina Näswall. "No Security: A Meta-Analysis and Review of Job Insecurity and Its Consequences." *Journal of Occupational Health Psychology* 7.3 (2002): 242–264.

van Vuuren, Tinka, Bert Klandermans, Dan Jacobson, and Jean Hartley. 1991. "Employees' Reactions to Job Insecurity" In *Job Insecurity: Coping with Jobs at Risk, ed.* Jean Hartley, Dan Jacobson, Bert Klandermans, and Tinka van Vuuren. (Newbury Park, CA: Sage, 1991), 79–103.

Critical Thinking

1. What was the psychological contract?
2. How has the psychological contract changed?
3. What do you think this means for the employee?
4. What do you think this means for the employer?
5. How does job insecurity affect the relationship between the employee and the employer?

COURTNEY KEIM received her BA in Psychology from Christian Brothers University and her MS in Psychology from the University of Memphis. She is currently a doctoral student in Experimental Psychology at the University of Memphis, with a concentration in Industrial and Organizational Psychology. Her research interests include occupational health and safety, with an emphasis on stress in the workplace.

UNIT 5

Implementing Compensation, Benefits, and Workplace Safety

Unit Selections

Learning Outcomes

After reading this Unit, you will be able to:

- Understand the difference between a paid and an unpaid position.

- Appreciate the controversy over executive pay.

- Know about the role the federal government is taking in executive pay for corporations.

- Understand the role of the Occupational Safety and Health Administration in enforcing workplace standards.

- Know about the growing movement concerning bullying in the workplace and how it is considered by many to be the new "sexual harassment."

- Understand why benefits are important to employees.

- Appreciate the importance of health care and the health reform efforts by the federal government and why they are so controversial.

- Know of ways organizations can help workers prepare for retirement.

Student Website

www.mhhe.com/cls

Internet References

BenefitsLink: The National Employee Benefits Website
www.benefitslink.com/index.php

CNN Money Retirement
www.money.cnn.com/retirement

Executive Pay
www.salary.com/compensation/executive_pay.asp

Job Stress
www.workhealth.org/news/nwprahn98.html

Individuals are usually paid what others perceive their work to be worth. This situation is not necessarily morally correct. In fact, it does not even have to be logical, but it is reality. Police officers and college instructors are often underpaid. They have difficult jobs, requiring highly specialized training, but these jobs do not pay well. Other professions pay better, and many illegal activities pay better than law enforcement or college teaching. When a company is trying to determine the salary of individuals, two markets must be considered. The first is the internal structure of the firm, including the wages that the company pays for comparable jobs. If the organization brings a new employee on board, it must be careful not to set a pay rate for that individual that is inconsistent with those of other employees who are doing the same or similar jobs. The second market is the external market for employees. Salary information is available from many sources, including professional associations and the federal government. Of course, both current and prospective employees, as well as organizations, can easily gain access to this information. To ignore this information and justify pay rates only in terms of internal structure is to tempt fate. The company's top producers are the ones in whom the competition is the most interested, and no organization can afford a mass exodus of its top talent. Organizations must obey the laws concerning compensation and be careful not to attempt to circumvent them as seen in "Bonus and Incentive Compensation Awards—Navigating Section 409A $1 Million Limit and Golden Parachute Rules."

One recent development in the area of compensation is a return to the concept of pay for performance. Many firms are looking for ways to directly reward their top performers. As a result, the idea of merit pay has gained wide acceptance in both industry and government. Pay for performance has been used in industry for a long time, most commonly in the sales and marketing area, where employees have historically worked on commission plans based on their sales productivity. Theoretically, merit pay and other types of pay for performance are effective, but they can easily be abused, and they are often difficult to administer because measuring performance accurately is difficult. Sales and production have numbers that are easily obtained, but research and development is a different situation. How does a firm measure the effectiveness of research and development for a particular year when such projects can often take several years for the results to be achieved? One issue that has evolved over the past several years is the question of pay for top executives as seen in "The Politics of Executive Pay." During times of economic recession, most workers are asked to make sacrifices in the form of reduced raises, pay cuts, cuts in benefits, other compensation reductions, or layoffs. Many of these sacrifices have not been applied to top management. Indeed, the compensation for top management has increased substantially during the past several years. Are chief executives overpaid, and if so, how did they get that way, and who should set their pay?

The fastest-growing aspect of employee compensation is benefits. Benefits are expensive for any firm, representing an ever-increasing burden to employers. As a result, many firms are reducing benefits and attempting to find more effective ways to spend their benefit dollars, Also, the needs of the employees are changing. As our society ages, there is greater interest in

© Comstock Images/Jupiterimages

health benefits and pensions and less interest in maternity benefits. Another facet of the issue is that employees are seeking greater benefits in lieu of salary increases, because the benefits, with some exceptions, are not usually taxed, a situation that is addressed in "Making Benefits Matter."

Health and safety are also major concerns of employers and employees. The workplace has become more violent as workers act out against their employers for unfairness—whether real or imagined. Some firms have had to address the anger of employees and other problems. The problems facing companies may even extend beyond the workplace, and employers may face liability when domestic violence comes to the workplace. Today, issues concerning safety and health in the workplace include AIDS, burnout, and substance abuse. These issues reflect not only changing social conditions but also a greater awareness of the threats presented by unsafe working conditions. An attempt to address some of these issues has been to practice what is essentially preventive medicine with wellness initiatives and other programs. While there was initially some doubt about their effectiveness, the results are now in, and wellness programs do work.

The landscape for healthcare has changed remarkably over the past year with the passage of the new healthcare bill by Congress. While the details of the massive bill are not yet clear, it is certain that this legislation will mean massive changes in the healthcare system in the United States. "Demystifying Health Reform Legislation" is still a goal that remains only partially achieved by the people of the United States and it remains to be seen how well it will be received. With the recent financial meltdown, the issue of retirement has become one of even greater concern. People who thought they were going to have a financially stable retirement now find themselves much less secure than they were just a few short months ago. Many of them are faced with having to work far beyond what they had originally planned. Others are finding themselves caught between being too old to be considered for retraining by their former employers, but too young to retire, so they have been laid off and left to fend for themselves in the worst recessions since the 1930s. The silver lining for these workers is that, in the long run, the workforce will shrink and they will be in demand. But, for now, they, like so many other workers, are finding it difficult coping.

There are those, who are fortunate enough to be able to work until they are eligible for retirement. These workers are interested in working until it is time for them to retire, but are interested in phasing into retirement. Retirement is a life-changing event and should not be taken lightly, so many people who are in this position are looking for ways to "Phase Into Retirement," so as to ease the transition.

All in all, salaries, wages, and benefits represent a major expense and a time-consuming management task for most firms, and health and safety requirements are a potential area of significant loss, in terms of both dollars and lost production.

Money makes the world go around . . . the world go around!
—From "Money" in the musical *Cabaret*

Where Have All the High-Paying Jobs Gone?

The labor market is slowly recovering, but with low-wage jobs. The US has lost at least 3 million high paid jobs forever.

JAMES C. COOPER

The United States labor market has been looking stronger in recent months. Since jobs began to increase in early 2010, private-sector companies have added two million workers, with the overwhelming bulk of the gains coming from small businesses. So far this year, payroll increases have accelerated to 214,000 per month, the strongest four-month pace in five years.

But there's a catch. The quality of the jobs the United States is creating right now in terms of pay, benefits, hours, and skills leaves a lot to be desired. The problem is not only the depth of the recession and the sluggishness of the recovery. It also reflects the changing structure of the United States economy, as more manufacturing operations shift to overseas locations, while service businesses, which often pay much less, take a more dominant role in job creation.

Previously high-paying jobs in manufacturing have gone the way of the Edsel. United States factories lost 3 million jobs from 2000 to 2004, jobs that did not return during the boom leading up to the recession, along with another 2.2 million from 2007 to 2010. Those are unlikely to come back, as well. Manufacturing jobs were 20 percent of private-sector payrolls in 1990, 15 percent in 2000, and just over 10 percent in April. Large multinational corporations have cut 2.9 million United States jobs over the past decade, while adding 2.4 million workers to their overseas operations.

Factory Pay Is Now below Average

More important, pay in manufacturing is not what it used to be. Hourly earnings of production and non-supervisory workers, which had held well above the private-sector average for decades, slipped below the average in 2006, and the ratio continues to trend gradually lower. In 2004, factory pay was about 3 percent above average. In April it was 2.4 percent below the $19.37-per-hour private-sector mark for production workers.

The recovery, so far, has generated a majority of lower paying jobs. Economists at UBS, who track payrolls in industries where hourly wages are above the overall average vs. sectors with pay below the average, say that job growth in low-wage industries has been generally faster since the recovery began in mid-2009. In particular, job gains in the retail-trade and leisure-and-hospitality sectors, where hourly pay is 32 percent and 43 percent, respectively, below the average for all private-sector employees, have accounted for 27 percent of this year's job growth.

At the other end of the pay scale, and in addition to the 5.2 million jobs already lost, the recession wiped out nearly three million high-paying jobs in construction and finance, where average hourly pay is 11 percent and 20 percent, respectively, above the $22.95 average for all private-sector employees, which includes both production workers and management. Those jobs are not coming back any time soon, if ever. One bright spot has been professional and business services, including legal, accounting, computer systems design, and consulting. Jobs there typically pay 20 percent higher than average, and they have accounted for 30 percent of all private-sector job growth over the past year.

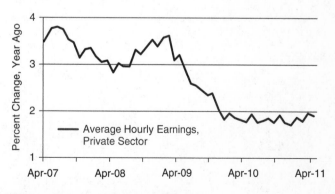

Wages Show No Sign of Picking Up

Source: Bureau of labor *statistics*

Small Businesses Hiring, but Offering Few Benefits

The big contribution to hiring by small business has been a blessing and curse. Since payrolls started to grow again in March 2010, companies with fewer than 500 employees have accounted for 97 percent of the growth in private-sector jobs, based on data from Automatic Data Processing. Companies with fewer than 50 workers have contributed nearly half, while growth at big firms with greater than 500 employees has been negligible. However, small companies don't generate as much income per worker, as bigger outfits, and offer far fewer benefits.

Small business hiring remained strong in April, but pay growth was sluggish, according to the Small Business Employment Index, developed by economist Susan Woodward with Intuit, a provider of payroll services for small and medium size businesses. The Intuit gauge covers companies with fewer than 20 employees, where employment has risen by 845,000 since October 2009, the company says. But over the past year average monthly pay has risen only 1.6 percent, to $2,653. "This upward trend is partly due to hourly employees working more hours while their hourly wages remain flat," says Woodward.

Given the unusually large slack in the labor force created by the recession, hourly pay across almost all industries is barely rising. Average hourly earnings for all private-sector employees in April were up only 1.9 percent from a year ago, according to the Labor Dept., close to the annual clip in late 2009 and below April's 3.2 percent inflation rate. With 13.7 million people—9 percent of the labor force—officially unemployed and another 10.6 million either too discouraged to seek work or forced to work only part time, it's going to be a buyer's market for a long time.

An economic recovery will not by itself lift the quality of United States jobs. Economists know that workers are paid based on the value of the products they make and their contribution to a company's production. That's a long-term problem requiring policy efforts that support investments in research and innovation, as well as human capital, which reflects education and skills. Such efforts will be key considerations as policymakers battle over how to cut future budget deficits.

Critical Thinking

1. What kind of jobs are being created in the United States?

2. What kind of jobs are being lost in the United States?

3. What does this mean for the long-term economic health of the United States?

This column first appeared on May 16, 2011 in the *Fiscal Times,* which also owns the copyright.

Bonus and Incentive Compensation Awards—Navigating Section 409A, $1 Million Limit, and Golden Parachute Rules

Edward E. Bintz and Douglas S. Pelley

As the area of executive compensation has become increasingly regulated, navigating applicable tax law requirements when granting compensation awards has become a growing challenge. This article provides an overview of some key aspects of Section 409A, the $1 million limit under Section 162(m), and the golden parachute rules under Section 280G that employers should keep in mind when making bonus and incentive compensation awards.

Section 409A

Annual bonus and other incentive compensation awards (collectively, "awards") can be designed to be either exempt from, or compliant with, Section 409A. In order to retain maximum flexibility with respect to modifying awards (such as accelerating payment, changing payment terms, or even canceling awards and replacing them with something else), it is generally preferable, where possible, to design awards to be exempt from Section 409A. Section 409A exemption/compliance alternatives for different types of awards are discussed below.

Annual Cash Bonuses

Several Section 409A strategies are available for annual cash bonuses:

- *Exempt Because No Legally Binding Right:* If the amount and payment of an annual bonus award is fully subject to an employer's discretion, the award should generally be exempt from Section 409A, because the recipient employee has no legally binding right to payment of the award until it is actually paid. Under Section 409A, unless an award grants a legally binding right to compensation in a later year, there is no deferral of compensation for purposes of Section 409A.

- *Exempt As Short Term Deferral:* Cash bonus awards are often designed to comply with the short term deferral exception to Section 409A. In general, the short term deferral exception will apply if a compensation award is required to be, and actually is paid, within two and a half months after the end of the year during which the executive obtains a vested right to the payment.

- *Comply with Section 409A Deferred Compensation Requirements:* If a bonus award is not exempt from 409A, it must, at the time of grant, (a) specify a permissible time of payment (a specified date or even year of payment is sufficient); (b) specify the form of payment (e.g., lump sum, installments, etc.); and (c) in the case of a publicly traded company, if the payment may in some circumstances be triggered by termination of employment (such as under the terms of an employment agreement), provide for a delay in payment of six months if the payment is to a "specified employee" (as defined under Section 409A) and is triggered by separation from service.

Stock Options

Stock options are almost always designed to be exempt from Section 409A. In order to be exempt from Section 409A, a stock option must satisfy the following requirements:

- *Option Must Cover Service Recipient Stock:* The stock covered by the option must be common stock (options on preferred stock are not allowed) of the employer (the legal entity actually employing the employee) or, generally, a direct or indirect parent thereof. Options may not be granted on the stock of a subsidiary of the corporation employing an employee.

- *Exercise Price Must Be Not Less Than Fair Market Value:* The exercise price must be not less than fair market value on the date of grant of the option. In the case of an option on stock traded on an established securities market, the regulations under Section 409A permit a number of pricing methodologies, all of which are based on actual market prices. In the case of an option on nonpublicly traded stock, fair market value must be determined by "the reasonable application of a reasonable valuation method." This is a higher standard than the "good faith" standard applicable to pricing incentive stock options (ISOs) at fair market value. The regulations under Section 409A provide a number of safe harbors that may be used to establish the fair market value of nonpublicly traded stock.
- *No Deferral Features:* The option cannot have any deferral features (beyond those inherent in an option), such as the ability to defer receipt of shares upon exercise of the option.

Restricted Stock

Restricted stock is exempt from Section 409A, because it constitutes the transfer of property subject to Section 83. This makes restricted stock particularly attractive from a Section 409A perspective.

Restricted Stock Units

Restricted stock units (RSUs), which involve the payment of stock or cash on a future date or event, are generally subject to Section 409A unless designed to comply with the short term deferral exception (as described above with respect to bonus awards). Although RSUs are, in many ways, economically equivalent to restricted stock, they are accorded fundamentally different treatment under Section 409A. Because restricted stock is exempt from Section 409A, an employer that utilizes restricted stock generally has more flexibility to make changes to its awards than an employer that utilizes RSUs.

$1 Million Limit Under Section 162(M)

In many cases, publicly held companies design compensation awards made to "covered employees" (and employees who may become covered employees prior to payment of an award) to comply with the performance based compensation exception to the $1 million limit under Section 162(m). Key requirements of that exception are as follows:

Grant and Certification by a Qualifying Compensation Committee

The award must be granted by a compensation committee comprised of at least two or more "outside directors." Except in the case of stock options and stock appreciation rights (SARs) that meet the requirements described below, the committee also must certify that the performance goals and any other material

terms of the arrangement were satisfied before payment is made. A director is an "outside director" only if he or she is not:

- A current employee of the publicly held corporation;
- A former employee of the corporation who is receiving compensation for prior services (other than benefits under a tax qualified pension plan);
- A former officer of the corporation; or
- Receiving remuneration from the corporation, either directly or indirectly, in any capacity other than as a director.

Performance Goal Requirement

Payment of the award must be contingent on the attainment of one or more pre-established objective performance goals. A performance goal is treated as "pre-established" if it is established by the compensation committee not later than 90 days after commencement of the period of service to which the performance goal relates, provided that the outcome is substantially uncertain and not more than 25 percent of the performance period has expired. A performance goal is objective only if a third party with knowledge of the relevant facts would be able to determine the extent to which the goal was satisfied and the amount of compensation that would be payable to the employee. A compensation committee may retain discretion to reduce the amount payable upon achievement of the performance goal(s).

Stockholder Approval Requirement

The award must generally be made under a stockholder approved plan that authorizes the performance goal(s) used in the award and contains a cap on the amount that can be paid to an executive during a specific period.

Special Rules for Stock Options and SARs

Special rules apply to stock options and SARs. Under these rules, a stock option or SAR is deemed to constitute qualifying performance based compensation if: (a) the grant is made by a qualifying compensation committee; (b) the plan under which the option or SAR is granted states the maximum number of shares with respect to which options or SARs may be granted during a specified period to any employee; and (c) the exercise price of the option or base price of the SAR is not less than the fair market value of the stock on the date of grant. If these requirements are not satisfied, a stock option or SAR may nonetheless satisfy the performance based exception if the grant of the option or SAR or its vesting is subject to achievement of one or more qualifying performance goals.

Golden Parachute Rules
Vesting Schedules

The accelerated vesting of compensation awards upon the occurrence of a change in control or termination of employment in connection with a change in control can increase the amount of an executive's parachute payments. In general, a longer vesting schedule results in increased parachute payments upon accelerated vesting, and accelerated vesting upon the occurrence of a change in control results in greater parachute payments than accelerated vesting only upon termination after a change in control (assuming termination does not occur immediately upon the change in control).

One Year Presumption

Awards made within one year prior to a change in control may be deemed to be parachute payments under the golden parachute rules.

Locking in Current Interest Rates for Accelerated Payments

Payment of compensation awards is often accelerated by a change in control. Under the golden parachute rules, the present value benefit of receiving payment of a compensation award on an accelerated basis is a parachute payment. For purposes of calculating present value, the interest rate (120 percent of the applicable federal rates compounded semiannually) in effect at the time of the change in control is generally used. An employer and employee may, however, agree in the contract providing for a parachute payment to use the interest rate in effect on the date of the contract. Because current interest rates are generally low by historical standards, locking in current interest rates for calculating parachute payments resulting from the accelerated

payment of awards can potentially reduce the amount of parachute payments an employee receives (thereby reducing the amount of excise taxes or the effect of golden parachute caps).

Nontax Considerations

Among the nontax considerations to be taken into account when making compensation awards are the accounting treatment of the awards, how the awards will be disclosed under the U.S. Securities and Exchange Commission's (SEC's) proxy and other disclosure rules, and institutional shareholder reaction.

Critical Thinking

1. What do you think about the $1 million dollar limit on executive salary?
2. Do you think it is effective?
3. How do executives get around it?
4. Do you think "golden parachutes" are appropriate?
5. Do you think incentive compensation works?

Edward Bintz is a partner specializing in employee benefits and executive compensation at Arnold & Porter LLP. **Douglas Pelley** is counsel and a member of the firm's compensation and benefits and tax, trusts, and estates practice groups. The authors may be contacted at edward.bintz@aporter.com and douglas.pelley@aporter.com, respectively.

Opening Keynote: Rethinking Pay for Performance

What have we learned about pay for performance in the current financial crisis that can help us do a better job in the future?

DEBRA PERRY

Our approach to executive compensation needs significant overhaul. At a time when several major financial institutions and industrial companies are on life support, shareholders have every right to question pay practices that have delivered outsized financial rewards to executives despite poor or *unsustainable* company performance. As the federal government has stepped in to backstop banks, auto manufacturers and our largest insurer, public outrage about executive pay has intensified.

The public acrimony over the AIG retention bonuses marks a new and alarming peak in anti-business sentiment that risks compromising the success of the measures being taken to repair the damage to our financial markets. It may also complicate our efforts to repair the economy. Private sector reliance on taxpayer-funded bailouts has also invited retaliatory legislative action on pay levels and pay policies. However, one-size-fits-all compensation rules crafted on Capital Hill are not likely to provide the right incentives to recruit and retain the skilled managers that we need to fix our companies and our economy. The recent executive compensation rules outlined in the stimulus package will further de-link pay from performance and over time, prompt an exodus of talented professionals from the very institutions in greatest need of managerial talent. This is not a good outcome for public companies' stakeholders—not the taxpayers who are now sizeable creditors and not the shareholders either.

This disconnect between pay and performance has occurred despite the hard work of many board compensation committees and outside consultants. Both have worked to more effectively align management rewards with shareholder value. But high levels of dissatisfaction with their work in the current environment demands some careful analysis.

What have we learned about pay for performance in the current financial crisis that can help us do a better job in the future? I believe that there are several takeaways for boards and for compensation committees.

Performance Goals That Govern Pay Should Be Set within Acceptable Risk Parameters

I believe that the compensation excesses of failed financial institutions are first and foremost a failure of risk oversight. Setting financial or operating performance objectives in the absence of clear and thoughtful risk parameters may be an invitation to bet the ranch. Companies make money by taking risk; the objective is not to eliminate risk but to take risks in ways that are quantifiable, manageable and in which the company has a competitive advantage. Strong financial performance in the short term may result from good operating management and risk governance—or alternatively from excessive risk taking. Looking back only three or four years, there are many examples of companies that recorded seemingly robust financial results by taking risks they could not analyze or quantify—and in some cases by taking risks that were not even on management's radar screen. Many of those companies have failed, been forced into mergers, or are operating with taxpayer support.

Compensation design and metrics should be informed by explicit risk parameters that have been reviewed and approved by the board. Risk tolerance should be defined not only in financial terms but also in terms of operational, legal and reputation risks that over time can result in franchise damage and high financial costs.

Incentive Compensation Should Be Related to the Time Frame Over Which Profits (or Loss) Emerge from the Business

The financial crisis has delivered countless examples of managers who were highly compensated for strategic decisions and new business production that later generated enormous losses.

Plan design needs to consider the time frame over which management performance can be accurately assessed. This can be a challenging issue.

In many industries, the performance horizon of a book of business or a product life cycle can be very long. In others, the performance horizon may appear to be short but in reality is the life of assets that were generated for sale to others. A timely example is the mortgage banking business that relies on asset securitization as its primary funding source. The turmoil in the residential mortgage market reflects not only a pervasive failure of risk management but many failures of risk transference. Without a substantially longer perspective on performance horizons, compensation plans encourage maximization of short term compensation opportunities that may result in unsustainable—or worse, ultimately destructive, risk taking.

Very High Senior Executive Pay Levels and Large Pay Differentials between CEOs and Other Officers May Not Be Sustainable without High Social Costs

The enormous loss in stock market capitalization and home values and rising unemployment have delivered a deep sense of economic insecurity to many Americans, including those deemed to be 'affluent.' Social tensions in our society appear to be growing as the deepening recession and subsequent rescue measures affect people in different ways. Pay differentials between senior executives and lower level employees will generate more anger and more public scrutiny in this environment, not less, especially when public funds are required to keep many companies operating. Boards ought to reassess absolute levels of compensation and pay differentials in their companies and in American business as a whole. What is at stake is more than bad 'optics' around compensation payouts but more fundamentally, preserving a sense of fairness that is essential to democratic society.

Talent Management and Succession Planning Are as Critical to Ensuring Strong and Stable Leadership as Compensation Strategy

The events of the past two years have provided distressing examples of boards of major companies searching on the outside for CEOs and other c-suite executives in moments of crisis. The lack of well-developed internal succession plans results in paying top dollar for outside leadership with the risk that a newly hired outsider can get his/her arms around

a complex and deteriorating situation in time to make a difference. There are few senior managers equipped to lead a company out of crisis, especially when they are unfamiliar with its people and operations. Boards need to focus on talent management and succession planning for key senior roles and should do so with a clear view of the company's strategy and risk parameters.

> **Boards ought to reassess absolute levels of compensation and pay differentials in their companies and in American business as a whole.**

It is time for boards to think deeply about compensation and leadership. We need a fundamental re-assessment of what pay for performance means—one that explicitly relates performance objectives to risk guidelines; that bases pay on meaningful performance horizons; and that addresses relative pay differentials and absolute compensation levels in a broader social context. Succession planning and talent management should be given equal consideration to compensation plan design. Ultimately, our success in restoring trust and confidence in business and in preserving boards' flexibility to reward operational excellence and entrepreneurial innovation will depend on getting pay for performance right.

Critical Thinking

1. Do you think the way senior executives are paid is fair?
2. Is there anything you would do to change it?
3. How do incentives play a role in motivating employees?

DEBRA PERRY is a corporate director who serves on the boards of Korn/Ferry International, a premier global provider of talent management solutions, and Conseco Inc., a life and health insurance company focused on the senior and middle markets. At Conseco, she chairs the board's Human Resources & Compensation Committee and also serves on the Governance & Strategy Committee. She is a member of the Korn/Ferry International Audit Committee. In addition, MS. PERRY is a member of the advisory board of Bridge Associates LLC, a turnaround and crisis management firm. Since becoming a corporate director, MS. PERRY has been a frequent speaker on Audit Committee oversight and on crisis management on boards. She is a member of the National Association of Corporate Directors, the International Corporate Governance Network, The Economic Club of New York and Women Corporate Directors. MS. PERRY holds a BA (Phi Beta Kappa) from the University of Wisconsin-Madison and a graduate degree from Yale University where she completed all course work for a PhD in European history.

The Politics of Executive Pay

Ideology, not "social justice," fuels calls for restraints on executive compensation.

JERRY W. MARKHAM

Current liberal ideology seeks "social justice" through the appropriation and redistribution of wealth—usually from members of the business class. Though we associate such redistribution schemes with places like the former Soviet Union, China, Cuba, North Korea, and Zimbabwe, it has a lengthy history in the United States. For example, in 1777, a Pennsylvania constitutional convention considered, but rejected, a provision that stated: "That, an enormous Proportion of Property vested in a few individuals is dangerous to the Rights, and destructive of the Common Happiness, of mankind; and therefore every free State hath a Right by its Laws to discourage the possession of such Property."

Today, the demand for wealth redistribution comes clothed in populist appeals to the unfairness of the gross disparity between executive pay and that of the average worker. This claim resonates well in the press, but efforts to redistribute wealth through taxes, mandatory public disclosure, and corporate governance "reforms" have all failed. Nevertheless, compensation politics continues unabated, as demonstrated by the latest fight over the Bush tax cuts.

Redistribution by Taxation

Liberals (in the American political sense) have long viewed disproportionate taxation as a "fair" way to redistribute the wealth of U.S. businessmen. The "progressive" income tax is based on an ability-to-pay principle—that is, the wealthy's higher income is reason enough for their being assessed higher tax rates.

Unsurprisingly, the wealthy have proved unwilling to part with their wealth and can avoid the worst effects of disproportionate taxes through various tax shelters. Anticipating the Laffer curve theory that lowering taxes can actually generate more revenue for government,

then-secretary of the treasury Andrew Mellon convinced Congress in the 1920s to lower the top income tax rate on investment income from 65 percent to 24 percent. Despite the cut, Mellon was able to reduce the national deficit.

Mellon's tax cutting efforts were cut short by the Great Depression, a period in which both political parties abandoned his common sense approach to taxation. President Herbert Hoover imposed a "temporary" increase in the top income tax rate to 63 percent in 1932. Revenues from the income tax promptly fell by about 50 percent. Calling businessmen a "stupid class," Franklin Roosevelt proclaimed that the American public wanted "their fair share in the distribution of the national wealth." He sought to give it to them through such legislation as the Revenue Wealth Tax Act of 1935, which raised the top marginal income tax rate on individuals to 75 percent. However, that and other punitive legislation directed against businessmen only served to worsen the economic situation during the Great Depression, as capital went into hiding. There was simply no incentive for businessmen to take risks when they would have to bear all of the losses and give the government most of the profits.

The highest marginal tax rate for individuals was raised to 94 percent during World War II, and the adoption of an "estate tax" applied another 50 percent tax on earnings that had already been taxed as income. Nevertheless, the wealthy continued to fight this wealth confiscation effort through various tax avoidance and evasion schemes. Indeed, higher taxes actually encouraged the preservation of wealth, rather than its redistribution. Before the estate tax, the successful formula for wealth redistribution in the United States was tried and true: "From rags to riches and back to rags again in three generations." Tax-motivated trusts, however, not only avoided the estate tax, but also derailed the rags-to-riches-to-rags natural order of wealth redistribution. Those trusts placed family wealth in the hands of professional money managers who could prevent it from being squandered by the third generation. Hence, the Kennedy and Rockefeller dynasties put trust fund babies into high offices and concentrated wealth for generations.

President Harry Truman reduced the marginal tax rates on individuals to 86.45 percent, tax rates on corporate earnings were cut from 90 percent to 38 percent, and tax revenues increased. President John F. Kennedy, himself a trust fund baby, lowered the top income tax rate during his administration to 70 percent. He contended that lower rates would reduce the motivation for engaging in tax evasion. Interestingly, Republican lawmakers opposed Kennedy's legislation because they believed lowering tax rates would increase the government deficit. Still, the high rate continued to provide a strong motive for tax avoidance, which became a cottage industry of oil depletion allowances, leveraged limited partnerships, and other schemes.

The Alternate Minimum Tax was another failed attempt at wealth redistribution. Congress enacted the AMT after it was revealed that 21 millionaires had paid not a single cent in income tax in 1967 because of various tax avoidance schemes. However, the AMT had little effect on wealth distribution. Instead, it is now increasingly falling on the middle class, as inflation sweeps more and more households into its arms.

President Ronald Reagan successfully launched a counter revolution against high marginal tax rates. He embraced "supply side" economics, which posits that reduced taxes spur economic growth. Reagan was able to convince Congress to slash income taxes on both individuals and corporations. Economic prosperity followed, and tax cutting thereafter became a centerpiece of Republican politics.

Reagan's successor, George H. W. Bush, learned the hard way that deviating from this Republican ideology can be costly. After he broke his "Read my lips" campaign pledge not to raise taxes, he lost the enthusiasm and support of many of his supporters, and ultimately his 1992 reelection bid.

His successor, Bill Clinton, then raised taxes. Clinton's action touched off a debate over whether taxes inhibit economic growth, because the economy boomed after the tax increase. Critics claim that the tax increase was, nonetheless, inhibiting because economic growth accelerated further after Congress enacted (minor) tax cuts during Clinton's second term. That accelerated growth came at a time when business cycles normally experience a slowing economy.

Bush Tax Cuts

In any event, George W. Bush took his father's loss to heart and promised tax reductions in his 2000 presidential campaign. Once in office, he convinced Congress to make significant tax reductions at all income levels, including those of the wealthiest. Capital gains and stock dividend taxes were reduced and the estate tax was phased out over a 10-year period. There was just one wrinkle in this program: it came with an expiration date of December 31, 2010.

"Bush tax cuts" became a term of derision and distaste for liberals because Bush had undercut their wealth redistribution efforts. Repealing the Bush tax cuts for the wealthy (those making over $250,000) became a centerpiece of the Democratic presidential campaign in 2008. As candidate Barack Obama told one skeptical voter (Joe "the Plumber" Wurzelbacher), Obama intended to "spread the wealth around" when he became president by raising taxes on the wealthy.

Candidate Obama also promised to increase capital gains taxes "for purposes of fairness," even though it was pointed out to him that the last two cuts in capital gains taxes had actually increased tax revenues. But it is unclear how increased rates would be fairer. The wealthy already bear the lion's share of the tax burden. The top 1 percent of earners received some 20 percent of income in 2007, but paid almost 40 percent of all income taxes; the top 5 percent of earners paid 60 percent of those taxes; the top 10 percent paid nearly 70 percent and the top 50 percent paid all but 3 percent of income taxes. This meant that nearly 50 percent of households paid no federal income tax.

Obama's wealth redistribution views were extreme, but he nonetheless won the White House. The repeal of the Bush tax cuts for the wealthy then seemed assured, since the Democrats also controlled both houses of Congress—but fate intervened. The Obama administration lost popularity before it could end the Bush tax cuts. The Tea Party-fueled victories by Republicans in the 2010 midterm elections forced the president to agree to extend the Bush tax cuts for two years and to reinstate the estate tax at a rate of only 35 percent, with an exemption for estates below $5 million. Although the Republicans won that fight, the timing of the expiration of those cuts will, undoubtedly, make them an important issue in the 2012 presidential election.

At the state level, there is also strong interest in increasing taxes on the wealthy, even though states that have done so have received much less revenue from the higher taxes than they expected. Oregon, for example, raised taxes on the wealthy in 2009, but received one-third less in revenue than was projected. The same phenomenon was observed in Maryland and California. Perhaps not coincidentally, the 2010 Census also showed a shift of population away from the high-tax states over the last 10 years, which portends an increase in Republican House seats.

Corporate Governance Reforms

Taxation is not the only arrow in the liberal quiver for wealth redistribution. Another arrow is attacking high executive compensation, under the questionable theory that reducing such compensation will mean higher wages for workers. These attacks have been disguised by the claim that restraining compensation would be good corporate governance reform.

Initially, it was claimed that high executive compensation constitutes a breach of the fiduciary duties owed by a corporation's managers to stockholders. The high-water mark for this theory was the 1933 Supreme Court decision in *Rogers v. Hill,* involving a compensation scheme at the American Tobacco Company that provided its president with compensation of over $1 million in 1930. The Supreme Court held that, at some point, excessive corporate compensation could constitute a waste of corporate assets in breach of the manager's fiduciary duties. However, the court offered no guidelines for determining at what point that breach occurs. The case was settled on remand with few changes, and a state court threw out a companion case because the court had no means of determining whether the compensation was excessive.

Fiduciary duty claims brought against executives at other companies were also unsuccessful. Those setbacks led Cornell law professor George T. Washington to conclude in the *Harvard Law Review* in 1941 that the courts had decided to leave the issue of the reasonableness of executive compensation to the judgment of the corporate board of directors. Washington's claim lay virtually uncontested until this century when shareholders of the Walt Disney Co. filed suit demanding that the courts stop what they claimed was an instance of excessive compensation. The lawsuit charged a breach of fiduciary duties when the Disney Board authorized a mind-boggling $130 million severance package for deposed Disney president Michael Ovitz. Although Ovitz had served only 14 unproductive months at Disney before being fired, the Delaware Supreme Court could find no breach of fiduciary duty. This will probably quiet attacks on executive compensation through fiduciary duty claims for a time, but—like wealth taxes—the issue will undoubtedly resurface in future decades.

Mandatory Disclosure

Another tax-the-rich scheme disguised as corporate governance reform is the requirement for "full disclosure" of executive compensation under the federal securities laws. The theory behind this requirement is that executives will eschew high compensation because they would be shamed by its public disclosure.

Ironically, this theory seems to have backfired on its proponents. Instead of being shamed, executives appear to relish having their compensation reported and to compete with each other over who gets the best deal. What shame they do experience seems to occur when they are topped by a competitor. Instead of reducing compensation, the disclosure requirement seems to have set off an "arms race" of spiraling executive compensation.

> **"Full disclosure" requirements appear to have backfired. Instead of being shamed, executives seem to relish having their compensation reported and to compete with each other over who gets the better deal.**

In 1992, the Securities and Exchange Commission substantially increased its executive compensation disclosure requirements. The result was that, by 2006, executive compensation had quadrupled. Incomprehensively, this caused the SEC to further increase its disclosure requirements. Executive compensation then continued to rise until the subprime crisis resulted in a somewhat minor decline in the overall level of executive pay.

Incentive Pay

Another effort to redistribute wealth was a proposal to require that executive pay be "aligned" with the interests of shareholders by basing most executive compensation on grants of options on company stock. It was theorized that this would give executives an incentive to increase their firm's share price, which would benefit shareholders as well as the executives. Congress assisted in this effort through a provision in the Omnibus Revenue Reconciliation Act of 1993 that limited the deductibility of corporate salaries (nonincentive pay) to $1 million, but placed no such limits on incentive pay in the form of stock options. A chairman of the SEC later ruefully remarked that this change in the tax laws "deserves pride of place in the Museum of Unintended Consequences."

Instead of a ceiling, the $1 million tax deduction limitation became the corporate executive's "minimum wage." Moreover, rather than curbing executive pay, options bestowed incredible amounts of wealth on executives as the stock market boomed in the 1990s. Another unintended consequence was that option-based compensation spurred management to manipulate company accounts in order to increase their company's stock price. Those machinations unraveled when the economy slowed in 2001. The resulting accounting scandals were legendary and included the bankruptcies of the energy firm Enron and the telecommunications firm WorldCom, where top executives had received hundreds of millions of dollars in options-based compensation.

The congressional response to the scandals was the Sarbanes-Oxley Act of 2002, which imposed much costly and unnecessary regulation on public companies and their managers. Not surprisingly, that legislation did nothing to halt the rise in executive compensation. It also did nothing to prevent or deter the scandals associated with executive compensation that arose during the subprime crisis.

Criminalizing Executive Compensation

Another response to the options-related accounting scandals was the high-profile criminal prosecutions of executives receiving large compensation packages, including Jeffrey Skilling at Enron and Bernie Ebbers at WorldCom. Those prosecutions exposed the dark side of compensation politics, as prosecutors and the press demonized the executives for the compensation they received. Those attacks prejudiced juries and were used to justify draconian prison sentences, which often exceeded those typically given to murderers and serial child molesters.

Prosecutors also employed some unseemly tactics to obtain convictions of business executives and to coerce them into guilty pleas. Executives were arrested in dawn raids and given a public pillorying through a "perp walk" in which they were shackled and paraded before the press. More charges were piled on if the executive refused to enter a guilty plea. Family members were threatened, and even indicted, in order to coerce guilty pleas. Prosecutors intimidated defense witnesses to discourage them from testifying by sending them so-called "target letters." The government also employed a convoluted legal theory under the mail and wire fraud statutes to obtain numerous executive convictions that were subsequently set aside by the Supreme Court.

Companies employing indicted executives were threatened with destruction by indictment if they did not "cooperate" with prosecutors. This meant that, in order to survive, public companies had to waive their attorney-client privilege. Prosecutors also illegally demanded that the companies cut off attorney fees for executives, even though they were required to pay those fees by law or contract. The companies were required to enter into "deferred prosecution" agreements in which they were allowed to escape indictment only after paying massive fines, making forced confessions worthy of a Stalinist show trial, and agreeing to the force hiring of former prosecutors and government officials as high-paid "corporate monitors."

The result of this criminalization of executive pay was a vast waste of government resources, enormous expenses to shareholders, and a disquieting loss of integrity on the part of prosecutors during the Bush administration. The Obama administration has continued this policy, but the acquittal of the managers of the failed Bear Stearns' hedge funds has made it more cautious. Nevertheless, pressure continues to mount in the press for more show trial prosecutions of executives at institutions that failed during the subprime crisis.

Proxy Reforms

Another corporate governance reform involves the use of SEC proxy rules. The rules require corporate managers to submit proposals from even small shareholders to a shareholder vote at the annual meeting. However, SEC rules contain a number of exemptions from the requirement, including the exclusion of proposals that would violate state law. That exemption was used historically to block shareholder votes on executive pay because state laws vest the board of directors with discretion to set executive pay, rather than shareholders.

In order to avoid this roadblock, corporate reformers demanded an "advisory" vote on executive compensation that would not violate state law because it was not binding on the board. The SEC adopted amendments to its rules to authorize such votes; Congress required such votes for firms receiving bailout funds under the 2008 Troubled Assets Relief Program, and the Dodd-Frank Act of 2010 endorsed that requirement. Several such "say-on-pay" votes have been conducted, but the results were generally supportive of management, thereby endorsing the very pay attacked by the proponents of the vote.

Board of Director Reforms

The next stop for the corporate reformers was to seek representation on corporate boards of directors where executives and their pay could be attacked directly. Historically, nominations for election to corporate boards were made through nominating committees selected, directly or indirectly, by the corporation's executives. Dissidents could wage a proxy fight to elect their own representatives, but such fights were enormously expensive and management was likely to prevail.

To avoid that obstacle, corporate reformers sought a change in SEC rules to require companies to include dissident nominations in company proxy materials at the company's expense. The SEC had previously rejected such a proposal in 1942, after a group of congressmen criticized it as being "communist" in nature. A similar proposal was rejected in 1992.

However, there has occurred a subtle, but revolutionary, change in shareholder activism as a result of pressures from labor unions and their pension funds. Union pension funds are now some of the largest institutional investors and their diversified holdings include most public companies. Unlike other passive institutional investors, union pension funds seek to actively manage companies in which they invest.

Congress gave a boost to the activist role of the union pension funds in 1995 through legislation that changed the manner in which the lead plaintiffs in class action lawsuits were selected. Specifically, the legislation changed the selection process from first-suit-filed to the plaintiff with the greatest stake in the litigation. The union pension funds usually had the largest stake, and they sought the lead plaintiff role in order to harass management and improve their returns. Today, any corporate setback will immediately be the target of a class action lawsuit led by a union pension fund. That harassment has proved to be costly to other shareholders, as the size and number of settlements ballooned in the union-directed class actions, to the detriment of other shareholders.

Today, any corporate setback will immediately be the target of a class action lawsuit led by a union pension fund. That harassment has proved to be costly to other shareholders.

The unions also seek to actively manage the entire spectrum of public companies through the SEC's proxy rules. Historically, most shareholders followed the "Wall Street rule," which posited that if you did not like management, you simply voted with your feet by selling the stock rather than cast a negative proxy vote. The unions sought to reverse the Wall Street rule and actively manage corporations through changes in the SEC's proxy rules. This was done in three steps:

First, the unions and other "reformers" convinced the SEC to require institutional investors to disclose their proxy vote policies and to adopt policies that would assure their proxy votes are in the best interest of their clients. Those institutions have no interest in managing the companies in which they invest. Therefore, in order to satisfy the SEC rule, many of those institutions delegated their proxy votes to the discretion of a group of corporate governance firms with questionable motivations and which are allied with the unions.

Second, the unions and other corporate governance advocates convinced the SEC to approve a change in stock exchange rules that prohibits broker-dealers from voting the shares of their non-objecting customers in board elections. Previously, because retail investors rarely voted their own proxies, their broker-dealers were allowed to act as the customers' proxy. The broker-dealers cast the vote of non-objecting shareholders in board elections for management-supported nominees. However, this rule change has now sidelined those votes.

Third, the SEC changed its proxy rules to allow the unions to nominate their own candidates for board elections in company proxies. The authority to impose that requirement was confirmed by the Dodd-Frank Act of 2010 and by a change in Delaware law. The SEC rule change seems to be specially designed for the union pension funds because it is limited to shareholders holding at least 3 percent of the company's stock for at least three years. Only time will tell how successful this union strategy will be or how much damage will be done to U.S. businesses as union board representatives seek to push corporate policy away from profits, toward other goals.

Risk Management

Another focus for compensation politics in recent years has been risk management. During the subprime crisis, an outcry arose over claims that executives were receiving bonuses that induced them to take excessive risks. That claim found its way into the TARP legislation, which established a "pay czar" to monitor executive compensation at bailed-out firms. The Dodd-Frank Act of 2010 also requires regulators to prohibit any bonus arrangement at financial services firms that "encourages inappropriate risks." Financial service regulators are now considering proposals to regulate bank bonuses so that they do not encourage such risk.

This latest assault on executive compensation raises a number of issues. For example, it was never shown that bonuses encouraged excessive risks. To the contrary, the banks were not seeking excessive risks through their subprime activities. They sold off the riskier tranches of the collateralized debt obligations that securitized the subprime mortgages that were of concern during the crisis. The massive asset write-downs of the large financial service firms during the crisis were mostly associated with the investment-grade tranches of the CDOs they retained on their books, including many that were rated AAA, just like federal government bonds. Federal regulators even allowed special treatment of those securities under bank capital requirements. It is, therefore, hard to claim that the banks were excessive risk takers.

More troubling is the thought that the government should regulate the proper level of risk incurred by a private company. Business is all about incurring risk. The amount of risk incurred will measure the success or failure of an enterprise—"no risk, no reward."

The unintended consequences of risk avoidance pressures could be serious. For example, if excessive business risk is to be avoided, pharmaceutical companies must stop their quest for new drugs to cure cancer or other deadly or debilitating diseases. Most such research will prove futile, and billions of dollars will be lost in the process. However, is that risk not worth the rewards of finding a successful drug that saves lives or eases suffering?

Compensation Politics

Interestingly, concerns about income inequality tend to focus on the compensation of executives, and not on the multi-millions earned by top entertainers and athletes. For instance, a December 26, 2010 *New York Times* article dismissed the outsize payments received by performers as being merely the product of technological innovations that enable performers to appear before larger audiences. Without pausing for breath, the article then launched an extended assault on increases in executive compensation, which it blamed on deregulation by the Reagan administration.

Congress and the SEC have made no effort to curb the pay of entertainers and athletes. Indeed, the SEC exempts the salaries of entertainers and athletes from its mandatory disclosure requirements in what has come to be known as the "Katie Couric" exemption. Yet, some of those payouts are astronomical. The average salary of an actor/performer is less than $50,000, but Oprah Winfrey has made at least $1 billion from her television talk show, shock jock Howard Sterns was paid nearly $600 million to move his talk show to satellite radio, and George Lucas recently made nearly $300 million in a single year without having to put out a new episode of *Star Wars*. The average salary in Major League Baseball is around $3.2 million; the average salary for a player in the NBA is over $5.3 million. Where is the outrage over those large payouts?

There are other unremarked-upon wealth disparities. Some authors become millionaires, or even billionaires in the case of J.K. Rowling, but most authors receive a pittance in royalties. Yet, no one is demanding that high-earning authors redistribute their earnings to those less successful. It is also notable that wide pay disparities exist in intellectual fields. University presidents and directors of elite museums and performing arts centers receive annual salaries in excess of $1 million, while the average income of a person holding a doctorate degree is less than $85,000 and most K–12 teachers earn under $60,000. Despite his paper's advocacy of social justice, *New York Times* publisher Arthur Sulzberger Jr. was paid over $10 million between 2006 and 2008, while the average pay of a reporter on that newspaper was around $85,000.

Conclusion

The dream of wealth redistribution from the business class was a disaster under the harsh lash of communist ideology. It has also failed to date under the modern doctrine of "social justice." Despite all the efforts of the wealth redistribution crowd, the concentration of wealth in the United States is now at the highest level since 1929. Nevertheless, the fight continues.

Critical Thinking

1. Why has executive pay become such a political issue?
2. Is executive compensation out of control?
3. Do top executives really earn their money, or are they just in the right place at the right time?
4. How would you measure their effectiveness?

JERRY W. MARKHAM is professor of law at Florida International University's College of Law.

From *Regulation*, Spring 2011, pp. 38–43 . Copyright © 2011 by Cato Institute. Reprinted by permission via Copyright Clearance Center.

Putting the Hurt On

OSHA enforcement is muscling up: Here's what you can do about it.

JONATHAN L. SNARE

Every April 28, Organized Labor Celebrates Workers' Memorial Day to honor workers harmed by job-site hazards and to commemorate the founding of the Occupational Safety and Health Administration. This year, workers' groups will celebrate a reinvigorated OSHA under new leadership committed to restoring the agency to what they believe is its rightful regulatory and enforcement stature.

Anyone who doubts the pro-enforcement mind-set of the new OSHA should consider a reference to New York's Triangle Shirtwaist Factory fire in a recent press release announcing a $230,000 citation against an employer with blocked exits at a retail location. Many employers might not see a true parallel between a situation that resulted in no deaths and the March 25, 1911, Triangle fire, in which 146 workers, mostly young immigrant women, died because the exits from their workplace were locked. (Triangle's owners were acquitted at trial.)

Yet, Dr. David Michaels, OSHA's new director and a former professor of occupational and environmental health, chose to draw a rhetorical and moral parallel—and back it up with a sizable fine, stating that "Blocked fire exits can be deadly. It is that simple." Asked about the release announcing the citation, Michaels replied that "regulation by shaming" can be "very effective."

> **When asked about a $230,000 citation for blocked exits at a retail location, OSHA director Dr. David Michaels said that "regulation by shaming" can be "very effective."**

Where shaming falls short, there is pending legislation in Congress. The Protecting America's Workers Act (H.R. 2067; S. 1580), if adopted, will significantly increase OSHA's punitive powers. PAW's provisions include raising the criminal penalty from a misdemeanor to a felony for a willful violation involving a fatality, and extending individual criminal liability to "any responsible corporate officer," as well as significantly raising OSHA's civil penalties.

What can you do to ensure that your company institutes best practices to safeguard itself from the sting of stepped-up OSHA enforcement? Several practical suggestions appear below. But first, some particulars as to what your company is going to be up against.

The aggressive, pro-labor agenda that is unfolding at OSHA is expected to have major consequences for employers beginning this year. Under Michaels, the agency is committed to more aggressively enforcing existing workplace standards with more inspections, more high-penalty citations for egregious violations, fewer unclassified settlements, and expanded use of the general duty clause in ergonomics and other areas. The newly reenergized OSHA is also intent on significantly scaling back compliance assistance and cooperative programs, and imposing new standards and requirements for employers through changes to OSHA's regulatory agenda.

Looking ahead, counsel for employers should expect to see all of the following: more enforcement, more inspections, and more citations for alleged misconduct.

To accomplish all this, OSHA is being beefed up by the Obama administration. OSHA's 2010 budget of $558 million is up nearly 12 percent, and the agency is already in the process of hiring up to 120 new enforcement personnel to dramatically boost work-site inspections. Last fall, just as the agency was levying the largest fine in its history (quadrupling the previous record), OSHA also expanded the use of its egregious violations policy to raise penalties. It issued seven of these egregious citations in the first quarter of fiscal 2010, compared with four in all of 2009.

The agency has also embarked on a historic departure from permitting willful citations in fatality cases to be reduced to Section 17 unclassified citations or settled. It will likely further constrict its use of settlements and the unclassified citations policy.

In addition, OSHA is expected to issue repeat citations for violations at multiple facilities of a single employer, and also to expand the use of repeat citations in performance standards such as the Process Safety Management Standard.

The agency is also on track to revise its EEP (Enhanced Enforcement Program). It plans to transform EEP into a Severe Violators Enforcement Program (SVEP) for employers with three or more willful or repeat violations, or those who experience fatalities or catastrophes. The biggest area of concern is that it could be much easier to be placed in this program and much harder to get out.

Finally, employers should watch out for expanded and new national, regional, and local emphasis programs. Reflecting OSHA leadership's belief that workplace injuries are significantly underreported, the agency has already announced a new National Emphasis Program to investigate the accuracy of employer reporting in certain high-hazard industries.

A nother looming cause for concern is a decrease in cooperation by the agency. In a departure from standing policy for 30 years, OSHA has begun to reduce the size and scope of its cooperative compliance programs. As a first step, OSHA announced a suspension of annual goal-setting for new Voluntary Protection Plan sites by its regional offices.

The agency has also announced its intent to revise exemptions from enforcement for (mainly) small employers in its consultation program in a new rule to be issued by August 2010. Employers who have been awarded Safety and Health Achievement Recognition Program status exemptions based on recent inspections will be included under that new rule.

There are some specific areas of activity to be especially vigilant about, and ergonomics heads the list. Michaels has often stated that musculoskeletal injuries and disorders (MSDs) are the largest source of injury and illness in the workplace, and that workplace injuries are significantly underreported. This has given rise to major concern among a broad swath of employers that a renewed focus by OSHA on ergonomics could be imminent.

In the past, Michaels has advocated broader use of the general duty clause where there is no existing OSHA standard in place (such as in ergonomics), partly to get around rule-making constraints. Whenever a hazard is serious and there are recognized measures to mitigate it, Michaels has stated that the agency doesn't need a new standard, but should use the general duty clause. The agency has already initiated rule-making to add a column to the OSHA 300 log for reporting MSDs. (The 300 logs are used to compile records of work-related injuries.)

Industrial workplaces and construction work are additional areas in which we should expect to see increased activity. During his nomination review, Dr. Michaels told the Senate Committee on Health, Education, Labor, and Pensions that instituting new rule-making on combustible dust was among his regulatory priorities. His other primary goals included speeding up rule-making with regard to beryllium, silica, cranes, and derricks, and also updating OSHA's hazard communication standard with a globally harmonized system.

Michaels is expected to add items to this agenda, creating new safety requirements. His past public testimony and writings suggest that he would also support a new comprehensive work place safety and health program standard as well as a comprehensive standard to cover many additional hazardous chemicals the agency does not currently regulate.

There's no need to give in to the gloom and doom outlined above. There are several prudent and proactive steps you can take to minimize the pain your company is likely to confront in dealing with the newly energized OSHA:

There are several steps you can take to MINIMIZE THE PAIN your company may confront in dealing with the newly energized OSHA.

- Ensure that your record-keeping is in order and that injuries and illnesses are reported accurately in OSHA 300 logs. Take necessary steps to train your employees who are responsible for OSHA record-keeping. Consider regular and random privileged audits conducted by inside or outside counsel to identify errors and take corrective action.
- Evaluate your safety incentive programs to ensure that they do not discourage employees from reporting injuries and illnesses.
- Take seriously the likelihood of OSHA inspections and citations at multiple facilities, and be prepared to take advantage of OSHA's new corporatewide settlement policy expected later this year.
- Be aware of national, regional, and local emphasis programs applicable to every facility, including locations impacted by OSHA state plans.
- Consider audits for specific issues and areas of potential concern to identify any vulnerability before OSHA inspectors arrive. If you have a significant OSHA citation history or may be the target under any emphasis programs, be particularly careful and take the necessary steps, including audits, to ensure that you are in full compliance.
- Prepare an inspection protocol designating staff in your organization responsible for dealing with OSHA, and make sure you are fully aware of your rights and responsibilities in the event that the agency pays a visit.
- If you receive an OSHA citation, exercise care in negotiating a settlement to minimize repeat, willful, and SVEP consequences. Consider using OSHA's new corporate settlement policy once it is released to the public.
- If you receive an OSHA citation, prepare for reinspections to verify abatement of the cited hazard.

We could hear a lot about The Protecting America's Workers Act this April 28. And if those driving the new OSHA agenda get their way, we may find that critical provisions of the bill have passed into law by Workers' Memorial Day 2011. You, and your company, should take steps now to make sure you are prepared for ramped-up OSHA enforcement and regulatory activity in the months and years ahead.

Critical Thinking

1. What is the role of the Occupational Health and Safety Administration?
2. How is OSHA implementing this role?
3. What does this mean for organizations?
4. How can these organizations deal with this new enhanced enforcement policy?

JONATHAN L. SNARE, a partner in the Washington, D.C., office of Morgan, Lewis & Bockius, served as acting assistant secretary of Labor for OSHA from January 2005 to April 2006, and as deputy assistant secretary for OSHA from December 2004 to July 2006.

Workplace Bullying Threatens Employers

Judy Greenwald

Employers should prepare for a flood of litigation if states approve legislation making it easier for employees to sue over workplace bullying, observers warn.

Anti-bullying bills were approved by the senates of the New York and Illinois legislatures this year, but the legislation stalled in their respective houses.

Observers expect, however, that anti-workplace bullying legislation will be reintroduced next year in those states and elsewhere, and some say eventual passage is likely.

Bullied workers can use existing laws to sue their employers under various causes of action, including sexual, gender, religious and disability discrimination laws. In addition, they can seek relief under federal Occupational Safety and Health Administration regulations. But, the legislation's proponents say, these laws still exclude many, if not most, instances of workplace bullying.

Opponents to the legislation, however, say the term bullying often is vaguely defined and could be inappropriately applied to a variety of behavior, including a lost temper or justifiable terminations or reprimands.

Workplace bullying is widespread, according to a widely quoted 2007 survey by Utica, N.Y.-based market research firm Zogby International, which was commissioned by the Bellingham, Wash.-based Workplace Bullying Institute. According to the survey, 37% of workers have been bullied, 72% of bullies are bosses and 62% of employers ignore the problem.

David C. Yamada, a professor at Suffolk University Law School and director of the New Workplace Institute, both in Boston, said most anti-bullying legislation, including the measures that failed to win passage in New York and Illinois, are based on a model he originally developed in 2002 called the Healthy Workplace Act, which has been updated several times since.

Many observers expect eventual passage of anti-bullying legislation in some states. Legislation is expected to be introduced in at least a dozen states next year, said Gary Namie, the Workplace Bullying Institute's co-founder and a supporter of the legislation.

"I think we're on the precipice of success," said Mr. Yamada. "We seem to be getting closer to eventual passage. I think it is just a matter of time."

"I think it's inevitable," said Robert Nobile, a partner with law firm Seyfarth Shaw L.L.P. in New York, noting several European countries already have anti-bullying laws.

Anti-bullying legislation has been defeated four times in Oregon, but "it's a matter of time before there is a statute," said Tamsen L. Leachman, a partner with law firm Dunn Carney Allen Higgins & Tongue L.L.P. in Portland, Ore.

The publicity surrounding the January suicide of 15-year-old Phoebe Prince, who hanged herself after being bullied by classmates, may increase pressure for passage of anti-bullying laws, say some observers.

A major court decision in this area was a 2008 opinion by the Indiana Supreme Court in *Daniel H. Raess, M.D. vs. Joseph E. Doescher* in which the court upheld a $325,000 jury verdict for an assault claim brought by Mr. Doescher.

The case involves a 2001 incident, in which Dr. Raess, a cardiovascular surgeon, became angry at Mr. Doescher, who runs an operating room heart/lung machine, causing Mr. Doescher to back up against a wall and raise his hands in defense, according to court documents.

"The legal issues in that case are mostly procedural and evidentiary, so they don't really establish any broad precedent in terms of bringing bullying-related claims," said Mr. Yamada, who believes this issue must be addressed through legislation rather than the court system.

Some observers believe, though, that there is no need for such legislation. "There are already existing laws that cover virtually every instance of workplace bullying if it's severe and intentional and consistent enough, including discrimination laws and OSHA regulations," said John S. Ho, an attorney with law firm Bond, Schoeneck & King P.L.L.C. in New York.

However, Seyfarth Shaw's Mr. Nobile said there is a gap in these existing laws. "They don't cover conduct that is not based on one's status in a protected group or class so, in effect, this type of legislation fills that gap if there is abusive treatment by a supervisor," said Mr. Nobile, who believes, though, that the issue can be controlled through the use of effective employer practices and training.

Many observers believe passage of anti-bullying legislation will lead to increased litigation against employers. Anti-bullying legislation could open the floodgates to litigation against employers "because every mean boss could create liability for a company," said Susan K. Lessack, a partner with law firm Pepper Hamilton L.L.P. in Berwyn, Pa.

D. Michael Reilly, a shareholder with the law firm Lane Powell P.C. in Seattle, said his concern is "the definition of bullying is not real clear, and because there is not a lot of case law" defining it, it's going to be tough for employers to know how to comply with the law. It will probably be a paradise for many people who would like to sue because it would be tough to get these cases resolved short of a full-blown trial."

An anti-bullying law will create a cause of action where one does not exist, said Garry G. Mathiason, a shareholder with the law firm Littler Mendelson P.C., San Francisco. Plaintiffs in such lawsuits may not win, but filing a lawsuit increases employers' costs, plus there is the potential cost of nuisance settlements, Mr. Mathiason said.

Jonathan T. Hyman, a partner with law firm Kohrman Jackson & Krantz P.L.L. in Cleveland, said such legislation also will hamstring employers because "they'll be afraid of being sued if they are being too harsh." It could result in employees having the potential to run the workplace because every petty slight or annoyance is going to be trumped up into this idea of bullying," he said.

Employers should prepare for possible legislation, say observers. Ms. Leachman said: "We're at the point where employers can choose to deal with this on their own terms, and not have a statute that mandates what they must do."

"Employers would be smart to review their harassment policies," said Mr. Ho. "A good harassment policy is not going to be limited to just sexual harassment," he said. And if a law eventually is passed, "you would have to specifically create a workplace bullying policy. What it looks like will obviously depend on the law as written," he said.

Critical Thinking

1. Have you seen examples of bullying in the workplace?
2. Do you think it is important to stop bullying in the workplace?
3. Will state governments pass legislation prohibiting bullying in the workplace?
4. How do you think these new laws, if passed, will be enforced?

Demystifying Health Reform Legislation

James C. Pyles

In March 2010, President Obama signed into law the most sweeping health care reform legislation in the nation's history. Those laws, entitled the "Patient Protection and Affordable Care Act," Public Law 111–148, and the "Health Care and Education Reconciliation Act," H.R. 4872, will be referred to collectively as PPACA, or the health reform legislation. This article is to provide you with an update on the status of implementation, the public's views with respect to the legislation, and the likely future of implementation.

The health reform legislation is likely to affect all mental health professionals throughout their lives, both as consumers and as practitioners of health care services. Many provisions of the new legislation remain to be implemented, and psychiatrists and psychoanalysts have been, and should continue to be, involved in shaping that implementation.

A Brief Overview

Generally, the health reform legislation provides for the following, implemented from 2010 through 2019:

- Prohibits health insurers from excluding enrollees because of a preexisting condition; prohibits insurers from rescinding coverage other than for fraud; requires insurers to renew insurance coverage; prohibits insurers from discriminating on the basis of health status, medical history, or genetic information; requires insurers to accept all employers or individuals in states that apply for coverage; and prohibits insurers from imposing lifetime or annual limits on payments(1)
- Requires insurers to pay a rebate to enrollees to the extent that payments for health care services are less than 80% of collected premiums in the small-group and individual market and 85% of collected premiums in the large-group market(2)
- Reduces the number of individuals without health insurance by 32 million to 34 million by adding 24 million who would obtain health insurance through state health insurance exchanges and 16 million who would obtain health insurance through Medicaid and the Children's Health Insurance Program (CHIP)(3)(p9),(4)(p3)

- Requires insurers to provide an "essential benefits" package that would have to include coverage for "mental health and substance use disorder services, including behavioral health treatment"(5)
- Requires insurers to provide "parity" in mental health coverage (6)
- Reduces the projected growth of Medicare by $577 billion (4)(p2)
- Increases the federal funding match for new Medicaid patients to 99% for 3 years, declining to 93% by the sixth year (4)(p4)
- Requires insurers to allow dependent children to remain on their parents' health insurance until age 26 (4)(p7)
- Cuts projected payments to Medicare Advantage (MA) plans (managed care) by $143 billion, thereby cutting MA enrollment by 50% by 2017 (4)(pp8,11)
- Would reduce the federal deficit by $143 billion (3)(p2)

Public Reaction

As of the end of the year, the public was roughly evenly divided with respect to whether it had a favorable or unfavorable opinion of the health reform legislation.

- Approximately 42% of Americans had favorable views of the health reform legislation, while 41% had unfavorable views. (7)(p1)
- The number of people withholding their opinion on the legislation has increased to 18%. (7)(p1)
- Three in 10 say they are angry about health reform, but 81% of those say their anger is at Washington in general rather than any specific provision of the reform legislation. (7)(p1)
- Three in 10 say they are enthusiastic about the law's passage. (7)(p1)
- What should the new Congress do about the health reform legislation? One in 5 wants to leave the law as it is, 1 in 5 wants to expand the law, 1 in 4 wants to repeal parts of the law and keep other parts, and 1 in 4 wants to repeal the law in its entirely. (7)(p2)
- What is the early impact of the law on individuals? 32% expect their family will be better off, 33% expect their

family will be worse off, and 28% do not anticipate any change. (7)(p3)

- Americans continue to have trouble paying for health care: 1 in 4 Americans says his or her household had trouble paying medical bills over the past year, 36% of those living in households with annual incomes of less than $40,000 and 48% of the uninsured had problems paying their medical bills over the past year, and 66% of low-income Americans and 85% of the uninsured have put off some sort of medical care because of cost. (7)(p5)

The Need for Health Reform

In December 2010, the Bipartisan Deficit Reduction Commission issued a report containing the following conclusions:

- Our nation is on an unsustainable fiscal path. Spending is rising and revenues are falling short, requiring the government to borrow huge sums each year to make up the difference. We face staggering deficits. In 2010, federal spending was nearly 24% of the gross domestic product (GDP), the value of all goods in the economy. Only during World War II was federal spending a larger part of the economy. (8)(p8)
- Over the long run, as the baby boomers retire and health care costs continue to grow, the situation will become far worse. By 2025, revenue will be able to finance only interest payments for Medicare, Medicaid, and Social Security. Every other federal government activity—from national defense and homeland security to transportation and energy—will have to be paid for with borrowed money. (8)(p9)
- Federal health care spending represents our single largest fiscal challenge over the long run. (8)(p31)

The legislation includes specific recommendations to reduce health care spending between now and 2020:

- Reduce Medicare payments to physicians (–$26 billion)
- Reform or repeal the Community Living Assistance Services and Support (CLASS) Act (–$76 billion)
- Increase funding to reduce Medicare fraud (–$9 billion)
- Reform (increase) Medicare cost sharing (–$110 billion)
- Restrict first-dollar coverage in Medicare supplemental insurance (–$38 billion)
- Extend drug rebates pharmaceutical companies are required to give Medicaid beneficiaries to beneficiaries eligible for both Medicaid and Medicare (–$49 billion)
- Reduce payments to hospitals for medical education (–$60 billion)
- Cut Medicare payments for bad debts (–$23 billion)
- Accelerate home health savings in health reform legislation (–$9 billion)
- Eliminate state gaming of Medicaid, which increases the federal funding match by increasing state taxes on hospitals (–$44 billion)
- Place dual eligibles in Medicaid managed care programs (–$12 billion)

- Reduce funding for Medicaid administrative costs (–$2 billion)
- Implement medical malpractice reform (–$17 billion)
- Pilot premium support through the Federal Employees Health Benefit Program–federal employees would get a fixed subsidy that would grow by no more than GDP plus 1% each year, to purchase insurance (–$18 billion)
- Implement payment reform pilots and demonstrations
- Eliminate provider carve-outs from the Independent Payment Advisory Board authority
- Establish a long-term global budget for total health care spending and limit growth to GDP plus 1% (8)(pp31–37)

Government Response

Congress. On January 5, the 112th Congress convened with the House in Republican control for the first time in 4 years and the Senate in Democratic control. (9) The change in control of the House from Democratic control to Republican control appears to have been based principally on public dissatisfaction with the status of the economy: "The economy was by far the most crucial issue. Nearly 9 in 10 said they were worried about the direction of the economy in the coming year, and a majority said the country was seriously on the wrong track. Those voters chose Republicans by large margins. About a quarter of voters said health care or the war in Afghanistan was the biggest concerns facing the country, and majorities of them favored Democrats . . . . " (10) House Majority Leader Eric Cantor (R-VA) introduced the "Repealing the Job-Killing Health Care Law Act" (H.R. 2) the health reform legislation in its entirety. It was scheduled for a vote in the House on January 12, but that vote was postponed indefinitely because of the shooting of Representative Giffords (D-AZ) and others on January 8.

It is expected that H.R. 2 will be approved by the House and not taken up by the Senate and would be vetoed by President Obama if it were to somehow pass the Senate. (11) House Republicans also plan to hold hearings and to try to withhold funding for specific provisions of the health reform legislation. (12)

On January 20, the House voted 245 to 189, generally along party lines, to approve H.R. 2 repealing the health reform legislation. On February 2, the Senate voted 51 to 47, again along party lines, to not adopt a bill repealing the health reform legislation.

On January 6, 2011, the nonpartisan Congressional Budget Office issued a letter to new Speaker of the House John Boehner (R-OH) providing a preliminary estimate of the effect of repealing the health reform legislation:

- It would increase federal deficits by "in the vicinity of $230 billion" between 2012 and 2021.
- It would increase federal deficits "in the decade after 2019 by an amount that is in a broad range around one-half percent of GDP."
- It would reduce the number of people who would have health insurance in 2019 by 32 million—"approximately 24 million people who would otherwise purchase their

own coverage through insurance exchanges would not do so, and Medicaid and the Children's Health Insurance Program would have roughly 16 million fewer enrollees."

- "Although premiums in the individual market would be lower, on average, under H.R. 2 than under the current law, many people would end up paying more for health insurance—because under current law, the majority of enrollees purchasing coverage in that market would receive subsidies via the insurance exchanges, and H.R. 2 would eliminate those subsidies."

- "Premiums for employment-based coverage obtained through large employers would be slightly higher under H.R. 2 than under current law . . . premiums for employment-based coverage obtained through small employers might be slightly higher or slightly lower. . . ." (13)

The Administration

The Obama administration appears to be committed to implementing as many of the health reform measures as possible in the next 2 years in the belief that measures that are already implemented will be difficult to repeal.

The Courts

There are 24 lawsuits pending in various courts across the country seeking to invalidate some aspect of the health reform legislation. (14) The allegations in these cases center around whether Congress has the authority under the "Commerce Clause" of the Constitution to require individuals to purchase health insurance or pay a tax under the individual mandate in the health reform legislation. (15) Article 1, section 8 of the Constitution authorizes Congress "to regulate Commerce . . . among the several states . . . ."

Four of these lawsuits have been decided–2 have upheld the constitutionality of the health reform law and 2 have found it unconstitutional. The federal district courts in Thomas More Law Center, et al v Barack Hussein Obama (16) and Liberty University, Inc. et al v Timothy Geithner, et al (17) both found that decisions by individuals to not purchase health insurance affect commerce among other citizens because the cost of their health care is then borne by those other citizens. The court in Commonwealth of Virginia, et al v Sebelius (18) found that neither the Supreme Court nor any Circuit Court has ever found that the Commerce Clause authorizes Congress to compel an individual to involuntarily enter the stream of commerce by purchasing a commodity in the private market. The court in State of Florida v US Department of Health and Human Services (HHS) (19) found that the individual mandate is not authorized under the Commerce Clause and invalidated the entire health reform legislation on the grounds that the unconstitutional provision was not severable from the rest of the legislation. That suit involved 26 states as plaintiffs because the status of the health reform legislation in those states is uncertain. This issue will likely have to be resolved by the Supreme Court.

Status of Health Reform Provisions

- High-risk insurance pools for individuals without insurance for 6 months and who have a preexisting condition (effective July 1, 2010, through January 1, 2014); more than 8000 people have enrolled (20,21)

- Federal reinsurance for early retirees age 55 or older but not eligible for Medicare (effective July 1, 2010, through January 1, 2014) (22)

- Elimination of lifetime limits on the dollar value of benefits and no "unreasonable" annual limits (23)

- No rescission of health plan or coverage other than in cases of fraud or intentional misrepresentation of a material fact (effective September 2010) (24)

- Health plans must provide coverage for and not impose cost sharing for preventive health services approved by the US Preventive Services Task Force (effective for private health plans in September 2010 and for Medicare January 1, 2011) (25)

- A plan that provides dependent coverage of children must make the coverage available to unmarried children until they turn 26 years of age (effective September 2010) (26)

- Health plans, including "grandfathered" plans cannot deny coverage to children on the basis of a preexisting condition (effective September 2010, applies to all persons in 2014) (27)

- HHS in conjunction with the states shall review health insurance premium increases to ensure that they are not "unreasonable" (for plan years beginning in 2010) (28)

- In 2010, Medicare beneficiaries will receive a $250 rebate on drugs that they pay for because they hit the "donut hole" in coverage under Part D of Medicare and will receive a 50% discount on such drugs beginning in 2011 (29)

- No exclusion of coverage on the basis of a preexisting condition (items 9-16 apply to health plans beginning on or after January 1, 2014) (30)

- Rating (price) of insurance premiums may be based only on whether the plan covers an individual or a family, the geographic rating area (to be established by the states), age (no more than 3 to 1), tobacco use (no more than 1.5 to 1) (31)

- Guaranteed acceptance of every employer and individual (32)

- Guaranteed renewability of coverage at the option of the plan sponsor or individual (33)

- Prohibition of discrimination in eligibility based on health status or medical history, including "medical condition (including both physical and mental illness)" (34)

- Prohibition of discrimination in participation against any provider acting within the scope of the provider's license or certification under state law (35)

- Insurers must offer coverage that includes the essential benefits package (36)
- Health plans in existence on the date of enactment do not have to comply with new insurance requirements, and nothing in the Act requires individuals to terminate that coverage (37)
- Requirements for "qualified health plans"
  - Contains the "essential benefits package," eg, coverage of mental health and substance use disorder services including behavioral health treatment (38)
  - Plans in the small-group market may have annual deductibles no higher than $2000 for an individual and $4000 for others; also limits on all cost sharing and premium adjustments (39)
  - Levels of coverage: bronze–coverage equivalent to 60% of full actuarial value of benefits; silver–coverage equivalent to 70% of full actuarial value of benefits; gold–coverage equivalent to 80% of full actuarial value of benefits; platinum–coverage equivalent to 90% of full actuarial value of benefits (40)
  - Mental health parity requirements apply (41)
- Tax credits for small business (no more than 25 full-time employees) of up to 50% of contributions to cost of health plan (42)
- Individual mandate: Beginning January 1, 2014, an individual will be liable for a penalty for any month in which the individual (and any dependents) do not have minimum essential health insurance in the amount of 1/12 of an "applicable dollar amount," which is $95 for 2014, $350 for 2015, and $695 thereafter, increased by the increase in the cost of living. For individuals under the age of 18, the amount is reduced by 50%. There are exceptions for individuals who cannot afford coverage, taxpayers with income below the filing threshold, members of Indian tribes, where coverage gaps are for less than 3 months and for hardships. The maximum penalty for any individual is the lesser of the sum of monthly penalties for a year or 300% of the "applicable dollar amount" for an individual. Minimum essential coverage is coverage under Medicare, Medicaid, CHIP, TRICARE, an employer-sponsored program, plans in the individual market, grandfathered plans, and other plans recognized by the Secretary of HHS. The penalty is payable on the individual's tax return. (43) Any taxpayer who fails to pay the penalty shall not be subject to any criminal prosecution and no lien shall be filed against his or her property.

Insurance Reforms Important to Mental Health Practitioners

- Mental health and substance use disorder services (including behavioral health treatment) in essential health benefits package. (44)
- Mental health parity required in coverage. (45)

- Medicaid coverage will be expanded to individuals at 133% of the federal poverty line (adding a projected 18 million individuals to the Medicaid rolls) and Medicaid coverage must include the essential benefits package (including mental health coverage) and mental health parity. (46)
  - Effective January 1, 2014: Federal funding match for "newly eligible individuals" is 100% for 2014, 2015, and 2016; 95% for 2017; 94% for 2018; 93% for 2019; and 90% for 2020 and thereafter.
- Beginning October 1, 2011, under the "Community First Choice Option," states may amend their Medicaid plans to provide home and community-based attendant services and supports for individuals whose income does not exceed 150% of the poverty level if the individuals require a level of care that but for this program, would be provided in a facility for the mentally retarded or an institution for mental disease. Covered services must be designed to assist the individual in accomplishing activities of daily living, instrumental activities of daily living (meal planning, managing finances, etc), and health-related tasks (those delegated or assigned by a licensed health care professional). The state may elect to also cover the costs (such as rent and transportation costs) necessary to allow an individual to make the transition to the home or community from an institution for mental illness or an intermediate care facility for the mentally retarded. As an incentive to adopt such options, the federal match for funding such programs is increased by 6%. (47)
- Beginning January 1, 2011, states may amend their Medicaid plans to add coverage for "health homes" for individuals with chronic conditions, which may include "1 serious and persistent mental condition." These services can be provided by a designated provider, a team of health care professionals operating with such a provider, or a health team that meets the requirements issued by the Secretary of HHS. The federal government will pay 90% of the costs of these programs for 2 years and provide $25 million to the states in planning grants. Nearly any entity can be approved by the state as a designated provider in this program. (48)

Regulations Specific to the Practice of Psychoanalysis

- A qualified health plan eligible to participate in a health insurance exchange "may contract with . . . "a health care provider *only* if such provider implements such mechanisms to improve health care quality as the Secretary may by regulation require (effective January 1, 2015)." (49) The Secretary may establish reasonable exceptions. (50)
- The Secretary cannot promulgate any regulation that creates any unreasonable barriers to the ability of

individuals to obtain appropriate medical care; impedes timely access to health care services; interferes with communications regarding a full range of treatment options between the patient and the provider; restricts the ability of health care providers to provide full disclosure of all relevant information to patients making health care decisions; violates the principles of informed consent and the ethical standards of health care professionals; or limits availability of health care treatment for the full duration of a patient's medical needs. (51)

- No individual, company, business, nonprofit entity, or health insurance issuer shall be required to participate in any federal health insurance plan created under the Act or any amendments to it or any such program expanded by the Act or any amendments. (52)

- A Patient-Centered Outcomes Research Institute is to be established to assist patients, clinicians, purchasers, and policy makers in making informed health decisions. The Secretary can only use the findings and recommendations of the Institute to make coverage determinations under Medicare if such use is "through an iterative and transparent process which includes public comment and considers the effect on subpopulations." None of the findings and recommendations of the Institute may be construed as "authorizing the Secretary to deny coverage of items or services under [Medicare] solely on the basis of comparative clinical effectiveness research. (53) Funding to be appropriated by Congress is the following: $10 million in fiscal 2010 increasing to $150 million in fiscal 2013 and thereafter.

References

1. Patient Protection and Affordable Care Act, 42 USC [section] 1001, [section] 1201 (2010).
2. Patient Protection and Affordable Care Act, 42 USC [section] 1001 (2010).
3. Congressional Budget Office letter. March 20, 2010.
4. CMS Office of the Actuary letter. April 22, 2010.
5. Patient Protection and Affordable Care Act, 42 USC [section] 1302(b)(1) (2010).
6. Patient Protection and Affordable Care Act, 42 USC [section] 1311(j) (2010).
7. Kaiser Family Foundation Health Tracking Poll. December 2010.
8. The National Commission on Fiscal Responsibility and Reform. The Moment of Truth. December 2010, p 8.
9. 112th Congress begins. The Hill. January 4, 2011. http://thehill.com/opinion/editorials/135979-112thcongress-begins. Accessed February 11, 2011.
10. Calmes J, Thee-Brenan M. Independents fueled GOP gains. New York Times. November 2, 2010. www.nytimes.com/2010/11/03/us/03exit.html. Accessed February 11, 2011.
11. Alonso-Zaldivar R. House takes symbolic step to repeal health law. Associated Press. January 7, 2011. http://news.yahoo.eom/s/ap/20110107/ap_on_re_us/us_health_care_repeal. Accessed February 11,2 011.
12. Pecquet J. CBO's repeal score throws GOP defunding strategy into question. The Hill. Healthwatch. January 10, 2011. http://thehill.com/blogs/healthwatch/health-reform-implementation/137065-cbos-repeal-score-throws-gop-deflmdingstrategy-into-question. Accessed February 11, 2011.
13. Letter from CBO to Speaker of the House, John Boehner. January 6, 2011.
14. Goldstein A. Status of legal challenges to Obama health care overhaul. Washington Post. December 15, 2010. www.washingtonpost.com/wp-srv/special/health-care-overhaul-lawsuits. Accessed February 11, 2011.
15. Patient Protection and Affordable Care Act, 42 USC [section] 1501 (2010).
16. Thomas More Law Center, et al v Barack Hussein Obama (SD Mich 2010).
17. Liberty University, Inc, et al v Timothy Geithner, et al (WD Va 2010).
18. Commonwealth of Virginia, et al v Sebelius (ED Va 2010).
19. State of Florida v US Department of Health and Human Services (ND Fla 2010).
20. Patient Protection and Affordable Care Act, 42 USC [section] 1101 (2010).
21. Kaiser Family Foundation, Health Reform Source. November 12, 2010.
22. Patient Protection and Affordable Care Act, 42 USC [section] 1102 (2010).
23. Patient Protection and Affordable Care Act, 42 USC [section] 1001 (2010), adding [section] 2711 of Public Health Services Act.
24. Patient Protection and Affordable Care Act, 42 USC [section] 1001 (2010), adding [section] 2712 of Public Health Services Act.
25. Patient Protection and Affordable Care Act, 42 USC [section] 1001 (2010), adding [section] 2713 of Public Health Services Act.
26. Patient Protection and Affordable Care Act, 42 USC [section] 1001 (2010), adding [section] 2714 of Public Health Services Act.
27. Patient Protection and Affordable Care Act, 42 USC [section] 1201 (2010), adding [section] 2704 of Public Health Services Act.
28. Patient Protection and Affordable Care Act, 42 USC [section] 1003 (2010), adding [section] 2794 of Public Health Services Act.
29. Patient Protection and Affordable Care Act, 42 USC [section] 3315 (2010).
30. Patient Protection and Affordable Care Act, 42 USC [section] 1201 (2010), adding [section] 2704 of Public Health Services Act.
31. Patient Protection and Affordable Care Act, 42 USC [section] 1201 (2010), adding [section] 2701 of Public Health Services Act.
32. Patient Protection and Affordable Care Act, 42 USC [section 2702 (2010).
33. Patient Protection and Affordable Care Act, 42 USC [section] 1201 (2010), adding [section] 2703 of Public Health Services Act.
34. Patient Protection and Affordable Care Act, 42 USC [section] 1201 (2010), adding [section] 2705 of Public Health Services Act.
35. Patient Protection and Affordable Care Act, 42 USC [section] 1201 (2010), adding [section] 2706 of Public Health Services Act.
36. Patient Protection and Affordable Care Act, 42 USC [section] 1201 (2010), adding [section] 2707 of Public Health Services Act.

37. Patient Protection and Affordable Care Act, 42 USC [section] 1251 (2010).

38. Patient Protection and Affordable Care Act, 42 USC [section] 1302 (2010).

39. Patient Protection and Affordable Care Act, 42 USC [section] 1302(c) (2010).

40. Patient Protection and Affordable Care Act, 42 USC [section] 1302(d) (2010).

41. Patient Protection and Affordable Care Act, 42 USC [section] 1311(j) (2010).

42. Patient Protection and Affordable Care Act, 42 USC [section] 1421 (2010).

43. Patient Protection and Affordable Care Act, 42 USC [section] 1501 (2010).

44. Patient Protection and Affordable Care Act, 42 USC [section] 1302(b)(1)(E) (2010).

45. Patient Protection and Affordable Care Act, 42 USC [section] 1311(j) (2010).

46. Patient Protection and Affordable Care Act, 42 USC [section] 2001 (2010).

47. Patient Protection and Affordable Care Act, 42 USC [section] 2401 (2010).

48. Patient Protection and Affordable Care Act, 42 USC [section] 2703 (2010).

49. Patient Protection and Affordable Care Act, 42 USC [section] 1311(h)(1)(B) (2010).

50. Patient Protection and Affordable Care Act, 42 USC [section] 1311(h)(2) (2010).

51. Patient Protection and Affordable Care Act, 42 USC [section] 1554 (2010).

52. Patient Protection and Affordable Care Act, 42 USC [section] 1555 (2010).

53. Patient Protection and Affordable Care Act, 42 USC [section] 6301 (2010).

Source Citation

Pyles, James C. "Demystifying health reform legislation." *Psychiatric Times* 28.3 (2011): 26. *General OneFile*. Web. 13 July 2011.

Critical Thinking

1. What are some of the major facts concerning the new health care bill?

2. How does the new health care bill change the current health care system?

3. Are these changes something that you would support?

JAMES C. PYLES is Washington Counsel for the American Psychoanalytic Association with the firm of Powers, Pyles, Sutter, and Verville, P.C., in Washington, DC.

Making Benefits Matter

We've all heard about it. from *NCB Nightly News* to *U.S. News & World Report* to *TIME* Magazine and beyond, the message has been consistent and it has been clear.

TORRY DELL

The "baby boomer" generation, born between the end of world War II and 1964, seventy-eight million strong, is retiring.

Demographics and Workforce Shortage

A pending wave of baby boomer retirements has been on the mind of many employers, and cooperative leadership is no exception. If you consider your own family and acquaintances, you'll probably notice that people are living longer and the population over sixty is growing. The Centers for Disease Control states that life expectancy is now 77.8 years, up from 77 just ten years ago. In 2006, the U.S. Census Bureau reported that almost eight thousand people a day—or about 330 an hour—turned sixty.

The force of baby boomers has been on the forefront of discussion for some time, so this news may not be surprising. We even watched as the first of a few notable baby boomers like Bill Clinton and George Bush make headlines for turning 60. These baby boomers will be followed by 4 million of their closest friends each year celebrating their 60th birthdays through the year 2025. When we look at the decline in birth rates and the increase in population for ages over 55 we start to see the real impact of increased longevity.

Workforce Dynamics for Electric Cooperatives

For today's electric cooperatives, an aging population brings about a more urgent issue: skilled workers. The rate at which the next generation is filling bucket trucks is looking alarmingly low. About half of the 400,000 current power industry workers are eligible to retire in the next five to ten years. Just as the need for energy is soaring, the outlook for skilled labor required for construction and maintenance is becoming more

and more grim. According to Russell Turner, NRECA's principal for human capital issues, "Despite some workers delaying retirements, cooperatives are facing increasing competition from Investor Owned Utilities and Muni's to retain existing workers while attracting a whole new generation of workers to deal with the technological challenges facing cooperatives."

For today's electric cooperatives, an aging population brings about a more urgent issue: skilled workers.

For electric utilities, the year 2012 will mean:

- 52% of generation technicians are expected to reach retirement eligibility
- An estimated 40% of line worker jobs will need to be filled
- 46% of engineering jobs are expected to be vacant

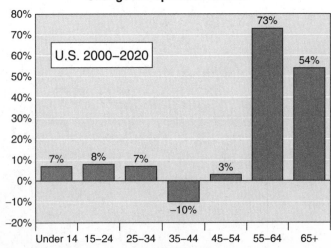

Change in Population Growth

U.S. 2000–2020

Age	Change
Under 14	7%
15–24	8%
25–34	7%
35–44	−10%
45–54	3%
55–64	73%
65+	54%

Even within the NRECA member community, the impact of an aging workforce is present.

Concerns about who will "fill the boots" of a retiring workforce has prompted many cooperatives to increase their focus on recruitment and training programs. As highlighted in *RE Magazine* in the April 2009 issue, solutions developed by co-ops include extensive partnerships with local vocational schools and colleges to offer training for new linemen. Norris Public Power District and Platte-Clay Electric are just a few with structured programs that work with vocational schools and colleges to offer certificate programs after classroom and field training is complete.

Randy Evans, operations manager for Norris Public Power, estimates the average age of his lineman team is 45 and he will likely see at least one member of the current team retire in each of the next five years. Randy summed up his concerns by saying: "We used to hire a lineman about every two to three years. In the last three years, we've hired five."

Danny Belcher, manager of safety & loss control of Trinity Valley Electric Co-op, echoed these same concerns: "I would say in the next six to eight years 50 percent of our lineworker knowledge will walk out the door."

Education programs and scholarships can help recruitment immensely but what are the factors that influence employees starting work today? And on the other hand, what can be done to slow the flood of skilled workforce moving toward retirement?

Benefits Matter More Than You May Think

The seemingly endless sources illustrating the crushing cost of healthcare and importance of insuring your own income in retirement is having an impact on the population entering the workforce. The Employee Benefits Research Institute (EBRI) cites in their 2009 Value of Benefits Survey that over 75% of employees today rank benefits high on the list of priorities when choosing an employer.

When it comes to identifying the most important benefit, healthcare tops the list, followed closely by retirement benefits. The trend that places healthcare first may change based on the final shakeout of new healthcare legislation. Once healthcare is guaranteed or even mandated to be offered by employers, we may find that retirement benefits become what differentiates employers.

No one will disagree with the importance that employees put in their benefit packages. But what is the real impact that benefits play in differentiating one employer from another? To get to the core of how much benefits can impact retention, we can look to the 30% of employees who accepted, quit or changed jobs because of benefits. That's over one fourth of all employees basing their decision on employment because of the benefit package.

Employers are taking note. In the past, phrases like "total compensation" were mainly used in human resources departments. Now those terms and related issues have expanded to include CFOs and CEOs. In fact, we saw executives defend their benefit plans even when markets became stressed. In 2009, Charles Schwab and CFO Research services found that 60% of employers planned to commit more to their 401(k) plans in the midst of great uncertainly and depressed markets.

In addition, employees are starting to see the impact that employer-offered benefits have on their overall livelihood—now and in the future. As such, employees are beginning to place as much value on benefits as they do salary.

Our corporate office is located in a university town and of course, money is always one of the top attractions for prospective employees but today, more individuals see the long-term advantages of a good benefit package as even more of an incentive to work for a company.

One key influence likely to be a factor in employee's increased focus on benefits is what has been occurring

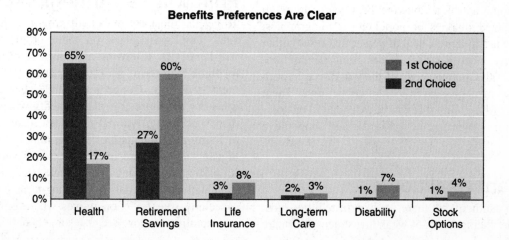

Benefits Preferences Are Clear

131

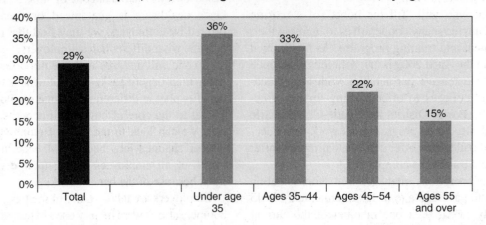

Benefits Play a Major Role in Employment Decisions Workers Who Accepted, Quit, or Change Jobs Because of Benefits, by Age

inside the homes of most Americans. Most American families are paying more for health insurance. In 2008, the U.S. average cost of family coverage premiums was $12,298. If you compare healthcare premiums as a percentage of median household income seven years ago to premiums two years ago, there is a dramatic increase in the percentage of household income going to cover healthcare premiums. Even more important, costs are projected to rise steadily.

Employers Are Getting Their Fair Share of Increased Cost

Increases are not just on the employee side. Most employers are paying significantly more for health insurance and are taking public steps to be sure that this is known and appreciated—in large part to help recruitment and retention.

Think about your own community. Do you know the employers who have reputations for providing strong benefit programs or have received community awards for providing noteworthy benefit programs? Probably so.

Cooperatives Are in a Position of Power

Employers can't control nationwide healthcare premium increases, financial markets or population demographics. However, there is still a great deal of power that rests within each cooperative when it comes to designing benefit programs that meet the unique needs of the workforce in each community and managing costs for the cooperative. There is also a range of flexibility that can be extended to customize these programs over time as workforce and cooperative needs change.

Retirement Realities

Customization can help, but there are benefit realities most cooperatives are facing. Years of weak investment return are

Year	Contributions in Billions for Single-Employer U.S. Pension Plans
2009	$ 36.3
2010	$108.6

* Towers Watson simulation of large single-employer U.S. Pension Plan

hard on the bottom line for defined benefit plans. Thanks to legislative efforts on their behalf, electric cooperatives have smoothing techniques in the RS Plan that allow the spreading of an investment loss from a single year over several years. However, periods of extremely low investment return, such as crisis years like 2008, translate to higher funding costs that cannot be avoided. Though RS Plan funding required a significant increase in contributions beginning in 2010, conditions were even worse for most non-cooperative plans which don't have smoothing techniques. Towers Watson, a prominent actuarial and employee benefits consulting firm, stated in a recent study that contributions due nationwide for U.S. single-employer pension plans in 2010 are triple the amounts due in 2009.

Following a Strategic Approach

To get the most out of benefit programs and the increased value employees place on these programs, cooperatives will benefit by following a strategic approach. The advice to "think long-term" isn't just for employees making investment decisions. Cooperatives and other employers have a history of improving plan benefits when market performance is strong. Normal retirement dates are earlier, cost of living adjustments are more common, benefit levels are higher and plans are overall more generous. This is good for participants but may be setting a benchmark for the long term without considering the long-term price tag. This is especially true for cooperatives where employee turnover is generally very low because some benefits, once awarded,

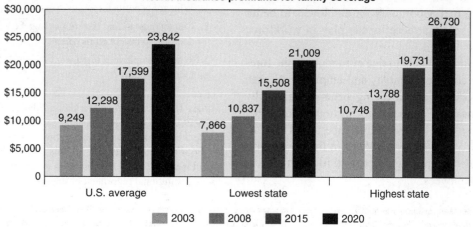

Premiums for Family Coverage 2003, 2008, 2015 and 2020

Health insurance premiums for family coverage

U.S. average: 9,249 (2003); 12,298 (2008); 17,599 (2015); 23,842 (2020)
Lowest state: 7,866 (2003); 10,837 (2008); 15,508 (2015); 21,009 (2020)
Highest state: 10,748 (2003); 13,788 (2008); 19,731 (2015); 26,730 (2020)

■ 2003 ■ 2008 ■ 2015 ■ 2020

2003: Lowest is North Dakota: highest is District of Columbia. 2008, 2015, and 2020: Lowest is Idaho; highest is Massachusetts Data sources: Medical Expenditure Panel Survey—Insurance Component (for 2003 and 2008 premiums); Centers for Medicare and Medicaid Services, Office of the Actuary, National Health Statistics Group, national health expenditures per capita annual growth rate (for premium estimates for 2015 and 2020).

Benefit Variation Is Expanding Between Global and Domestic Focused Firms—and by Workforce Focus

Employers That Are Global
Low Base Pay

High Incentive Pay

Frozen DB or Cash Balance or None

401(k) Savings and Profit Sharing

High Deductible Health Plans

No Retiree Health Benefits

Large Employers That Are Domestic–NRECA Co-ops
Base Pay Emphasis

Low Incentive Pay

Strategic Defined Benefits Plans

401(k) Savings and Profit Sharing

Range of Health Plans

Strategic Retiree Health Benefits

Targeted Hiring and Tenure Focused Employers Are Keeping DB Plans and Retiree Health

are protected and must remain in place even if changes are made for future benefit accruals.

It helps to view employee benefit trends with an eye for what is most relevant in order to recruit and retain electric cooperative employees. Benefit features and forces affecting global employers are now reflected in employee benefit trends but may show trends that aren't applicable for electric cooperatives. For example, employees in other countries with a different cultural focus on elder care or centralized healthcare systems may be less concerned about pension benefits or retiree medical. Domestic-based employers such as public, investor-owned utilities and electric cooperatives are impacted by a different set of cultural and social values and are likely to see benefits from offering a range of health plans, defined benefit options and strategic retiree medical.

It is also beneficial to consider the benefit offerings of regional competitors and other community employers. Just don't forget that this comparison should serve as a guide, not a roadmap. Following the herd and making benefit cuts

to programs which cooperative employees tie to their livelihood can have devastating effects and diminish employee productivity.

The Personal Finance Employee Education Foundation reports that one-third of Americans in the workforce report that money concerns hamper work performance and/or keep them away from work. How? Employees experiencing financial strain are more likely to skip preventive wellness exams that can keep them healthy and reduce medical plan costs. They take extended work breaks to get advice about what to do from co-workers. They miss work to meet with bankers to seek loan alternatives and they become distracted and make mistakes. A distracted lineman working in a storm at 50 feet above ground is not an individual most cooperatives want in their crews.

Opportunities for Employers

Legislation and public policy may dictate change or mandate minimum coverage of certain benefits. However, as Cynthia Mallet, vice president, Product & Market Strategies for MetLife stated, "With benefits, on average, representing one-third or more of the money spent to compensate each employee, there's a real opportunity for employers to better grasp the strategic role that benefits can play in workforce management."

Employee benefits are likely to rise even more to the forefront of employer conference tables and employee kitchen tables. Keeping focused on balancing benefits valued by employees with providing a total compensation package that can be supported over the long term by cooperatives is a formula that should leave most cooperatives in the best condition over time while also paying off tenfold for both current and prospective employees.

Critical Thinking

1. Why are benefits important to employees?
2. Can an outstanding benefit package be a deciding factor in a decision to accept employment?
3. Why do employees often want increased benefits rather than increased salary?

TORRY DELL is a Senior Marketing Advisor for retirement programs at NRECA and provides financial education tools to participants and cooperatives promoting positive retirement savings and investing habits. Prior to joining NRECA in 2008, Torry managed clients for Principal Financial Group and served as a participant education consultant for an institutional retirement business

---

Ways to Phase Retirement

Reducing hours for employees nearing separation can be good for them—and for business.

ERIC KRELL

The use of phased retirement programs among U.S. companies appears to be waning, even though there may be no better time for HR managers to develop flexible work arrangements geared toward employees age 50 and older.

The Society for Human Resource Management's *2010 Employee Benefits* survey report indicates that only 6 percent of U.S. companies operate formal phased retirement programs, down from 13 percent in 2006. HR professionals without such programs may want to consider developing them before recuperating 401(k) balances help spark a wave of retirements.

The negative impact on organizations of "flash retirement"—the departure of large numbers of retirement-eligible employees in a short period—"could be eased by well-planned phased retirement programs offering a mix of extended employment and other benefits," notes Warren Cinnick, a Chicago-based director in PricewaterhouseCoopers' people and change advisory services practice.

Organizations have limited the likelihood of flash retirement, stimulated knowledge transfer and leadership development, and enhanced employee satisfaction through the use of formal and informal phased retirement offerings. Organizational culture and the extent to which it embraces flexible work arrangements are key to operating a phased retirement program, says John Daniel, SPHR, chief HR officer at First Horizon National Corp. In annual workplace surveys at his company, "each year, 'my supervisor supports a flexible schedule' rates among the highest-scoring items in terms of satisfaction," Daniel says.

The bank holding company, known by its main brand First Tennessee Bank, was named by the AARP in 2009 as one of the "Best Employers for Workers Over 50," in part for the flexible work arrangements it offers older employees.

These phased retirement programs "start with an assessment of the labor market and its talent management needs," Daniel says. "When it comes to execution, the biggest issue is cultural."

If an organization does not already have policies, procedures and executive support for flexible schedules, Daniel says the introduction of phased retirement programs creates a "major change management challenge."

Waiting on Government

Until recently, the primary hurdle related to phased retirement programs was not cultural but regulatory. The passage of the Pension Protection Act (PPA) of 2006 helped clarify some of the legal issues involved in phased retirement, yet confusion remains due to the slow gears of the federal government as well as the evolving nature of phased retirement itself.

"Phased retirement means different things to different people," says Pierce Noble, a partner at Mercer who testified before the U.S. Department of Labor's 2008 advisory council on phased retirement.

"There is no universal definition of phased retirement," according to The Conference Board report *Phased Retirement After the Pension Protection Act,* an authoritative guide on the practice. Despite the ambiguity, most phased retirement programs share common features, including:

- Offering reduced-hours schedules for employees nearing retirement.
- Enabling employees who are eligible for retirement to collect pension benefits while continuing to collect their salary in compliance with the act.
- Rehiring retired employees as full-time workers, part-time workers or consultants directly or through third parties.

While the law created some new phased retirement options for organizations with defined benefit retirement plans, the future tax implications on companies that compensate retirement-age employees who collect pension benefits remains unclear. The Internal Revenue Service may yet take action related to the PPA's phased retirement provisions by amending the Internal Revenue Code. Currently the PPA does not specify any length of time a retired employee must remain away from the organization before the employee can be rehired into a formal phased retirement program that enables the employee to collect pension payments.

These issues may soon be resolved as discussions on the use and structure of phased retirement programs continue to crop up in Washington, D.C., including hearings held by the Senate Finance Committee in mid-July. Until then, experts suggest that companies proceed with common *sense* when creating formal phased retirement programs.

For example, some retirement consultants suggest that companies include a sunset clause for enrollment when creating formal programs. By closing enrollment after one year, the company can create new guidelines for later phased retirees if the IRS' forthcoming rules prove too onerous from a tax perspective.

Noble expects the IRS to include nondiscrimination rules in a future amendment. A formal program allowing part-time employment for people "between the ages of 55 and 65," for instance, likely would qualify as age discrimination. Instead, the program should be open to employees age "55 and older."

Structural Snapshots

Richmond-based Bon Secours Virginia Health System's phased retirement program requires employees younger than 65 who retire to wait three months before returning to work for a minimum of 16 hours a week. This "waiting period" reduces any ambiguity related to the "retired" classification. Retired employees who take advantage of this option are eligible for medical, dental and vision coverage as well as tuition reimbursement. In the health care provider's Richmond health system, roughly 40 percent of employees are age 50 or older.

"Employers committed to a culture of aging must proactively address why older workers leave," says Bonnie Shelor, SPHR, senior vice president of human resources. "Flexibility addresses nearly all of them. Preventing attrition through flexibility involves creative thinking and a willingness to try new ways of doing things."

By soliciting employee feedback, Shelor and her HR team designed phased retirement options that include allowing:

- Full-time retirement-age workers to move to part-time schedules of less than 24 hours per week and continue to receive pension checks.

- Employees older than 70½ to begin receiving their retirement checks regardless of their employment status.

- Employees to retire and then be rehired at a later date while still collecting their retirement checks.

At First Tennessee, workers nearing retirement can enter the company's "prime-time program," which consists of a flexible schedule of between 20 and 40 hours per week accompanied by full benefits. The program is available to all employees, and Daniel says it currently serves as an informal phased retirement option.

For example, the banking company's compensation and benefits manager, who reports to Daniel, is 63 and currently works four days a week through the primetime program; in 2011, the manager will further reduce his weekly hours before retiring in September.

"He still has responsibility to help us build programs, respond to regulations and mentor his successor," Daniel explains. "The mentoring is the key activity … and he is helping us to mentor several other professionals on our HR staff."

Veteran employees who gear down to phased schedules before leaving the workforce for good have a chance to manage a major transition in a more gradual manner. "Traditional retirement can feel like jumping off a cliff for some people," notes John Grounard, administrative director for Bon Secours Virginia Health System. "Phased retirement can help the organization as well as the individuals."

Paul Bursic, director of Cornell University's benefit services, agrees that phased retirement programs can be mutually beneficial.

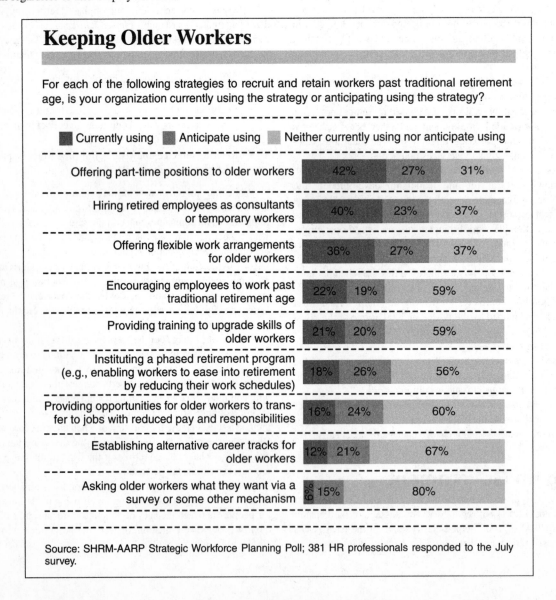

Keeping Older Workers

For each of the following strategies to recruit and retain workers past traditional retirement age, is your organization currently using the strategy or anticipating using the strategy?

■ Currently using   ■ Anticipate using   ■ Neither currently using nor anticipate using

Strategy	Currently using	Anticipate using	Neither
Offering part-time positions to older workers	42%	27%	31%
Hiring retired employees as consultants or temporary workers	40%	23%	37%
Offering flexible work arrangements for older workers	36%	27%	37%
Encouraging employees to work past traditional retirement age	22%	19%	59%
Providing training to upgrade skills of older workers	21%	20%	59%
Instituting a phased retirement program (e.g., enabling workers to ease into retirement by reducing their work schedules)	18%	26%	56%
Providing opportunities for older workers to transfer to jobs with reduced pay and responsibilities	16%	24%	60%
Establishing alternative career tracks for older workers	12%	21%	67%
Asking older workers what they want via a survey or some other mechanism	6%	15%	80%

Source: SHRM-AARP Strategic Workforce Planning Poll; 381 HR professionals responded to the July survey.

"We place an emphasis on making sure that the agreement represents a good business model in each individual case," says Bursic, who helps oversee a formal phased retirement program for faculty members and staff. "Does it make sense for the faculty member or the staff member to step out this way? Does it make sense for the university to have this person doing the types of things he or she can do on a phased basis?"

Cornell University and Bon Secours Virginia Health System also appear on the AARP's 2009 list of the "Best Employers for Workers Over 50." At Cornell, faculty and staff members may request to take part in the program. They work "half-effort," and receive half of their full-time salary and all benefits. The university must agree with the request. Professors who enter the program agree to relinquish tenure. Phased retirees can access pension payouts from their 403(b) plans as soon as they sign their agreements, which generally last two to three years.

The length of the agreement and specific working arrangements that constitute "half-effort" are worked out between individuals and their supervisors or deans. The underlying uniformity of the program is important, Bursic notes, because it helps prevent the perception among faculty and staff that another colleague is receiving special treatment. Yet, the flexibility on defining "half-effort" is important, he adds, to ensure that the situation makes sense on both sides.

Key Steps

In some cases, particularly in small companies, it may make sense to provide "special treatment" to certain employees nearing retirement age. Anna Rappaport, a retirement consultant, actuary and co-author of The Conference Board report, notes that very small companies, particularly those without defined benefit plans, are well-served by informal phased retirement arrangements tailored to individual situations. For example, a small manufacturing company may design a part-time schedule with increased mentoring responsibilities for a soon-to-be-retiring engineer, without creating a formal program.

The format of a phased schedule varies in practice, according to the needs of the company and the desires of the phased retiree. From an employee perspective, working reduced-hours, alternating full-time, project or seasonal schedules may be more or less appealing depending on the employee's lifestyle. For instance, are they starting a side business? Do they plan to travel? Do they want to spend more time with grandchildren? Do they care for elderly parents? For most employers, an alternating week schedule is probably harder to manage effectively, Cinnick notes, especially with knowledge workers.

HR professionals should address scheduling design after taking other steps, including the following:

Assess Cultural Readiness

The introduction of a phased retirement program may require a major change management effort in organizations where flexible work arrangements are relatively rare. "Work on the cultural piece first," Daniel suggests. "That starts with educating managers on the business benefits of the approach. This should be filtered through a business perspective as much as it is filtered through a personal perspective." Although flexible schedules are prevalent among most health care companies, Bon Secours Virginia Health System's CEO Peter Bernard still makes an effort to emphasize the value of mature employees and the importance of their scheduling needs. Bernard routinely hosts lunches for workers age 50 and older to listen to their concerns, discuss developments that may interest them and answer questions, Shelor reports.

Review Talent Management Strategy

Rappaport says HR professionals considering offering phased retirement arrangements should begin by understanding what their organizations are trying to achieve from a talent management perspective. The review should also include a survey of existing knowledge transfer efforts; Rappaport points out that phased retirement programs should be integrated with knowledge transfer. "After you address what you're trying to accomplish at a strategic level, then you can get to the question of how you structure the arrangement," she explains. "And then, pay and benefits become important."

Dig into Procedural Issues

From a legal and compliance perspective, HR professionals should review the PPA, review relevant age discrimination risks and keep tabs on any amendments the IRS makes to its tax code related to the PPA's phased retirement provisions. Noble encourages HR professionals to conduct a top-down review of all compensation and benefits programs, HR policies and procedures to ensure that they support part-time employment. For example, some companies currently do not provide health care coverage to employees who work less than 30 hours a week. "If people lose their health benefits when they enter into a flexible arrangement," Rappaport asserts, "the program is going to be dead on arrival."

> **Conduct a top-down review of all compensation and benefits programs, HR policies and procedures to ensure that they support part-time employment.**

Leave Some Leeway

Bursic and Daniel suggest that formal phased retirement programs should provide supervisors flexibility to structure the job and schedule to meet the needs of the employee and the organization. "Our role in phased retirement," Daniel adds, "is to help foster a culture where it can thrive while maintaining flexible policies and support."

While Cornell University's formal phased retirement program may look fairly proscribed, upon closer inspection the final agreement relies on a substantial amount of vetting, discussion and collaboration. Cornell's HR function provides a well-defined policy and support, but it leaves the definition of "half-effort" up to the phased retirees and their supervisors.

Despite numbers suggesting that phased retirement program offerings are on the decline, companies that use such formal and informal programs may well be ahead of the game when the economy stabilizes.

Critical Thinking

1. Why is phasing-in retirement important to the employee?
2. Why is phasing-in retirement important to the employer?
3. What are some of the things that can be done to help employers and employee phase-in retirement?

ERIC KRELL is a business writer based in Austin, Texas, who covers human resource and finance issues.

UNIT 6

Fostering Employee/ Management Relationships

Unit Selections

Learning Outcomes

After reading this Unit, you will be able to:

- Understand the importance of corporate misconduct.

- Develop a plan to address some of the aspects of corporate misconduct.

- Appreciate the importance of due process when dealing with misconduct in the organization.

- Know about the historic development of using temporary employees.

- Look for creative ways to address employee needs and the needs of the organization when it comes to keeping people employed.

- Appreciate the personal sacrifices made by principled individuals fighting for integrity in the corporate world.

- Understand the importance of creating a culture of ethics in an organization.

Student Website
www.mhhe.com/cls

Internet References

Business Corporate Ethics
www.washingtonpost.com/wp-dyn/business/specials/corporateethics

Corporate Governance
www.corpgov.net

Employee Relations
www.opm.gov/er

SmartPros Legal & Ethics
http://corporate.smartpros.com/ethics/index.html

The American labor movement has a long history dating back to the start of the Industrial Revolution. That history has been marked by turmoil and violence, as workers sought to press their demands on business owners, whether represented by managers or entrepreneurs. The American labor movement exists because working conditions, pay, and benefits were very poor during the early years of the Industrial Revolution in both the United States and the rest of the world. It should be remembered that the American labor movement is only a small part of a broader, world-wide labor movement that includes most Western and European societies. The working conditions under which the first American industrial workers labored would be unacceptable today. Child labor was common. There are documented instances of 6- and 7-year-old children, chained to machines for 12 hours a day, 6 days a week, who threw themselves into the machines—choosing death over life in the dehumanized and mechanized existence of the early factory. Conditions in some factories in the North prior to the Civil War were so infamous that Southern congressmen used them as a justification for the institution of slavery. Slaves sometimes lived in better conditions than the factory workers of New England and many other Northern states.

Unions exist because workers sought a better working environment and a better standard of living. Companies often took advantage of employees, and the government sided with management and the owners, frequently quelling strikes and other forms of labor protest initiated by the workers. Such incidents as the Pullman Strike, the Haymarket Square Riot, and the Homestead Strike exemplify the struggle of the American labor movement to achieve recognition and success in the attempt to improve the lives of all workers, whether unionized or not. The victories of labor have been hard fought and hard won. But, labor has not been without blemish in the struggle for worker's rights. The Marion County Turkey-Shoot, in Southern Illinois, probably the most violent day in American labor history, involved coal miners deliberately chasing and killing strikebreakers from the mines.

During the past hundred years, the fortunes of the American labor movement have varied, and now their fortunes may be taking an even deeper downward turn, with attempts at unionization even more difficult. Unions have been able to achieve their gains through the mechanism of collective bargaining. The individual has very little bargaining power when compared to a company, especially huge companies such as United Technologies or General Electric. Collective bargaining allows workers to pool their collective resources and power to bargain with the corporation on a more equal footing. Unfortunately for the unions, many of the industries in which they are strongest are in decline, but it would seem that there might be help coming from the Obama administration and Congress with the possibility of new laws making it possible for unions to organize more easily. It remains to be seen if these new laws will be passed and what their impact would be, but new leadership is certainly necessary if the American labor movement is to survive and rebound in the next century, and if it is to serve as a useful organ of society. A union's ultimate weapon in contract negotiations, the strike, represents a complete breakdown of discipline from management's perspective. Disciplinary situations are almost always unpleasant, and today they can

© Stockbyte/Punchstock Images

often lead to court cases, with all of the attendant legal questions and problems. A key to effective disciplinary action is documentation of the employees' actions and the steps that were taken to correct them. Management needs to implement procedures and policies to assure employees are treated fairly and equitably in the workplace.

The American labor movement has come a long way since the first strike by printers in Philadelphia in 1786. The journey, although difficult, has led to greater justice in the workplace and an increased standard of living for the nation as a whole. Unions have experienced both declines and increases in membership, but they have endured as a powerful social, political, and economic force. Whether they will again successfully "reinvent" themselves and adapt to a changing environment is a major question.

During the past twenty years, primarily as a result of the dislocations in the job market, temporary and part-time workers became available to organizations. There are certain advantages to this situation for the employer, but employers must manage these temporary and part-time employees on a permanent basis. A recent twist on this is the ability in some states for workers to collect unemployment while continuing to work part-time for their employer. This arrangement is presented in "Sharing Work and Unemployment Benefits."

There is also the issue of ethics. How companies treat their employees and their customers is going to be of increasing concern in the future. Ethical behavior will be at a premium, and managers know that it will be part of the job. Unfortunately, some managers of organizations will always make the economic/legal calculation that doing something that is illegal or unethical at best will benefit them, if not their shareholders, customers, and/or employees. "Strategic Human Resource Management as Ethical Stewardship" points out a way that organizations can reduce the temptation to cut corners and do the easy, less than completely ethical thing when faced with those kinds of choices. Someone will always try to get away with some sort of illegal, unethical, or dishonest gain. Flawed human nature will always play a role. But there will be those who will try to do something about it, even in the face of difficult resistance as celebrated in "Fighting the Good Fight."

The underground and lower end labor market also plays a role in the ethical treatment of employees. With an estimated twelve to twenty million undocumented aliens in the United States, these people have to work somewhere and often for less than minimum wage. They do it because they work for unethical employers, who know that they are in the United States illegally and therefore are not protected by employment laws; thus the workers are exploited. This is creating an underclass of workers who perform at below the legal wage. This is not only subsidizing these unethical employers, but it is giving them an unfair advantage in the marketplace by lowering their costs when competing against employers paying legal wages, and driving down the wages of legitimate workers in the economy.

Employee-management relations are always going to be complicated. There will never be a simple solution because people are complicated and their needs and wants will be in constant flux. Dealing with these changes will present human resource professionals constant challenges.

Finding and Fixing Corporate Misconduct

What 300,000 employees said about unethical cultures.

DAN CURRELL AND TRACY DAVIS BRADLEY

In 2009, senior management teams restructured departments and business units, and in many cases dramatically reduced the size of their companies. Upset by these changes, employees became cynical about their companies' ethical cultures and the integrity of the people who work with them. That cynicism translated directly into a rise in serious instances of fraud and misconduct.

In 2008, as the economy worsened, misconduct rose by 20% during the second half of the year. In 2009, by contrast, overall misconduct levels reportedly declined from the first half of the year to the second half.

But a survey conducted by the Corporate Executive Board's Compliance & Ethics Leadership Council (CELC), provides compelling evidence for why this finding does not tell the whole story.

According to the results from more than 300,000 employees in over 75 countries, this "decline" in misconduct during 2009 is actually misleading, as it pertains to less severe and risky behaviors such as the misuse of company resources or other "inappropriate behavior."

In fact, the real story in 2009 was that more serious types of misconduct (e.g., conflicts of interest, insider trading and improper payments) rose during the year. Observations of bribery and corruption were up more than 100%, and observations of insider trading were up 300%. At a time when regulators are on the warpath for precisely these kinds of violations, such behaviors tremendously increased risk for companies.

Consistent with this trend, and with the ongoing recession, CELC research found that the number of highly disengaged employees increased in 2009. At the beginning of the year, the proportion of such employees was one in ten. But by the end of 2009, it rose to one in five. (The data is based on the attitudes and work habits of thousands of employees.) Based on CEB's productivity models, this widespread disengagement not only created fertile ground for misconduct, but also decreased employee output by about 5%.

The fact is that while many have reported that overall misconduct was on the decline, the most troubling types of misconduct are actually on the rise. And they have increased to a staggering degree. Companies must not just be on guard, but learn how to prevent employees from wanting to skirt the rules—or even the law—in the first place. Prevention starts from within.

The Culprit: Employee Perceptions of Culture

Misconduct levels were shown to reveal themselves in employee perceptions of culture. Business units with the weakest ethical cultures had the highest levels of misconduct—in 2009, these units experienced five times more misconduct than those with the strongest ethical cultures. When employees perceive a weak ethical culture, misconduct does not just increase—it multiplies.

In contrast to popular opinion, CELC research also found that misconduct does not vary by region. Europe and North America, for example, have nearly identical overall levels. That said, different business units in different locations within a company often do show varying levels of misconduct. But this disparity is not a national culture issue—it is a business culture issue. Weak business units within an otherwise average company can have sky-high misconduct levels.

Perhaps more disconcerting is that misconduct is rarely reported. This means that companies need to be diligent, creative and persistent in their efforts to detect and mitigate serious compliance risks and uncover information about employee misconduct.

A companywide assessment is a good place to start. By comparing business units' performance on such ethical culture measures as clarity of expectations, tone at the top, comfort speaking up, and levels of observed misconduct, companies can pinpoint business units that present a cultural risk to the company.

When it comes to perceptions of ethical culture, employees can generally be divided into four ethical risk groups: "Integrity Champions," who are most positive about the culture, and present the least risk; "Casual Supporters," who are somewhat positive about the culture and present minimal cultural risk; "Agnostics," who are on the fence about their company's ethical culture and present a cultural risk to the company; and "Disaffected," who have the most negative perceptions of the culture at their company and thus present the greatest cultural risk.

Agnostics and Casual Supporters, in particular, report greater levels of uncertainty about observing instances of misconduct than other employees, and also report the misconduct that they do observe at much lower rates than do Integrity Champions. Their lack of certainty about what they are observing, and their possible negativity about their firm's ethical culture, suggests that awareness and education are the keys to reaching these Agnostic and Casual employees. Targeted communication and training can greatly impact the reporting rates for this segment of a company's population.

Organizational Justice for a Culture of Integrity

So how can executives restore a strong culture of integrity? Looking at the best-performing business units, it is clear that the key to a strong culture of integrity is an element called organizational justice. Organizational justice has two parts: (1) the belief among employees that the company does not tolerate unethical behavior, and (2) the belief that management responds quickly and consistently to unethical behavior when it occurs.

In other words, organizational justice is strong when employees believe that their company will take action on its policies and values. And it encapsulates the maxim that actions speak louder than words.

Organizational justice is singularly powerful in driving a culture of integrity throughout the company. When employees believe that the company has strong organizational justice, the company's integrity index (an overall measure of integrity) rises, and misconduct drops significantly. And while every aspect of culture affects employees' perceptions of corporate integrity, organizational justice is by far the most powerful single factor—accounting for more index movement than all other cultural factors combined.

How can management teams enhance organizational justice? The key is for the organization to visibly enforce the company's ethical commitments. This is no small task. Many management teams are either unwilling to do this or just do not know what to do.

For those firms willing to do what is necessary, there are three key steps: (1) equip managers to decisively deal with unethical behavior, (2) show the whole employee population—using real instances from within the company—that the company deals decisively with misconduct, and (3) close the loop with employees who report misconduct so that they know that appropriate actions were taken.

Companies need to be accountable, consistent and transparent when taking action on misconduct. These efforts should focus on the top and middle leadership of the organization. Employees who believe that their senior leaders have high integrity feel more connected to the values of the company. Viewing it at another level, an employee who believes that his or her manager behaves ethically and demonstrates corporate values will consistently show better performance in the workplace—including working harder and longer hours.

Evolutionary Stages in Your Corporate Culture of Integrity

The best way to prevent employee misconduct is not a draconian enforcement strategy. It is promoting a culture of integrity and openness.

Enron famously had a "no harm, no foul" culture where potential whistleblowers were either too apathetic or too concerned about their own advancement and profit to care what others were up to. Whether it was simply looking the other way or actual ignorance, most workers were unaffected by the executive pillaging going on across all levels of the business. And once that becomes endemic, it is tough to reverse course.

Creating and nurturing a culture where malfeasance cannot occur is not easy. But your best resources are right in front of you: your employees. By recognizing where your workers are in this evolution, you can start to determine how high the hill is that you have to climb.

These are the four general employee types that you can either identify as a part of the solution—or a part of the problem.

Integrity Champions

Those who are very positive about the culture. These are the key influencers in the company who can help turn others into positive employees.

Casual Supporters

Employees who are somewhat positive about the culture but not particularly engaged one way or the other.

Agnostics

"Fence-sitters," these people may present some cultural risk to the company and can be influenced if the culture takes a change for the better—or for the worse.

Disaffected

These employees with the most negative perceptions of the culture at their company present the greatest risk.

Corporate values in action lead to a more ethical work environment, and possibly even better corporate performance. With some hard data in hand, we now know with precision how corporate integrity, corporate misconduct and corporate performance relates to one another. These connections are clear, and they are too strong to be ignored.

Critical Thinking

1. What role does corporate culture play in corporate misconduct?

2. Do you think that senior management plays a role in establishing the corporate culture?

3. How can a corrupt corporate culture be changed?

DAN CURRELL is managing director of the Compliance and Ethics Council at the Corporate Executive Board. **TRACY DAVIS BRADLEY,** PhD, is senior director of the council at CEB.

Harassment Goes Viral—What Can HR Do to Prevent It?

Lynn D. Lieber

A mere 20 years ago, "sexual harassment" frequently constituted a male supervisor making lewd comments or sexual propositions to a female subordinate. It is astonishing how far and fast "unlawful harassment" has evolved over the last two decades. Long gone are the days of someone filing a harassment claim after receiving a pornographic fax. Today's workplace now includes unlawful harassment through e-mails, instant messaging, texting, and the gigantic, unwieldy realm of social networking, including Facebook, LinkedIn, Twitter, MySpace, YouTube, and many more such sites that will literally be created before the publication of this column.

Social networking is evolving with ferocious speed, with Facebook releasing the following statistics about its users: 400 million active users; 50 percent of active users log on to Facebook in any given day; and individuals spend over *500 billion* minutes per month on Facebook. Many of those millions of Facebook users are also your employees.

Twitter, blogs, and text-messaging services have cited similarly burgeoning usage. On the flip side, social media has seemingly endless benefits to business. It is successfully being used for marketing and sales purposes, for brand recognition and information dissemination, and for recruitment and hiring. However, every day more and more unlawful harassment is perpetrated via these electronic communication mediums, and employers are paying the price, which can be exorbitant.

How have employers reacted to quell the endless tsunami of unlawful harassment through these electronic methods? According to recent statistics, not very well: only 10 percent of employers have a policy specifically addressing social networks; more than 50 percent of employers do not have a policy to address employees' use of social-networking sites outside of work; more than 25 percent of employers have already disciplined an employee for improper activities on such sites; and most employers do no monitoring of their employees' use of these sites.[1]

This article describes the broad scope of online harassment issues that exist in today's electronic workplace, the response of the court system to online harassment cases, the key components of a social-networking policy that every organization should institute, and other policies and procedures HR should create or revise to prevent online harassment.

What Potential Online Harassment Issues Exist in Today's Workplace?

A simpler question might be the reverse—what potential online harassment issues do *not* exist in today's workplace? The varieties of possible employment-related online harassment issues that exist are "virtually" limitless. This fact has not gone unnoticed by disgruntled employees, workers who have been laid off or terminated, or hungry, creative plaintiffs' counsel. Perhaps the extent of online harassment issues can best be illustrated by this recent posting on a plaintiff attorney's website, eliciting electronic-workplace harassment claims from potential plaintiffs:

Has any of the following happened to you?

A coworker(s)/supervisor(s) has computer porn on his or her screen.

A coworker(s)/supervisor(s) "tags" you on a Facebook page.

A coworker(s)/supervisor(s) sends you/others inappropriate jokes by e-mail or text that relate to any of the protected categories—race, religion, national origin, age, etc.

A coworker(s)/supervisor(s) e-mails or texts you religious quotations, symbols, verses, or other propaganda.

A coworker(s)/supervisor(s) has "friended" you on Facebook and subjected you to inappropriate content related to the protected categories.

A coworker(s) sends you e-mails or text messages of a sexual nature and you are sick of it.

A coworker(s) is stalking you either physically or electronically (texting, e-mails, etc.).

Online unlawful harassment comes in many forms, and is ever-evolving. Some of the most common forms of unlawful online harassment—spam, e-mails, texts, instant messaging, voice mails, blogs, social-media-related harassment, and cyber-stalking—are described in detail in the sections that follow.

Unwanted Electronic Mail (Spam)

There has been a recent, exponential increase in the receipt of unsolicited "commercial" e-mails, commonly known as "spam," by employees of all types of organizations. Spam has obvious business-related detriments but is also a leading unlawful harassment claim from employees. Obviously, the initial problem is receipt of unwanted spam and viewing of it by others in the workplace. However, another serious danger occurs when employees forward spam to others, creating potential harassment issues as the spam makes its way through the organization and to third parties outside the organization as well.

Courts have routinely held that pornographic images in the workplace can create a hostile environment for employees. It is likely that courts will soon be called on to decide whether and under what circumstances an employer can be liable for failing to implement appropriate safeguards to limit workplace-related pornographic spam.

Electronic Communications

Welcome to 2010, the Golden Age of "electronic" unlawful harassment. Offensive e-mail, texts, instant messages, "tweets," and voice-mail messages are now routinely used by plaintiffs as corroborative evidence of a hostile work environment, as well as the basis of electronic harassment claims. Workplace electronic media has been and will continue to be used by employees to unlawfully harass other employees and third parties. Offensive and inappropriate use of electronic workplace media runs the gamut from sexual jokes e-mailed around the office to raunchy tweets about the latest reality shows to sexually related instant messages from coworkers having an affair.

Most employees also fail to realize that their personal e-mails may be the subject of discovery in a legal claim or lawsuit. If an employee is a party to an unlawful harassment-based lawsuit, or even is a witness in such a case, any personal e-mails related to inappropriate workplace conduct could be subject to the discovery process. This includes "throwaway" forms of electronic communications, such as instant messages.

Add to these burgeoning issues the seemingly uncontrollable issue of employees "surfing" the Internet during business hours, especially viewing inappropriate websites. A shocking number of employees still do not realize that Internet surfing leaves a digital trail. Internet providers routinely record each individual's use of websites, surfing history, and e-mails. Employees should be instructed at every opportunity that the organization's Web browser creates files that record all of a user's interactions. Copies of downloaded data including pictures may also be stored in cached files. Employees who use the Internet leave a trail that employers can track to discover where that employee has been in cyberspace, often with shocking consequences to employees.

Blogging

Recently, blogs have presented a new issue for employers: whether an employer can limit its employees' access to blogs through the employer's computer and Internet service, or personally. A significant number of employee terminations have occurred for violations of an organization's blogging, social networking, and related acceptable-use policies.

For example, to be *dooced* is to be terminated because of comments about the organization (or a coworker or supervisor) by an employee on a personal blog or other message forum. *PC Magazine*'s encyclopedia of technology terms notes that blogger Heather Armstrong coined the phrase in 2002 after being terminated because of blog entries about work. Coworkers called her

"Dooce" because she made so many misspellings typing *doode* as a joke to emphasize the "oo" in *dude*. Nine percent of large U.S. companies that Proofpoint (a provider of e-mail security systems) surveyed said that they had terminated an employee for violating blog or message-board policies in the past 12 months. About 72 percent of companies report that they have formal acceptable-use policies for blog and message-board postings.

Not all employees, however, easily submit to terminations over their blogging. A former Delta flight attendant—the self-proclaimed "Queen of the Sky"—filed suit in an Atlanta federal court claiming sex discrimination.[2]

She claimed that while the airline company terminated her for alleged inappropriate pictures on her personal blog (one picture featured the attendant with her Delta uniform blouse partly unbuttoned and exposing a glimpse of her bra), it did not punish her male colleagues who had potentially insensitive material on their own websites.

The State of Kentucky is currently being sued by a state employee who is challenging the state's decision to prohibit state employees from accessing blogs, including their own personal blogs, from state-owned computers.[3]

Social-Networking-Related Activities

Employees are astonishingly unaware that their social-networking activities are public—that *nothing* on the Internet is private. Employees do not realize that even if their Facebook page profile is set to "private," it can be accessed by employers, potential employers, coworkers, supervisors, the government, or governmental administrative agencies.

Employers are increasingly disciplining and terminating employees for an employee's inappropriate use of social-networking sites. Again, such terminations are giving rise to new workplace-related terminology. For example, to be *Facebook fired* is to be terminated because of an inappropriate posting to a social network such as Facebook. Another word to add to our 2010 workplace technology vocabulary is the term *twerminated*—to be terminated over a post to a short-message service such as Twitter.

In a recent case, the plaintiff told his Facebook friends to misrepresent to the Equal Employment Opportunity Commission (EEOC) that he was terminated by his employer because of his race. The plaintiff's Facebook page setting was on "private," leading him to believe that his communications were private. The EEOC discovered his Facebook admonitions to his "friends" and subsequently dismissed his case.

Cyber-Stalking

Cyber-stalking, the use of electronic communication to harass, threaten, or pursue a victim, is increasing as a form of workplace harassment and violence. Law enforcement agencies estimate that electronic communications are a factor in 20 to 40 percent of all stalking cases.[4]

Cyber-stalking watchdog organizations report that cyber-stalking frequently occurs in the workplace, either because the perpetrators are unhappy with their organization, management, or coworkers or because they have been laid off, terminated, or not hired. Many additional cases are reported when employees feel they have been passed over for a promotion or raise, treated differently from other employees, or denied a job benefit.[5]

How Have the Courts Viewed Online Harassment Issues?

The legal landscape regarding electronic media, unlawful harassment, employee privacy issues, and employer obligations is developing in a slow and ad hoc manner. Courts have addressed some issues, while others remain largely unresolved. This inconsistent development of laws regarding the electronic workplace is undoubtedly complicated by the continued rapid growth of technology and Internet applications.

One thing courts have consistently held is that the open viewing of sexually explicit websites in the workplace may be sufficient to create a "hostile working environment." For example, a court allowed a female Chicago police officer's case to proceed to trial in a sexual harassment lawsuit where she claimed she was exposed to pornographic images on computer monitors at work and harassed by her coworkers regarding the pornography.[6]

Reducing Employees' Expectation of Privacy

Most court decisions to date regarding online unlawful harassment focus on whether employers have sufficiently reduced employees' reasonable expectation of privacy in workplace-related electronic mediums. Courts have routinely upheld employers' termination decisions for employees' violations of electronic systems when the employers have clearly and repeatedly given employees notice that their use of the organization's systems may be monitored by the employer at any time to ensure compliance with the organization's policies.[7]

An employer's rights in this area are, however, limited. Some states, including California and Connecticut, have laws forbidding employer surveillance and monitoring of employees in certain situations. Again, of critical importance is that employers reduce employees' expectations of privacy in the workplace.[8]

In *United States* v. *Ziegler,*[9] the Ninth Circuit held that an employer who installed a firewall, monitored its employees' computer usage, and apprised its employees of the company's monitoring efforts maintained control of an employee's computer located in a private office. The court held that the employer could consent to government agents entering the private office, removing the computer hard drive, and copying that drive, even though the employee had downloaded personal files onto the workplace computer.

Court Rulings on Electronic Evidence

Electronic evidence is a pressing issue confronting courts around the country. Courts are routinely upholding employers' rights to regulate the use of their electronic resources and asserting that employees do not possess an expectation of privacy in documents and communications created, received, saved, or sent over the employer's electronic systems. Where an employer maintains e-mail policies stating that documents and electronic communications are not confidential and that the employee has no personal privacy right in this information, the employee may not be able to claim the information is privileged.

The court in *In re Asia Global Crossing, Ltd.* identified four factors to determine whether an employee's electronic communications are privileged: (1) does the organization maintain a policy banning personal or other objectionable use; (2) does the organization monitor the use of the employee's computer or e-mails; (3) do third parties have a right of access to the computer or e-mails; and (4) did the corporation notify the employees, or was the employee aware, of the use and monitoring policies.[10]

What Are the Key Components of an Electronic-Resources-Use Policy?

In late 2009, the Society of Corporate Compliance and Ethics (SCCE) reported that many employers were surprised by the extent to which employees use social media in the workplace, and their organizations' policies have not yet caught up with this phenomenon. Increasingly, however, companies are now creating and implementing policies to address the issue.

Most prudent employers currently have an e-mail/Internet/IT policy. Such employers are now establishing comprehensive electronic-resources-use policies that encompass e-mail, voice mail, Internet access, cell phones, pagers, PDAs, laptops, headphones, and employees' use of social media at work or on behalf of their employer. An electronic-resources-use policy is more than a good idea—it is imperative in today's workplace. The key reason behind such a policy is to reduce employees' "reasonable expectation of privacy," as courts have deemed critical based on the case law described earlier.

Much to certain employees' chagrin, lack of a comprehensive electronic-use policy does not prevent employers from disciplining or terminating employees who engage in unlawful online harassment. Organizations often rely on a code of conduct, unlawful-harassment policy, e-mail/Internet/IT policy, confidentiality-of-information policy, or the like to discipline or terminate employees who use social networking, tweeting, blogging, and similar activities for inappropriate uses that negatively affect the workplace.

Some of the following are critical components of any organization's updated electronic-communications policy:

- The organization should first specify what electronic systems are covered by the policy, including e-mail, texts, instant messages, Internet, blogs, phone systems, cell phones, PDAs, organization-owned laptops, and so on. As technology is evolving more rapidly than organizations' policies, every policy should have a catch-all phrase or sentence about emerging technology so employees cannot circumvent the policy on a technical omission of an electronic form of communication.
- Organizations should clearly specify that employee use of the organization's computer systems is for business purposes only, and all files and messages belong to the organization. Should some personal use of electronic media be permitted by the organization, the policy should specifically prohibit personal use that interferes with the employee's work/work time or that of others, as well as conduct that could be a conflict of interest with the organization and its business operations.
- Perhaps most critically, organizations should notify employees that any misuse of electronic systems will subject the employee to discipline, up to and including termination. Policies must clearly inform employees that their organization may access, search, and monitor voice mail, e-mail, or organization files that are created, stored, or deleted from the organization's computer systems.

- Policies should explicitly prohibit inappropriate use of technology, including downloading, transmitting, or forwarding material that is harassing, discriminatory, inflammatory, defamatory, insulting, offensive, pornographic, or obscene. Policies should prohibit employees from copying and sending any confidential or proprietary information, or software that is protected by copyright and other laws protecting intellectual property. Additionally, it is imperative to prohibit unauthorized access by employees of other employees' electronic communications.

- Policies should inform and instruct employees that they should not expect their communications or use of their organization's computer information systems to be confidential or private. Employees should (at least yearly) sign a policy, acknowledgment, or notice on acceptable usage of their organization's electronic use and related policies.

- Employers should reduce the employees' expectation of privacy in the employer's electronic-related systems at every opportunity, including policies, meetings, online training, screen savers, and so on. Monitoring and enforcement processes can be greatly enhanced by the creation of a duty to report misconduct. Thus, an employee who witnesses a coworker viewing sexually explicit information on his or her computer screen has an affirmative obligation to report it to the organization.

- More important, a well-established policy is largely irrelevant without correct implementation, repeated training, and consistent enforcement at all levels and departments of the organization.

What Other Policies and Procedures Should HR Institute or Revise to Prevent Online Harassment?

Online harassment relates to a surprising number of policies that most organizations currently have in place. For example, organizations should now revise many provisions in their codes of conduct to accommodate electronic forms of communication. Some examples of code provisions that may need rethinking and modification include those pertaining to personal conduct, conflict of interest, outside employment, privacy, use of organization resources/assets, unlawful harassment, workplace violence, document retention, and many more provisions depending on the organization and its industry.

Other policies and handbook provisions t̶ should reanalyze in light of the current workplace ele̶ sion include confidentiality of information and trade secr̶ trading (where applicable), employee and former employee̶ ences, and use of organization time.

Notes

1. Society of Corporate Compliance and Ethics and the Health Care Compliance Association Survey, September 25, 2009.

2. Tierney, M. (2005, September 8). Ex-flight attendant sues Delta over blog. Atlanta Journal-Constitution, p. 1E. See also http://queenofsky.journalspace.com.

3. Nickolas v. Fletcher, 2007 U.S. District LEXIS 23843 (E. D. Ky. Aug. 9, 2007).

4. National Conference of State Legislatures, State Computer Harassment or "Cyber-Stalking" Laws, March 29, 2007, available at www.ncsl.org/programs/lis/cip/stalk99.htm (listing each state's stalking and cyber-stalking provisions).

5. National Center for Victims of Crime, Cyberstalking, available at www.ncvc.org.

6. Williams v. City of Chicago, 325 F. Supp. 2d 867 (N.D. Ill. 2004).

7. Lowell, B., Matson, E., & Weiss, L. (2001, Fall). Big brother or modern management: Email monitoring in the private workplace. Labor Lawyer, 17(2), 311–326.

8. 92 A.L.R. 5th 15 (expectation of privacy in Internet communications).

9. 474 F. 3d 1191–1192 (9th Cir. 2007).

10. 322 B.R. 247 (Bankr. S.D.N.Y., March 21, 2005).

Critical Thinking

1. What are some of the ways employees can be harassed outside the corporate environment?

2. What can the organizations do about it?

3. How does this affect the work environment?

4. What are some of the legal implications?

LYNN D. LIEBER, Esq., is founder and CEO of Workplace Answers, a San Francisco-based provider of Web-based legal compliance training. Lieber is a seasoned employment law attorney and a nationally recognized spokeswoman on harassment and discrimination law. Workplace Answers delivers Web-based training in human resources, unlawful harassment prevention, and financial and ethics compliance. The company helps client organizations build an effective affirmative defense under local, state, and federal employment law. She may be contacted at www.workplaceanswers.com.

panding Role of Temporary Help Services from 1990 to 2008

During the 1990–2008 period, employment in the temporary help services industry grew from 1.1 million to 2.3 million and came to include a larger share of workers than before in higher skill occupations; employment in this industry has been very volatile because temporary workers are easily hired when demand increases and laid off when it decreases

TIAN LUO, AMAR MANN, AND RICHARD HOLDEN

Workers in the temporary help services industry, also referred to as contingent, contractual, seasonal, free-lance, just-in-time, or "temp" employees, are those whose salaries are paid by a temporary help services agency that supplies them, upon request, to employers looking to fill a temporary full- or part-time staffing need.[1] Though the term of employment can range from a day or less to several years, a key feature is that the contractual employment relationship for temps is with their employment services firm and not with the requesting firm. Over time, temporary workers have grown in importance as firms have relied on them to meet their changing labor needs. Once known as a source of stopgap labor used primarily for routine clerical assignments, temp help services now plays an important role in the U.S. economy as a bridge to permanent employment[2] for those who are out of work or changing jobs and as an indicator of the overall job market closely watched by the Federal Reserve and other financial institutions as well as by policymakers.[3]

Using employment and wage data from the BLS Quarterly Census of Employment and Wages and Occupational Employment Statistics programs, this article examines the evolving role of the temp help services industry in the national economy and regional economies during the 1990-to-2008 period, which encompasses the explosive growth of temporary help services in the 1990s culminating in the 2000 peak in temp employment, as well as the economic recessions that began in 1990, 2001, and 2007. It also examines the factors that have contributed to the high growth and volatility seen in temp help services. The analysis also considers how employers' use of temps has evolved over the past two decades and the extent to which temp help services employment has expanded into a diversified base of industries, occupations, and geographic regions over the 18-year period.

The temporary help services industry is considered an indicator of the overall economy because movements in temp employment often have been a precursor to changes in the broader labor market.[4] As firms have increased their use of temporary workers over the past two decades, the use of temp help services has become an indicator of how businesses operate. In fact, around both the time of the 2001 recession and that of the recession that began in December 2007, temporary employment declined before total employment did and temp help services experienced employment growth before the overall job market did.[5] The shifts in temp help services appear to signal employment growth, employment shifts across regions within particular industries, and the demand for particular skills in an evolving labor market.

Overview of Temporary Help Services

Temporary help services is an industry within the employment services industry group, and it makes up about 70 percent of employment in that group.[6] The other industries within the group are employment placement agencies and professional employer organizations.

Employment Growth

The temporary help services industry is a relatively new player in the U.S. economy. Not until after World War II did the temporary help services industry develop into its modern form. In 1956, there were only about 20,000 employees in the employment services industry, and the industry's primary focus was to place employees in clerical and factory positions that involved routine or repetitive tasks.[7] By the early 1970s, the number of workers in the temporary help services industry had grown to approximately 200,000 but represented less than 0.3 percent of total U.S. employment. In the following decades, the industry experienced tremendous growth both absolutely and as a percentage of national employment. By 1990, the industry comprised slightly more than 1 million employees and accounted for 1.0 percent of total employment. Following 1990, temp employment experienced another decade of phenomenal growth, expanding to 2.7 million employees and accounting for 2.0 percent of U.S. employment by 2000. That year marked the

Index
[1990 = 100]

Index
[1990 = 100]

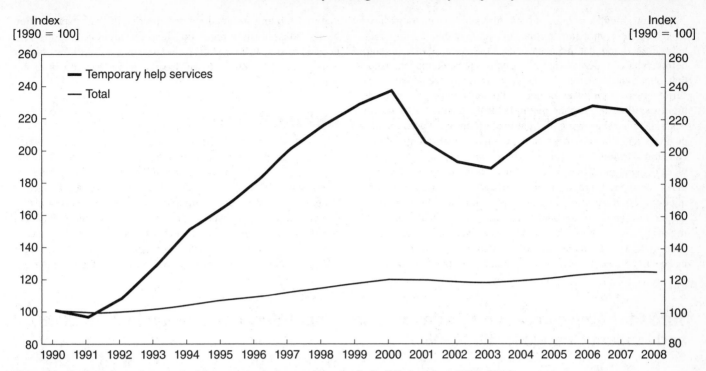

Figure 1   Indexed employment of temporary help services and of all industries, 1990–2008

Source: QCEW data.

peak in both employment for temp help services and the industry's share of total employment. (See Figure 1.)

The growth of temp employment in the 1990s can be attributed to a variety of factors, including business' increased emphasis on specialization and their increased focus on gaining flexibility in response to changes in consumer demand.[8] The high turnover rate[9] and consequent lack of a long-term relationship between employer and employee also made temporary workers attractive to firms. As more businesses began to use temporary workers to quickly and efficiently address changing labor needs, other firms took note of this source of inexpensive[10] and flexible labor and altered their hiring patterns to make greater use of just-in-time labor.[11] Furthermore, staffing firms introduced new technologies for matching employees to jobs and expanded the services offered to clients to include more training. Matching workers to employers for specific geographic regions and industries became more efficient as partnerships formed between niche temp agencies and larger staffing firms.[12]

As both the demand for and supply of temporary employees grew, employers became more sophisticated about their use of temporary employees as a clutch to downshift during periods of lower demand and to upshift when demand rose, allowing the employers to insulate permanent employees from economic fluctuations.[13] The use of temp workers by employers as a buffer to obtain numerical flexibility during labor contractions and expansions[14] is demonstrated by the disproportionate share of job loss incurred by temp help services during and after the 2001 recession. Between 2001 and 2003, temp employment dropped by over 20 percent, or by approximately 550,000 workers. During the same period, total employment declined by 1.6 percent. In fact, more than 25 percent of all jobs lost during that period were in temporary help services, despite their accounting for less than 2 percent of total employment. That such a small sector

could absorb such a large proportion of net job losses attests to the uniquely important function of temporary workers during periods of restructuring and of changes in the business cycle.[15] Similarly, since 12 months before the beginning of the most recent recession, temporary workers have shouldered a larger-than-average share of jobs lost. From December 2007 to December 2008, temp employment dropped by over 484,000 jobs, or about 19 percent, while total employment dropped by 2.3 percent.

Occupational Trends in Temporary Employment

Over the past two decades, temporary employment has moved into a much wider array of occupations, and in more recent years, it has moved towards higher paying occupations. By 2008, temporary workers in clerical positions such as those of secretary, typist, receptionist, data-entry operator, and office clerk (the types of positions most commonly associated with temp work) represented less than a quarter of overall temp help services industry employment and accounted for only 16 percent of the industry's revenue.[16] The occupational employment distribution of employment services is shown in table 1.[17] Approximately 65 percent of jobs in the employment services industry in 2008 were in three occupational groups: office and administrative support, transportation and material moving, and production occupations. The next-largest occupational groups, which make up about 15 percent of temp help services employment, are the following: construction and extraction, healthcare practitioner, and business and financial operations occupations. According to a previous assessment,[18] office and administrative support occupations accounted for most of temp employment in 1984. By 2008, the occupational share of office occupations had shrunk by more than one-half, and the share of other occupations had risen.

149

Previous studies have found that high-skill occupations have started making up a larger share of employment in temporary help services and that they have caused the average wage in temp help services to increase.[19] Similarly, the present analysis finds that employment in employment services in recent years has shifted away from lower skilled and lower paying jobs to more highly skilled and higher paying staffing positions. In recent years, the fastest growing occupational groups have been legal;[20] business and financial operations; computer and mathematical; education, training and library; and community and social services occupations. (See table 1.) All of these groups have wages that exceed the average for all occupations. The fastest declining occupational groups were farming, fishing and forestry; food preparation and serving; and transportation and material moving occupations, all of which have below-average annual wages. (See table 1.) The most marked shift in employment services has been the recent fall in the employment of transportation and

material moving occupations and the rise in that of production occupations. In short, temporary help services occupations have been diversifying and shifting towards higher skill and higher paying jobs over the last two decades and especially in recent years.

Industry Trends

This section expands the previous analysis and determines which industries are prominent users of temporary workers and how the use of temps across industries has shifted over time. Temporary workers, regardless of their particular industry, are grouped together under one industrial code: temporary help services. Because of this generalization of temp workers, no direct data on their numbers in specific industries exist. To circumvent this issue, an econometric approach is needed to estimate the magnitude of temp help utilization in individual industries. By correlating the employment

Table 1 Employment and Wages in Employment Services Occupations for 2008, and Percent Change for 2004–08

	2008			Percent Change, 2004–08	
	Employment	Percent of Total	Mean Annual Wage	Employment	Real Wage
All occupations, all industries	135,185,230	. . .	$42,270	5.5	0.2
All occupations, employment services	3,408,230	100.0	32,530	−.1	5.6
Office and administrative support	843,560	24.8	27,890	1.1	−2.0
Transportation and material moving	660,530	19.4	22,460	−21.6	3.6
Production	654,030	19.2	23,700	18.4	1.8
Construction and extraction	186,590	5.5	30,360	−4.9	8.8
Healthcare practitioner and technical	168,270	4.9	62,770	113	−1.1
Business and financial operations	156,300	4.6	57,640	49.7	7.5
Sales and related	102,930	3.0	37,560	13.3	8.3
Building and grounds cleaning and maintenance	91,970	2.7	21,730	−12.5	1.1
Healthcare support	79,940	2.4	26,200	−8.8	−3.2
Computer and mathematical	77,970	2.3	71,020	41.2	−7.4
Food preparation and serving related	74,490	2.2	20,800	−23.5	5.1
Management	58,090	1.7	97,990	−5.0	3.9
Installation, maintenance, and repair	54,880	1.6	35,600	10.4	2.1
Architecture and engineering	47,460	1.4	66,260	7.2	−2.6
Personal care and service	37,190	1.1	21,670	26.0	−3.4
Education, training, and library	30,930	.9	43,240	40.5	−2.9
Arts, design, entertainment sports, and media	26,320	.8	49,670	23.3	−9.5
Life, physical, and social science	15,830	.5	52,130	11.3	12.4
Protective service	14,580	.4	24,220	24.8	−2.0
Legal	10,950	.3	80,650	87.2	14.7
Community and social services	7,940	.2	34,570	39.8	−1.8
Farming, fishing, and forestry	7,490	.2	23,030	−75.3	23.1

Source: OES data

concentration of certain industries within particular counties with the employment concentration of temp help services within those same counties, the industry assignments for temporary workers and the existence and strength of relationships between temp help services and other industries can be tested.

The model developed to estimate the utilization of temps across industries measures the marginal effects (or the effects when all else is constant) of the employment concentrations of individual industries on the employment concentration of temp help services. The results of this model identify those industries in which positive or negative employment changes tend to have a significant positive or negative effect on temporary employment. See Appendix B for more information about the model.

Results from the model of county-level data from the Quarterly Census of Employment and Wages show that, from 1990 to 2008, counties with higher concentrations of employment in manufacturing; trade, transportation and utilities (henceforth referred to simply as "trade"); financial activities; and professional and business services (P&B) also tended to have higher concentrations of temporary employment. Consequently, it appears that these four industries tended to use temporary employees more heavily than other industries. Furthermore, during the same period, the relationships between the concentrations of manufacturing, trade, and P&B employment and the concentrations of temporary help services employment in the same counties strengthened, suggesting that the use of temporary employment intensified and that these industries were developing an even greater reliance on temporary workers. Studies from the 1980s and 1990s indicated that the largest users of temporary workers in office and administrative support occupations were in the manufacturing, trade, and financial activities industries.[21] (See table 2.)

Manufacturing

The analysis in this article indicates that, throughout the 1990s and 2000s (until 2008), the manufacturing industry has shown a statistically significant reliance on temporary workers. The analysis also shows that the use of temporary workers in manufacturing steadily intensified in the 1990s before sharply increasing in the early 2000s. Compared with the model results for 1990, the marginal effect of manufacturing employment concentration on temp help services employment concentration was 4.5 times greater in 2005. The model results show that, while manufacturing's share of total national employment fell from 16.2 percent in 1990 to 9.8 percent in 2008, manufacturing's use of temporary workers greatly intensified. A two-sample t-test also verifies that the difference between the parameter estimates of 1990 and 2008 is statistically different from zero, indicating that the observed increase in the use of temporary employment from 1990 to 2008 is statistically significant. (See Figure 2 and tables A1–A4 of Appendix C.)

The model results support estimates from a previous study which found that temp workers accounted for about 4 percent of total employment in the manufacturing sector in 1997, compared with only 1 percent in 1992.[22] Other studies have shown that many manufacturing firms have become more "flexible," or dependent on just-in-time workers.[23] The combination of lower costs for flexible labor inputs—due to increased efficiency in matching temporary workers with firms—and the growth in networks of temp help services firms has contributed to manufacturing firms' increased reliance on and use of temporary workers.[24] Manufacturing plants tend to choose temporary workers over permanent workers when they expect output to fall, allowing them to avoid the costs of laying off permanent workers. Generally speaking, higher levels of uncertainty regarding output are associated with greater use of temporary workers.[25]

Table 2   Relationships Between the Concentration of Temporary Help Employment and the Concentrations of Employment in Other Industries

Industry	Relationship with Temporary Help			Change in Strength of Relationship	
	1990	2000	2008	1999–2000	2000–08
Natural resources and mining					
Construction					
Manufacturing	+	+	+	+	+
Trade, transportation, and utilities	+	+	+	+	+
Information					
Financial activities	+	+	+		
Professional and business services	+	+	+	+	
Education and health services					
Leisure and hospitality			–		
Other services			–		
Public administration					
R^2	0.73	0.77	0.70		

Note: A plus sign indicates a significantly positive relationship, a minus sign indicates a significantly negative relationship, and blank cell indicates that the relationship is not significantly different from zero. Significance testing is at $\alpha = 0.05$.

Source: Model results calculated with QCEW data.

Parameter
Estimate

Parameter
Estimate

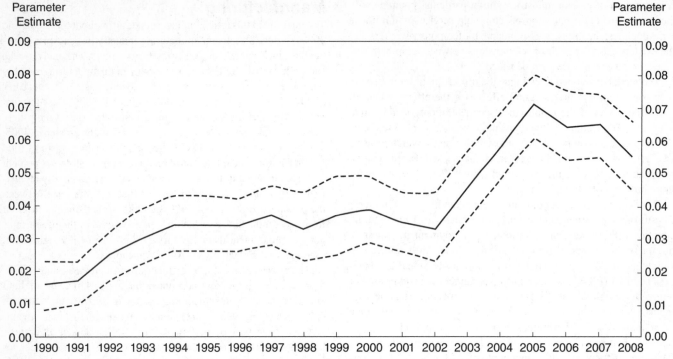

Figure 2   Parameter estimates for manufacturing, 1990–2008

Note: The dashed lines indicate a 95 percent confidence interval. The parameter estimate for a particular industry is the marginal effect (or the effect when all else is constant) of that industry's employment concentration on the concentration of temporary employment, Larger parameter estimates suggest greater reliance on temps.

Source: Model results calculated with QCEW data.

Trade, transportation, and Utilities

The use of temp help services in the trade industry also significantly intensified between 1990 and 2008. In 2008, the marginal effect of increased concentration of trade industry employment on temp help services was 5 times the level seen in 1990. Statistical tests verify that this intensification is statistically significant at the 95 percent confidence level. (See Figure 3 and tables A1–A4 of Appendix C.)

The model results—which point towards the growth of the use of temporary help in this industry—are consistent with estimates from a previous study which found that the share of temporary employment in the transportation and utilities sector increased from about 1.5 percent to 2.5 percent during the mid-1990s, while the employment share for trade remained fairly stable at around 0.7 percent.[26] The estimate of increasingly positive correlation between employment in trade, transportation, and utilities and employment in temp help services is also consistent with data showing an increase in the use of temps in material moving and retail sales occupations in recent years.[27]

Professional and Business Services

The use of temporary workers in the professional and business services industry intensified in the 1990s and then weakened, but remained positive, during most of the 2000s. Despite the fluctuations, the professional and business industry made significant use of temporary workers throughout the 1990-to-2008 period. A separate two-sample t-test shows that the intensification in the use of temps during the 1990s is statistically significant at the 95 percent confidence level. (See Figure 4 and tables A1–A4 of Appendix C.) The statistical test also shows that the use of temps by P&B has grown less intense in recent years. This is substantiated by evidence that the share of clerical and data-entry operator positions occupied by temporary workers has dropped in recent years, as explained in the section on occupational trends in temporary employment. In addition, lower skilled occupations in P&B such as filing clerks and data-entry operators have been outsourced or eliminated in many firms because of greater automation and digitization of business records.

Financial Activities

Model estimates also show that the concentration of financial activities employment was a significant determinant of the concentration of temporary employment over most of the 1990–2008 period. This indicates that the financial activities sector was a major employer of temps during this timespan. Throughout the 1990s, the use of temps in financial activities was fairly stable. In the early 2000s, however, the use of temporary workers decreased, and it then intensified from around 2003 onwards. Statistical testing shows that this intensification was statistically significant at the 95 percent confidence level. (See Figure 5 and tables A1–A4 of Appendix C.)

The model results corroborate estimates from a previous study which found that the proportion of temporary employment in finance increased from about 0.5 percent in the early 1980s to about 2.5 percent by 1990 then remained stable during the 1990s.[28] Following the passage in 2002 of the Sarbanes-Oxley Act, which enhanced financial accounting standards, demand soared for financial accounting professionals able to navigate firms through the new legislation. Instead of remaining tied down to one firm, many of these finance professionals became temporary or contract workers and were able to demand greater pay and flexibility.[29] This article's model estimates are also corroborated by the growth of employment services jobs in business and financial operations occupations, shown in table 1.

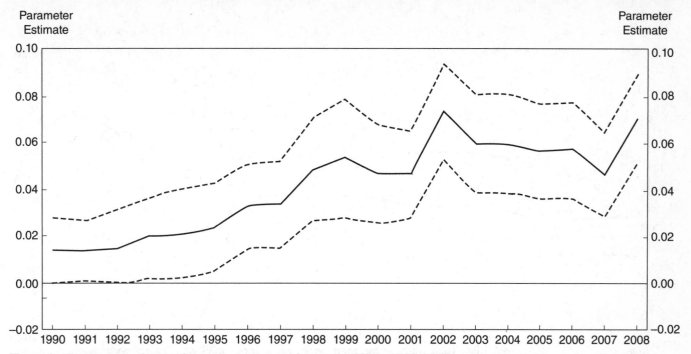

Figure 3   Parameter estimates for trade, transportation, and utilities, 1990–2008

Note: The dashed lines indicate a 95 percent confidence interval. The parameter estimate for a particular industry is the marginal effect (or the effect when all else is constant) of that industry's employment concentration on the concentration of temporary employment, Larger parameter estimates suggest greater reliance on temps.

Source: Model results calculated with QCEW data.

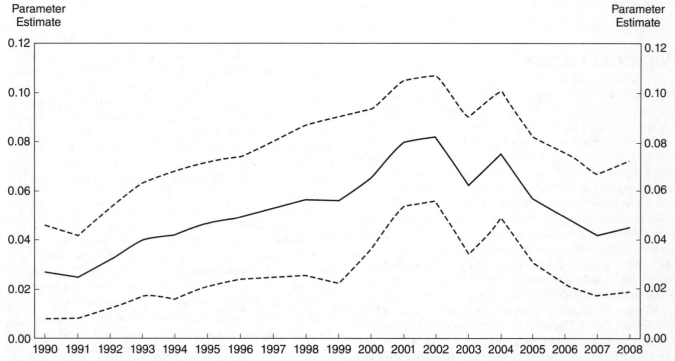

Figure 4   Parameter estimates for professional and business services, 1990–2008

Note: The dashed lines indicate a 95 percent confidence interval. The parameter estimate for a particular industry is the marginal effect (or the effect when all else is constant) of that industry's employment concentration on the concentration of temporary employment. Larger parameter estimates suggest greater reliance on temps.

Source: Model results calculated with QCEW data.

Other Industries

The analysis in this article of the 1990-to-2008 period indicates that other industries such as natural resources and mining, construction, information, education and health services, leisure and hospitality, other services (except public administration), and public administration were not significant factors in the concentration of temp help services employment in the average county in nearly all years.

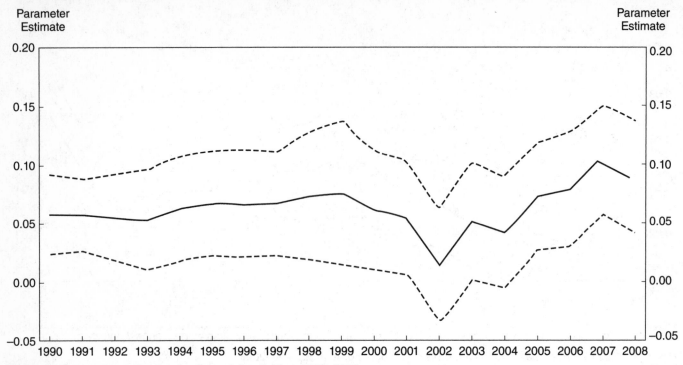

Parameter Estimate

Parameter Estimate

Figure 5   Parameter estimates for financial activities, 1990–2008

Note: The dashed lines indicate a 95 percent confidence interval. The parameter estimate for a particular industry is the marginal effect (or the effect when all else is constant) of that industry's employment concentration on the concentration of temporary employment. Larger parameter estimates suggest greater reliance on temps.

Source: Model results calculated with QCEW data.

Regional Trends

In addition to being associated more with certain industries than with others, the temporary help services industry is associated with counties with certain characteristics and with particular regions. As discussed later in this section, temp help services has evolved and grown differently in different counties and regions of the United States. Building upon the analysis of changes in temporary help services by occupational group and industry, this section shows how the growth of employment in temp help services has varied on the basis of the size of temp employment in given areas in 1990 and has varied by region as well.

Temp employment growth rates by 1990 temp employment level. Over the past two decades, the distribution of temporary employment has shifted towards areas with lower initial (i.e., 1990) employment in temporary help services. The average percent growth of temp employment from 1990 to 2008 was much greater in counties with fewer than 1,000 temporary employees in 1990 than in counties with higher initial employment in temp help services.[30] (See Figure 6.) Counties with temp help employment of 10,000 or more in 1990 grew by an average of 55 percent over the next 18 years. During the same period, counties that had 1990 temp employment of 5,000–9,999 had average growth of 62 percent, and those with 1990 temp employment of 1,000–4,999 nearly doubled their temporary employment. Finally, counties with temporary employment of fewer than 1,000 had an average growth rate of over 450 percent. Therefore, smaller counties have been the emerging markets for temporary employment while larger counties have grown more slowly in temp employment, probably because they were closer to the saturation point.

This larger relative growth of temp help services employment in counties with lower 1990 temp employment has greatly increased the share of temporary employment in these counties. (See Figure 7.) In 1990, the 20 counties with the highest employment in temporary help services contained over 30 percent of all temp employment in the Nation, and the 100 counties with the highest temp employment had about 60 percent. By 2008, the top 20 counties held less than a quarter of total temp employment, and the share for the top 100 counties had fallen to less than half.

Temporary help services employment by region. Temporary help services employment has distinct patterns in its growth that differ by region of the country. Between 1990 and 2008, among the four U.S. Census regions,[31] the South had the largest employment growth, at 126 percent, followed by the Midwest (117 percent), the West (88 percent), and the Northeast (68 percent). (See Figure 8.)

In the South, the concentration of temporary help services employment has stayed consistently above the national average. The gap between temporary employment concentration in the South and that in the Nation as a whole has increased since 1990 because of a larger-than-average growth rate in temp employment in the South. Despite a steep decline after 2006 in the concentration of temp employment, the South region still had temp employment of nearly 900,000 in 2008, or 39 percent of all temporary employment in the country.

The concentration of temporary employment in the Northeast region has stayed consistently below the national average. (See Figure 9.) The gap between temp help services concentration

Temp.employment level

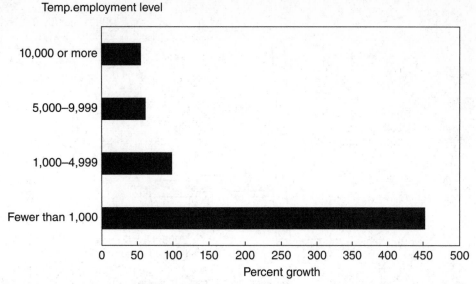

Percent growth

Figure 6   Average growth from 1990 to 2008 in temporary employment for counties grouped by level of temporary employment in 1990

Source: QCEW data.

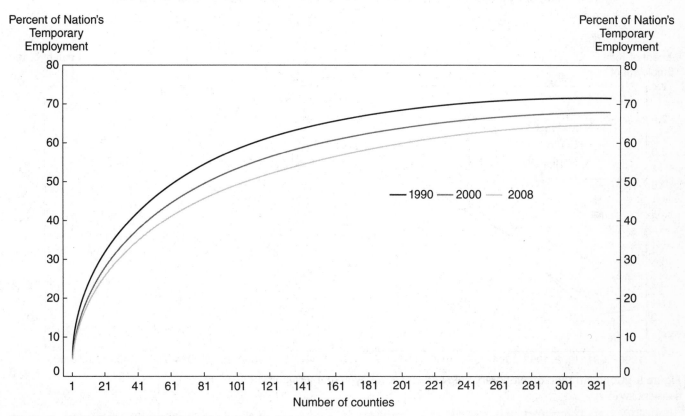

Figure 7   Cumulative distribution of temporary help services employment among the 329 counties with the most such employment, 1990, 2000, and 2008

Source: OCEW data.

in the Nation as a whole and that in the Northeast was larger in 2008 than it was in 1990 because the employment concentration of temp help services grew more slowly in the Northeast during the 1990–2008 period as a whole. Despite this slower growth, temp help employment concentration in the Northeast stood at nearly 1.4 percent in 2008, considerably higher than the 1990 figure of 0.9 percent.

In the West, the concentration of temp help services employment stayed above the national average during most of the 18-year period. In 2007 and 2008, though, the concentration of temps in the

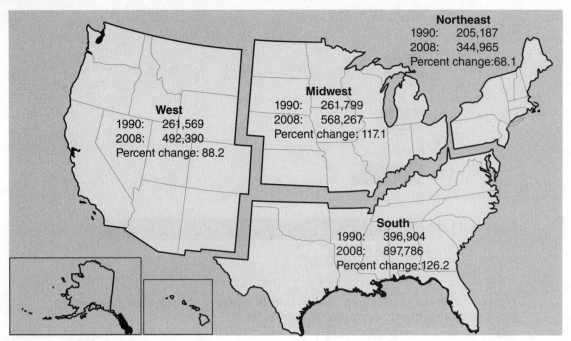

Figure 8   Temporary employment by region in 1990 and 2008, and 1990–2008 percent change
Source: QCEW data.

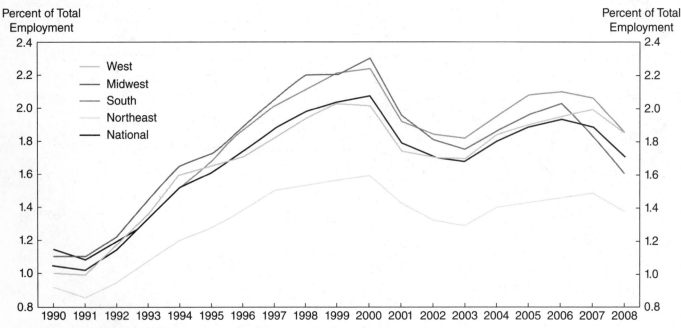

Figure 9   Concentration of temporary help services employment, by region, 1990–2008
Source: QCEW data.

West region was below the national average. One factor that may have played a role in the recent decline in the concentration of temporary help services employment in the West is the large decline in construction employment following the housing bubble, which was most acute in the West region. Temporary workers allowed construction firms to scale production up during the housing boom and scale it down following the collapse in housing prices in order to meet increases and decreases in demand without incurring the costs associated with hiring or laying off permanent workers.[32]

The concentration of temporary worker employment in the Midwest stayed similar to that in the Nation as a whole for much of the 1990–2008 period. However, somewhere around 2006 a gap in temp employment concentration between the Midwest and the Nation as a whole opened up, with the Midwest's concentration overtaking the national average, and the gap was more pronounced in 2007 and 2008.

The tremendous growth of temporary help services has been driven by the flexibility and low labor cost of temporary workers.

From 1990 to 2008, total temporary employment in the United States went from 1.1 million to 2.3 million, and in 2008 it represented 1.7 percent of total U.S. employment. Traditionally, temporary workers have worked in lower paying occupations such as office and administrative support, transportation and material moving, and production occupations; however, temporary help services has gained prominence in recent years in higher skilled and higher paying occupations.

The analysis in this article indicates that industries which typically employ temporary workers include manufacturing; trade, transportation, and utilities; financial activities, and professional and business services. The use of temporary workers intensified in manufacturing between 1990 and 2005 but decreased slightly after 2005. In the trade, transportation, and utilities industry, the use of temporary workers has intensified since 1990. The use of temps in the professional and business services industry increased between 1990 and 2001 but decreased significantly in subsequent years. In the financial activities industry, the use of temporary workers remained fairly stable between 1990 and 2001 but significantly increased after 2001.

Regional differences in temp employment also are apparent. In the South, temp employment grew by 126 percent during the 1990–2008 period, and the region had a higher concentration of temporary workers than any other region of the United States for much of the period. Until recently, the concentration of temps in the West region also was higher than the national average. The growth and concentration of temporary employment were lower in the Northeast than in the rest of the Nation throughout the 18-year period analyzed, while the Midwest maintained a concentration of temp help services employment similar to that of the Nation as a whole.

Despite a steep decline in temporary employment in recent years, the industry has remained an important indicator of the overall economy. Employers rely on temporary workers to achieve greater workforce flexibility. During economic expansions, temp workers are among the first to be hired, and during times of recession, temporary workers are laid off in disproportionate numbers.[33] Hence, temporary help services has grown in importance not only with respect to the industries and occupations associated with it and the areas where it is found, but also because of its function as a macroeconomic buffer during periods of economic volatility.

Notes

1. Wayne J. Howe, "Temporary help workers: who they are, what jobs they hold," *Monthly Labor Review,* November 1986, pp. 45–47; and Anne E. Polivka and Thomas Nardone, "On the definition of 'contingent work," *Monthly Labor Review,* December 1989, pp. 9–14.

2. See page 129 of Lewis M. Segal and Daniel G. Sullivan, "The Growth of Temporary Services Work," *Journal of Economic Perspectives,* spring 1997, pp. 117–36, citing a study which states that 38 percent of temporary workers were offered permanent jobs at the firms where they worked as temps.

3. Edward A. Lenz, "Staffing Industry's Positive Role in U.S. Economy" (Alexandria, Virginia, American Staffing Association, Mar. 4, 2008) on the Internet at www.americanstaffing.net /legalandgovenment/issue_papers/Staffing_Industry_Positive_Role .pdf (visited Aug. 2, 2010).

4. Jamie Peck and Nik Theodore, "Flexible recession: the temporary staffing industry and mediated work in the United States," *Cambridge Journal of Economics,* March 2007.

5. Around the time of the 2001 recession, year-over-year percent change for temp employment switched from positive to negative 7 months before the switch for total nonfarm employment; around the time of the recession that started in December 2007, the switch occurred 17 months earlier for temp employment than for total nonfarm employment.

6. During the 1998–2008 period, employment in temporary help services made up on average 69.8 percent of employment services employment, although it exceeded 70 percent in all months from the last calendar quarter of 2004 through at least the end of 2008, when it was 73.2 percent.

7. Martin J. Gannon, "Preferences of temporary workers: time, variety, and flexibility," *Monthly Labor Review,* August 1984, pp. 24–28.

8. Katharine Abraham and Robert McKersie, ed., *New Developments in the Labor Market: Toward a New Institutional Paradigm* (Cambridge, Massachusetts, MIT Press, 1990), chapter 4; Dwight R. Lee, "Why is Flexible Employment Increasing?" *Journal of Labor Research,* December 1996, pp. 543–53; and Barbara A, Wiens-Tuers, "Employee Attachment and Temporary Workers," *Journal of Economic Issues,* March 2001, pp. 45–60.

9. Jeffrey B. Wenger and Arne L. Kalleberg, "Employers' Flexibility and Employment Volatility," *American Journal of Economics and Sociology,* April 2006, pp. 347–82. On page 352, the authors estimate that less than one-third of temporary workers are likely to be employed in the industry a year later.

10. In 1990, the average annual wage for temp help services was $12,500, compared with $23,600 for overall national employment. By 2008, both temp help services wages and national average wages doubled, to $25,500 and $45,600, respectively. Real wage growth in this period was 23.9 percent for temp help services and 17.2 percent for overall employment.

11. Angela Clinton, "Flexible labor; restructuring the American work force," *Monthly Labor Review,* August 1997, pp. 3–27.

12. Based on an internal BLS report.

13. Rachel Krantz, "Employment in business services: a year of unprecedented decline," *Monthly Labor Review,* April 2002, pp. 17–24.

14. Wenger and Kalleberg, "Employers' Flexibility and Employment Volatility"; Lonnie Golden, "The Expansion of Temporary Help Employment in the U.S., 1982–1992: A Test of Alternative Economic Explanations," *Applied Economks,* September 1996, pp. 1127–41; and Karylee Laird and Nicolas Williams, "Employment Growth in the Temporary Help Supply Industry," *Journal of Labor Research,* December 1996, pp. 663–81.

15. Nik Theodore and Jamie Peck, "Temporary downturn? Temporary staffing in the recession and the jobless recovery," *Focus,* spring 2005, pp. 35–41; Nik Theodore and Jamie Peck, "The Temporary Staffing Industry: Growth Imperatives and Limits to Contingency," *Economic Geography,* October 2002, pp. 463–93; and Peck and Theodore, "Flexible recession."

16. Revenue was estimated by Staffing Industry Analysts, Inc.; data were provided to the authors by Jon Osborne, vice president of research at Staffing Industry Analysts, on Feb. 17, 2010.

17. See Appendix A for notes on these data.

18. Max L. Carey and Kim L. Hazelbaker, "Employment growth in the temporary help industry," *Monthly Labor Review,* April 1986, pp. 37–44.

19. Elizabeth Dietz, "A Look at Temporary Help Wage Rates," *Compensation and Working Conditions*, September 1996, pp. 46–50; and Patrick Kilcoyne, "Occupations in the Temporary Help Services Industry," in *Occupational Employment and Wages, May 2004*, Bulletin 2575 (Bureau of Labor Statistics, September 2005), on the Internet at www.bls.gov/oes/2004/may/temp.pdf (visited Aug. 4, 2010) pp. 6–9.

20. According to estimates from Staffing Industry Analysts, Inc., legal occupations also had the largest revenue growth from 2004 to 2008.

21. Carey and Hazelbaker, "Employment growth in the temporary help industry"; and Marcello M. Estevao and Saul Lach, *The Evolution of the Demand for Temporary Help Supply Employment in the United States,* NBER Working Paper W7427 (Cambridge, MA, National Bureau of Economic Research, December 1999).

22. Estevao and Lach, *The Evolution of the Demand for Temporary Help.*

23. Donald S. Allen, "Changes in Inventory Management and the Business Cycle," Federal Reserve Bank of St. Louis *Review*, July/August 1995, pp. 17–26.

24. Segal and Sullivan, "The Growth of Temporary Services Work."

25. Yukako Ono and Daniel Sullivan, *Manufacturing Plants' Use of Temporary Workers: An Analysis Using Census Micro Data*, WP 2006-24 (Federal Reserve Bank of Chicago, originally published in 2006 and revised in February 2010).

26. Francoise Carré, Marianne A. Ferber, Lonnie Golden, and Stephen A. Herzenberg, eds., *Nonstandard Work: The Nature and Challenges of Changing Employment Arrangements* (Champaign, IL, Industrial Relations Research Association, 2000), chapter 4; and Marcello and Lach, *The Evolution of the Demand for Temporary Help,* p. 131.

27. This increase was calculated by use of the same Occupational Employment Statistics dataset used for the analysis of individual occupations.

28. Estevao and Lach, *The Evolution of the Demand for Temporary Help.*

29. Conversation with Jon Osborne, director of research at Industry Staffing Analysts, on Feb. 12, 2010.

30. QCEW county-level annual data were used for these calculations. The data pertain to temporary employment in 330 counties across the Nation for the years 1990, 2000, and 2008.

31. The U.S. Census Bureau divides the United States into regions: the West, Midwest, South, and Northeast; see www.censns.gov/geo/www/us_regdiv.pdf (visited Aug. 6, 2010).

32. "Current Trends in Construction Employment," *Issues in Labor Statistics* (Bureau of Labor Statistics, Oct, 5, 2007), on the Internet at www.bls.gov/opub/ils/pdf/opbils62.pdf (visited Aug. 6, 2010).

33. Peck and Theodore, "Flexible recession."

Appendix A: Data Notes

The two main datasets used in this paper are those of the Quarterly Census of Employment and Wages (QCEW) and Occupational Employment Statistics (OES) programs, both of which are part of the Bureau of Labor Statistics. County-level, State-level, and national-level data were used for years 1990 through 2008 from the QCEW database, and national-level data were used for years 2004 and 2008 from the OES database. The following list displays the industries that are used for the analysis of this article. They all are are either supersectors or NAICS sectors except for temporary help services, which is classified as a NAICS industry.

- Natural resources and mining
- Construction
- Manufacturing
- Trade, transportation, and utilities
- Information
- Financial activities
- Professional and business services
- Temporary help services
- Education and health services
- Leisure and hospitality
- Other services (except public administration)
- Public administration

Note: NAICS groups establishments into industries on the basis of the activities in which they are primarily engaged. In this article, professional and business services employment excludes temporary help services employment.

QCEW data notes. The QCEW program produces a comprehensive set of employment and wage data for workers covered by State unemployment insurance laws and Federal workers covered by the Unemployment Compensation for Federal Employees program. The program serves as a near census (covering 98 percent of U.S. jobs) of monthly employment and quarterly wage information; the data are organized by six-digit NAICS industry at the national, State, and county levels.

OES data notes. The OES program produces employment and wage estimates for over 800 occupations. The OES survey is currently constructed from a sample of 1.2 million establishments that are surveyed over six semiannual "panels." These panels are combined in a weighted fashion and benchmarked to May of the survey year. The occupational trends section of this paper uses a tabulation of the OES database for years 2004 and 2008 to analyze recent occupational patterns in the temporary staffing industry. Because of the unavailability of data at the temporary help services industry level, the employment services industry is analyzed instead.

The OES survey was converted from an annual survey to a semiannual survey in November 2002, making May 2003 the first time that BLS created estimates for a 3-year period that included two semiannual panels; it did so by incorporating data from the two semiannual panels with data from two annual panels. Unfortunately, the May 2003 estimates for employment services do not include data on two major occupational groups and thus could not be compared with estimates from May 2008. The occupational analysis in this article is based on a comparison of the staffing patterns in May 2004 and May 2008. May 2008 is the most recent month for which data are available, and May 2004 is far enough away in time that data from the two periods do not include any overlapping panels.

Appendix B: Multivariate Linear Regression Model

A cross-sectional, multivariate linear regression model was used to estimate the relationship between the concentration of a given industry's employment in a given area and the concentration of temporary help services employment in the same area. The equation used is

$$THS_{it} = \beta_1 MINING_{it} + \beta_2 CONSTR_{it} + \beta_3 MANUF_{it} + \beta_4 TTU_{it} + \beta_5 INFO_{it} + \beta_6 FINANCE_{it} + \beta_7 (P\&B - THS)_{it} + \beta_8 EDUC_{it} + \beta_9 LEISURE_{it} + \beta_{10} OTHER_{it} + \beta_{11} GOV_{it} + \varepsilon_{it}$$

where THS_{it} is the concentration of temporary help services employment in county i at year t, and each independent variable is the concentration of the employment of the industry in question. This model was run for each year from 1990 to 2008. The model does not include an intercept, because temporary employment can be attributed to all of these industries. Since temporary workers serve other industries by nature, it is assumed that no temporary workers are employed independently of another industry.[1]

The sign and significance of each coefficient shows the direction and strength of the relationship between the employment concentration of each industry and the concentration of temporary employment. In a multivariate regression framework,[2] cross-industry correlations are controlled. "β_k is the change in the expected value of y if x_k is increased by one unit and the other xs are held fixed."[3] For example, if the estimate for β_3 is positive and significant, then an area with a higher concentration of manufacturing employment would, on average, have a higher concentration of temp help services employment than an area with a lower concentration of manufacturing employment concentration, assuming constant concentrations of other industries' employment.

The increase in the strength of a parameter estimate[4] of the linear model across time demonstrates the change in the use of temporary help services by industries across counties. Furthermore, a significantly positive coefficient means that the employment concentration of an industry is positively related to the concentration of temp employment, suggesting that the industry tends to rely on temporary workers. A positive coefficient which increases in value suggests that an industry is increasing its reliance on temporary workers.[5]

Appendix C: Additional Tables

Table A1   Model Estimates for 1990

Industry	Parameter Estimate	t-Statistic	Statistical Significance
Natural resources and mining	−0.008	−0.86	
Construction	.024	1.39	
Manufacturing	.016	4.25	****
Trade, transportation, and utilities	.014	1.94	*
Information	−.003	−.10	
Financial activities	.058	3.34	***
Professional and business services	.027	2.81	****
Education and health services	−.006	−.60	
Leisure and hospitality	−.004	−.36	
Other services	−.012	−.25	
Public administration	−.007	−.71	

Note: * significant at the 10 percent a level, ** significant at the 5 percent a level, *** significant at the 1 percent a level, **** significant at the 0.1 percent a level

Table A2   Model Estimates for 2000

Industry	Parameter Estimate	t-Statistic	Statistical Significance
Natural resources and mining	0.005	0.28	
Construction	−.005	−.19	
Manufacturing	.039	7.53	****
Trade, transportation, and utilities	.047	4.46	****
Information	.045	1.04	
Financial activities	.061	2.33	**
Professional and business services	.065	4.45	****
Education and health services	−.018	−1.30	
Leisure and hospitality	−.006	−.46	
Other services	−.090	−1.23	
Public administration	.000	.02	

Note: * significant at the 10 percent a level, ** significant at the 5 percent a level, *** significant at the 1 percent a level, **** significant at the 0.1 percent a level

Table A3   Model Estimates for 2008

Industry	Parameter Estimate	t-Statistic	Statistical Significance
Natural resources and mining	0.008	0.63	
Construction	−.020	−1.00	
Manufacturing	.055	10.40	****
Trade, transportation, and utilities	.071	7.43	****
Information	−.003	−.07	
Financial activities	.089	3.54	****
Professional and business services	.045	3.39	****
Education and health services	−.014	−1.51	
Leisure and hospitality	−.025	−2.32	**
Other services	−.226	−4.19	****
Public administration	−.017	−.80	

Note: * significant at the 10 percent a level, ** significant at the 5 percent a level, *** significant at the 1 percent a level, **** significant at the 0.1 percent a level

Table A4   Changes in Parameter Estimates, 1990–2000 and 2000–2008

Industry	1990–2000			2000–2008		
	Difference, in Percent	t-Statistic	Statistical Significance	Difference, in Percent	t-Statistic	Statistical Significance
Natural resources and mining	1.3	0.68		0.3	0.17	
Construction	−2.9	−0.94		−1.5	−.48	
Manufacturing	2.3	3.65	****	1.6	2.21	**
Trade, transportation, and utilities	3.3	2.60	***	2.4	1.69	*
Information	4.9	.90		−4.9	−.74	
Financial activities	.3	.09		2.8	.77	
Professional and business services	3.7	2.14	**	−1.9	−.98	
Education and health services	−1.2	−.69		.4	.25	
Leisure and hospitality	−.3	−.15		−1.9	−1.08	
Other services	−7.8	−.90		−13.7	−1.51	
Public administration	.8	.30		−1.8	−.56	

Note: * significant at the 10 percent a level, ** significant at the 5 percent a level, *** significant at the 1 percent a level, **** significant at the 0.1 percent a level

Notes

1. Note that the estimates for P&B exclude temp help services employment.

2. A multiple regression model is used to accommodate many explanatory variables that may be correlated, and allows one to explicitly control for many other factors that simultaneously affect the dependent variable. A least squares model with multiple regressors captures the variation in temporary employment that is due to the variation in a particular industry only; that is, it captures the partial effect of that industry's employment concentration on temporary employment concentration. See Jeffrey M. Wooldridge, *Introductory Econometrics: A Modern Approach,* fourth edition (Cincinnati, OH, South-Western, 2009), p. 61.

3. John A. Rice, *Mathematical Statistics and Data Analysis,* third edition, (Belmont, CA, Duxbury, 2007), p. 545.

4. To test for significance in changes in a parameter estimate between two periods, a two-sample *t*-test with unequal variances was used.

The difference in the parameter estimate is statistically significant if the following is true:

$$\frac{\left|\beta_i^{t=1} - \beta_i^{t=0}\right|}{\sqrt{SE^2_{\beta_i^{t=1}} + SE^2_{\beta_i^{t=0}}}} > t_{\frac{a}{2}, df}$$

5. In a perfect world where, in every county, each industry's use of temporary help services is exactly proportional to the employment of the industry, an industry s employment concentration is either (surely) significantly positive (if that industry uses temporary workers, even a little), or is not significantly different from 0 (if that industry does not use temps). However, in reality, it is not the case that each industry in each county employs temporary workers at the same rate; therefore, an insignificant result may not be associated only with an industry s non-employment of temps. It is not possible to distinguish whether statistical insignificance indicates that some industries employ substantial numbers of temps and others do not or insignificance indicates that no industries have a substantial number of temps, but one can reasonably assume that each industry employs at least some temporary workers.

Critical Thinking

1. Why do you think temporary help services have expanded from 1990 to 2008?

2. Do you think this trend will continue? Why or why not?

3. Why would an organization use a temporary firm instead of hiring full-time employees?

TIAN LUO is an economist, **AMAR MANN** is a supervisory economist, and **RICHARD HOLDEN** is a regional commissioner, all at the Bureau of Labor Statistics' West Regional Office for Economic Analysis and Information in San Francisco, California.

Acknowledgments—The authors thank David Hiles, David Talan, George Stamas, Laurie Salmon, Sheryl Konigsberg, and Phoebe Yung from the BLS Office of Employment and Unemployment Statistics, and Richard Cerri, Jay Mousa, and Michael Dolfman from the BLS Office of Field Operations for their thoughtful comments, review, and guidance.

Sharing Work—and Unemployment Benefits

In 18 states, workers whose hours are cut to part time become eligible for unemployment benefits.

DIANE CADRAIN

As the nation's employers continue to stagger under a load of financial misery, HR professionals at some companies have found a powerful retention tool that enables them to avoid layoffs and hang on to trained employees.

They're setting up work-sharing programs, using a little-known feature of the unemployment laws in 18 states. Work sharing, shared work or short-time compensation programs, as they're variously known, soften the blow of full layoffs by allowing employers to reduce hours for full-time employees, who then may collect prorated unemployment benefits for the lost hours. Rather than lay off 20 percent of the full-time workforce, for example, an employer might reduce everyone's hours by 20 percent. Some employers that implement work sharing continue to fund employee benefits while the program is in place.

"With all the publicity about layoffs due to the uncertain economy, our employees have embraced our use of work sharing as an alternative to layoffs," explains Pam Thayer, director of human resources at the New Buffalo Shirt Factory, a Clarence, N.Y., manufacturer of high-tech, screen-printed garments.

"It's a win-win," adds Dave Randall, personnel and safety director for Columbia Steel Castings, a Portland, Ore., foundry. "We get to keep our trained workforce, and employees maintain their standard of living."

To make this happen, a participating employer in a state that allows work sharing has to submit a plan to state officials. The employer must also get a green light from any unions. Employers may institute work sharing plantwide or in a specific department or unit.

In general, with some variation among the states, plans must reduce work hours between 10 percent and 40 percent, involve only regular full-time employees, and identify participating employees by names and Social Security numbers.

Unlike the usual requirements for receiving jobless benefits, employees in work-sharing programs are not required to demonstrate that they're seeking work and are available for it, but they are required to be available for their normal workweek.

The programs are relatively simple for employers, too. "All we do is fill out a master form every Monday," says Andy Nowakowski, president and chief executive officer of Tri-Star Industries, a Berlin, Conn., manufacturer of metal components, "and employees don't have to go to the Labor Department, log in, and prove they're available and looking for work. That makes it easier on them."

Bob Scodari, chief financial officer of Better Packages Inc., a Shelton, Conn., manufacturer of packaging equipment with 35 employees, agrees: "It's completely easy administratively—once a week, we send information to the [state] Labor Department."

For Columbia Steel's 350 employees, Randall says administration of the work-sharing program "is a little bit of a headache because we have to review the payroll and attendance to make sure people qualify. For example, if a person was sick for one day, they don't qualify because they're not available for their usual work," he explains. "But it's a price I'm willing to pay because it's good for the company."

Unemployment officials in states that allow work sharing say employer participation is up this year—way up. In Connecticut, where 50 companies had work-sharing programs in effect a year ago, the number is now 300, says Nancy Steffens of the state's Labor Department.

In Oregon, in any given year about 50 employers normally have programs, says Carol Fisher, benefits adjustment unit manager of the Bureau of Labor and Industry. As of March 13, 372 employers were participating.

And in Rhode Island, where 154 employers participated in 2007, 1,800 companies participated in 2008, says Ray Filippone, director of unemployment insurance for the state Department of Labor and Training.

Experience Ratings

Shared-work benefits are charged against employers' experience rating accounts in the same way as other unemployment benefits. But employers say they take the increases in stride, considering the alternative.

"Our unemployment contributions went up slightly, but they would have gone up more with full layoffs," says Scott Hollander, vice president of human resources for Latham International, a manufacturer of packaged swimming pools and components with 240 employees at two plants in Latham and Scotia, N.Y. "Layoffs would be more of a hit without work sharing. It's a very small price to pay."

Rob Calef, HR manager for ChemArt, a Lincoln, R.I., manufacturer of high-end Christmas ornaments, is similarly unconcerned. "Obviously, there's going to be an effect on our experience rating, but it's all relative in light of the costs of recruitment and training of new employees," he says.

"It's pay now or pay later," notes Bob Cartwright, SPHR, president and CEO of Intelligent Compensation LLC in Austin, Texas. "The rule of thumb is that the cost of replacing an employee is three times the cost of annual pay. Your experience rate goes up somewhat [with work sharing], but you keep the talent."

It's pay now or pay later. . . . Your experience rate goes up somewhat [with work sharing], but you keep the talent.

The Benefit of Benefits

Some state laws require employers to maintain benefits such as health coverage and pension plans during a work-sharing period. Others don't.

Oregon law doesn't require continuation of benefits, but Randall says his company has decided to maintain benefits anyway. "Continuing to pay employee health care premiums is costing the company, but having these employees move to other industries would generate significant recruiting and training costs when business levels increase," he says.

"Maintaining benefits is not a requirement, but our department encourages it," adds Filippone of Rhode Island. "We'll say to an employer, 'Instead of reducing hours 10 percent, why don't you reduce them 20 percent and use the extra money toward health coverage?'"

One Rhode Island employer that continues to fund employee benefits is ChemArt. "We're a familial work environment," explains Calef of his 85-employee plant. "Most employees have been here six years or more. Retention is high. We see employees as people first and employees second. To start pulling the rug out from under people in the long run does more harm than good." He believes that the cost of maintaining benefits is "insignificant" in the grand scheme of things.

"Florida law doesn't require employers to continue paying health or other benefits to workers in an approved plan," says Robbie Cunningham, communications director for the Agency for Workforce Innovation in Tallahassee. "However, employers participating in short-time compensation plans are typically employers who want to keep their workforces intact rather than undergo layoffs. Short-time compensation employers generally have an investment of skill and training in their staffs that would be costly to replace. Consequently, employers would likely not want to adversely affect workers' benefits since this could be impetus for workers to leave the companies."

The cost of maintaining benefits is more than made up by levels of quality and productivity, says Latham's Hollander. "Our work-sharing program helped us avoid $1 million in costs over the past four years—not only productivity and quality, but turnover, staffing and retraining" skilled laborers.

Effect on Productivity

Columbia Steel's foundry work environment is hot and the work is heavy, physical labor, says Randall. "With work sharing, employees working three or four days a week aren't as tired. They're relaxed and ready to work."

Columbia Steel employee Tony Davis agrees: "We're running full tilt. Work-share employees are more focused."

Consultant Cartwright says work sharing "works in favor of the company because employees feel better off and more willing to work hard."

Choosing Employees

While employers cannot designate individual employees for a program, they do have some flexibility.

"We chose work-sharing employees based on an increase in inventory—we had fewer orders, so the product was accumulating," says Scodari of Better Packages. "That's why we started with manufacturing employees. We hoped it would be short-lived and that manufacturing would be enough, but then we had to extend it to administrative employees. Most are working 40 percent, a two-day week."

Last year, ChemArt "chose all hourly manufacturing and assembly employees" with work of a cyclical nature for its work-sharing program, says Calef. "This year, we expanded it to sales and marketing, graphics, IT, and accounting."

Joel Shaughnessy, personnel director of Starrett Manufacturing, a precision tool-maker in Athol, Mass., says, "Originally, it was our entire production facility, based on sales and tools shipped. Everyone went to 32 hours." Today, 449 of Starrett's 700 employees are on work sharing.

Tri-Star Industries "picked all hourly staff, companywide—21 or 22 of them," says Nowakowski. "We had to sign an agreement with the [Connecticut] Department of Labor not to reduce benefits and promise that the program would be departmentwide, with no picking and choosing," he says. He adds that employees' contributions to their health coverage and their 401(k) accounts remain at the levels they would pay if they were working a 40-hour week.

Columbia Steel's "work-sharing employees were chosen by skill and ability, not seniority," says Randall. "We have both union and nonunion employees, and the union had to buy off on the concept. It was a little bit of a sell at first with the union. But when [union officials] understood the benefit, they bought on quickly."

What Kinds of Companies?

A variety of companies participate in work sharing, says Chris Swenson, who runs the program for the Massachusetts Department of Labor and Workforce Development. "But there are more manufacturing employers because the scheme fits well with their operations—the employees are skilled and work the same number of hours each week. The program was designed for that kind of operation."

Carol Fisher, benefits adjustment unit manager of Oregon's Bureau of Labor and Industry, says, "Manufacturers are our biggest group." She notes, "We have a lot of manufacturers of RVs and mobile homes. But we also have a number of builders and other companies based on lumber, some architectural and engineering firms, and some travel and title companies. Some have as many as 600 employees. There's a big variety of employer sizes."

New Buffalo Shirt Factory's Thayer says, "We chose all hourly workers. They're divided into units within departments, and as production needs dictate, an entire unit will be on shared work on a given day."

Employees' Reactions

"The only negative is that employees are supposed to get their [state] checks in 10 days, but they're not on time," Nowakowski says. "I think the [Labor Department] is overwhelmed."

Calef says Rhode Island's unemployment agency "is dealing with four to five times the workload this year, with no staff increases. That slows processing. Checks are sometimes a couple of days late. But at least employees know they're coming."

Randall admits that "Sometimes there are administrative hassles with paper-work. Employees have to fill out forms every week, and sometimes there's a glitch, but the problem usually comes back to the employee himself, such as a change of address."

Despite occasional hassles, "I love work sharing," says Rick Kaliszewski, a master shipper with Better Packages. "I work three days, I get two days off, and I only miss one day's pay. Health benefits aren't affected, so that's great. The checks are on time every Saturday. And I still have my job."

It's a great benefit, says Heather McGinnis, a key account executive in ChemArt's Business Development Department. "I picked up an extra job for my off day, and I get to spend more time with my aging parents."

Columbia Steel's Davis agrees: "It's working out really well: There's been no glitch in payments, I'm thankful to have the supplemental income, and I get my job back."

Nowakowski says "Employee compensation for the days off ranged from 65 percent to 75 percent of a normal day's pay." Another advantage: Employees "save the gas for the drive to work."

Employees at Better Packages aren't shy about showing their appreciation. "Employees stop the company president, they pull him aside and thank him," says Scodari. "They think it's great, especially the medical benefits. They're extremely appreciative."

Critical Thinking

1. Do you think employees, working part-time, should receive unemployment benefits?
2. Why would a state government agree to do this?
3. Why would an organization enter into this kind of a program?

The author is an attorney and writer based in West Hartford, Conn., and a member of the Human Resource Association of Central Connecticut.

Fighting the Good Fight

Harry Markopolos used his instinct, wits, and knowledge to expose Bernie Madoff in what is one of the largest and most far-reaching Ponzi schemes in history.

RUSSELL A. JACKSON

Harry Markopolos, a former Boston investment firm equity derivatives portfolio manager, went from relatively unknown to well-known after pointing out that the emperor had no clothes. Currently on an international speaking tour—including a stop at The IIA's International Conference this month—Markopolos is promoting his book, *No One Would Listen: A True Financial Thriller* (Wiley). The book details his globe-trotting, harrowing, and ultimately ignored pursuit of the truth regarding Bernard Madoff, the emperor in question who brazenly ripped off senior citizens, not-for-profits, and other vulnerable investor classes in what's probably the biggest fraud of its kind.

What's less-well-known about Markopolos is his internal audit background. Much of his investigation, in fact, involved many of the same tasks internal auditors perform every day. Now Markopolos is giving back to the internal audit community, offering his often provocative views and advice for anyone who thinks something's fishy but can't get management's support.

Q: Your bosses tasked you with reverse engineering Madoff's hedge fund so your firm could offer one just like it. How quickly did you switch from trying to figure out how to replicate the fund's success to trying to prove it was a scam?
It took about five minutes of reading through a one-page Madoff marketing brochure to know it was a fraud scheme. Keep in mind that everything about the case was the *Twilight Zone,* and the things that happened to my team over the years never made sense unless, of course, you knew Madoff was a fraud. We quickly learned that if something seemed rational we should immediately discard it, because it couldn't be a part of the case. Madoff had built up a web of lies that were layered upon each other, so we had to pick our way through the lies by using our wits and math skills, disproving each lie one at a time.

Q: What were the specific clues that convinced you that Madoff was a fraud?
There were three glaring red flags I saw during my initial five-minute analysis of Madoff's marketing brochure. One was that in

his strategy paragraph, his portfolio construction techniques were so flawed that he would have needed to pick stocks that only went up or stayed the same; he couldn't afford for a single stock to go down by very much. No one in recorded human history has been able to do that. The second red flag was the fact that his performance line went up at a 45-degree angle—and those angles only exist in high school geometry classes. In finance, the markets can move in three directions: up, down, or sideways. Madoff's returns moved in only one direction—up—which was a dead giveaway. Anytime something doesn't look like anything ever before seen in an industry, a good internal auditor should immediately suspect fraud—not genius—and start investigating. The third red flag was that Madoff reported positive returns for more than 96 percent of the months he reported on—which would be akin to a Major League Baseball player batting .960. How the feeder funds didn't spot the obvious is beyond me—unless they didn't want to know where the performance came from.

> **"Madoff reported positive returns for more than 96 percent of the months he reported on—which would be akin to a Major League Baseball player batting .960."**

Proving Madoff was a fraudster took four hours of mathematical modeling. I ran a least-squares regression and calculated some summary financial statistics related to risk–reward ratios, and it all came clearly into focus. I had run smack into the largest single fraud case in history. At that point, I recruited two of my co-workers to join me in what would become almost a nine-year pursuit of Madoff across two continents. A lot of the investigation took place in Europe, and having a team that traveled extensively and knew how to ask leading questions was necessary to solve the case.

Q: Your bosses weren't very supportive when you told them the Madoff fund was a fraud. How did you press forward to make them understand what you were uncovering?

After I reported Madoff as a fraud to my bosses and they didn't listen, my team and I continued our investigation secretly. Knowing that something is a fraud doesn't mean you're forced to commit career suicide or quit your job. You have to handle such things intelligently and exercise reasonable caution whenever you continue to investigate matters that management doesn't want you looking into.

Q: You sent detailed evidence to the U.S. Securities and Exchange Commission (SEC) at least five times over nearly 10 years. Why didn't the SEC respond?

By December 2005, I had outlined 30 separate red flags for the SEC, some of which were mathematical proofs that Madoff's hedge fund couldn't exist. The SEC's examiners and enforcement attorneys are, for the most part, untrained in finance, financial mathematics, portfolio construction techniques, accounting, and derivatives. The SEC pays its people very poorly and doesn't have any meaningful bonus system to reward its staff for taking on large, difficult cases against the largest Wall Street firms. The SEC's performance metrics measure how many audits are completed in a year—which any internal auditor knows is a worthless statistic that ignores the quality of the audit or the amount of fraud uncovered.

Q: What encouragement can you offer to auditors who may feel frustrated at the lack of credibility they're getting as they try to report on fraud and abuse?

If internal auditors find evidence of criminal fraud at their company, and it's apparently taking place with management's blessing, they should look at it as if they're playing a hand of poker against company management. Every piece of evidence acquired is a card. The better the evidence, the higher the card. Once you've collected overwhelming evidence of the fraud, you should safeguard it outside of the workplace and weigh your next moves. Once you control enough high cards—and if you play your hand right, with an outside lawyer's advice—management will have to listen to you. Smart internal auditors who come across fraud should end up winners, not losers—but only if they play their cards right and realize that knowledge really is power. Oftentimes, if it's a C-suite fraud, you will either have to take your evidence to the authorities or to the press—or maybe even both, whichever your lawyer recommends. The key is to not let the bad guys win and to outthink them every step of the way. Internal auditors can and should be as brave as the quality of their evidence allows them to be.

Q: What advice do you have for auditors who need to convince their bosses of the value an experienced auditor can bring to fraud investigations?

Collect press clippings of fraud cases where companies' management was replaced, billions in shareholder value were wiped out, and the enterprises went bankrupt thanks to a lack of effective controls. The auditor should embark on a rigorous, self-directed professional development program. The truly great internal auditors have a passion for the field and read settled cases and new criminal case filings against companies accused of fraud to learn about new types of fraud schemes. Internal auditors also need to read every good fraud book that comes out and assemble a first-rate fraud library. As soon as an experienced internal auditor reads about a new fraud case in the newspaper, he or she should analyze the elements of the scheme and ask, "Could someone at my company do that? And if so, how?"

Madoff's Scheme

Bernard Madoff was operating a simple Ponzi scheme, Harry Markopolos explains. "He was robbing Peter to pay Paul, so he needed a continual new stream of incoming cash to pay off the old investors," he says. "Investors who got in early would tell their friends and family how great a money manager Madoff was, so they'd want to invest as well." The problem is, in a Ponzi scheme there is no underlying investment activity or service provided. It's all, as Markopolos notes, a charade. On the surface, Ponzi schemes offer alluring, steady returns. But the cold, hard truth, as he puts it, is "those investment returns exist only on the monthly investor statements because they're fiction. The returns generated by most Ponzi schemes on paper are so good that if you are not a professional investor you would definitely be tempted to invest 100 percent of your retirement money in them." That's, in fact, what makes them so lethally effective: It takes tremendous discipline and financial knowledge to successfully avoid them.

Madoff enabled his US $65 billion scam by enlisting the apparent complicity of close to 350 "feeder funds"—companies that marketed his Ponzi scheme for him in more than 40 countries and that, in effect, "fed" him new "investors." Since Markopolos' investigation began almost a decade ago, close to 80 feeder funds have been identified in the United States, along with more than 75 in Switzerland; more than 50 in the United Kingdom; about 25 each in Italy, Brazil, and Germany; and 15 in the Isle of Man. "It's obvious his next frontier was Asia," Markopolos says. "Given a few more years, he would have had similar numbers of feeders operating there." Those funds all pretended to conduct exhaustive due diligence, he adds, such as checking into each manager's background, inspecting his or her operations, verifying the assets, and vetting the strategy. "But in reality, they were likely earning the lion's share of the fees—and the reason Madoff paid them so handsomely was so they would willingly look the other way and not conduct any of their promised due diligence checks," he says. They were the accomplices that enabled the scheme to get as large as it did and go on for as long as it did, he adds. "Madoff alone would never have been able to reach US $65 billion without their help." That's how much it's estimated that he stole from innocent investors.

Good internal auditors also review internal controls while asking, "How could I beat them? How many employees would have to collude to commit fraud?" Internal controls are static, while the criminal mind is always learning new tricks. So internal auditors need to learn new tricks at a faster rate than the fraudsters.

Q: What do you think of the Office of Inspector General's (OIG's) proposed changes to the SEC's bounty program for rewarding whistleblowers?

I wholeheartedly support all of the OIG's recommended changes to the bounty program. On March 10, 2009, I recommended to SEC Chair Mary Schapiro that the SEC copy the best practices of the Department of Justice and the Internal Revenue Service whistleblower bounty programs—and it has. The SEC needs to quickly obtain large cases against big Wall Street players to restore its reputation, and the only way to get those big cases is to pay rewards to whistleblowers who bring in well-developed cases with a high quality and quantity of specific evidence proving fraud. Rewards are necessary to make whistleblower programs work, because if a whistleblower gets found out by his or her company, that company almost always retaliates, despite laws on the books punishing companies that do so.

Critical Thinking

1. What is the role of whistleblowers?
2. Why is it so difficult?
3. What do you think of the experience of Harry Markopolos?
4. How was Bernie Madoff able to get away with his scheme for all those years and why?

From *Internal Auditor,* June 2010. Copyright © 2010 by Institute of Internal Auditors. Reprinted by permission.

Strategic Human Resource Management as Ethical Stewardship

Cam Caldwell et al.

Research about the strategic role of human resource management (HRM) has exponentially increased over the last decade (Hartel et al., 2007), with scholars and practitioners acknowledging the critical importance of ethical issues in HRM as key factors in aligning and guiding organizational success (Hernandez, 2008; Werhane et al. 2004). Scholars have also noted that the strategic focus of human resource systems is more effective when aligned with an organization's mission, purposes, values, and structure (Becker and Gerhart, 1996; Becker and Huselid, 2006; Huselid and Becker, 1997). This article examines the ethical duties associated with the implementation of HRM systems in helping organizations to achieve their potential (cf. Payne and Wayland, 1999) and identifies the leadership roles which make up an ethical stewardship approach to organizational systems.

We begin by citing the strategic human resource management (SHRM) literature to provide a contextual framework for examining the importance of the alignment and congruence of HRM systems (Becker and Huselid, 2006; Pfeffer, 1998) with the strategic goals of an organization (Becker et al., 2001). We then examine the nature and duties of ethical stewardship (Caldwell et al., 2008) related to the effective governance of organizations. Integrating the importance of SHRM with this framework of ethical stewardship, we identify important but sometimes implicit leadership roles that human resource professionals (HRPs) ought to contribute in optimizing the ability of their organizations to achieve that long-term wealth creation (Senge, 2006). We conclude by identifying the contributions of our article and offer comments about the importance of ethical leadership in creating the work systems, cultures, and the high level of employee commitment that are essential for organizations in today's global workplace (Pfeffer, 1998, 2007).

Strategic Human Resource Management

Understanding of the important role of SHRM in the modern organization provides an important context to understanding the ethical duties owed by HRPs. The most effective HRPs add value to their organization's effectiveness by linking people, strategy, values, and performance (Becker et al., 2001). This linking of an organization's overall strategy with aligned human resource systems is critical to the maximization of performance outcomes (Ulrich and Brockbank, 2005) in a world that is increasingly dependent upon the initiative, creativity, and commitment of employees to succeed (Covey, 2004; Senge, 2006). A growing body of empirical evidence has suggested that aligned systems in combination create superior organizational outcomes as compared to the implementation of individual human resource practices, although many scholars note that an incremental approach is more likely to occur (Pfeffer, 1998; Sun et al., 2007). However, the goals of effective organizations are not simply instrumental or outcome oriented. Great organizations are also normative, or value-based, and achieve their greatness because of their commitment to values and principles which guide employees (Collins, 2001; Collins and Porras, 2004) and which create strong and effective employee cultures (Schein, 2004).

Becker and Huselid (1999) noted that integrating key human resource functions to reframe an organization's internal environment results in significantly higher organizational outcomes and financial performance that is superior to what firms can attain by implementing individual human resource program elements piecemeal. The three key functions that Becker and Huselid (1999) cited as most important were (1) a management culture aligned with the corporate strategy; (2) operational and professional excellence in conducting key tasks; and (3) a human resource structure focusing on human resource managers as business partners to other departments. These three organizational factors are interrelated (Becker and Huselid, 1999; Paine, 2003) and organizational cultures can enrich human lives as well as increase profitability (Cameron, 2003; Senge, 2006).

Empirical evidence by an award-winning HRM study (Huselid, 1995) demonstrated that high performance HRM systems had a significant positive impact upon overall financial performance, productivity, and turnover. Pfeffer (1998) has provided a comprehensive body of business evidence citing studies that demonstrate that strategically crafted HRM systems can generate organizational wealth when effectively integrated with organizational goals. More importantly, Pfeffer's research and that of other scholars provides valuable insight about *how to implement* those systems. Pfeffer (1998, p. xv) noted that "enormous economic returns (can be) obtained through the implementation of what are variously called high involvement, high performance, or high commitment management practices."

Unfortunately, many HRPs and organizational leaders have consistently lacked the know-how to design and implement systems and policies that mesh with organizational goals. (2005). As Pfeffer (1998, p. 14) and Kouzes and Posner (2007, p. 75) have emphasized in their discussions of the roles of organizational leaders, the key to effective organizational change is execution. Becker and Huselid (2006, p. 99) called HR architecture, "the systems, practices, competencies, and employee performance behaviors" of SHRM a key element to "building sustainable competitive advantage and creating above-average financial performance." Ulrich and Beatty (2001, p. 293) have explained that the critical contribution made by human resources in accomplishing strategic goals required that they fill the roles of coach, architect, facilitator, conscience, and contributing leader—rising from the status of subservient "partners" to substantial "players." In order to achieve that higher level of status and impact, Beer (1997, pp. 49–51) noted that a successful transformation of the human resource function focused on three key change factors:

Focus on cost-effectiveness: Reframing the human resource function to deliver services at a reduced cost made the HRM function more financially accountable.

Merger of the HRM function with the strategic role: Aligning core processes—the key tasks performed by organizations—so that when systems mesh rather than conflict the entire organization is able to utilize people efficiently and effectively.

Development of new knowledge: Empirical studies (e.g., Collins and Porras, 2004) confirmed that organizational culture, financial performance, and goal achievement were interdependent elements of successful organizations—and that valuing people and treating them well improved the bottom line.

Successful SHRM "involves designing and implementing a set of internally consistent policies and practices that ensure that employees' collective knowledge, skills, and abilities contribute to the achievement of its business objectives" (Huselid et al., 1997, p. 172). If HRPs lack the knowledge and skill to craft these policies and practices and implement them in their organizations, then they fail to honor their professional duties and ethical obligations to the organizations they serve.

Historically, HRPs have traditionally played the role of internal service provider and deliverer of programs for operating departments (Beer, 1997; Lawler III, 2008). Organizational leaders and HRPs have apparently been slow to either understand the benefits of implementing high performance and high commitment systems, or they simply lack the skills required to implement such systems (Pfeffer, 1998). Pfeffer (1998, Part II) thoughtfully examines the consistent failure of HRPs and organizational leaders to apply the best thinking and empirical research that affirms proven principles of HRM, and clearly identifies the need for today's organizations to raise the standard of their performance in applying those principles. Yet the sub-optimization of organization performance persists and organization leaders miss opportunities to effectively serve their employees, shareholders, and society at large (Pfeffer, 1998, Chapter 1).

Increasingly, today's HRPs acknowledge that they can earn a place at their organization's strategic policy making table only if they understand how to measure the added value of employee contributions—the "decision science" of human resources—and help create organizational programs and systems that reinforce desired employee behaviors (Boudreau and Ramstad, 2005, p. 17). Clardy (2008) has suggested that to manage the core competencies and human capital of the entire firm, HRPs must clearly understand the strategic goals of the firm and must then play a key leadership role in taking advantage of those competencies. Despite this obligation, HRPs are often unprepared to help their organizations to optimize the use of human capital and today's organizations fail to perform effectively (Lawler III, 2008). This inability to respond to the needs of the modern organization is an implicit but often unacknowledged and unintended violation of the responsibilities and duties owed to the organizations that those HRPs serve (Hosmer, 2007).

The HR Professional as Ethical Steward

The role of the leader as a steward in the governance of organizations has received increasing attention in the post-Enron era (cf. Carroll and Buchholtz, 2007; Caldwell et al., 2008; Hernandez, 2008; Hosmer, 2007). In articulating the relationship that exists between organizations and their employees, Block (1993) described leaders as stewards who owed a complex set of duties to stakeholders. These duties achieve long-term wealth creation which ultimately benefits all stakeholders and honors the obligations owed by business to society (Caldwell and Karri, 2005; Solomon, 1992). DePree (2004, Ch. 1) and Pava (2003, Chapter 1) have described the duties of organizational leaders as "covenantal" in nature, suggesting that the relationship that organizations owed to employees was akin to both a contact and a sacred obligation.

Ethical stewardship has been defined as "the honoring of duties owed to employees, stakeholders, and society in the pursuit of long-term wealth creation" (Caldwell et al., 2008, p. 153). Ethical stewardship is a theory of organizational governance in which leaders seek the best interests of stakeholders by creating high trust cultures that honor a broad range of duties owed by organizations to followers (Caldwell and Karri, 2005; Pava, 2003). Covey (2004) has described the stewardship role as value-based, principle-centered, and committed to the welfare of all stakeholders. In pursuit of the best interests of each stakeholder, Covey has emphasized that the duty of leaders is to optimize outcomes, rather than settling for a compromise position that overlooks opportunities—a phrase Covey (2004, pp. 204–234) has described as "Win–Win or No Deal."

Both Block (1993) and DePree (2004) viewed the ethical obligations of organizations as neither idealistic nor soft. Block (1993, pp. 91–97) has argued that the responsibility of organizations was to fully disclose critical information and to clearly identify threats facing an organization as well as the accompanying implications of those threats upon employees. Block (1993, pp. 25–26) advocated treating employees as "owners and partners" in the governance process and emphasized that in the highly competitive global that relationship encompassed sharing honest and extensive communication. DePree (2004, p. 11) emphasized that "(t)he first task of the leader is to define reality"—a reality that included an obligation to tell all of the truth to employees, rather than withholding key information that might treat the employees as mere hirelings or the means by which the firm achieved its goals.

The moral position of ethical stewardship is that organizational leaders have the obligation to pursue long-term wealth creation by implementing systems that strengthen the organizational commitment of each stakeholder (Caldwell and Karri, 2005). Ethical stewards in HRM demonstrate the insights of great organizations that transform their companies into human and humane communities which emphasize inclusion, shared partnership, empowerment, and leadership trustworthiness (Kanter, 2008). This transforming culture occurs when followers believe that systems will enable employees to achieve desired outcomes and that social contracts will be honored (Caldwell and Karri, 2005; Caldwell et al., 2008). Such a culture is also achieved by treating employees as "yous" or as valued individuals and organizational partners, rather than as "its" or a mere organizational commodity with a human form (cf. Buber, 2008).

Grossman (2007) has noted that the HR professional must become a steward in framing an organization's culture and in facilitating change. Although some scholars have advocated that HRPs become ethical advocates (Payne and Wayland, 1999), the scope of that advocating role and the ethical values to be incorporated therein have been a source of debate (Guest, 2007; Legge, 2000; Palmer, 2007; Schultz and Brender-Ilan, 2004). Nonetheless, human resource managers have not typically reported performing a major role as ethical educators within their organizations nor have they been successful when they attempted to perform that role (Coltrin, 1991). HRPs would benefit to understand that organizations owe a complex set of duties to multiple stakeholders, and that they must be accountable to help organizations understand the ethical implications of their actions (Hosmer, 2007). In providing a glimpse into the ethics of management and the duties of organizations to society, Hosmer (2007) is just one of many ethics scholars who have addressed the responsibilities of organizational leaders to constantly examine the moral calculus of leadership in evaluating consequences of a firm's behaviors to diverse stakeholders.

If the HRP is to function as an ethical steward in the modern organization, she/he must combine a profound knowledge (Deming, 2000) of the operations of the firm, an understanding about how to implement systems by which organizations can maximize human performance (Becker and Huselid, 2006), an understanding of the empirical value and cost/benefit contribution of high performance systems (Pfeffer, 1998), and the ability to communicate effectively to top management and Boards of Directors in a convincing manner so that those policy makers will adopt policies and systems essential for creating integrated and effective HRM systems that support organizational goals (Lawler III, 2008).

HRPs and the Duties of Leadership

As organizational leaders HRPs have responsibilities that require insight, skills, wisdom, experience, and a profound knowledge of their organizations (Becker and Huselid, 1999). In this section of our article, we suggest that HRPs are "transformative leaders" (Bennis and Nanus, 2007) who honor a broad set of ethical duties in their role as ethical stewards.

The HRPs demonstrate principles of *transformational leadership* when they combine a commitment to helping both individuals and organizations to achieve unprecedented excellence (Kupers and Weibler, 2006). Dvir et al. (2002) found that transformational leaders had a positive impact on followers' development and performance and the accomplishment of organizational priorities, affirming Bass and Avolio's (1990, p. 22) claim that transformational leaders "elevate the desires of followers for achievement and self-development while also promoting the development of groups and organizations." Citing the example of the U.S. Naval Academy graduate, Jim Schwappach, Kouzes and Posner (2007, pp. 118–119) describe Schwappach as a leader who was effective at listening deeply to others and involving others in developing solutions that empower employees while greatly increasing the effectiveness of an organization in accomplishing organizational goals. HRM practices that view employees as valued assets and contributors to the creation of strategic competitive advantage empower people to enhance their potential to contribute to the organization's success while simultaneously improving employees' skill sets along the way (Becker and Gerhart, 1996; DePree, 2004). Empowering employees maximizes commitment and enables employees to become a source of strategic competitive advantage that competitors rarely can duplicate (Becker et al., 2001).

Becker et al. (2001, p. 4) have noted that "(w)e're living in a time when a new economic paradigm—characterized by speed, innovation, short cycle times, quality, and customer satisfaction—is highlighting the importance of intangible assets." The intangible human assets essential for sustaining competitive advantage depend on whether a firm's leadership understands how to integrate people into the achievement of organizational goals (Becker and Huselid, 1998, 2006). The ability of transformational leadership to simultaneously pursue both individual needs and organizational goals has long been considered a critical element of organizational success (Barnard, 1938), and is widely regarded as an important characteristic of high performance organizations (Cameron, 2003).

The HRPs also honor their duties to others when they apply principles of charismatic leadership. *Charismatic* leaders are ethical stewards to the degree that they personally inspire others to achieve worthy goals (Caldwell et al., 2007). Charismatic leadership is "an attribution based on follower perceptions of their leader's behavior," and reflects the followers' "perception of their leader's extraordinary character" (Conger et al., 2000, p. 748). House (1977) described charismatic leadership as being characterized by high emotional expressiveness, self-confidence, self-determination, freedom from internal conflict, and a conviction of the correctness of the leader's own beliefs. Kouzes and Posner (2007, p. 133) emphasized that inspiring leaders appeal to common ideals and animate an organization's vision in a way that resonates deeply within the hearts of others.

Charismatic leaders recognize that it is in resonating with people at the emotional level that creates the greatest personal commitment (Boyatzis and McKee, 2005). While writing of effective human resource leadership, Pfeffer (1998, p. 125) cited the case of Elmar Toime of the New Zealand Post who implemented high trust practices based upon close relationships with individual employees. Toime's style demonstrates the influence of charismatic leadership in implementing human resource practices which transformed the New Zealand Post "from a typical government bureaucracy to a profitable state-owned enterprise and the most efficient post office in the world" (Pfeffer, 1998, p. 125).

The HRPs, who demonstrate the ability to create a personal charismatic connection with organizational employees, and who maintain that connection by honoring commitments, honor the duties of ethical stewardship by encouraging the hearts of employees (Kouzes and Posner, 2007, Chapters 11 and 12). That ability to create high commitment and high trust is at the heart of high performing organizations (Senge, 2006) and is a key responsibility of effective leadership.

In honoring ethical duties, HRPs are also principle-centered. *Principle-centered* leadership incorporates foundations of ethical stewardship to the degree that it seeks to integrate the instrumental and normative objectives of an organization while being congruent with universal principles demonstrated by effective leaders. Covey (1992, 2004) argued that leadership is the most successful when it adheres to a patterned set of well-accepted principles of effectiveness and respected moral values. According to Covey (1992, p. 31), principle-centered leadership is practiced "from the inside out" at the personal, interpersonal, managerial, and organizational levels. Principle-centered leaders earn trust based upon their character and competence (Covey, 2004). Kouzes and Posner (2003b, 2007) have noted that great leaders sustain their credibility based upon their consistency in modeling correct principles and in honoring values that demonstrate personal integrity.

The principle-centered leader recognizes that virtuous outcomes supersede adherence to rules (Kohlberg, 1985) and that moral purposes complement best practices in achieving stewardship goals (Caldwell and Karri, 2005). Principle-centered leaders model organizational values (Kouzes and Posner, 2007) and recognize that effective leadership is ultimately the integration of both ends and means (cf. Burns, 1978). In their classic study of the most successful businesses of the past century, Collins and Porras (2004, pp. 131–135) noted the emphasis that Procter and Gamble placed on creating a strong principle-based culture based on core values and a core ideology.

The HRPs honor the obligations of ethical stewards when they develop a knowledge of guiding principles that characterize great organizations (Pfeffer, 1998), and when they help organizations to create aligned organizational cultures that match actual behaviors with espoused values (Schein, 2004). This commitment to values and principles of principle-centered leadership is a key element in establishing and implementing human resource systems that earn employee commitment and trust (Covey, 2004).

The HRPs that demonstrate principles of servant leadership build trust and inspire the confidence of others. *Servant* leadership is at the heart of ethical stewardship (Caldwell et al., 2007) and exemplifies its depth of commitment to serving the individual. DePree (2004, p. 11), one of the most highly regarded advocates of servant leadership, opined that organizational leaders had the ethical responsibility to be "a servant and a debtor" to employees by establishing policies that demonstrate the organization's commitment to the welfare of each employee. Hamilton and Nord (2005, p. 875) describe servant leadership as "valuing individuals and developing people, building community, practicing authenticity, and providing leadership that focuses on the good of those who are being led and those whom the organization serves."

Greenleaf (2004, p. 2) emphasized that the great leader is a servant first because that commitment to serving others is his identity "deep down inside." Servant leadership honors each individual as a valued end, rather than simply as a means to organizational outcomes (cf. Buber, 2008; Hosmer, 1995). The servant leader puts the needs, desires, interests, and welfare of others above his or her self-interest (Ludema and Cox, 2007, p. 343) while also honoring duties owed to the organization (DePree, 2004). Pfeffer (1998, pp. 91–92) noted that Herb Kelleher, the former CEO of Southwest Airlines, and Sam Walton,

the founder of Wal-Mart, were both known for valuing employees as critical to the success of their organizations and for adopting a leadership philosophy incorporating principles of servant leadership. This valuing of employees at both Wal-Mart and at Southwest Airlines balanced a consideration for employees' welfare with a recognition that treating employees well increases their commitment in return.

The HRPs who demonstrate a commitment to the "welfare, growth, and wholeness" (Caldwell et al., 2002, p. 162) of stakeholders are servant leaders and ethical stewards. It is this commitment to stakeholder interests that makes leaders credible and trustworthy (Kouzes and Posner, 2003a). HRPs, who fail to create policies that demonstrate a commitment to serving employees, and who do not behave congruently with those values, undermine the trust of employees and inhibit the ability of organizations to maximize long-term wealth creation (Senge, 2006).

The HRPs are Level 5 leaders when they demonstrate their fierce commitment to the success of the organization while creating systems that recognize employee contributions and give credit to employees for achieving an organization's success. *Level 5* leaders demonstrate a leadership insight that willingly shares both power and the credit for accomplishments while accepting personal responsibility for organizational failures (Collins, 2001). In his study of great corporations, Collins (2001, pp. 17–40) found that the leaders of the organizations that evolved "from good to great" were typified by high commitment coupled with great personal humility. In discussing these Level 5 leaders, Marcum and Smith (2007) explained that Level 5 leaders avoided the counterfeit leadership qualities of egoistic self-interest that typified high profile leaders in many organizations. Collins (2001, p. 27) emphasized that Level 5 leaders were not "I-centered" leaders who pursued self-serving goals or who viewed themselves as the upfront personification of their organization's success. Instead, they tended to be described by those who worked with or wrote about them as *"quiet, humble, modest, reserved, shy, gracious, mild-mannered, self-effacing, understated, did not believe his own clippings;* and so forth" (Collins, 2001, p. 27).

Collins (2001, p. 30) reported that Level 5 leaders also possessed a "ferocious resolve, an almost stoic determination to do whatever needs to be done" to serve the organization and to make it great. Werhane (2007, p. 433) also noted that the most successful leaders in her study of effective women leaders were Level 5 leaders who "seem to care more about the sustained success of their organization than their own legacy." Level 5 leaders are transformative in demonstrating humility about their own accomplishments, giving credit to others in their organization for success while accepting full responsibility for the errors made by an organization and working unceasingly to address those errors (Collins, 2001, 2005). Citing the case of AES Corporation's CEO, Dennis Bakke, Pfeffer (1998, pp. 99–103) emphasized that effective organizations do not achieve short-term profitability by short-changing employees. Working for the long-term success of an organization and creating policies and systems that reward employees for laying the foundation to achieve long-term growth rather than a short-term appearance of growth takes courage and integrity in the face of pressures to achieve short-term results in today's distorted business environment (Pfeffer, 1998).

Human resource professionals act as both ethical stewards and Level 5 leaders when they create human resource systems and processes that are fully aligned with the normative and instrumental goals of the organization while giving employees credit for their role in the accomplishment of those goals (Caldwell et al., 2007). These aligned and congruent systems and processes balance the needs of the organization with a commitment to the best interests of its stakeholders (Pauchant, 2005) and create reward systems that also reward employees for contributing to organizational success.

When HRPs model the behaviors of covenantal leadership, they help organizations create new knowledge which enables firms to create and maintain competitive advantage and constantly improve. *Covenantal* leadership integrates the roles of the leader as a servant, role model, a source of inspiration and as a creator of new insight and meaning (Caldwell et al., 2007; Pava, 2003). Covenantal leadership encompasses the pursuit of a noble purpose, often described as rising to the level of a contractual or even a sacred duty (Barnett and Schubert, 2002; DePree, 2004; Pava, 2003). Covenantal leaders seek not only to enhance the skills and abilities of those with whom they associate, but also to "unleash the great human potential which is often dormant and silent" in organizations (Pava, 2003, p. 26). Striving to serve both individuals and the organization, sharing knowledge, inspiring by personal example, and learning with others, covenantal leadership is attuned to the importance of continuous learning (Pava, 2003).

Covenantal leadership incorporates ethical stewardship's commitment to creating new solutions to problems, creating new wealth and value, and working for the welfare of stakeholders (Caldwell et al., 2006). It is in this ability to help people to discover new truths and achieve the best within themselves at both the individual and organizational levels, enabling organizations to optimize wealth creation (Senge, 2006) and honor their role as covenantal leaders and ethical stewards (Caldwell and Dixon, 2007; Caldwell et al., 2007). Kouzes and Posner (2007, p. 317) cited the example of Bob Branchi, the Managing

Director of Western Australia's largest network of automobile dealerships, in teaching a delivery driver that his value as an individual and his role in the organization were also important to the organization's success—thereby helping that individual not only to share in the organization's accomplishments but also to redefine himself.

Sung-Choon et al. (2007) have emphasized the vital role of knowledge creation in firms as an important element of the human resource architecture and have advocated the importance of adopting a learning organization culture to create a sustainable competitive advantage. HRPs become covenantal leaders when they focus on individuals, empower them to increase their level of commitment to themselves and to the organization, and create opportunities for creating new knowledge and insight that benefits both the organization and the individual (cf. Pava, 2003; Senge, 2006).

As HRPs adopt the characteristics of ethical stewardship, they help their organizations add value to the lives of individuals and organizations. Solomon and Flores (2003, p. 6) have called leaders who demonstrate high commitment to others and to their organizations "authentic" and praise the trustworthiness and integrity of those who lead unselfishly and effectively. Kolp and Rea (2005, pp. 154–158) have also cited the character of such leaders and have described their accomplishments as balancing "value and virtue" in creating cultures where employees feel empowered to take risks and achieve unprecedented results. HRPs who adopt the leadership behaviors of ethical stewardship understand the value of the individual as well as the organization while holding both people and the organization in high regard.

By integrating the best elements of leadership, HRPs honor their role as ethical stewards and contribute to the capability of their organizations while profoundly benefiting the employees who work in those organizations. As contributors to the optimal strategic accomplishment of an organization's mission, HRPs who exhibit transformative leadership behaviors have the opportunity to serve the needs of a multiple set of stakeholders in honoring a broad range of ethical duties (Hosmer, 2007). HRPs can help organizations to build trust and commitment in the pursuit of long-term wealth creation (cf. Senge, 2006) as ethical stewards when they serve their organizations as transformative leaders.

Contributions of Our Article

Today's modern organizations desperately need leaders who they can trust if their organizations are to be successful in a highly competitive global market place (Cameron, 2003). Those leaders include highly competent, knowledgeable, and skilled HRPs who understand how to align

HRM programs with corporate objectives and strategic plans (Becker et al., 2001). We argue that the leadership skills of these HRPs must encompass the moral perspectives of ethical stewardship and the unique contributions of transformative leadership.

We suggest that our article contributes to the SHRM literature in four significant ways.

1. *We affirm the importance of SHRM as a vital element of successful organizations when aligned with the overall goals, values, and priorities of that organization. We note, however, that many HRPs either fail to understand this strategic role of HRM or lack the abilities to align HRM systems to serve their firms.* Human resource management practices that are integrated in a manner that reinforces strategic objectives can play a major role in enabling organizations to utilize employees as the source of strategic competitive advantage (Hartel et al., 2007; Konzelmann et al., 2006). Although designing aligned human resource systems and framing a well-conceived strategy are important, it is in implementing these systems that a firm achieves desired organizational outcomes (Pfeffer, 1998; Sun et al., 2007). The failures of organizations to create aligned and congruent organizations with HR systems that mesh with strategic objectives are well documented by management scholars (Lawler III, 2008; Pfeffer, 1998, 2007).

2. *We describe and clarify the role of SHRM as it relates to the principles of ethical stewardship and emphasize the implicit ethical duties owed by HRPs to their organizations.* Ethical stewardship is a philosophy of leadership and governance that optimizes long-term wealth creation and that honors duties owed to all stakeholders (Caldwell and Karri, 2005; Pava, 2003). As a framework that integrates both normative and instrumental ethical values (cf. Paine, 2003), the principles of ethical stewardship build both the trust and the commitment of followers (Caldwell et al., 2008). HRPs owe their organizations a set of obligations and duties that include helping the top management team to contribute to the strategic effectiveness of the firm while simultaneously meeting the needs of organizational members (Barnard, 1938; Becker and Huselid, 1999). Rarely are organizations able to earn the trust of employees if HRM systems and processes conflict with the strategic goals of the firm (Pfeffer, 1998). Congruent and effective leadership and consistent policies help organizations to obtain the commitment from employees which is the key to long-term wealth creation (Senge, 2006).

3. *We identify the importance of the ethical duties inherent in best leadership practices as essential elements of the HRPs' responsibilities in honoring their organizational roles.* The leadership obligations and responsibilities of HRPs incorporate the best elements of transformational leadership, charismatic leadership, servant leadership, Level 5 leadership, and covenantal leadership. Each of these six leadership perspectives of leadership is normatively and instrumentally consistent with the scope and duties of SHRM (Pfeffer, 1998, 2007) and facilitate both social and financial outcomes of organizations (cf. Collins, 2001; Hosmer, 2007; Paine, 2003). These ethical responsibilities demonstrate the importance of aligned and congruent organizational systems and are consistent with the empirical evidence that affirms the importance of high performing organizations in creating long-term wealth (Collins, 2001; Paine, 2003; Senge, 2006).

4. *We reinforce the importance of human resource professionals elevating their contribution to organizations professionally, ethically, and strategically.* HRPs have often been ineffective at contributing to the success of organizations because they have failed to demonstrate the requisite knowledge and skills to help organizations to achieve objectives that are vital to their role as business partners and major decision makers (Lawler and Mohrman, 2000). In today's highly competitive business environment, the role of employees has become increasingly important to achieving strategic competitive advantage, and the opportunity for organizations to create that advantage by unlocking employee potential is often the key difference for both competitive advantage and increased profitability (Pfeffer, 2007). HRPs who help create organizational cultures based on normatively virtuous principles can increase the ability of their companies to earn the high trust and employee commitment which leads to better quality, improved customer service, and increased profitability (Cameron, 2003). The roles of HRPs in organizations enable their companies to be more professional and more successful strategically while enabling the companies to honor the implicit ethical duties owed to employees.

The clear message of management scholars who study today's organizations is that "good" is not good enough and is, in fact, "the enemy of great" (Collins, 2001, p. 1). The challenge for today's leaders is to move from "effectiveness" to "greatness" (Covey, 2004, pp. 3–4) to optimize the potential of the modern organization.

Conclusion

Only when HRPs are perceived as competent and ethical will they be able to merit the trust of those organizational stakeholders with whom they work (Graham and Tarbell, 2006). Adopting the standards of ethical stewardship and the best practices of leadership may be a daunting challenge for HRPs. Nonetheless, this challenge is consistent with the needs of organizations that must compete in an increasingly competitive world that is heavily dependent on the skills and commitment of employees to create value and long-term wealth (Covey, 2004; Pfeffer, 2007).

Although the role of HRM has changed substantially over the past 20 years, HRPs continue to have opportunities to broaden and strengthen their role in helping organizations maximize productivity, govern more ethically, and compete more effectively (Pfeffer, 2007). In understanding their role as transformative organizational leaders, HRPs have the obligation to prepare themselves to accomplish the goals of their organizations by honing their expertise about organizational goals, developing the skills of organizational members, and creating aligned systems that are critical to the success of modern organizations (Hosmer, 2007; Werhane et al., 2004). Such preparation demands that HRPs also develop insights about ethical and moral issues and that they set the example as ethical leaders (Kouzes and Posner, 2007; Pinnington, et al., 2007).

The willingness of organizations to pursue systematically the twin goals of achieving organizational mission and assisting employees to achieve their personal goals is an implicit obligation of ethical stewardship and organizational leadership (Barnard and Andrews, 2007; Caldwell et al., 2008). The resource-based view of the firm emphasizes the importance of meeting the needs of employees to retain them as a resource-based source of competitive advantage (Barney and Wright, 1998). Scholarly research about successful organizations has increasingly suggested that the most successful companies are those that balance *instrumental* or outcome-based and *normative* or value-based objectives (Cameron, 2003; Collins, 2001; Pfeffer, 1998). Measuring results and maintaining a commitment to people are well-respected elements of high performance systems that balance the instrumental and normative priorities of organizations (Pfeffer, 1998, 2007).

Organizations that integrate principles of ethical leadership with a strategic approach to HRM optimize the maximization of values and outcomes and achieve results which pay off long-term (Collins and Clark, 2003; Paine, 2003). By honoring their duties as ethical stewards and incorporating principles of transformative leadership, HRPs can make a major contribution to their organization's financial success while helping their organizations honor the implicit duties owed to organization members (DePree, 2004; Paine, 2003).

References

Barnard, C. I.: 1938, *Functions of the Executive* (Harvard Business School Press, Cambridge, MA).

Barnard, C. I. and K. R. Andrews: 2007, *Functions of the Executive: 30th Anniversary Edition* (Harvard University Press, Cambridge, MA).

Barnett, T. and E. Schubert: 2002, 'Perceptions of the Ethical Climate and Covenantal Relationships,' *Journal of Business Ethics* **36**(3), 279–290.

Barney, J. B. and P. M. Wright: 1998, 'On Becoming a Strategic Partner: The Role of Human Resources in Gaining Competitive Advantage,' *Human Resource Management* **37**(1), 31–46.

Bass, B. M. and B. J. Avolio: 1990, 'Developing Transformational Leadership: 1992 and Beyond,' *Journal of European Industrial Training* **14**(5), 21–27.

Becker, B. E. and M. A. Huselid: 1998, 'High Performance Work Systems and Firm Performance: A Synthesis of Research and Managerial Implications,' in G. Ferris (ed.), *Research in Personnel and Human Resources Management,* Vol. 16 (JAI Press, Greenwich, CT), pp 53–101.

Becker, B. E. and B. Gerhart: 1996, 'The Impact of Human Resource Management on Organizational Performance, Progress, and Prospects,' *Academy of Management Journal* **39**(4), 779–801.

Becker, B. E. and M. A. Huselid: 1999, 'Overview: Strategic Human Resource Management in Five Leading Firms,' *Human Resource Management* **38**(4), 287–301.

Becker, B. E. and M. A. Huselid: 2006, 'Strategic Human Resource Management: Where do we go from Here?,' *Journal of Management* **32**(6), 898–925.

Becker, B. E., M. A. Huselid and D. Ulrich: 2001, *The HR Scorecard: Linking People, Strategy, and Performance* (Harvard Business School Press, Boston, MA).

Beer, M.: 1997, 'The Transformation of the Human Resource Function: Resolving the Tension Between Traditional Administrative and a New Strategic Role,' *Human Resource Management* **36**(1), 49–56.

Bennis, W. G. and B. Nanus: 2007, *Leaders: Strategies for Taking Charge* (Harper, New York).

Block, P.: 1993, *Stewardship: Choosing Service over Self-Interest* (Jossey-Bass, San Francisco, CA).

Boudreau, J. W. and P. M. Ramstad: 2005, 'Talentship, Talent Segmentation, and Sustainability: A New HR Decision Science Paradigm for a New Strategy Definition,' *Human Resource Management* **44**(2), 129–136.

Boyatzis, R. and A. McKee: 2005, *Resonant Leadership: Renewing Yourself and Connecting with Others Through Mindfulness, Hope, and Compassion* (Harvard Business School Press, Boston, MA).

Buber, M.: 2008, *I and Thou* (Hesperides Press, New York).

Burns, J. M.: 1978, *Leadership* (Harper & Row, New York).

Caldwell, C., S. J. Bischoff and R. Karri: 2002, 'The Four Umpires: A Paradigm for Ethical Leadership,' *Journal of Business Ethics* **36**(1/2), 153–163.

Caldwell, C. and R. Dixon: 2007, Transformative Leadership—An Integrative Theory of Ethical Stewardship. Paper Presented at the Fourteenth Annual International Conference on Ethics in Business at DePaul University on November 1, 2007.

Caldwell, C., L. Hayes, P. Bernal and R. Karri: 2008, 'Ethical Stewardship: The Role of Leadership Behavior and Perceived Trustworthiness,' *Journal of Business Ethics* **78**(1/2), 153–164.

Caldwell, C. and R. J. Karri: 2005, 'Organizational Governance and Ethical Systems: A Covenantal Approach to Building Trust,' *Journal of Business Ethics* **58**(1), 249–259.

Caldwell, C., R. Karri and P. Vollmar: 2006, 'Principal Theory and Principle Theory: Ethical Governance from the Follower's Perspective,' *Journal of Business Ethics* **66**(2–3), 207–223.

Caldwell, C., C. Voelker, R. D. Dixon and A. LeJeune: 2007, *Transformative Leadership: An Ethical Stewardship Model for Healthcare* (Healthcare, Business, and Policy, Fall Edition, Organizational Ethics), pp. 126–134.

Cameron, K. S.: 2003, 'Ethics, Virtuousness, and Constant Change,' in N. M. Tichy and A. R. McGill (eds.), *The Ethical Challenge: How to Lead with Unyielding Integrity* (Jossey-Bass, San Francisco, CA), pp. 185–194.

Clardy, A.: 2008, 'The Strategic Role of Human Resource Development in Managing Core Competencies,' *Human Resource Development International* **11**(2), 183–197.

Collins, J.: 2001, *Good to Great: Why Some Companies Make the Leap . . . and Others Don't* (HarperCollins, New York).

Collins, J.: 2005, 'Level 5 Leadership: The Triumph of Humility and Fierce Resolve,' *Harvard Business Review* **83**(7/8), 136–146.

Collins, C. J. and K. D. Clark: 2003, 'Strategic Human Resource Practices, Top Management Team Social Networks, and Firm Performance: The Role of Human Resource Practices in Creating Organizational Competitive Advantage,' *Academy of Management Journal* **46**(6), 740–751.

Collins, J. and J. I. Porras: 2004, *Built to Last: Successful Habits of Visionary Companies,* 2nd Edition (Harper-Collins, New York).

Coltrin, S. A.: 1991, 'Ethics—More than Legal Compliance,' *Human Resource Management* **26**, 1–12.

Conger, J. A., R. N. Kanungo and S. T. Menon: 2000, 'Charismatic Leadership and Follower Effects,' *Journal of Organizational Behavior* **21**(7), 747–767.

Covey, S. R.: 1992, *Principle Centered Leadership* (Simon & Schuster, New York).

Covey, S. R.: 2004, *The 8th Habit: From Effectiveness to Greatness* (Free Press, New York).

Deming, W. E.: 2000, *Out of the Crisis* (MIT Press, Cambridge, MA).

DePree, M.: 2004, *Leadership is an Art* (Doubleday, New York).

Dvir, T., D. Eden, B. J. Avolio and B. Shamir: 2002, 'Impact of Transformational Leadership on Follower Development and Performance: A Field Experiment,' *Academy of Management Journal* **45**(4), 735–744.

Graham, M. E. and L. M. Tarbell: 2006, 'The Importance of the Employee Perspective in the Competency Development of Human Resource Professionals,' *Human Resource Management* **45**(3), 337–355.

Greenleaf, R. K.: 2004, 'Who Is the Servant-Leader?,' in L. C. Spears and M. Lawrence (eds.), *Practicing Servant Leadership: Succeeding Through Trust, Bravery, and Forgiveness* (Jossey-Bass, San Francisco), pp. 1–7.

Grossman, R. J.: 2007, 'New Competencies for HR,' *HR Magazine* **52**(6), 58–62.

Guest, D. E.: 2007, 'HRM and Performance: Can Partnership Address the Ethical Dilemmas?,' in A. Pinnington, R. Macklin and T. Campbell (eds.), *Human Resource Management: Ethics and Employment* (Oxford University Press, Oxford), pp. 52–65.

Hamilton, F. and W. R. Nord: 2005, 'Practicing Servant-Leadership: Succeeding Through Trust, Bravery, and Forgiveness,' *Academy of Management Review* **30**(4), 875–877.

Hartel, C., Y. Fujimoto, V. E. Strybosch and K. Fitzpatrick: 2007, *Human Resource Management: Transforming Theory into Innovative Practice* (Pearson Education, Australia).

Hernandez, M.: 2008, 'Promoting Stewardship Behavior in Organizations: A Leadership Model,' *Journal of Business Ethics* **80**(1), 121–128.

Hosmer, L. T.: 1995, 'Trust: The Connecting Link Between Organizational Theory and Behavior,' *Academy of Management Review* **20**, 379–404.

Hosmer, L. T.: 2007, *The Ethics of Management,* 6th Edition (McGraw-Hill, New York).

House, R. J.: 1977, 'A 1976 Theory of Charismatic Leadership,' in J. G. Hunt and L. L. Larson (eds.), *Leadership: The Cutting Edge* (Southern Illinois University Press, Carbondale, IL), pp. 189–207.

Huselid, M. A.: 1995, 'The Impact of Human Resource Management Practices on Turnover, Productivity, and Corporate Financial Performance,' *Academy of Management Journal* **38**, 635–672.

Huselid, M. A. and B. E. Becker: 1997, The Impact of High Performance Work Systems, Implementation Effectiveness, and Alignment with Strategy on Shareholder Wealth. Academy of Management Proceedings.

Huselid, M. A., S. E. Jackson and R. S. Schuler: 1997, 'Technical and Strategic Human Resource Management Effectiveness as Determinants of Firm Performance,' *Academy of Management Journal* **40**(1), 171–188.

Kanter, R. M.: 2008, 'Transforming Giants,' *Harvard Business Review* **86**(1), 43–52.

Kohlberg, L.: 1985, 'The Just Community Approach to Moral Education in Theory and Practice,' in M. W. Berkowitz and F. Oser (eds.), *Moral Education: Theory and Practice* (Erlbaum, Hillsdale, NY).

Kolp, A. and P. Rea: 2005, *Leading with Integrity: Character Based Leadership* (Atomic Dog Publishing, New York).

Konzelmann, S., N. Conway, L. Trenberth and F. Wilkinson: 2006, 'Corporate Governance and Human Resource Management,' *British Journal of Industrial Relations* **44**(3), 541–567.

Kouzes, J. M. and B. Z. Posner: 2003a, *Credibility: How Leaders Gain and Lose It, Why People Demand It,* 2nd Edition (Wiley & Sons, San Francisco, CA).

Kouzes, J. M. and B. Z. Posner: 2003b, *Encouraging the Heart: A Leader's Guide to Rewarding and Recognizing Others* (Jossey-Boss, San Francisco, CA).

Kouzes, J. M. and B. Z. Posner: 2007, *Leadership Challenge,* 4th Edition (Wiley & Sons, San Francisco, CA).

Kupers, W. and J. Weibler: 2006, 'How Emotional is Transformational Leadership Really? Some Suggestions for a Necessary Extension,' *Leadership & Organizational Development Journal* **27**(5), 368–385.

Lawler, E. E. III: 2008, 'The HR Department: Give It More Respect,' *Wall Street Journal—Eastern Edition* **251**(57), R8.

Lawler, E. E. III and S. A. Mohrman: 2000, 'Beyond the Vision: What Makes HR Effective?,' *Human Resource Planning* **23**(4), 10–20.

Legge, K.: 2000, 'The Ethical Context of HRM: The Ethical Organisation in the Boundaryless World,' in D. Winstanley and J. Woodall (eds.), *Ethical Issues in Contemporary Human Resource Management* (MacMillan Press, London), pp. 23–40.

Ludema, J. D. and C. K. Cox: 2007, 'Leadership for World Benefit: New Horizons for Research and Practice,' in S. K. Piderit, R. E. Fry and D. L. Cooperrider (eds.), *Handbook of Transformative Cooperation: New Designs and Dynamics* (Stanford Business Books, Palo Alto, CA), pp. 333–373.

Marcum, D. and S. Smith: 2007, *egonomics: What Makes Ego Our Greatest Asset (or Most Expensive Liability)* (Fireside Publishing, Wichita, KS).

Paine, L. S.: 2003, *Value Shift: Why Companies must Merge Social and Financial Imperatives to Achieve Superior Performance* (McGraw-Hill, New York).

Palmer, G.: 2007, 'Socio-Political Theory and Ethics in HRM,' in A. Pinnington, R. Macklin. T. Campbell (eds.), *Human Resource Management: Ethics and Employment* (Oxford University Press, Oxford), pp. 23–34.

Pauchant, T. C.: 2005, 'Integral Leadership: A Research Proposal,' *Journal of Organizational Change Management* **18**(3), 211–229.

Pava, M.: 2003, *Leading with Meaning: Using Covenantal Leadership to Build a Better Organization* (Palgrave MacMillan, New York).

Payne, S. L. and R. F. Wayland: 1999, 'Ethical Obligation and Diverse Value Assumptions in HRM,' *International Journal of Manpower* **20**(5/6), 297–308.

Pfeffer, J.: 1998, *The Human Equation: Building Profits by Putting People First* (Harvard Business School Press, Boston, MA).

Pfeffer, J.: 2007, 'Human Resources from an Organizational Behavior Perspective: Some Paradoxes Explained,' *Journal of Economic Perspectives* **21**(4), 115–134.

Pinnington, A., R. Macklin and T. Campbell: 2007, 'Introduction: Ethical Human Resource Management,' in A. Pinnington, R. Macklin and T. Campbell (eds.), *Human Resource Management: Ethics and Employment* (Oxford University Press, Oxford), pp. 1–20.

Schein, E. H.: 2004, *Organizational Culture and Leadership* (Jossey-Bass, San Francisco, CA).

Schultz, T. and Y. Brender-Ilan: 2004, 'Beyond Justice: Introducing Personal Moral Philosophies to Ethical Evaluations of Human Resource Practices,' *Business Ethics: A European Review* **13**(4), 302–316.

Senge, P. M.: 2006, *The Fifth Discipline: The Art and Practice of the Learning Organization* (Doubleday, New York).

Solomon, R. C.: 1992, *Ethics and Excellence: Cooperation and Integrity in Business* (Oxford University Press, New York).

Solomon, R. C. and F. Flores: 2003, *Building Trust: In Business, Politics, Relationships, and Life* (Oxford University Press, New York).

Sun, L.-Y., S. Aryee and K. S. Law: 2007, 'High-Performance Human Resource Practices, Citizenship Behavior, and Organizational Performance: A Relational Perspective,' *Academy of Management Journal* **50**(3), 558–577.

Sung-Choon, K., S. S. Morris and S. A. Snell: 2007, 'Relational Archetypes, Organizational Learning and Value Creation: Extending the Human Resource Architecture,' *Academy of Management Review* **32**(1), 236–256.

Ulrich, D. and D. Beatty: 2001, 'From Partners to Players: Extending the HR Playing Field,' *Human Resource Management* **40**(4), 293–299.

Ulrich, D. and W. Brockbank: 2005, 'The Work of HR Part One: People and Performance,' *Strategic HR Review* **4**(5), 20–23.

Werhane, P. H.: 2007, 'Women Leaders in a Globalized World,' *Journal of Business Ethics* **74**(4), 425–435.

Werhane, P. H., T. J. Radin and N. E. Bowie: 2004, *Employment and Employee Rights* (Blackwell Publishing, Oxford).

Critical Thinking

1. Why do you think that organizations that behave ethically are more profitable in the long run?

2. What role can HR professionals play in this effort?

3. Is being the ethical steward an appropriate role for HR professionals?

CAM CALDWELL University of Georgia, Athens, GA, U.S.A. E-mail: cam.caldwell@gmail.com **DO X. TRUONG, PHAM T. LINH** and **ANH TUAN** Vietnam National University, Hanoi, Vietnam

UNIT 7

International Human Resource Management

Unit Selections

Learning Outcomes

After reading this Unit, you will be able to:

- Understand the reasons for outsourcing and offshoring.

- Have an appreciation of some of the trends that will affect the coming decades.

- Realize the implications of having offshore ownership.

- Appreciate the problems associated with having employees from multiple countries in multiple international locations.

- Understand why American workers and other workers in the rest of the post-industrialized world are under pressure.

Student Website

www.mhhe.com/cls

Internet References

Global Trade Information Services
www.gtis.com/english

Global Trade Watch
www.citizen.org/trade

Global Trading
http://globaltrading.com

Offshoring May Slow Impending US Economic Recovery
http://gbr.pepperdine.edu/093/offshoring1.html

Trade: Outsourcing Job
www.cfr.org/publication/7749/trade.html

The world is changing and getting smaller all the time. At the beginning of the twentieth century, the Wright brothers flew at Kitty Hawk, and some 25 years later, Charles Lindbergh flew from New York to Paris, alone, nonstop. In 1969, the spacecraft *Eagle One* landed on the moon, and Neil Armstrong said, "One small step for man, one giant leap for mankind."

Indeed, the giant leaps have become smaller. The world has shrunk due to transportation and communication. Communication is virtually instantaneous—not as it was during the early part of the 1800s, when the Battle of New Orleans was fought several weeks after the peace treaty for the War of 1812 had been signed. For centuries, travel was limited to the speed of a horse or a ship. During the nineteenth century, however, speeds of 60 or even 100 miles an hour were achieved by railroad trains. Before the twentieth century was half over, the speed of sound had been exceeded, and in the 15 years that followed, humans circled the globe in 90 minutes. Less than 10 years later, human beings broke free from Earth's gravity and walked on the Moon. The exotic became commonplace. Societies and cultures that had been remote from each other are now close, and people must now live with a diversity unknown in the past.

A shrinking world also means an expanding economy, a global economy, because producers and their raw materials and markets are now much closer to each other than they once were. People, and the organizations they represent, often do business all over the world, and their representatives are often members of foreign societies and cultures. Human resource management in just the domestic arena is an extremely difficult task; when the rest of the world is added to the effort, it becomes a monumental undertaking.

Workers in the United States are competing directly with workers in other parts of the world as discussed in "Business Is Booming: American's Leading Corporations Have Found a Way to Thrive Even if the American Economy Doesn't Recover: This Is Very Bad News." Companies often hold out for the lowest bidder in a competition for wage rates. This often forces the wage rates down for higher-paying countries, while only marginally bringing up the wages of the lower paying societies—a development that is bound to have a direct impact on the standard of living in all of the developed countries of the world. "Global Outsourcing" and offshoring have been key developments in global trade. It is part of what firms have to do to be able to compete in the hyper-competitive global economy.

In the United States, immigration has become a major issue as more illegal/undocumented immigrants from lesser developed countries pour into the United States to take the low-end jobs, creating an almost separate society within the country. On the other hand, the United States needs immigrants to help build the society and is missing out on many of these talented individuals because of very restrictive legal immigration policies. As more firms become involved in world trade, they must begin to hire foreign workers. Some of these people are going to stay with the firm and become members of the corporate cadre. In the global economy, it is not uncommon for Indian employees to find themselves working for American or European multinational corporations in, say, Saudi Arabia. This presents the human resource professional with

© Andersen Ross/Blend Images LLC

a problem of blending the three cultures into a successful mix. In this example, the ingredients are a well-educated Asian, working in a highly traditional Middle-Eastern society, for a representative of Western technology and culture. The situation involves three different sets of values, three different points of view, and three different sets of expectations on how people should act and be treated. A people strategy, as discussed in "Multiple Choice," that spans the globe is necessary to any organization doing business on a worldwide scale. There is bound to be a blending of ideas on such issues as compensation, benefits, and pensions. Not only on a regional level, such as the EU or NAFTA, but, probably on a global level in the future as organizations vie for top talent, no matter where they may originally come from.

American industry does not have a monopoly on new ideas in human resources. Other societies have successfully dealt with many of the same problems. While U.S. firms certainly will not adopt every idea (lifetime employment as practiced in Japan seems the most obvious non-candidate), they can learn much from organizations outside the United States. Human resource managers need to engage in learning from their overseas counterparts if they are going to meet the needs of their employees and contribute to the success of the corporation. Faster and better communication and transportation are leading to a more closely knit social, cultural, and economic world, where people's global abilities can make the difference between the success or failure of an organization. But this closer world is also a more dangerous world. The recent events of the War on Terror have demonstrated the dangers associated with doing business abroad, outside the confines of one's home country. Family and personal security have become a far larger issue than they were in the past, and security is now a consideration for all individuals whether they are working domestically or outside of their home country. But we cannot turn our back on the world. The world, because it is the one largely created by the success of western culture, ideas, and technology, is going to come to the United States and Europe whether the West wants it or not. The only alternative is to be ready for it. As it says in the *Art of War,* "That which you cannot change, accept with open arms."

Global Outsourcing

It's hit the $4 trillion mark, which means US outsourcing is rapidly deepening. The question is, how will it impact the US economy?

Sheryl Nance-Nash

Outsourcing used to be thought of as yet another management fad . . . but, obviously, it isn't.

Outsourcing spending has continued to climb at 10 to 20 percent for the last decade. The size of the outsourcing industry has grown to $4 trillion annually in the United States and $6 trillion globally, according to the International Association of Outsourcing Professionals® (IAOP®), the standard-setting organization and advocate for the outsourcing profession.

"Outsourcing is here to stay as long as Fortune 2000 companies continue to view it as a viable means of achieving their growth strategy targets," says Sally Wright, president of Alliance Consulting Group.

The chief motivation for outsourcing has been and remains cost savings, especially as the United States continues to claw its way out of the recession.

"Organizations need to be more competitive in an increasingly competitive world. This is often coupled with the demands by stockholders for increased profits," says Fred Maidment, professor with the Department of Management at Ancell School of Business at Western Connecticut State University. "Prices are driven down in a global economy, so companies must become efficient. Labor is often a chief component in the production of goods and services. If the cost of labor can be reduced while maintaining or enhancing productivity and quality, then attempting to do that is only good business. Simply put, do you want to pay Wal-Mart prices or Nieman Marcus prices for the same good?" he asks.

Outsourcing is an integral aspect of American corporate success, and without it, "we'd be in trouble," says David Poole, head of Capgemini's Business Processing Outsourcing (BPO) North America organization in Chicago. "Any real action to restrict outsourcing is antiquated and unsustainable. A company that outsources is increasingly nimble, with the ability to reinvest savings and zero-in on innovation and their core competencies. Ultimately, this is what will help American companies and the country emerge completely from this economic slump."

Cost savings is part of the picture, but not the whole picture. The true benefits of outsourcing are achieved by taking a strategic look at the business structure and functions, determining which functions are better kept in-house, and defining areas where outsourcing can increase productivity and invigorate local economies. In most cases, outsourcing back-office functions helps companies manage costs, streamline business operations and stimulate revenue growth, says Poole.

"Since most businesses don't gain an advantage with administrative activities, why waste time and money trying to make them unique?" he asks. While it's true that staffing cuts may result from outsourcing, advocates contend that the funds saved can be allocated to highly strategic business areas, and remaining staff are better able to focus on their core competencies.

"As we've seen too frequently, companies that are not focused eventually fail, causing the greatest job loss of all. When considering the long term, outsourcing is a crucial catalyst for growth and job creation," Poole explains.

Outsourcing is increasingly a value play, adds Dwayne Prosko, KPMG LLP advisory director. "It's about having access to better talent and better capabilities, and being able to free up staff from transactional activity so they can concentrate more on being a business partner."

According to the results of IAOP's global membership surveys, conducted with support from Accenture over the past 18 months, outsourcing has established itself as a strategic management practice that leading companies around the globe are increasingly using for high-value, knowledge-based processes.

"Increasingly, companies are outsourcing to do more than cut costs, but to add value, increase business flexibility and prepare for future growth," said IAOP Chairman Michael Corbett. "Companies that are using outsourcing are poised to emerge from the current economic crisis stronger."

A Growing Trend

It's not just big companies that are outsourcing. Mid-market and even smaller companies are looking at outsourcing as a way to reduce costs and gain access to skills they can't afford in-house.

Historically, manufacturing and banking, financial services and insurance industries outsourced the most, but today organizations in almost all industries are engaged in outsourcing to some degree, says Gabriel Tinti, global marketing manager for Stefanini IT Solutions, a provider of onshore and nearshore IT consulting.

Another trend, says Maidment, is that more work is being outsourced and offshored farther up the food chain. In other words, more complicated job functions, such as HR, accounting and legal, are jumping on the outsourcing bandwagon.

Outsourcing arrangements are also becoming more integrated. Prosko explains that, "In the past, there may have been a very functionally oriented arrangement, but now across the organization people see the value in coordinating and governing outsourcing arrangements in a similar way."

But for all the wonders of outsourcing, it's far from a perfect system. "When it comes to risk, the jury is still out," says Prosko. "Companies expect an outsider to add value, but that outsider may not be motivated to add value—to do things faster and better. They may be focused on keeping the shop running and operating well, but not necessarily on doing what you need to do to take your company to the next level, year after year after year. Companies have to realize that these deals have to be closely managed; they don't manage themselves. Work is required."

The Small Print

While it's possible to craft custom and complex agreements of almost any kind, it's extremely difficult to staff and manage those complex agreements. "So many firms are looking to standardize as much as possible in the marketplace. When that happens, the options for clients moves from a custom order to ordering 'off the menu,'" explains Thomas Young, partner and managing director of infrastructure for sourcing advisory firm TPI. "Additionally, outsourcing agreements are multi-year in nature, so it's critical to build flexibility into the relationship so that firms can adapt to the changing marketplace."

Research is a must. "'Strategic Overshoot©'" is the tendency to operate in another country, often China these days, before careful analysis of the actual business and market conditions rationalizes the decision. "The real solution is often much closer to home," says Michael L. Hetzel, vice president, Americas for Pro QC International. "Nothing gets more valuable on a boat," he says, adding that, "For manufacturing outsourcing it's also important to consider the locations of offshore markets and potential markets, along with proximity to your customers' supply chain elements. Outsourcing architecture must be based on a matrix rather than a flat model."

"Both outsourcing and offshoring are planned strategic moves on the part of the organization," says Maidment. "They are not to be done in a panic to save money when the organization is in trouble. If they are done that way, they are almost certain to fail. These are strategic decisions not to be taken lightly and organizations must plan these moves. It's not unusual for the planning to take a year or more."

Then there's the loss of control over the outsourced function to consider. When it was performed in-house, the organization had direct control over personnel, resources, methods and processes. But when the function is outsourced to an outside provider, that control is lost. Many companies simply aren't prepared for the culture shock.

"I advise my clients that the success of outsourcing transactions hinges on not only structuring and negotiating good contracts, but also implementing effective, flexible processes for governing the relationships with their outsourcing service providers that accommodate and address the inevitable changes that occur in these relationships," says Jeff Andrews, a senior partner specializing in outsourcing with the law firm of Thompson & Knight.

Think, for example, of the classic example where US toy manufacturers found high lead content in the paint being used to manufacture their toys in China. "This is a quality control issue that ruined toy company sales," explains Maidment.

There are other common problems, including delivery challenges, rejects and poor vendor interface. When offshoring is added into the mix, problems may impinge upon currency, overseas deliveries, customs and all the other things that go hand in hand with international commerce. Additionally, says Maidment, you can run into problems with Human Rights Watch if you don't carefully monitor your vendor to make sure it isn't exploiting workers. "Nobody wants to be another Nike!" he exclaims.

And there certainly have been some unpleasant surprises. "For any buyers concerned just with cost savings benefits, reality was nothing but shocking. Cheapest rates often mean failure to deliver the required level of quality," says Alex Golod, VP of global delivery and managing partner with Intetics, a global sourcing company.

Realize the complexity of what you're getting into. "Outsourcing transactions are inherently challenging. They combine all the complexities of M&A transactions with those of long-term service relationships," says Andrews. "The scope and evolution of services; the transfer of personnel and assets; the licensing and ownership of intellectual property; resource-based pricing; performance standards and credits; compliance with laws; termination rights; and allocating risk through representations, warranties and indemnities, are but a few of the difficult issues that have to be addressed to achieve a successful outsourcing relationship."

Outsourcing & Economic Growth

Given the potential economic impact of outsourcing, the pressure for companies to get it right is enormous.

"Outsourcing creates jobs for Americans. A company that outsources is able to reinvest its savings to focus on innovation, which is what this country desperately needs. Over time, the business can build, expand and emerge from the economic slump in a stronger position because it has been able to focus on its core business," says Poole.

A strong company at the beginning of a growth cycle will enrich the local and national economies by adding higher-level jobs, services and functions, all born of the intelligent and strategic application of outsourcing, he adds.

Outsourcing Glossary

Onshore outsourcing:

"The process of engaging another company within your own country for BPO or ITO services. For the US, it means hiring a US-based company to provide services."

Offshoring:

"The transfer of business or IT processes to other countries. Dominant offshoring locations include India, China and the Philippines."

Nearshoring:

"The transfer of business or IT processes to companies in a nearby country, often sharing a border with your own country. In the US, nearshoring describes work sent to Canada and Mexico. Nearshoring is a popular model for companies that don't want to deal with the cultural, language or time zone differences involved in offshoring."

Rural sourcing:

"Sending work to service providers in domestic locations where salaries and operating expenses are lower (such as the Midwest for the United States). An alternative for companies that want to avoid the negative aspects of offshoring."

Cited from Sourcingmag.com

"While it's a small comfort to those who lose their jobs in the short term, the US economy stands to gain as a whole in the long term. Offshoring benefits US consumers by lowering the costs of goods and services," Andrews explains.

What's more, outsourcers are increasingly offering the option of rural sourcing, which involves outsourcing within the United States in communities outside large cities that have the talent and capability to take on large projects. "A combination of nearshore and rural sourcing works for many companies," says Tinti.

"Offshoring is a two-way street," says Maidment, "and not all the jobs that are going around the world are leaving the developed world and heading for the developing world. Many of those jobs are going from one developed country to another, and some are going from the developing world to the developed world."

Although Americans may be distrustful of companies that practice outsourcing, says Wright, "They can't deny that it stimulates the economy by keeping those companies in business."

Critical Thinking

1. Do you think global outsourcing is a good idea?
2. How is global outsourcing an indication of the global economy?
3. What are the long-term implications of global outsourcing?
4. What is the role of the United States in global outsourcing?

America's Other Immigration Crisis

The United States has a pressing immigration problem. But it's not the one you hear about on cable chat shows. **VIVEK WADHWA** explains how we are bringing the world's smartest minds to our shores, training them, and then pushing them away.

VIVEK WADHWA

From his early childhood, Sanjay Mavinkurve dreamed of coming to America and making it big. So his parents, who are from India, sent him to boarding school in Cleveland, Ohio when he was 14. He did so well that he gained a scholarship to Harvard, where he completed both a bachelor's and a master's degree in computer science. In his spare time, he helped conceive the design for Facebook and wrote its first computer code. After graduating, Sanjay joined Google and designed key parts of their mapping software for mobile devices.

Then Sanjay fell in love and had to choose between his heart and the American dream. He was in the United States on a temporary visa and was years away from obtaining permanent resident status. His fiancee had graduated from a top university in Singapore and started work as an investment banker. The only U.S. visa they could obtain for her would not allow her to work, and that would force her to abandon her ambitions. Instead, they decided to abandon America and move to Canada, which welcomed them with open arms.

Over a million skilled workers and their families in the U.S. are waiting for permanent resident visas. But few visas are available and the backlog is rapidly increasing.

The U.S. immigration system allows highly educated workers to enter the country for up to six years on a visa called the H-1B. But this visa imposes many restrictions. If these workers want to stay longer and enjoy the same rights as Americans, they need to obtain a permanent resident visa. And then after five years as a permanent resident, they can apply to become naturalized American citizens.

The problem is that there are more than a million skilled workers and their families in the United States who are waiting for these permanent resident visas, but there are hardly any visas available and the backlog is rapidly increasing. So, over the next few years, Sanjay's story is likely to be repeated many times.

These engineers, scientists, doctors, and researchers entered the country legally to study or to work. They contributed to U.S. economic growth and global competitiveness. Now we've set the stage for them to return to countries such as India and China, where the economies are booming and their skills are in great demand. U.S. businesses large and small stand to lose critical talent, and workers who have gained valuable experience and knowledge of American industry will become potential competitors.

My team at Duke University has been researching the impact of globalization on U.S. competitiveness and the sources of the U.S. advantage. We had many surprises in store when we looked at the role of immigrants in the tech sector.

In 1999, AnnaLee Saxenian of the University of California at Berkeley published a groundbreaking report on the economic contributions of skilled immigrants to California's economy. She found that Chinese and Indian engineers ran a growing share of Silicon Valley companies started during the 1980s and 1990s and that they were at the helm of 24 percent of the technology businesses started from 1980 to 1998. Saxenian concluded that foreign-born scientists and engineers were generating new jobs and wealth for the California economy.

We decided to update and expand her study and focus on engineering and technology firms started in the United States from 1995 to 2005. Over a period of two years, we surveyed thousands of companies and interviewed hundreds of company founders.

Visit a state-of-the-art lab in China and you will meet many highly skilled workers who received their education and training in top U.S. universities and corporations.

We found that the trend Saxenian documented had become a nationwide phenomenon. In over 25 percent of tech companies founded in the United States from 1995 to 2005, the chief executive or lead technologist was foreign-born. In 2005, these companies generated $52 billion in revenue and employed 450,000 workers. In some industries, such as semiconductors, the numbers were much higher—immigrants founded 35 percent of start-ups. In Silicon Valley, the percentage of immigrant-founded start-ups had increased to 52 percent.

When we looked into the backgrounds of these immigrant founders, we found that they tended to be highly educated—96 percent held bachelor's degrees and 74 percent held a graduate or postgraduate degree. And 75 percent of these degrees were in fields related to science, technology, engineering, and mathematics.

The vast majority of these company founders didn't come to the United States as entrepreneurs—52 percent came to study, 40 percent came to work, and 6 percent came for family reasons. Only 1.6 percent came to start companies in America. They found that the United States provided a fertile environment for entrepreneurship.

Even though these founders didn't come to the United States with the intent, they typically started their companies around 13 years after arriving in the country.

We uncovered some puzzling data in the World Intellectual Property Organization (WIPO) database, which is the starting point for obtaining information on global intellectual property protection. In 2006, foreign nationals residing in the United States were named as inventors or co-inventors in an astounding 26 percent of patent applications filed in the United States. This increased from 8 percent in 1998. Some U.S. corporations had foreign nationals contribute to a majority of their patent applications—such as Qualcomm at 72 percent, Merck at 65 percent, GE at 64 percent, and Cisco at 60 percent. Over 40 percent of the international patent applications filed by the U.S. government had foreign authors.

In 1998, 11 percent of these global patent applications had a Chinese inventor or co-inventor. By 2006 this percentage had increased to almost 17 percent. The contribution of Indians increased from 9 percent to 14 percent in the same period. To put these numbers into perspective, it is worth noting that Indians and Chinese both constitute less than 1 percent of the U.S. population, and census data show that 82 percent of Indian immigrants arrived in the United States after 1980.

But our concern was that these were foreign nationals and there was no certainty that they would stay and become U.S. citizens. These foreign-national inventors were also not from the same immigrant group that was founding high-tech companies—those were permanent residents or naturalized citizens. These inventors were likely to be Ph.D. researchers on student visas and employees of U.S. corporations on temporary visas like the H-1B, as Sanjay Mavinkurve was.

The question was: Why was the number of foreign-national inventors increasing so dramatically—337 percent over 8 years?

To answer this, we had to develop our own methodology to estimate the population of skilled immigrants from which such inventors may originate.

We found that at the end of 2006, there were 200,000 employment-based principals waiting for labor certification, which is the first step in the U.S. immigration process. The number of pending I-140 applications, the second step of the immigration process, stood at 50,132. This was over seven times the number in 1996. The number of employment-based principals with approved I-140 applications and unfiled or pending I-485s, or the last step in the immigration process, was 309,823, a threefold increase from a decade earlier. Overall, there were 500,040 employment-based principals (in the three main employment visa categories of EB-1, EB-2, and EB-3) waiting for legal permanent residence. And the total including family members was 1,055,084.

These numbers are particularly troubling when you consider there are only around 120,000 visas available for skilled immigrants in the EB-1, EB-2, and EB-3 categories. To make things worse, no more than 7 percent of the visas are allocated to immigrants from any one country. So immigrants from countries with large populations like India and China have the same number of visas available (8,400) as those from Iceland and Poland.

This means that immigrants like Sanjay who file for permanent resident visas today could be waiting indefinitely. H-1B visas are valid for up to six years and can be extended if the applicant has filed for a permanent resident visa. The problem is that once these workers have started the process, they can't change employers or even be promoted to a different job in the same company without taking the risk of having to restart the application process and move to the back of the line. Their spouses aren't allowed to work or obtain Social Security numbers, which are usually needed for things like bank accounts and driver's licenses. And these workers can't lay deep roots in American society because of the uncertainty about their future.

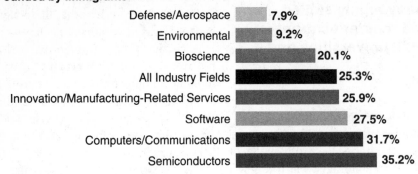

Percentage of Companies Founded by Immigrants

Defense/Aerospace	7.9%
Environmental	9.2%
Bioscience	20.1%
All Industry Fields	25.3%
Innovation/Manufacturing-Related Services	25.9%
Software	27.5%
Computers/Communications	31.7%
Semiconductors	35.2%

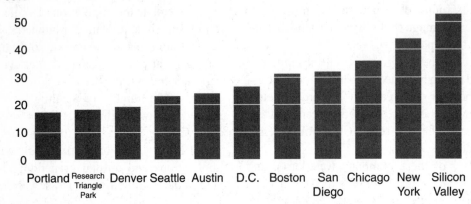

Immigrant-Founded Start-Ups
as Percent of Total in Tech Centers

Portland, Research Triangle Park, Denver, Seattle, Austin, D.C., Boston, San Diego, Chicago, New York, Silicon Valley

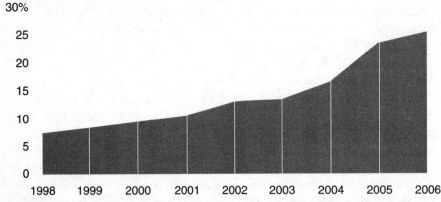

Foreign-National Contribution to U.S. Global Patent Applications,
1998–2006

1998 1999 2000 2001 2002 2003 2004 2005 2006

Sources: Top and bottom charts: Vivek Wadhwa, AnnaLee Saxenian, Ben Rissing, and Gary Gereffi, "America's New Immigrant Entrepreneurs: Part 1," the Kauffman Foundation, January 2007; middle chart: Wadhwa, Saxenian, Rissing, and Gereffi, "Education, Entrepreneurship, and Immigration: America's New Immigrant Entrepreneurs, Part II," The Kauffman Foundation, June 2007.

We also researched the trends in globalization and what was happening in India and China. We met dozens of executives of top companies in several industries in these countries and toured their R&D labs.

In Hyderabad, India, companies like Satyam Computer Services and Hindustan Computers are designing navigation control and in-flight entertainment systems and other key components of jetliners for American and European corporations. In New Delhi, Indian scientists are discovering drugs for GlaxoSmithKline. In Pune, Indians are helping design bodies, dashboards, and power trains for Detroit automakers. In Bangalore, Cisco Systems, IBM, and other U.S. tech giants have made the Indian city their global base for developing new telecom solutions.

China is already the world's biggest exporter of computers, telecom equipment, and other high-tech electronics. Multinationals and government-backed companies are pouring hundreds of billions of dollars into next-generation plants to turn China into an export power in semiconductors, passenger cars, and specialty chemicals. China is lavishly subsidizing state-of-the-art labs in biochemistry, nanotech materials, computing, and aerospace.

Visit any of these labs, and you will meet dozens of workers returned from the United States—highly educated and skilled workers who received their education and training in top U.S. universities and corporations. In GE's Jack Welch Technology Center in Bangalore, 34 percent of the R&D staff have returned from the United States. So have 50 percent of those with a Ph.D. at IBM research in Bangalore. And so are the managers of Chinas top engineering, technology, and biotech companies.

These returnees have fueled much of the innovation and growth in R&D in China and India. And the executives of these companies will tell you that the number of resumes they receive from the United States has increased tenfold over the last few years.

We need to do all we can to attract and keep skilled immigrants rather than bring them here temporarily, train them, and send them home.

Most students and skilled temporary workers who come to the United States want to stay, as is evident from the backlog for permanent resident visas. Yet we're leaving these potential immigrants little choice but to return home. "The New Immigrant Survey," by Guillermina Jasso of New York University and other leading academics, found that approximately one in five new legal immigrants and about one in three employment principals either plan to leave the United States or are uncertain about remaining. These surveys were done in 2003, before the backlog increased so dramatically.

Additionally, there are over 250,000 foreign students studying in our universities. In our engineering schools, 60 percent of Ph.D. candidates and 42 percent of master's candidates are foreign nationals. These students are often the best of their home countries. But there are few visas available for U.S. companies to hire these students when they graduate. Foreign students can work temporarily when they graduate on practical training visas. But if they want to stay long term, they need to get H-1B visas and then file for permanent residence.

The yearly allocation of H-1B visas for foreign students who graduate at the master's level and above is 20,000. But 31,200 people filed applications for these visas in the first week they became available in April of this year. Bachelor's-level graduates had even worse odds, as they had to compete in the general pool with only 65,000 visas available, less than half the number of applications for that visa category.

The result is that employers are now reluctant to hire foreign students. Why recruit and train new hires when there is less than a 50 percent chance that they will be able to stay? These students are getting increasingly frustrated and applying for jobs back home or in other countries.

So we have set the stage for hundreds of thousands of highly educated and skilled workers to become our competitors. Indian and Chinese industry benefited in a big way from the trickle of returnees over the last few years. Now we're looking at a flood.

Immigration has been a hot topic in the media, but the focus has been on the plight of the estimated 12 million unskilled workers who entered the United States illegally. Emotions have been running high on the issues of amnesty and border control.

In 2006, foreign nationals residing in the U.S. were named as inventors or co-inventors in an astounding 26 percent of patent applications filed in the U.S.

At the same time, a debate rages about H-1B visas and this gets considerable press coverage. Companies such as Microsoft, Intel, and Oracle have been lobbying for visas to bring in skilled immigrants, but have focused on expanding the numbers of H-1B visas available. Why? Perhaps because workers on these visas are desirable, as they are less likely to leave their employers during the decade or more they are waiting for permanent residence.

Moreover, I know from my experience as a tech CEO that H-1Bs are cheaper than domestic hires. Technically, these workers are supposed to be paid a "prevailing wage," but this mechanism is riddled with loopholes. In the tech world, salaries vary widely based on skill and competence. Yet the prevailing wage concept works on average salaries, so you can hire a superstar for the cost of an average worker. Add to this the inability of an H-1B employee to jump ship and you have a strong incentive to hire workers on these visas. (To be fair, the lobbying platform of these tech companies does include recommendations that the government expand the number of permanent resident visas.)

Opponents of H-1B visas complain that these visas cause job losses and damage the engineering profession. To some extent, they are right. If we bring in too many workers at the lower end of the scale, we could end up causing a reduction of salaries to the point that Americans don't consider the profession worthwhile. And there are indications that enrollments in computer science have already dropped. The fact is that if we flood the market with workers with any skill, we end up hurting individual members of the profession; if we brought in 100,000 doctors, dentists, or plumbers, we would cause salaries to drop, create unemployment, and discourage Americans from studying these professions.

So we want skilled immigrants, but we want them to come on the right visas as permanent residents. The battles being fought are about bringing in more people with H-1B visas—not about those who are already here with them and stranded in "immigration limbo." Which means that we're going to be compounding the hardship on workers who are already here and forcing more, like Sanjay, to abandon America.

Unlike many of the problems facing the United States, this one isn't hard to fix. All we have to do is to increase the number of visas offered to skilled workers in the EB-1, EB-2, and EB-3 categories from 120,000 to around 300,000 per year. And we need to remove the per-country limits. Instead of requiring graduates from top universities who receive jobs from American corporations to go through the tedious H-1B visa process, we should provide a direct path to permanent residence. We are now competing with the rest of the world for the best talent. We need to do all we can to attract and keep skilled immigrants, rather than bring them here temporarily, train them, and send them home.

Critical Thinking

1. Why are some of the non-U.S. citizens who study in America not being allowed to stay in the United States upon graduating from American universities?

2. What does that mean from American industry?

3. How can this system be changed?

VIVEK WADHWA is Executive in Residence at Duke University's Pratt School of Engineering and a Wertheim Fellow at Harvard Law School's Labor and Worklife Program.

Trends Shaping Tomorrow's World
Forces in the Natural and Institutional Environments

MARVIN J. CETRON AND OWEN DAVIES

Introduction

For nearly half a century, Forecasting International has been tracking the forces that shape our future. Some 20 years ago, we codified our observations into a list of trends that forms the basis for much of our work. For each of our projects, we compare the specific circumstances of an industry or organization with these general trends and project their interactions. This often allows us to form a remarkably detailed picture of what lies ahead.

This is Part Two of FI's periodic trend report. It covers trends in energy, the environment, technology, management and institutions, and terrorism. (Part One, published in the May-June 2010 issue of THE FUTURIST, tracked economic, population, societal, family, and work trends.)

Because this forecast project is ongoing, the authors—and the World Future Society—welcome your feedback.

Energy Trends

Despite efforts to develop alternative sources of energy, oil consumption is still rising rapidly.

- The world used only 57 million barrels of oil per day in 1973, when the first major price shock hit. By 2008, it was using 86 million barrels daily, according to the U.S. Energy Information Administration (EIA). This was slightly more than it produced that year.
- The United States alone consumed about 19.5 million barrels of oil per day in 2008 (22.8 percent of world total), down from 20.7 million in 2004 (25.1 percent of world total). U.S. petroleum consumption is projected to increase to 22 million barrels per day by 2035.
- In 2008, China consumed 7.8 million barrels of oil per day, making it the second-largest user of oil in the world. Its oil demand has grown by 7 percent per year, on average, since 1990. Most of China's imported oil (more than 3.1 million barrels a day) comes from the Middle East.
- However, oil's share of world energy consumption has begun to decline: It is expected to drop from 40 percent in 1999 to about 37 percent in 2020.

Assessment and Implications:

Consumption is expected to reach 97 million barrels daily by 2015 and 118 million by 2030. These projections seem likely to prove reasonably accurate.

Oil prices now are high enough to provide an incentive to develop new fields, such as the Arctic National Wildlife Refuge and the deep fields under the Gulf of Mexico.

Environmentally sensitive areas will be developed using new drilling techniques, double-walled pipelines, and other precautions that make it possible to extract oil with less damage to the surroundings. But they will be developed.

Any prolonged rise of oil prices to triple digits will erode support for environmental protections in the United States, leading to widespread development of whatever energy sources are most readily available regardless of the long-term consequences.

Contrary to popular belief, the world is not about to run out of oil.

- As a result of intensive exploration, the world's proven oil reserves climbed steadily since the 1980s and hovered around 1.3 trillion barrels in 2007, the most recent figure currently available.
- Recent discoveries of major oil fields in Canada, Brazil, and under the Gulf of Mexico have substantially increased the world's known oil reserves. Exploitation of oil in Venezuela has barely begun. Reserves there may be even larger than those in Saudi Arabia, according to some estimates. However, it is more expensive to refine and use,

because it contains much higher levels of sulfur than the Middle Eastern oil currently in production. India also is believed to own substantial reserves of oil in deposits beneath the Indian Ocean.

- OPEC officials claim that the 11 member countries can provide for the world's energy needs for roughly the next 80 years. OPEC supplies about 40 percent of the world's oil and holds 60 percent of the known oil available internationally. Even 80 percent of OPEC's estimated supply would still be oil enough to supply the world for the next 64 years.

Assessment and Implications:

Talk of "peak oil," the suggestion that crude production has topped out or soon will, is unjustified and, in FI's view, unjustifiable.

Higher oil prices should make it cost effective to develop new methods of recovering oil from old wells. Technologies already developed could add nearly 50 percent to the world's recoverable oil supply.

OPEC will continue to supply most of the oil used by the developed world. According to the U.S. Department of Energy, OPEC oil production will grow to about 57 million barrels of oil per day by 2020.

Russia and Kazakhstan will be major suppliers if the necessary pipelines can be completed and political uncertainties do not block investment by Western oil companies. Russia has been the world's second-largest oil producer since 2008.

Alternative energy sources face problems with economic viability. Barring substantial incentives, this will inhibit efforts to stem global warming for the foreseeable future.

A generalized war in the Middle East after the United States leaves Iraq could drastically reduce the region's oil output. This is unlikely, but the impact of such a conflict would be too large to ignore the possibility.

The spread of fundamentalist Islamic regimes with a grudge against the West also could keep OPEC oil out of the American market.

If the United States loses access to Middle Eastern oil, it will buy even more from Canada and Venezuela, tap the Arctic National Wildlife Reserve, and develop the deep-water fields under the Gulf of Mexico much faster than expected.

In a prolonged energy emergency, America also would be likely to develop its vast reserves of oil shale, which have long been economically viable at crude prices over $40 per barrel. New technology reportedly makes it profitable at any price over $17 per barrel. With enough shale oil to supply its own needs for 300 years, the United States could become one of the world's largest petroleum exporters.

Developing shale would devastate the environment, but with crude oil prices in triple digits during a Middle Eastern war, the environment will be considered expendable.

When not perturbed by political or economic instability, oil prices will average around $65 per barrel.

- The International Energy Agency's World Energy Outlook 2007 concurs.
- Prices approaching $100 per barrel in the fall of 2007 were an aberration caused by a global shortage of refinery capacity and by fears of instability triggered by the Iraq war. New energy demand from the fast-growing economies of China and India has raised the floor that until 2004 supported oil in the $25 per barrel range. The "risk premium" built into the price of oil is estimated at $10 to $15 per barrel.
- Yet, in the long run, other factors will tend to depress the price of oil toward its former levels. New refineries in Saudi Arabia and other countries scheduled to come online by 2012 will ease the tight supply–demand balance for oil. New oil supplies are being found or developed in many parts of the world. The 20 most-industrialized countries all have at least three-month supplies of oil in tankers and underground storage. Most have another three months' worth in "strategic reserves." In times of high oil prices, customer nations can afford to stop buying until the costs come down. And OPEC has stated that it prefers to see the price of oil in the neighborhood of $45 per barrel.

Assessment and Implications:

Barring an American invasion of Iran, any excursions beyond $100 per barrel will be extremely brief. Given continued concerns about instability in the Middle East, oil prices will slowly decline to $60 or so per barrel.

In response to high (by American standards) gas prices, the U.S. government probably will boost domestic oil production and refining to increase the reserve of gasoline and heating oil. This stockpile would be ready for immediate use in case of future price hikes. This will make it easier to negotiate with OPEC.

A key step in controlling oil prices, and an indicator of Washington's seriousness about doing so, would be development of at least four new refineries around the country by the government, probably for lease to commercial producers. We rate the odds at no more than 50:50.

The United States almost certainly will drill for oil in the Arctic National Wildlife Reserve, though efforts will be made to minimize environmental damage. For example, drilling would take place only in the winter, when the tundra is rock hard.

By 2020, the new fields under the Gulf of Mexico will come online, putting even more pressure on oil prices.

Growing competition from other energy sources also will help to limit the price of oil.

- Nuclear power is growing rapidly. Nuclear plants supply about 15 percent of Russian electricity. By

2020, Russia will consume 129 billion kWh of nuclear energy per year. Plans call for construction of 26 more nuclear plants by 2030, when 25 percent or more of the nation's electricity will be nuclear. In early 2004, China had only nine operating nuclear power plants. It plans to build 30 more by 2020, bringing nuclear energy consumption from 16 billion kWh in 2000 to 142 billion kWh. By 2020, Canada will use 118 billion kWh. Even the United States is weighing the construction of new reactors.

- Renewable sources accounted for about 14 percent of the world's energy in 2005. However, more than half of the world's renewable energy came from hydroelectric dams. Hydroelectric power generation has been declining since its peak of 727.62 billion kWh in 1996.

- Worldwide wind-power generating capacity grew by 30 percent annually in the decade ending in 2005, to a total of 59,000 MW, according to the Earth Policy Institute and the World watch Institute. This is a 12-fold increase in 10 years.

- Photovoltaic solar energy production has been growing at a steady 25 percent per year since 1980. Commercial solar cells are now cheap enough to compete with other power sources, especially in sunny regions.

- Natural gas burns cleanly, and there is enough of it available to supply the world's total energy demand for at least the next 200 years. Consumption of natural gas is growing by 3.3 percent annually, compared with 1.8 percent for oil. Proven natural gas reserves stood at about 237 trillion cubic feet in 2009, about 1 percent more than a year earlier, but the total gas available is believed to be more than 2,000 trillion cubic feet. The United States has been described as "the Saudi Arabia of natural gas." Its shale gas accounts for an estimated 35 percent of the world's total natural gas supply. New technologies have made it economically practical to develop this supply.

- Although most of the world's scientists gave up on cold fusion long ago, the U.S. Navy has continued work on the process. Its researchers have announced development of a reproducible cold-fusion system that consistently releases more energy than it consumes.

- According to the DOE's Energy Information Agency, shifting 20 percent of America's energy supply to renewable resources by 2020 would have almost no impact on the total cost of power. At present, less than 5 percent of the energy used in the United States comes from renewable resources.

Assessment and Implications:

Though oil will remain the world's most important energy resource for years to come, two or three decades forward it should be less of a choke point in the global economy.

Solar, geothermal, wind, and wave energy will ease power problems where these resources are most readily available, though they will supply only a very small fraction of the world's energy in the foreseeable future.

Declining reliance on oil eventually could help to reduce air and water pollution, at least in the developed world. By 2060, a costly but pollution-free hydrogen economy may at last become practical.

Fusion power remains a distant hope.

Cold fusion also remains a long shot for practical power, but FI believes it can no longer be discounted. Reported confirmations of the phenomenon, including the one by the U.S. Navy, seem highly credible. If they prove to be correct, power plants based on the process could begin to come online by 2030.

Environmental and Resource Trends

People around the world are becoming increasingly sensitive to environmental issues as the consequences of neglect, indifference, and ignorance become ever more apparent.

- The World Health Organization estimates that 3 million people die each year from the effects of air pollution. In the United States, an estimated 64,000 people a year die of cardiopulmonary disease caused by breathing particulates. In sub-Saharan Africa, the toll is between 300,000 and 500,000 deaths per year. Pollution-related respiratory diseases kill about 1.4 million people yearly in China and Southeast Asia.

- In developing countries, indoor air pollution is an even bigger problem. Indoor smoke from burning fuels such as dung and wood—which more than half the world's population relies on for cooking and other basic energy needs—creates particulates that penetrate deeply into the lungs. An estimated 1.6 million people a year die from indoor air pollution, according to WHO.

- Contaminated water is implicated in 80 percent of the world's health problems, according to WHO. An estimated 40,000 people around the world die each day of diseases directly caused by contaminated water, more than 14 million per year. In India, an estimated 300 million people lack access to safe drinking water, due to widespread pollution of rivers and groundwater. The European Parliament estimates that 70 percent of the Continent's drinking water contains dangerous concentrations of nitrate pollution. In the United States, there is growing concern that pollutants such as perchlorate, the gasoline additive MTBE, and even the chlorine used to kill waterborne pathogens may present significant health concerns.

- Though some debate remains about the cause, the fact of global warming has become undeniable. At Palmer Station on Anvers Island, Antarctica, the average annual temperature has risen by 3°C to 4°C since the 1940s, and by an amazing 7°C to 9°C in June—early winter in that hemisphere.

- Pew Research Center's 2007 Global Attitudes Project survey of 46 countries found much more concern for the environment than in the 2002 survey. In the United States, the number citing environmental problems as the top global threat rose from 23 percent to 37 percent. In India, the number went from 32 percent to 49 percent. In both Japan and China, 70 percent of respondents said environmental problems were the greatest global threat to the world.

- Many governments are taking more-active measures to protect the environment. For instance, after years of ineffective gestures, Costa Rica has incorporated about 25 percent of its land into protected areas, such as national parks. In an effort to promote cleaner energy technologies and to slow global warming, most European nations now tax carbon emissions or fossil fuels. Anticipating a three-foot rise in sea levels, the Netherlands is spending $1 billion to build new dikes.

Assessment and Implications:

A solid majority of voters throughout the developed world now recognize the need to clean up the environment, and especially to control greenhouse warming. Throughout most of the world, polluters and private beneficiaries of public assets will increasingly confront restrictive regulations designed to serve the interests of the community at large.

Carbon dioxide will remain a problem for many years to come. If air pollution were halted instantly, it would take an estimated 200 years for CO_2 and other greenhouse gases to return to preindustrial levels.

Impurities in water will become an even greater problem as the population of the developed countries ages and becomes more susceptible to infectious diseases.

Recent analyses say there is a 90 percent chance that the planet's average annual temperature will rise between 3°C and 9°C over the next century. This will cause severe dislocations both for plant and animal populations and for many human activities.

Environmental policies will provoke a political backlash wherever they conflict with entrenched interests, as they have long done in the American West.

Industrial development still trumps environmental concerns in many parts of the world.

- The Pew study cited above found that less than one-fourth of respondents in any African country rated environmental problems as the world's most important threat. In Ethiopia, where desertification is at its worst and drought is a constant threat, only 7 percent did so.

- Beijing has made repairing the environment a national priority. Yet, 70 percent of the energy used in China comes from coal-burning power plants, few of them equipped with pollution controls. The country intends to build more than 500 additional coal-fired plants in the next 10 years. Scientists estimate that by 2025 China will emit more carbon dioxide and sulfur dioxide than the United States, Japan, and Canada combined.

Assessment and Implications:

Broad regions of the planet will be subject to pollution, deforestation, and other environmental ills in the coming decades.

Acid rain like that afflicting the United States and Canada will appear wherever designers of new power plants and factories neglect emission controls.

India is covered by a haze of sulfates and other chemicals associated with acid rain. Look for this problem to appear in most other industrializing countries.

Diseases related to air and water pollution will spread dramatically in the years ahead. Already, chronic obstructive pulmonary disease is five times more common in China than in the United States. As citizens of the developing countries grow to expect modern health care, this will create a growing burden on their economies.

This is just a taste of future problems, and perhaps not the most troublesome. Even the U.S. government now admits that global warming is a result of human activities that produce greenhouse gases. It now seems that China and India soon will produce even more of them than the major industrialized nations. Helping the developing lands to raise their standards of living without creating wholesale pollution will require much more aid and diplomacy than the developed world has ever been willing to give this cause.

Water shortages are a growing problem for much of the world.

- In many regions, they are severe already. The northern half of China, home to perhaps half a billion people, already is short of water. The water table under Beijing has fallen 200 feet since 1965. Australia's Murray-Darling river system, which supplies water for 40 percent of the country's crops and 80 percent of its irrigation, no longer carries enough water to reach the sea without constant dredging. Salinity in the Murray is rising so quickly that the water is expected to be undrinkable in 20 years.

- There is worse to come. According to UN studies, at least 3.5 billion people will run short of water by 2040, almost 10 times as many as in 1995. By 2050, fully two-thirds of the world's population could be living in regions with chronic, widespread shortages of water. One-third of the population of Africa and most of the major cities in the developing world will face water shortages, according to the United Nations. Many climatologists believe that global warming will make drought in the United States much more frequent—even the norm—west of the Mississippi River.
- Water usage is causing other problems as well. For example, irrigation water evaporates, leaving minerals in the soil. By 2020, 30 percent of the world's arable land will be salty; by 2050, 50 percent. Salinization already is cutting crop yields in India, Pakistan, Egypt, Mexico, Australia, and parts of the United States.
- An estimated 38 percent of the world's land is threatened with desertification, owing mostly to overgrazing, overcultivation, and deforestation. Northern Africa, the Middle East, southwestern China, and the western edge of South America are at the greatest risk.

Assessment and Implications:

Providing adequate supplies of potable water will be a growing challenge for developing and developed countries alike.

Such problems as periodic famine and desertification can be expected to grow more frequent and severe in coming decades.

In many lands, including parts of the United States, growing water shortages may inhibit economic growth and force large-scale migration out of afflicted areas.

Climate change is expected to reduce the flow of Australia's parched Murray River by a further 5 percent in 20 years and 15 percent in 50 years.

Countries dependent on hydropower face growing shortages of electricity. Most are relatively poor lands in Africa and Asia, which will find economic development even more challenging. Venezuela has already rationed electricity, owing to low reservoir levels behind the Guri Dam, which produces 70 percent of the country's electric power.

Water wars, predicted for more than a decade, are a threat in places like the Kashmir: Much of Pakistan's water comes from areas of Kashmir now controlled by India.

Recycling has delayed the "garbage glut" that threatened to overflow the world's landfills, but the threat has not passed simply because it has not yet arrived.

- Americans now produce about 4.5 pounds of trash per person per day, twice as much as they threw away a generation ago. In 2005, they sent about 245 million tons of municipal solid waste to landfills. Seventy percent of U.S. landfills will be full by 2025, according to the EPA.
- Japan expects to run out of space for municipal solid waste by 2015.
- In London and the surrounding region, landfills will run out of room by 2012.
- In some other regions, simply collecting the trash is a problem. Brazil produces an estimated 240,000 tons of garbage daily, but only 70 percent reaches landfills. The rest, 72,000 tons per day, accumulates in city streets, where it helps to spread disease.
- Recycling has proved to be an effective alternative to dumping. Some 37 percent of London's municipal waste is recycled, with a target of 45 percent by 2020. Seattle, with one of the most effective recycling programs in the United States, recycles about half of its solid waste. As of 2005, Germany recycled 60 percent of its municipal solid waste, 65 percent of manufacturing waste, 80 percent of packaging, and 87 percent of construction waste, according to the Federal Ministry for Environment, Nature Conservation and Nuclear Safety. Largely as a result, the number of landfills for domestic waste has been reduced from about 50,000 in the 1970s to just 160.

Assessment and Implications:

Recycling and waste-to-energy plants are a viable alternative to simply dumping garbage.

Expect a wave of new regulations, recycling, waste-to-energy projects, and waste management programs in the United States and other countries in an effort to stem the tide of trash. In the United States it will of course begin in California, a jurisdiction often cited by policy forecasters as a bellwether of change.

State and local governments will tighten existing regulations and raise disposal prices in Pennsylvania, South Carolina, Louisiana, and other places that accept much of the trash from major garbage producers such as New York.

Trash producers in the developed world will ship much more of their debris to repositories in developing countries. This will inspire protests in the receiving lands.

Beyond 2025 or so, the developing countries will close their repositories to foreign waste, forcing producers to develop more waste-to-energy and recycling technologies. Ultimately, it may even be necessary to exhume buried trash for recycling to make more room in closed dump sites for material that cannot be reused.

Waste-to-energy programs will make only a small contribution to the world's growing need for power.

Species extinction and loss of biodiversity will be a growing worry for decades to come.

- An estimated 50,000 species disappear each year, up to 1,000 times the natural rate of extinction, according to the United Nations Environmental Program. By 2100, as many as half of all species could disappear. Twelve percent of birds, 21 percent of mammals, 30 percent of known amphibians, and 32 percent of all conifers and cycads are estimated to be nearing extinction. Some 17,291 species are now listed as threatened, according to the 2009 Red List of the International Union for Conservation of Nature and Natural Resources. The real list is likely much larger, as the group has evaluated only 47,677 of the 1.5 million species on its list. Amphibian populations are in decline throughout the world, for reasons that remain poorly understood.

- Coral reefs throughout the world are dying rapidly. Caribbean reefs have lost 80 percent of their coral cover in the past three decades. In Indonesia, home to one-eighth of the world's coral reefs, more than 70 percent of the reefs are dead or dying. Most scientists believe that climate change is largely responsible for killing coral. Other suspected culprits are overfishing and pollution.
- Twenty-five so-called "hot spots" covering 11 percent of the world's surface have lost 70 percent of their original vegetation. These hot spots are home to 1.2 billion people, or one-fifth of the world's population.
- What is left in its natural state, about 2 percent of the planet's surface, is home to 44 percent of all plant species and 35 percent of all vertebrates other than fish.
- The chief cause for species loss is the destruction of natural habitats by logging, agriculture, and urbanization. Some 30 million acres of rain forest are destroyed each year. More than half the world's rain forests are already gone. At current rates, the rest could disappear in the next 40 years.
- Though commercial fishing is not known to have exterminated any species—largely because the last few members of a species are too costly to catch—it is turning out to be one more important cause of species depletion. Stocks of cod, tuna, swordfish, marlin, and sharks are down 90 percent since modern industrialized fishing began 40 years ago.

Assessment and Implications:

Saving any significant fraction of the world's endangered species will require much more effort and expense than many governments find acceptable. For species such as corals, whose loss is attributable largely to climate change, it may not be possible.

Species loss has a powerful negative impact on human well-being. Half of all drugs used in medicine are derived from natural sources, including 55 of the top 100 drugs prescribed in the United States. About 40 percent of all pharmaceuticals are derived from the sap of vascular plants. So far, only 2 percent of the 300,000 known sap-containing plants have been assayed for useful drugs. Most of the species lost in the years ahead will disappear before they can be tested.

The Indonesian economy loses an estimated $500,000 to $800,000 annually per square mile of dead or damaged reef.

Australia may lose even more as degradation of the Great Barrier Reef continues. The UN Intergovernmental Panel on Climate Change predicts that the reef will be "functionally extinct" by 2030.

Diverse ecosystems absorb more carbon dioxide than those with fewer species. Loss of biodiversity is thus a potential cause of global warming.

Urbanization, arguably the world's oldest trend, continues rapidly.

- Forty-eight percent of the world's population currently lives in cities, according to the Population Reference Bureau's World Population Data Sheet. By 2030, that figure will grow to 60 percent, as some 2.1 billion people are added to the world's cities. More than three-fourths of the populations in developed countries live in cities. North America's urbanization is the highest, at 79 percent. But cities are growing fastest in the developing world.
- The big are getting bigger. In 1950, there were just eight mega-cities (populations exceeding 5 million) in the world. By 2015, there will be 59 megacities, 48 of them in less-developed countries. Of these, 23 will have populations over 10 million, all but four in the developing lands.
- Natural increase now accounts for more than half of population increase in the cities; at most, little more than one-third of urban growth results from migration.
- Up to 1 billion city dwellers lack adequate shelter, clean water, toilets, or electricity. The United Nations estimates that these problems cause 10 million needless deaths annually.
- Urbanization has significant environmental consequences: Fuels burned in cities account for 75 percent of global carbon emissions from human activity, according to the Worldwatch Institute. NASA scientists point out that urbanization also tends to put buildings and blacktop on the most fertile land, eliminating significant quantities of carbon-absorbing plants. Urbanization also deprives surrounding areas of water: Instead of sinking into the ground, rain is collected, piped to the city, used, treated as gray water, and then discarded into the ocean. In some regions, such as near Atlanta, water levels in local aquifers are declining rapidly because the water that once replenished them now is lost.

- The United States is the one major exception to the global urbanization trend. This automobile-reliant society built one of the best highway systems in the world and has relatively little mass transit, so more Americans live in the suburbs than in the cities.

Assessment and Implications:

Continuing urbanization will aggravate most environmental and social problems. Cities' contribution to global warming can only increase in the years ahead.

As the world's supply of potable water declines, people are concentrating in those areas where it is hardest to obtain and is used least efficiently. This trend will aggravate water problems for so long as it continues.

Many more people will die due to shortages of shelter, water, and sanitation. Epidemics will become still more common as overcrowding spreads HIV and other communicable diseases more rapidly.

Since urban growth is now due more to natural increase than to migration, programs designed to encourage rural populations to remain in the countryside may be misplaced. Education and family planning seem more likely to rein in the growth of cities.

Technology Trends

Technology increasingly dominates both the economy and society.

- New technologies are surpassing the previous state of the art in all fields, and technological obsolescence is accelerating.
- For most users, computers have become part of the environment, rather than just tools used for specific tasks. With wireless modems, portable computers give us access to networked data wherever we go. Internet-equipped cell phones are even more convenient for access to e-mail and websites.
- Robots are taking over more and more jobs that are routine, remote, or risky, such as repairing undersea cables and nuclear power stations. Flexible, general-service personal robots will appear in the home by 2015, expanding on the capabilities of devices such as robotic vacuum cleaners and lawn mowers.
- By 2015, artificial intelligence, data mining, and virtual reality will help most companies and government agencies to assimilate data and solve problems beyond the range of today's computers. AI applications include robotics, machine vision, voice recognition, speech synthesis, electronic data processing, health and human services, administration, and airline pilot assistance.
- Superconductors operating at economically viable temperatures will be in commercial use soon after 2015.

Assessment and Implications:

Technologically related changes in society and business seen over the last 20 years are just the beginning of a trend that will accelerate at least through this century.

New technologies should continue to improve the efficiency of many industries, helping to keep costs under control.

However, this increased productivity has retarded U.S. job creation since at least 2002. Other developed countries are likely to feel the same effect in the future.

Technology made international outsourcing possible. It will continue to promote outsourcing, to the benefit of the recipient countries, but causing painful job losses in the donor lands.

New technologies often require a higher level of education and training to use them effectively. They also provide many new opportunities to create businesses and jobs.

Automation will continue to cut the cost of many services and products, making it possible to reduce prices while still improving profits.

This will be critical to business survival as the Internet continues to push the price of many products to the commodity level.

The United States is losing its scientific and technical leadership to other countries.

- "The scientific and technical building blocks of our economic leadership are eroding at a time when many other nations are gathering strength," the National Academy of Sciences warns. "Although many people assume that the United States will always be a world leader in science and technology, this may not continue to be the case in as much as great minds and ideas exist throughout the world. We fear the abruptness with which a lead in science and technology can be lost—and the difficulty of recovering a lead once lost, if indeed it can be regained at all."
- According to the National Science Board, R&D spending grows by 6 percent per year in the United States, on average. China spends 20 percent more on R&D each year.
- China is now second to the United States in the number of research articles its scientists publish each year and gaining rapidly.
- In patents earned each year, Americans are now in sixth place and falling.
- Military research now absorbs much of the money that once supported basic science. Since 2000, U.S. federal spending on defense research has risen an average of 7.4 percent per year, compared with only 4.5 percent for civilian research. The Defense Advanced Research Projects Agency has been legendary for its support of "blue sky" research that led to dramatic technical advances, including the creation of the Internet. Today it focuses

increasingly on immediate military needs and low-risk development efforts.

- More than half of American scientists and engineers are nearing retirement. At the rate American students are entering these fields, the retirees cannot be replaced except by recruiting foreign scientists. According to the National Academy of Engineering, the United States produces only about 7 percent of the world's engineers. Only 6 percent of American undergraduates are engineering majors, compared with 12 percent in Europe and 40 percent in China. Of the doctoral degrees in science awarded by American universities, about 30 percent go to foreign students. In engineering, it is 60 percent.

- By inhibiting stem-cell research, cloning, and other specialties, the United States has made itself less attractive to cutting-edge biomedical scientists. The United Kingdom is capitalizing on this to become the world's leader in stem-cell research. In the process, it is reversing the brain drain that once brought top British scientists to the United States. More than 70 leading American biomedical researchers have moved to the U.K. along with many less noted colleagues. Latin America also has been receiving scientific émigrés from the United States.

- About 25 percent of America's science and engineering workforce are immigrants, including nearly half of those with doctoral degrees. During the 15 years ending in 2007, one-third of the American scientists receiving Nobel Prizes were foreign-born.

- According to Purdue University President Martin Jischke, more than 90 percent of all scientists and engineers in the world live in Asia.

Assessment and Implications:

If this trend is not reversed, it will begin to undermine the U.S. economy and shift both economic and political power to other lands. According to some estimates, about half of the improvement in the American standard of living is directly attributable to research and development carried out by scientists and engineers.

Demand to import foreign scientists and engineers on H-1b visas also will continue to grow. Publicity about the H-1b program, and about the offshoring of R&D to company divisions and consulting labs in Asia, in turn will discourage American students from entering technical fields. This has already been blamed for shrinking student rolls in computer science.

In 2005, China for the first time exported more IT and communications goods ($180 million) than the United States ($145 million). Its lead has grown each year since then.

Transportation technology and practice are improving rapidly.

- The newest generation of aircraft, such as the Boeing 787 and future Airbus A350 XWB, are using lightweight materials and more efficient engines to cut fuel costs, stretch ranges, and increase cargo capacity.

- The airline industry is developing technical advances such as improved satellite navigation and communications, runway collision avoidance systems, and safer seat designs. These advances will allow planes to fly closer together, increasing the carrying capacity of air routes.

- Rail travel is getting faster. The TGV Est line, which runs 300 km (180 miles) from Paris to Frankfurt, operates at 320 kph (198.8 mph) inside France, compared with 300 kph (186.4 mph) on other parts of the TGV system.

- Advances in automobile technology are reaching the marketplace, such as road-condition sensors, continuously variable transmissions, automated traffic management systems, night-vision systems, and smart seats that tailor airbag inflation to the passenger's weight.

- European researchers are experimenting with "auto trains," in which a long line of cars automatically trails after a leader. This allows tighter, more efficient spacing of vehicles and fewer delays.

- The United States has finally committed to funding its first relatively high-speed rail line, between Tampa and Orlando, Florida.

Assessment and Implications:

These advances will make travel faster, cheaper, and safer by land, sea, and air.

One of the fastest-growing transport industries is trucking, thanks to the expanded use of just-in-time inventory management and Internet-based companies that rely on trucks to deliver their products. This field will grow more efficient as GPS-based truck tracking, RFID-based cargo management, more efficient engines, and other new technologies spread through the industry.

To reduce the number and severity of traffic accidents, trucks on the most heavily used highways will be exiled to car-free lanes, and the separation will be enforced.

New hybrid car models will begin to gain significant market share from traditional gas guzzlers between 2010 and 2015.

Following European practice, even "legacy" air carriers in the United States will begin to replace the spokes of their existing hub-and-spokes systems with high-speed trains for journeys of 100 to 150 miles.

By 2015, improved technologies and concerns about the long-term costs of energy will lead even the rail-resistant United States to begin modernizing its train system.

New aircraft navigation and safety technologies will reduce the number and severity of crashes.

In Europe, smart-car technologies will begin to reduce deaths due to auto accidents in 2010, and, in the United States, a few years later.

Cities increasingly will struggle to reduce auto congestion by limiting the use of private automobiles, as in Munich, Vienna, and Mexico City; by taxing auto use in congested areas, as in London; or by encouraging the development and use of mass transit, as in Copenhagen and Curitiba, Brazil.

Technology may offer other alternatives. One proposal is "dual-mode transportation," in which private cars would be used normally on short hauls but would run on automated guideways for long-distance travel.

The pace of technological change accelerates with each new generation of discoveries and applications.

- In fast-moving engineering disciplines, half of the cutting-edge knowledge learned by college students in their freshman year is obsolete by the time they graduate.
- The design and marketing cycle—idea, invention, innovation, imitation—is shrinking steadily. As late as the 1940s, the product cycle stretched to 30 or 40 years. Today, it seldom lasts 30 or 40 weeks. Almost any new consumer product can be exactly duplicated by Chinese factories and sold on eBay within a week after it is introduced.
- Eighty percent of the scientists, engineers, technicians, and physicians who ever lived are alive today—and exchanging ideas in real time on the Internet.

Assessment and Implications:

Subjectively, change will soon move so rapidly that we will no longer recognize its acceleration, save as an abstract concept.

All the technical knowledge we work with today will represent only 1 percent of the knowledge that will be available in 2050.

Industries will face much tighter competition based on new technologies. Those who adopt state-of-the-art methods first will prosper. Those who ignore them eventually will fail. Products must capture their market quickly, before the competition can copy them. Brand names associated with quality are becoming even more important in this highly competitive environment.

Lifelong learning is a necessity for anyone who works in a technical field—and for growing numbers who do not.

In what passes for the long run—a generation or two—the development of true artificial intelligence is likely to reduce human beings to managers. Rather than making new discoveries and creating new products, we will struggle to understand and guide the flow of novelties delivered by creations we cannot really keep up with.

Important medical advances will continue to appear almost daily.

- Genetic research has accelerated advances in medicine and in the growth of medical knowledge. Early results include possible cures for hemophilia, cystic fibrosis, familial hypercholesterolemia, a number of cancers, and AIDS. Eventually, some 4,000 hereditary disorders may be prevented or cured through genetic intervention. At Sangamo Biosciences in California, researchers have experimented with rewriting the patient's own DNA, rather than replacing it, to correct hereditary errors. The technique may lead to practical therapies sooner than conventional gene splicing. Also in the works: gene-based diagnostic tests that may identify cancer early and tell which drugs are most likely to benefit individual patients with heart disease, cancer, and other ills. Already, roughly 1,000 clinical trials of gene therapy are under way in the United States alone.
- A process called RNA interference, which deactivates individual genes, is quickly revealing the genes' functions. It also may be used to disable disease-causing genes, perhaps making it possible to cure cancer, viral illnesses, and some hereditary disorders. One potential cure for HIV/AIDS is expected to be ready for human testing in 2010.
- In research performed outside the United States, stem cells promise to repair damaged brains and other organs. Embryonic stem cells have already been found to repair damaged heart muscle.
- Growing knowledge of biochemistry, aided by advanced computer modeling, has made it possible to design drugs that fit specific receptors in the cell. Drugs created through this technology often are much more effective than natural derivatives and have fewer side effects. Nearly 400 anticancer compounds are being tested in people, almost all of them "designer drugs." In 1995, only 10 anticancer drugs were being tested, all either natural products or derivatives of existing drugs.
- Other transplanted tissues come from cloning and related technologies used to grow stem cells. Radical new treatments for diabetes, Parkinson's disease, perhaps Alzheimer's, and many other disorders are expected to arrive within the next five to 10 years.
- Brown fat, found in many animals and in human babies, is converted almost immediately to body heat; it does not cause obesity. White fat goes straight to the waist and other bulging body parts. Scientists at Boston's Dana-Farber Cancer Institute have found the gene controlling brown fat production, perhaps opening the way to end the epidemic of obesity.
- Surgeons working via the Internet can now operate on patients in remote areas, using experimental robot manipulators to handle their instruments.
- Nanotechnology research is beginning to produce medically useful products, such as nanoparticles that can carry medication into the cell. Much more complicated devices for both diagnosis and treatment are in the concept stage.
- Scientists are beginning to understand the fundamental processes of aging, bringing the

possibility of averting the diseases of old age and perhaps aging itself.

Assessment and Implications:

Biomedicine will be to the twenty-first century what computers were to the twentieth, a force that transforms our lives beyond anything our parents could have conceived. By 2020, medicine will finally understand and be able to control such mysteries as our need for sleep, the cancerous transformation of cells and the spread of tumors to remote parts of the body, Alzheimer's and Parkinson's diseases, and some forms of mental illness. It also will produce drugs to improve memory and concentration and extend our lives to age 110 or more with mid-life health and vigor. What it will offer even farther into the future, we can hardly guess.

In the next 10 years, we expect to see more and better bionic limbs, hearts, and other organs; drugs that prevent disease rather than merely treating symptoms; and body monitors that warn of impending trouble. These all will reduce hospital stays.

Outside the United States, transplants of brain cells, nerve tissue, and stem cells to aid victims of retardation, head trauma, and other neurological disorders will enter clinical use by 2012. Laboratory-grown bone, muscle, and blood cells also will be employed in transplants.

Expect also the first broadly effective treatments for viral diseases, experimental regeneration of lost or damaged human tissues, and effective ways to prevent and correct obesity.

By 2025, the first nanotechnology-based medical therapies should reach clinical use. Microscopic machines will monitor our internal processes, remove cholesterol plaques from artery walls, and destroy cancer cells before they have a chance to form a tumor.

Forecasting International believes that cloning and related methods will be accepted for the treatment of disease, though not to produce identical human beings.

Even without dramatic advances in life extension, baby boomers are likely to live much longer, and in better health, than anyone now expects. However, this trend could be side-tracked by the current epidemic of obesity, which threatens to raise rates of hypertension, diabetes, heart disease, and arthritis among boomers if a cure is not found quickly enough.

High development and production costs for designer pharmaceuticals, computerized monitors, and artificial organs will continue to push up the cost of health care far more rapidly than the general inflation rate. Much of these expenses will be passed on to Medicare and other third-party payers.

Severe personnel shortages can be expected in high-tech medical specialties, in addition to the continuing deficit of nurses.

A growing movement to remove barriers to stem-cell research in the United States could speed progress in this critical field. This could be expected to produce new treatments for neurological disorders such as Parkinson's and Alzheimer's disease and many other illnesses now incurable

or untreatable. It also would recover one aspect of America's lost lead in science.

A significant extension of healthy, vigorous life—to around 115 or 120 years as a first step—now seems more likely than no extension at all.

The Internet continues to grow, but at a slower pace.

- In mid-2009, Internet users numbered about 1.7 billion, up less than 50 percent in two years.

- Most growth of the Internet population is now taking place outside the United States, which is home to only 13 percent of the world's Internet users (but who now account for about 74 percent of the U.S. population). In mid-2009, data showed 162 million Internet users in China (27 percent of the population), 81 million in India (7 percent), and 96 million in Japan (75.5 percent). Internet penetration is lagging badly in Africa, where only 6.8 percent of the population is online (up from just 3.8 percent two years earlier). Africa's Internet users are mainly in the North African countries or in the Republic of South Africa. In between, Internet connections are scarce.

- When it comes to percentage of broadband users, the United States ranks only fifteenth among the developed lands and twenty-fourth over all. About 70 percent of U.S. Internet users have broadband service, compared with 90 percent in South Korea. Americans also get poorer service, with broadband speed eighteenth worldwide and some service providers throttling download speeds for heavy users.

- E-commerce is still recovering from a downturn in the third quarter of 2008. In the United States, online sales in the second quarter of 2009 came in at about $32.4 billion, up 2.2 percent at a time when total retail sales shrank by 4.4 percent.

- Not long ago, the Internet was predominately English-speaking. In mid-2007, English and "Chinese" (we assume, but cannot confirm, that this combines mainland Mandarin, Taiwanese Mandarin, and Cantonese) were tied at 31.7 percent of Internet users. More than 5 percent of Netizens spoke Spanish, Japanese, German, or French.

Assessment and Implications:

Americans will continue to dominate the Internet so long as they produce a substantial majority of Web pages—but that is not likely to be very long.

Analysts believe that growth of Internet use will not accelerate again until broadband service becomes less expensive and more widely available. This is a matter of government policy as much as of technology or basic costs.

Demands that the United States relinquish control of the Internet to an international body can only gain broader support and grow more emphatic as Americans make up a smaller part of the Internet user population.

The Internet has made it much easier and cheaper to set up a profitable business. An online marketing site can be set up with just a few minutes' work at a cost of much less than $100. This is fostering a new generation of entrepreneurs.

Internet-based outsourcing of U.S. jobs to other countries has only just begun. Growth in this field will accelerate again as service firms around the world polish their workers' English, French, and German and find even more business functions they can take on.

Cultural, political, and social isolation has become almost impossible for countries interested in economic development. Even China's attempts to filter the Internet and shield its population from outside influences have been undermined by hackers elsewhere, who provide ways to penetrate the barriers.

Management and Institutional Trends

More entrepreneurs start new businesses every year.

- In the United States, about 11 percent of workers are self-employed. Self-employment has been growing in about two-thirds of the OECD countries.

- Women comprise a growing proportion of the self-employed in the United States, up from about 27 percent in 1976 to 36 percent in 2009, according to the Bureau of Labor Statistics (BLS).

- Many women are leaving traditional jobs to go home and open businesses, even as they begin a family. At least half of the estimated 10.6 million privately held firms in the United States are owned by women, employing 19.1 million people and generating $2.46 trillion in sales annually.

- Workers under 30 would prefer to start their own company, rather than advance through the corporate ranks. Some 10 percent are actively trying to start their own businesses, three times as many as in previous generations.

- Most simply distrust large institutions and believe that jobs cannot provide a secure economic future in a time of rapid technological change.

- Firms with fewer than 500 employees accounted for 64 percent (or 14.5 million) of the 22.5 million net new jobs (gains minus losses) between 1993 and the third quarter of 2008, according to BLS figures. "While small firms create a majority of the net new jobs, their share of employment remains steady since some firms grow into large firms as they create new jobs," notes the Small Business Administration.

- However, jobs also disappear fastest from small companies, which are much more likely to fail than larger companies.

Assessment and Implications:

This is a self-perpetuating trend, as all those new service firms need other companies to handle chores outside their core business. It will remain with us for many years, not only because it suits new-generation values, but also because it is a rational response to an age in which jobs can never be counted on to provide a stable long-term income.

It is driven as well by the attitudes and values of Gen X and the millennials and by the rapid developments in technology, which create endless opportunities for new business development.

Specialty boutiques will continue to spring up on the Internet for at least the next 15 years.

This trend will help to ease the poverty of many developing countries, as it already is doing in India and China.

Government regulations will continue to take up a growing portion of the manager's time and effort.

- In 1996, the U.S. Congress passed regulatory reform laws intended to slow the proliferation of government regulations. Nonetheless, by 2001 more than 14,000 new regulations were enacted. Not one proposed regulation was rejected during this period.

- In 2008, the Federal Register, which records regulations proposed and enacted, ran to more than 80,200 pages. To keep up with the flow, it is published daily. It has not missed a day since its first edition in 1936.

- The Brussels bureaucrats of the European Union are churning out regulations at an even faster rate, overlaying a standard regulatory structure on all the national systems of the member countries.

- The growth of regulations is not necessarily all bad. A study by the Congressional Office of Management and Budget estimated that the annual cost of major federal regulations enacted in the decade ending September 2002 (the most recent data we have been able to locate) amounted to between $38 billion and $44 billion per year. However, the estimated benefits of those regulations added up to between $135 billion and $218 billion annually.

Assessment and Implications:

Regulations are necessary, unavoidable, and often beneficial. Yet, it is difficult not to see them as a kind of friction that slows both current business and future economic growth.

The proliferation of regulations in the developed world could give a competitive advantage to countries such as India and China, where regulations that impede investment and capital flow are being stripped away, while health, occupational safety, and environmental codes are still rudimentary or absent.

However, there is a significant penalty for the kind of risk that comes from inadequate regulation. China pays an estimated risk penalty of 6.49 percent for international borrowing. Per capita GDP, access to capital, foreign direct investment, and other measures of a country's economic health all decline directly with a rising Opacity Index, which is heavily influenced by the lack of effective regulations to guarantee a level playing field for those doing business there.

Nonetheless, lands such as Russia will remain at a competitive disadvantage until they can pass and enforce the regulations needed to ensure a stable, fair business environment.

Multinational corporations are uniting the world—and growing more exposed to its risks.

- The continuing fragmentation of the post–Cold War world has reduced the stability of some lands where government formerly could guarantee a favorable— or at least predictable—business environment. The current unrest in Iraq is one example.
- Multinational corporations that rely on indigenous workers may be hindered by the increasing number of AIDS cases in Africa and around the world. Up to 90 percent of the population in parts of sub-Saharan Africa reportedly tests positive for HIV in some surveys. Thailand is almost equally stricken, and many other parts of Asia show signs that the AIDS epidemic is spreading among their populations.
- One risk now declining is the threat of sudden, extreme currency fluctuations. In Europe, at least, the adoption of the euro is making for a more stable financial environment.

Assessment and Implications:

It is becoming ever more difficult for business to be confident that decisions about plant location, marketing, and other critical issues will continue to appear wise even five years into the future. All long-term plans must include an even greater margin for risk management. This will encourage outsourcing, rather than investment in offshore facilities that could be endangered by sudden changes in business conditions.

Countries that can demonstrate a significant likelihood of stability and predictable business outcomes will enjoy a strong competitive advantage over neighbors that cannot. Witness the rapid growth of investment in India now that deregulation and privatization have general political support, compared with other Asian lands where conditions are less predictable.

Although Russia has continued to attract Western investment, particularly in its energy industry, the increasingly autocratic governance by President Dmitry Medvedev and Premier Vladimir Putin, and probably any future successors, could eventually discourage foreign companies from doing business there or require much more favorable terms to justify accepting the associated risks.

Consumers increasingly demand social responsibility from companies and each other.

- More than two-thirds of people around the world surveyed by the World Economic Forum say that the current economic crisis is a crisis of values. Similar numbers believe that people do not live the same values in their business as they do in their personal lives. Nearly 40 percent of respondents identified honesty, integrity, and transparency as the most important values for the global political and business systems.
- While the current recession may have temporarily reduced the significance of "social responsibility" in much consumer spending, companies are continuing to invest in corporate responsibility programs, because they increasingly are being judged on issues such as how they treat the environment.
- Many are changing their business practices as a result. For example, home-improvement retailers Home Depot and Lowe's have stopped buying wood from countries with endangered forests.
- With 5 percent of the world's population and 66 percent of the lawyers on the planet, American citizens do not hesitate to litigate if their demands are not met. Other countries, such as India and China, are beginning to see more legal actions on behalf of citizens' causes.
- In an effort to get ahead of this trend, companies are now trying to make good citizenship part of their brand. Unlike traditional "good works," this movement aims for profit and long-term corporate success, not just reputation-polishing.
- In addition to traditional performance measures, *Fortune* now ranks its 500 companies according to "how well they conform to socially responsible business practices."
- In a survey of nearly 1,200 companies, 81 percent of companies—and 98 percent of large firms—said corporate citizenship is a priority; 84 percent said that being socially responsible has improved their profits.

Assessment and Implications:

This trend is well established in the industrialized world, but only beginning in the developing world. It can be expected to grow more powerful as the no-nonsense, bottom-line-oriented Gen Xers and millennials gain influence.

Government intervention will likely supplant deregulation in the airline industry (in the interest of safety and services), financial services (to control instability and costs), electric utilities (nuclear problems), and the chemical industry (toxic wastes).

As the Internet spreads Western attitudes throughout the world, consumers and environmental activists in other regions will find more ways to use local court systems to promote their goals. Litigation is likely to become a global risk for companies that do not make the environment a priority.

On average, institutions are growing more transparent in their operations and more accountable for their misdeeds.

- Many different forces are promoting this change in various parts of the world.
- In the United States, the wave of business scandals in 2004, the controversy over child abuse within the Catholic Church, and the unwillingness of the Bush administration to accept effective oversight by Congress all inspired demands for greater transparency and accountability. Public ire over the bank failures of 2008, and the subsequent bailouts, may yet trigger another round of regulations designed to shed light on secretive corporations.
- China, rated by Kurtzman Group as the most opaque of the major nations, was forced to open many of its records as a precondition for joining the World Trade Organization.
- In India, a country often regarded as one of the world's most corrupt, the Central Vigilance Commission has opened the country's banking system to more effective oversight. Lesser "vigilance commissions" now oversee many parts of the Indian economy and government.
- More generally, wars against terrorism, drug trafficking, and money laundering are opening the world's money conduits to greater scrutiny. They also are opening the operations of nongovernmental organizations that function primarily as charitable and social-service agencies but are linked to terrorism as well.

Assessment and Implications:

There are roughly as many reactions against this trend as there are governments, agencies, or individuals with something to hide. Yet, the benefits of transparency are so clear that the general decline of barriers to oversight is likely to continue until societies develop a consensus about how much—or little—secrecy is really necessary.

Countries with high levels of transparency tend to be much more stable than more opaque lands. They also tend to be much more prosperous, in part because they find it easier to attract foreign investment.

Greater transparency reduces the operational effectiveness of the world's miscreants. It impedes drug traffickers and terrorist organizations, and also dishonest governments and bureaucrats.

Institutions are undergoing a bimodal distribution: The big get bigger, the small survive, and the mid-sized are squeezed out.

- Economies of scale enable the largest companies to win out over mid-sized competitors, while "boutique" operations can take advantage of niches too small to be efficiently tapped by larger firms.

- By 2012, there will be only five giant automobile firms. Production and assembly will be centered in Korea, Italy, and Latin America.
- The six largest airlines in the United States today control 65 percent of the domestic market, leaving roughly one-third to be divided among many smaller carriers. Many of these are no-frills carriers with limited service on a few routes where demand is high or competition is unusually low.
- Where local regulations allow, mergers and acquisitions are an international game. The continuing removal of trade barriers among EU nations will keep this trend active for at least the next decade.
- We are now well into the second decade of micro-segmentation, as more and more highly specialized businesses and entrepreneurs search for narrower niches. These small firms will prosper, even as mid-sized, "plain vanilla" competitors die out. This trend extends to nearly every endeavor, from retail to agriculture.
- "Boutique" businesses that provide entertainment, financial planning, and preventive medical care for aging baby boomers will be among the fastest-growing segments of the U.S. economy.

Assessment and Implications:

No company is too large to be a takeover target if it dominates a profitable market or has other features attractive to profit-hungry investors. No niche is too small to attract and support at least one or two boutique operations. Thanks in part to technology, this trend is likely to be a permanent feature of the business scene from now on.

Thus far, industries dominated by small, regional, often family-owned companies have been relatively exempt from the consolidation now transforming many other businesses. Takeovers are likely even in these industries in the next decade.

This consolidation will extend increasingly to Internet-based businesses, where well-financed companies are trying to absorb or out-compete tiny online start-ups, much as they have done in the brick-and-mortar world.

However, niche markets will continue to encourage the creation of new businesses. In Europe as of 2006, no fewer than 48 small, no-frills airlines in 22 countries had sprung up to capture about 28 percent of the Continental market share. Only 15 offered more than 50 flights per day.

Terrorism Trends

Militant Islam continues to spread and gain power.

- It has been clear for years that the Muslim lands face severe problems with religious extremists dedicated to advancing their political, social, and doctrinal views by any means necessary.

- Most of the Muslim lands are overcrowded and short of resources. Many are poor, save for the oil-rich states of the Middle East. Virtually all have large populations of young men, often unemployed, who are frequently attracted to violent extremist movements.

- Despite this, according to a Pew survey, the number of Muslims who say that suicide bombing is "often/ sometimes justified" has shrunk significantly since its post-9/11 peak. Only 15 percent of Egyptians supported suicide bombing in 2009, down from 28 percent in 2006. In Lebanon, only 38 percent supported it, compared with 74 percent in 2002.

- During its proxy war with the Soviet Union in Afghanistan, the United States massively fortified the Muslim extremist infrastructure by supplying it with money, arms, and above all training.

- It made a similar mistake in Iraq, where the American occupation inspired a new generation of jihadists, who now are migrating to Afghanistan and Pakistan.

- In a now-declassified National Security Estimate, the U.S. intelligence community concluded that al-Qaeda was more powerful in 2007 than it had been before the so-called "war on terror" began—more dangerous even than it had been when it planned the attacks of September 11, 2001.

- Afghanistan, Pakistan, and Somalia all face growing Muslim insurgencies.

Assessment and Implications:

Virtually all of the Muslim lands face an uncertain, and possibly bleak, future of political instability and growing violence. The exceptions are the oil states, where money can still buy relative peace, at least for now.

These problems often have spilled over into the rest of the world. They will do so again. The West, and particularly the United States, must expect more—and more violent—acts of terrorism for at least the next 20 years.

Europe faces a significant homegrown Muslim extremist movement, and the United States may do so in the near future. Thanks largely to waves of immigration since the 1980s, Islam is the fastest-growing religion in both regions. Extremist clerics in Europe are recruiting young Muslims to the cause of jihad against their adopted homes. So far, their colleagues in the United States have been much less successful. That may not always be true.

Muslims living in Great Britain have recently launched a grassroots peace campaign (www.LoveForAll HatredForNone.org) to counter extremist views and to promote a positive image of Islam. The campaign comes at a time when Islamophobia is at a height. A recent survey by an independent agency found that a quarter of respondents had described Islam as the "worst religion" on earth, the group reports.

In a 1994 terrorism study for the Department of Defense and other government clients, Forecasting International predicted that by 2020 a majority of the world's 25 or so most important Muslim lands could be in the hands of extremist religious governments. At the time, only Iran was ruled by such a regime. That forecast still appears sound.

Iraq is likely to become the next fundamentalist Muslim regime. Once U.S. forces leave, Iran will support the establishment of a Shiite regime much like its own in Baghdad.

There is a one-in-ten chance that this will set off a general war in the Middle East, as Sunni-dominated states intercede to protect Iraqi Sunnis against Shi'a domination. However, Iraq and Saudi Arabia already are negotiating to keep this situation under control.

Any attempt to reduce the commitment of Western forces to the task of stabilizing Afghanistan will result in the restoration of the Taliban to power.

International exposure includes a greater risk of terrorist attack.

- State-sponsored terrorism has nearly vanished, as tougher sanctions made it more trouble than it was worth. However, some rogue states may still provide logistical or technological support for independent terrorist organizations when opportunities present themselves.

- Nothing will prevent small, local political organizations and special-interest groups from using terror to promote their causes. These organizations have found inspiration, and many have found common cause, in the successes of al-Qaeda.

- Until recently, attacks on U.S. companies were limited to rock-throwing at the local McDonald's, occasional bombings of bank branches and of U.S.-owned pipelines in South America, and kidnappings. Since September 11, U.S.-owned hotel chains have experienced major bombings, in part because U.S. government facilities overseas have been effectively hardened against terrorist assault.

- As the United States has been forced to recognize, the most dangerous terrorist groups are no longer motivated primarily by specific political goals, but by generalized, virulent hatred based on religion and culture.

- Terrorism has continued to grow around the world as the Iraq war proceeds, even as the rate of violence in Iraq itself has, at least temporarily, declined.

- Risks of terrorism are greatest in countries with repressive governments and large numbers of unemployed young men.

Assessment and Implications:

On balance, the amount of terrorist activity in the world will continue to rise in the next 10 years. Terrorism against the West is likely to grow, not decline, when fighters trained and bloodied in the Iraq war are able to turn their attention elsewhere.

Western corporations may have to devote more of their resources to self-defense, while accepting smaller-than-expected profits from operations in the developing countries.

Like the attacks on the World Trade Center and Pentagon, the U.S. embassies in Kenya and Tanzania before them, and the bombings of the Madrid rail system and London subways since then, any attacks on major corporate facilities will be designed for maximum destruction and casualties. Bloodshed for its own sake has become a characteristic of modern terrorism.

Where terrorism is most common, countries will find it difficult to attract foreign investment, no matter how attractive their resources.

Though Islamic terrorists form only a tiny part of the Muslim community, they have a large potential for disruption throughout the region from Turkey to the Philippines.

The economies of the industrialized nations could be thrown into recession at any time by another terrorist event on the scale of 9/11. This is particularly true of the United States. The impact would be greatest if the incident discouraged travel, as the 9/11 attacks did.

As technology grows more complex, the world is growing more fragile.

- Vulnerabilities do not grow with the size of a system, but in proportion to the number of its interconnections. Thanks to the Internet, much of the world is almost infinitely interconnected.
- Anyone with a personal computer knows how often operating systems, programs, and hardware break down owing to unforeseen interactions between one part of the programming and another.
- Unforeseen, and often unforeseeable, drug interactions abound in older patients, who may be taking one medication to control their blood sugar levels, two or three drugs to keep their cholesterol and blood pressure under control, something for their arthritis, and half a dozen over-the-counter pharmaceuticals and supplements. One physician we know is also a PhD pharmacologist. He declares: "If a patient is taking more than three drugs, even if they aren't supposed to interact, you don't have any idea what is going on."
- Early in October 2009, a breakdown in Britain's air traffic control system grounded transatlantic flights at Gatwick and Heathrow, in London. In mid-November, a breakdown in critical computer systems in Salt Lake City and Atlanta sent air traffic controllers back to entering information into their computers manually. Flights were delayed for hours.
- Counterterrorism experts tell us that most of the electrical power west of the Mississippi could be taken offline for months if terrorists destroyed just

four critical lines in the right sequence, with proper timing. Again, this is a result of the ways in which some components of a complex system interact with the rest.

Assessment and Implications:

Nothing will stop the world's technological systems from becoming more complex every day.

Spontaneous breakdowns in critical systems will grow more common with each passing year. Picture a malfunction in the systems controlling traffic on an automated highway or the pilotless airliners proposed for 2030.

Opportunities for sabotage also will proliferate.

Operators of mundane systems, such as sewage plant controls or fire alarm monitors, may find they need to implement quality assurance protocols as complex as the ones NASA developed for the space program.

System security is likely to be a high-growth field for well-trained specialists in the coming decades.

Cyberattacks are spreading rapidly.

- In the run-up to Russia's battle with Estonia in May 2007, a massive denial-of-service attack brought most of the Estonian economy to a halt. The incident has never been proved to have originated with the Russian government.
- A similar attack struck computers in Georgia when relations with Russia became uncommonly tense.
- Canadian researchers reported that they had uncovered more than 1,000 attacks on sensitive computer systems carried out by hackers working through Chinese servers. Targets included embassies and consulates, academic networks, and the office of the Dalai Lama.
- U.S. security officials reported discovery of illicit software buried in computers that control the nation's electrical grid. The routines, which authorities said must have been installed by one or more foreign governments, would have allowed hackers to shut down the power system in time of emergency.
- Cyber-gangs in eastern Europe have been attacking small and mid-sized companies in the United States, transferring funds from out of the target accounts. Victims who have come forward include an electronics testing firm in Baton Rouge, Louisiana, that was robbed of nearly $100,000; a Pittsburgh-area school district that lost $700,000; and a Texas company that was defrauded of $1.2 million.
- In 2007, government computersecurity specialists discovered that someone had broken into networks operated by the departments of Defense, State, and Commerce, and probably NASA and the Department of Energy—"all the high-tech agencies, all the military agencies," as Jim Lewis, director of the

Center for Strategic and International Studies, put it. The intruders downloaded a mass of sensitive information roughly equivalent to the contents of the Library of Congress.

- Several major power outages in Brazil—in 2005, 2007, and 2009—have been blamed on computer hackers who sabotaged the electric company's control systems.
- In November 2009, cybersecurity officials from the U.S. Strategic Command reported that the number of malicious attempts to break into Defense Department computer networks had jumped by 60 percent from the previous year, to 43,785 in the first six months of 2009.
- Cyberterrorism specialists worry that computer chips bought from foreign sources could include extra circuitry that would give hackers a "back door" into supposedly secure computer systems. The chips could be used to download secret data or shut down critical hardware in time of war. At least one such attack is believed to have been successful.

Assessment and Implications:

Cyberattack is a simple, low-cost, deniable way to give an adversary grief during peacetime as well as in war. It will be a favorite tool for anyone with the skill to use it.

The United States is not prepared to safeguard itself against cyberattack by a foreign power. Neither is any other country whose classified or sensitive computer networks are connected to the Internet.

Classified information on Internet-connected computer systems should be regarded as already compromised.

Although there is no evidence that international terrorist organizations have yet adopted cyberwarfare to further their goals, they will do so as soon as they gain the necessary skills. At that point, real-world destruction by cyberwarfare will become a significant threat. Possible attacks include hacking into air traffic control systems, chemical plant and refinery controls, power systems, and other critical and potentially lethal infrastructure.

Critical Thinking

1. What are some of the trends that will impact the global economy?
2. How will they impact institutions?
3. Why is this important?
4. What can HR do to deal with about trends?

MARVIN J. CETRON is president of Forecasting International Ltd. in Virginia. He is also a member of the World Future Society board of directors. **OWEN DAVIES** is a former senior editor of *Omni* magazine and is a freelance writer specializing in science, technology, and the future. This article is excerpted from their report, "52 Trends Shaping Tomorrow's World;" the first half was published in the May-June 2010 issue of *The Futurist*. The full report (print or PDF) is available from the World Future Society, www.wfs.org.

Offshored Headquarters

**Global human resources becomes a top priority—
fast—when foreign companies buy U.S. operations.**

ALLEN SMITH

It's not every day that companies such as General Motors (GM)—once the largest private employer in the world—go bankrupt. Sichuan Tengzhong Heavy Industrial Machinery Co.'s purchase of the Hummer brand as part of GM's bankruptcy plan, announced June 2, may not be just the end of an era for GM. It may signal the purchase of other U.S. businesses by companies based abroad, a trend that shouldn't be too surprising in light of the global economy.

Of the four most populous countries—China, India, the United States and Indonesia—only the United States was predicted to have a shrinking gross domestic product (GDP) in 2009. Last June, the Organisation for Economic Co-operation and Development, based in Paris, projected that the GDP in China would grow by 7.7 percent in 2009, India's would rise 5.9 percent and Indonesia's 3.5 percent.

Would you be ready if your corporate headquarters suddenly went offshore? Any merger can be challenging for HR professionals, but that's especially true when the C-suite suddenly flies across the globe.

Fortunately, HR leaders can learn lessons from those who have been through this. When Doosan, based in Seoul, South Korea, bought the Bobcat unit from Ingersoll Rand Co. in 2007, the acquired company launched a familiarization program for employees on both sides of the Pacific, even sending U.S. employees to Seoul to immerse themselves in Korean culture, says Bonnie Guttormson, SPHR, director of compensation and benefits at Doosan in West Fargo, N.D.

Bridging cultural differences is not the only challenge, according to Jay Warren, an attorney with Bryan Cave LLP in New York. During foreign takeovers, HR leaders must run on "a compliance track and business-culture track." One challenge on the compliance track: the need to "manage upward," which means not simply telling executives what they may want to hear but instead informing them if standard business operating procedures in their countries would lead to legal challenges in the United States.

After hearing bits and pieces about the at-will rule, owners of foreign companies may overestimate how much leeway U.S. employers have in dismissing employees, cautions Laurence Stuart, an attorney with Stuart & Associates PC in Houston and a member of the Society for Human Resource Management (SHRM) Labor Relations Special Expertise Panel. Stuart has come across a "cowboy mentality" among some new foreign owners of U.S. businesses—purchasers who assume that when an employee must be terminated, "anything goes."

Beginners' Mistakes

"There will be a huge difference" among foreign buyers that have US. operations and foreign buyers purchasing their first U.S. ventures, according to Donald Dowling Jr., an attorney with White & Case LLP in New York.

For HR professionals who already have been through mergers, much about foreign takeovers may seem the same as with new U.S. owners. Dowling says many urgent issues remain largely the same: post-merger integration, layoffs, internal restructuring, new reporting relationships, alignment of HR offerings and policies, and so forth.

That said, HR employees will face additional layers of complexity when purchasers are based abroad, Dowling says, noting that his wife works at a French-owned company. "When the foreign-based buyer has other existing U.S. operations, it will likely aim toward integrating this new operation with its other U.S. business lines," he says. "When the foreign-based buyer is taking its first steps into the U.S. via this acquisition, that is where the cultural and HR problems are likely to be most acute."

Stuart "has seen activity among foreign buyers looking for U.S. companies." He suspects this trend will intensify "if other economies get strong before us." In Texas, he sees the most activity among owners of international private equity firms based in Europe who are eyeing energy-related businesses.

Different Lens

Many foreign professionals have the "misconception that the U.S. employment market is not heavily regulated. That obviously is not correct," Stuart notes.

While the United States does not have the kinds of national and local severance and termination protection common in the European Union (EU), he says many U.S. laws protect classes of individuals from discrimination. That "makes the U.S. market more heavily regulated than Europe, but the risks aren't as obvious."

Foreign executives may be used to more-unionized settings but unfamiliar with laws such as the Americans with Disabilities Act and the Family and Medical Leave Act. Consequently, he cautions, sometimes "they don't understand the role documentation procedures and policies have in reducing risks."

> **Foreign executives may be used to more-unionized settings but unfamiliar with laws such as the Americans with Disabilities Act and the Family and Medical Leave Act.**

Stuart recommends employment law training to familiarize new owners with US. laws and their applications.

Dowling notes that "EU executives come from a culture that has complex and intrusive employment regulations—far more so than under U.S.-style employment at will." But, he says misunderstandings arise because the at-will rule has given rise to a highly evolved—to a European, a disproportionate—series of equal employment opportunity, discrimination and harassment regulations.

As a result, European executives purchasing U.S. businesses "need to reorient their thinking" about employment law compliance, according to Dowling. From the European perspective, "the good news is that the U.S. state and federal systems impose far fewer employment laws and rules than they are used to. The bad news is that Americans look at employment relationships through the lens of discrimination." And, he says, "To a European executive, Americans appear over-concerned with what the European might see as political correctness."

However, Dowling doesn't think foreign executives necessarily are surprised by the compliance risks in the United States: "European executives hear horror stories about U.S. court judgments—multimillion-dollar verdicts, runaway juries, class actions and unpredictable results," he notes. But they still "will need to be shown where the land mines lie."

Dowling adds that U.S. unionization laws constitute a separate issue, and he advises incoming businesses to develop a U.S. union strategy.

Stuart recalls several foreign-based clients that have unions in Europe and have been "pushed into signing global codes of conduct" that simply weren't practical for U.S. operations. For example, in global codes of conduct, foreign businesses may have provisions prohibiting mandatory overtime, even though mandatory overtime may be an industry norm in the United States and a feature many workers want. Or, global codes of conduct may specify the intervals for employees to have days off, even though seven-day workweeks while employees are offshore are common in the energy sector, he adds.

Stuart recommends that U.S. HR professionals and attorneys conduct due diligence and look into overseas policies that would be unlawful if applied in the United States. For example, mandatory retirement is common overseas.

HR professionals shouldn't be surprised if colleagues at acquiring companies do not understand the exempt/nonexempt distinctions under federal and state wage and hour laws, as well as other state-specific requirements, according to Baker & McKenzie attorneys Susan Eandi, Ute Krudewagen, John Raudabaugh and Carole Spink.

In addition, foreign employers often do not understand that employee benefits are provided at the employer's discretion in most circumstances, or that the amount and quality of benefits a company provides affects its ability to attract and retain employees, the Baker & McKenzie attorneys add.

Face to Face

There's much for U.S. employees to learn about the prevailing culture of an overseas purchasing company's C-suite.

At Bobcat, employees were used to having the C-suite overseas even before Doosan purchased it, since Bobcat was owned by Ingersoll Rand, a global construction equipment business based in Ireland. But, to help get employees on the right cultural track, some Bobcat employees were paid to travel to Seoul following Doosan's acquisition. Guttormson says the company started flying over top-level executives and is working its way down the organization. She is slated to be in the next group to visit.

Guttormson recommends familiarization training for employees in the United States as well as for those in the purchasing company, even if the purchaser seems to be a good match, as was the case with Doosan. Familiarization training might include an introduction to cultural differences. For example, Guttormson notes that Korean culture is "very hierarchical, so where here in the United States we're very free to talk with higher officials about differences, there the process is to go through the hierarchy."

To smooth the way for foreign travelers in the United States, Dowling recommends that employers start getting visas early.

Employees' Fears

Cultural differences intimidate some, according to Thomas Belker, SPHR, GPHR, managing director of HR for OBI—one of the world's largest home improvement companies, located in 15 countries—based near Cologne, Germany. "We say it is a global world, but nonetheless many line managers have never been exposed to dealing with cultural differences," he notes. "Nor do they necessarily understand anything about foreign laws and their impact on HR processes. There is quite normally a huge gap caused by resentment or a lack of understanding of foreign HR issues."

Belker, a member of the SHRM Global Special Expertise Panel, recommends starting with minor changes and paying close attention to employees' initial reactions.

Online Resources

For more about HR professionals' role when a foreign business buys domestic operations, see the online version of this article at www.shrm.org/hrmagazine. For other resources on employment law, visit www.shrm.org/law.

Michelle Haste, an attorney with Crowell & Moring in London, recommends that HR leaders stay in "close contact with U.S. employees who may be fearful of acquisition by a foreign entity." She says HR executives from the purchaser and the seller should cultivate relationships that enable "full and frank communication on the differences."

Reset Expectations

One point of discussion should be the cultural work expectations, such as whether employees can speak freely or are expected to be subordinate to managers, advises Brenda Cossette, SPHR, HR director for the City of Fergus Falls, Minn., and a member of the SHRM Labor Relations Special Expertise Panel.

The foreign company can have very different values, and it may put a premium on running extremely efficient operations compared to some of our U.S. companies, Cossette says. "Employee loyalty to the new brand name or new company is a real difficult issue since many smaller companies are often bought up by foreign companies," she explains. "These small companies are proud of being a local company, and now a foreign company only sees them in terms of sales or diversification of their product lines."

According to Cossette, many Asian companies don't have big bonuses and stock plans for leaders, raising concerns among U.S. executives who depend on those plans—assuming these executives aren't laid off following the purchase.

Role Clarification

Stuart notes that in some jurisdictions, the HR function may even "be purely administrative as opposed to being strategic business partners."

HR leaders should be sure they understand what the decision-making process will be following the acquisition. Will all decisions flow through headquarters abroad, or will the new C-suite choose not to get involved in day-to-day activities?

HR leaders should be sure they understand what the decision-making process will be following the acquisition.

The answer affects liability in lawsuits, says Warren, explaining that if a foreign company acquires a publicly traded U.S. company through stock acquisition but does not get involved in decision-making, the parent company would have no legal liability.

However, if the foreign purchaser doesn't trust U.S. officers to make decisions and starts calling the shots, it would be treated as liable, he cautions. So, the acquiring company "may want to keep itself separate."

Managing Upward

Managing upward always is a challenge, but particularly with officers based abroad—and when there are cultural and linguistic divides.

"Most of us try to listen to get to what the boss wants," Warren notes. But HR leaders should be quick to recognize when bosses overseas are inadvertently asking them to implement changes that would fly in the face of domestic law. Warren says that takes "active and patient listening."

The challenge, he notes, is to respond "in a way that does not lead to friction, not to say, 'That's not the way we do things here.'" He recommends that HR professionals make sure they understand what bosses are asking—and then, make sure it's legal stateside.

Critical Thinking

1. How are mergers with offshored companies more complicated than simply domestic companies?

2. Why are cultural considerations important?

3. What are some of the implications for HR?

Multiple Choice

Should global employers standardize their employee benefits packages?

Lori Chordas

For Informa's employees in India, private health insurance, flexible benefits and dependent coverage are top commodities. But in the United Kingdom, the international provider of information and services sees wellness programs such as gym memberships and health screenings as highly valued benefits.

That's a common theme among multinational corporations: Geography has a huge influence on employee benefits design. But while locales dictate differences, are global companies looking to standardize employee benefits globally?

That's highly unlikely, said Robyn Cameron, who leads Mercer's International Health and Benefits Specialty Group. "It's not a one-size-fits-all approach."

Each country has its priorities when it comes to benefits. "In the United Kingdom, it would be odd not to offer three or four times annual earnings on death-in-service life benefits," said Pam Enright, vice president and director of international benefits for Lockton Benefits Group. "But that would be completely over the top in most other countries. Another example is the dearness allowance, which is a standard part of the compensation model in India, hut as such would not he offered in any other country." (Dearness allowances help offset inflation.)

Multinationals need to look locally when designing benefits programs, Cameron said. "While some companies do set some overarching global guidelines for benefits, most will then take a country-by-country approach for designing benefits, taking into account the local social benefits, and typical market practice."

And, she added, corporations want to have a greater role in understanding what programs are out there, and some central oversight on decision-making on benefit design and financing.

More companies are asking whether their benefits programs are compliant with local laws. In the past, they would have left that to locals to worry about, said Cameron.

Rather than standardizing global benefits, most multinational companies are attempting to prioritize how they approach looking at their benefit programs through transparency of benefit structures, said Christopher Burns, chief executive officer of Willis Group Holdings' global employee benefits practice.

> - **The Trend:** A growing number of organizations are becoming multinational.
> - **The Significance:** Employers are offering a variety of employee benefits to a growing global work force with very diverse needs.
> - **What Needs to Happen:** Multinational employers need to ensure that benefits address local needs and governance concerns.

"Employers need to determine where they want to be in terms of their competition on benefit structures in the local marketplace. Then they can alter the structure of those benefit programs accordingly," he said.

"Companies that are just venturing into global markets should follow the simple mantra: Think globally and act locally."

—Rudy Bethea,
MetLife

To India's predominantly young work force, "retirement benefits aren't as top of mind as health care and flexible benefits."

—Francis Coleman,
Watson Wyatt

Offering the United Kingdom's traditionally generous death-in-service life benefits "would be completely over the top in most other countries."

—Pam Enright,
Lockton Benefits Group

Meeting a Need

The benefits global employees are looking for differ almost as much as cultural and language barriers themselves.

For instance, a U.S. employee would expect an employer to offer private health insurance, but that would be a lesser priority for a U.K. worker, according to a Hewitt Associates report.

Employees in countries such as the United States, India and Mexico continue to value health insurance as a top priority, according to MetLife's 2007 *Study of International Employee Benefits Trends*.

The need of multinational employers to offer benefits, however, seems to speak a more common language: They're concerned about work force shortages and competition for top talent in mature economies, the study found. That's prompted many to reconsider their benefits strategies and find new ways to attract and retain highly skilled workers.

Many of those strategies are focused on emerging markets such as the "BRIC" countries of Brazil, Russia, India and China.

"They're predominantly areas with huge, inexpensive talent pools," said David Martin, employee benefits practice leader for Hub International.

China and India remain two of the biggest markets, largely due to their size.

BRAZIL: This country is quickly becoming a developed benefits environment, said Francis Coleman, international practice leader in Watson Wyatt's West region. Not only have many employers moved to defined contribution plans and enacted pro-employee protection laws, but supplemental health care has become nearly fully saturated among employees. Life, disability and supplemental retirement insurance also are a growing part of many employers' programs.

RUSSIA: There's been an increase in demand for supplemental retirement plans, especially among multinational companies, Coleman said. However, given the declining life expectancy among Russian males, retirement benefits aren't necessarily the highest priority.

INDIA: "India already has a sophisticated benefits structure in place, with most retirement benefits mandated by the government. But we expect the government to cut back more and private enterprise to take over," said Francois Choquette, Aon Consulting's Global Benefits Practice Leader for the Americas.

He said the decades-long monopoly of the insurance sector in the country has virtually dissipated, allowing more carriers to come in and provide choice to employers with Indian operations.

Housing and transportation allowances also are significant benefits offerings in India, Coleman said. "On top of that, a lack of government providers and hospitals has made private health care very popular. Employees there don't get the same choices you find in other countries."

Added to that, there's a predominantly young work force in India, Coleman said. "So retirement benefits aren't as top of mind as health care and flexible benefits among those workers."

Family also is highly revered, so some employers have begun offering deep discounts on health care coverage for dependents.

CHINA: Private health coverage is becoming one of employees' most highly requested benefits, said Coleman. "But any legislation enacted by the Chinese government often has different interpretations in each city, resulting in variations in benefits plans and tax rulings."

Benefits brokers also are keeping a close watch on other emerging markets such as the Middle East and what Coleman calls "the second layer of emerging markets," such as Vietnam and Bangladesh.

Francis Coleman, international practice leader in Watson Wyatt's West region, said it's nearly impossible to design an exact package in every location.

"What country would you base that on? If based on the United States, employers would be providing very rich benefit plans. Most multinationals come up with a set of guiding principles or a philosophy stating what core benefits they should be providing globally and adapt this to each location," Coleman said.

Making It Work

In the current economic environment, multinational employers are focused on using their bulk purchasing power globally to reduce their benefits costs with global insurance providers, said Burns.

Added to that is the need for some flexibility to adjust to each region so employers aren't overpaying on benefits, said Coleman.

He said countries now recognize the need to provide more favorable conditions for supplemental retirement plans, which hasn't always been the case. "Social Security is essentially going out of business in most countries, so they need to incentivize third-pillar savings, whether it be employee or individual savings plus employer. Many countries recently changed legislation to enable companies to set up supplemental plans for individuals or employers on a tax-efficient basis."

Multinationals need to ensure programs are financed as efficiently as possible, said Cameron. "They can do that by taking advantage of things like the use of multinational pooling and captives for risk benefits, and ensuring that consulting and brokerage dollars are being spent wisely."

Multinational pooling works by allowing global companies to spread the risk associated with local benefit plans around the globe, along with offering more favorable underwriting standards, a single point of contact for domestic and international employee coverage, and detailed information on subsidiary insurance plans, said MetLife Multinational Solutions Vice President Rudy Bethea.

MetLife Multinational Solutions' pooling is handled through MAXIS, a global employee benefits network of insurers in more than 75 countries that delivers local coverage to international employees.

One of the biggest trends in global benefits has been the growing switch from defined benefit plans to defined contribution plans.

"Historically, defined benefit retirement plans had been the rule in the United States and much of Europe. But the past several years there's been a switch due to cost rationale and more predictability on the bottom line for companies," said Burns.

The plans also help employers better manage their liabilities, Coleman added. "Switching obligation to defined contribution is easier for employers from a budgetary standpoint, as opposed to having to calculate the widely fluctuating liabilities that come with defined benefit plans."

On the health side, inadequacy of some socialized medical systems in many countries is giving rise to supplemental health plans, said Burns. The challenge, he said, is that health care costs in most private systems now are outpacing the local consumer price index in many countries—a trend he fears likely will continue.

That's where benefit brokers can step in to help. Many multinational employers are turning to outside consultants to help develop a global benefits strategy.

The first step often begins with a benefits audit, said Burns.

"We collect details regarding current benefit programs and costs, along with bringing transparency around compliance and helping clients use their bulk purchasing power to negotiate with global insurance carriers. Then we review the details to ensure they comply with local laws in each country. That helps uncover if a program is out of synch with local regulations; for instance, discovering a company's retirement age of 62 doesn't match up with a country's legal retirement age of 65."

While the need for global benefits continues to grow, multinational employers are feeling the pinch of the global financial downturn.

"That's caused some companies to cut back benefits in some countries or cost-shift to employees," said Cameron.

Clients always are watching their bottom line, said Enright.

"But that can be challenging in industries and markets where a competitive—and expensive—benefits and pay package is necessary," Enright said. "Attracting and retaining the best candidates for key positions usually trumps the need to offer a low-cost benefit plan."

Employers will need to be smarter about how they spend their benefit dollars going forward, said Bethea.

That's where financial vehicles such as captives and multinational pooling can help, he added.

For companies just venturing into global markets, Bethea suggests following a simple mantra: Think globally and act locally.

"Employers start out trying to come up with an overarching program to cover everyone around the globe to make it simple."

But that actually increases the level of complexity, Bethea said.

"They should begin with a global strategy and then allow flexibility to meet the demands of a global, diverse work force."

Critical Thinking

1. Why do employees from different countries and cultures have different expectations from their employers?

2. How can HR deal with this?

3. Why is it important?

4. What are some of the strategies that HR can employ to address those needs?

Business Is Booming

America's leading corporations have found a way to thrive even if the American economy doesn't recover. This is very, very bad news.

HAROLD MEYERSON

When he was CEO of General Electric, in 1998, Jack Welch pithily summarized his vision for corporate America: "Ideally, you'd have every plant you own on a barge to move with currencies and changes in the economy."

Since then, corporations have discovered that they don't need barges in order to unmoor themselves from the American economy. As corporate profits skyrocket, even as the economy remains stalled in a deep recession, Americans confront a grim new reality: Our corporations don't need us anymore. Half their revenues come from abroad. Their products, increasingly, come from abroad as well.

Consider, for example, the crucial role that a company called Foxconn plays in the American economy. Scarcely any Americans had heard of Foxconn until a wave of worker suicides shook its immense factory complex in China's city of Shenzhen last spring. Within the space of a few months, 10 workers inside the company's walled-off Longhua industrial village, a 1.2-square-mile development where 400,000 employees live and work, killed themselves.

What made the stories particularly troubling, though, were the revelations about Foxconn's place in the American industrial system. It's at Longhua that Apple's iPhones and iPods are manufactured (which is why Longhua is also referred to as "iPod City"). At Longhua and Foxconn's other Chinese factory complexes, 937,000 employees also make computers for Dell, games for Nintendo, and several products for Hewlett-Packard. Indeed, the number of Foxconn employees who assemble these companies' products often exceeds by a wide margin the number of workers these companies employ directly in the United States. At Apple, the ratio of Foxconn employees at work on Apple products to United States-based Apple employees is 10-to-1: 250,000 Foxconn workers to 25,000 Apple workers. The same ratio exists at Dell.

The role that even the most widely admired American companies, such as Apple, Hewlett-Packard, and General Electric, have played in offshoring American jobs has long been a subject of controversy. Their zeal for offshoring has lowered the prices of the goods Americans buy while increasing our trade deficit,

shrinking our manufacturing sector, and flattening our wages. But to look at the employment numbers at Foxconn, Apple, Dell, or IBM—whose total worldwide workforce expanded from 329,000 employees in 2005 to almost 400,000 in 2009, while its United States workforce shrank from 134,000 employees to 105,000—is to come away with an even more disquieting thought: With each passing year, and even more so during the recession, America's leading corporations grow more and more decoupled from the American economy. Their interests grow increasingly detached from those of our workers, our consumers—and our economic future.

This growing detachment is certainly reflected in their revenues. In 2001, 32 percent of the income of the firms on Standard & Poor's index of the 500 largest publicly traded United States companies came from abroad. By 2008, that figure had grown to 48 percent. Although precise figures on offshoring are unavailable from either companies or governmental bodies, the evidence of the growth of offshoring is overwhelming. A 2008 survey of 1,600 companies conducted by Duke University's Fuqua School of Business and the Conference Board (a group of leading corporations) found that 53 percent had an offshoring strategy—up from just 22 percent in 2005. "Very few" companies, the survey concluded, "plan to relocate activities back to the United States."

The implications of this shift in the conduct of American big business are profound—and terrifying. At a time when small business can't expand because high unemployment and the decline of home values have depressed consumer demand, big business is increasingly committed to expanding its sales and production abroad rather than at home. That's why the current downturn is different from its predecessors: Unlike any recession in American history—including the Great Depression—this one has come at a time when America's leading employers can return to profitability without rehiring large numbers of American workers.

This grim new reality has yet to inform our discussion over how to come back from our mega-recession. The existing debate pits those who believe that the downturn is cyclical and that public spending can restore prosperity, against those who believe that it's structural—that we have too many carpenters, say, and not enough nurses—and that we should leave things be while American workers acquire new skills and enter different lines of work. But there's another way to look at the recession: that it's institutional, that it's the cumulative consequence of our leading banks and corporations investing in job-creating enterprises abroad rather than in the United States Thus, the disjuncture between the record-high profits of American corporations and the otherwise dismal indices of national economic health. Corporate profits for the third quarter were the highest on record—$1.659 trillion—and were 28 percent higher than third-quarter profits one year previous, the highest year-to-year increase on record, beating the old record set in the previous three months.

This rise in profits, however, has not been accompanied by a rise in employment, wages, or national income. Official unemployment hovers just under 10 percent, and the Federal Reserve is predicting that it will stay at around 9 percent throughout 2011. Gross domestic product increased by just 2.5 percent during the third quarter of 2010. *The Wall Street Journal* has calculated that as a result of this combination of high profits and stalled prosperity, after-tax second-quarter profits of American companies as a percentage of national income were the third-highest of any quarter since 1947.

The multinationals' profits depend not just on their sales and production overseas but also on reducing labor costs in the United States by pushing down wages and the size of their United States workforce. In theory, a robust recovery in the United States, boosting demand and thus revenues, would be an event they would welcome. In practice, many of our leading corporations don't need it: They have developed a business model for a globalized economy in which they can chug along happily even if the American economy continues to stagger.

With small business floundering at home, and big business flourishing abroad, where, exactly, will the economic recovery come from? Who will do the hiring? America's private-sector economy is no longer structured to generate anywhere near the number of jobs it would take to return us to the levels of employment we had in 2007, before the crash.

When the financial crisis hit, America's employers laid off many more workers than did their counterparts in other mature economies, and they haven't rehired them. It's not because the overall economy has contracted more steeply here. Between 2008 and 2009, the United States GDP dropped 2.4 percent, compared to 2.6 percent in France and roughly 5 percent in Germany, Japan, and Britain. But United States unemployment has increased by approximately 5 percentage points since 2007, compared to an increase of just 1 point in France and Japan and 2 in Britain. In Germany, unemployment has actually dropped a point since the downturn began and now stands a full 2 points lower than ours.

Discharging workers can't be a permanent pillar of profitability—companies cannot slip beneath certain employment levels. But keeping labor costs low in the United States—by avoiding rehiring, substituting temporary for fulltime workers, increasing productivity, depressing wages, and shifting employment abroad—can be an ongoing boost to a company's bottom line, particularly if its revenues increasingly derive from foreign rather than domestic consumers. America's leading employers are pursuing all of these strategies.

The high level of joblessness has obscured another troubling story: the declining incomes of the employed. The median annual wage of American workers declined by $159 in 2009 from the previous year, to a mere $26,261 (that means half of all employed American workers make even less than that). The hourly wage for new hires in manufacturing plants, both union and nonunion, today is roughly $15—about half of what it was just a few years ago.

One way American employers depress wages and avoid benefits is to hire temps. Indeed, of the 1.4 million net jobs created since the economy bottomed out in September 2009, 494,000 have been temporary. In November 2010, employers hired 40,000 temps—a number exceeding the total of 39,000 net new jobs created that month.

As a result of these trends, profits and wages have recently moved in sharply different directions. As Andrew Sum and Joseph McLaughlin of Northeastern University's Center for Labor Market Studies have documented, pretax corporate profits increased during this period—the second quarter of 2009 to the first quarter of 2010—by a whopping $388 billion, while wages increased by just $68 billion. This disparity stood in sharp contrast to the experience of earlier recoveries. At a comparable point in the 1981–1982 recession and recovery, corporate profits constituted just 10 percent of the combined uptick in profits and wages. This time around, they amounted to 85 percent.

But in 1981–1982, workers in the private sector, roughly 25 percent of whom belonged to unions compared to just 7 percent today, had more power to defend their pay levels than they do now. The same goes for health-care costs. According to a September survey by the Kaiser Family Foundation and the Health Research & Educational Trust, employee insurance premiums rose by 13.7 percent in the preceding year, while employer contributions dropped by 0.9 percent. Employers have been free to impose the costs of the recession and the costs of doing business on their workers—and keep all the proceeds for themselves.

The hiring that is going on, moreover, isn't located in the higher-wage manufacturing sector, which has been declining steadily as a percentage of the workforce as a result of both offshoring and productivity increases. We are, in effect, trading good jobs for lower-paying jobs. According to a survey this summer from the National Employment Law Project, only a third of the jobs lost in 2008–2009 were in industries paying less than $15 an hour, but fully three-quarters of the job growth in 2010 came in these same low-wage industries. Among the industries that grew in 2010, the top three occupations were retail sales clerks, cashiers, and food preparers with a median hourly wage of less than $10.

The recovery, in other words, is every bit as alarming as the recession. The America emerging from the financial crisis of 2008 is distinctly downwardly mobile.

The recovery is every bit as alarming as the recession. The America emerging from the financial crisis of 2008 is distinctly downwardly mobile.

In earlier times, downwardly mobile American consumers would have posed a huge problem for American corporations. Today, as those corporations look abroad for their sales and labor, that problem is much diminished.

From 1995 to 2008, The American economy grew by a yearly average of 2.9 percent. During that time, the yearly economic growth rates in the world's two largest nations, China and India, averaged 9.6 percent and 6.9 percent, respectively. Increasing United States presence in the Chinese and Indian markets followed as the night the day.

As growth in the United States economy continues to lag behind that of much of the rest of the world, those United States-based companies able to sell more abroad gain a clear advantage over those companies whose sales are more domestic. An analysis by *The Wall Street Journal*'s Justin Lahart of the 30 companies included in the Dow Jones industrial averages concluded that the 10 with the largest share of their sales abroad were projected to increase their revenues by an average of 8.3 percent over last year, while those with the lowest share of sales abroad were looking at increased revenues of just 1.6 percent. This puts Coca-Cola, which gets 75 percent of its sales overseas, at a distinct advantage over the Dr Pepper Snapple Group, which gets 90 percent of its sales in the United States

In industry after industry, foreign markets are offering more opportunity than domestic ones. The foreign affiliates owned in part or in full by United States-based multinationals now bring in just about as much money to their parent corporations as their domestic counterparts. A study published last year by the Business Roundtable and the United States Council Foundation concluded that in 2006, 48.6 percent of profits of United States-based multinationals came from their foreign affiliates, compared to just 17 percent in 1977 and 27 percent in 1994. What this means is that the equilibrium between production, pay, and purchasing—the equilibrium that Henry Ford famously recognized when he upped his workers' wages to an unheard-of $5 a day in 1914, the equilibrium that became the model for 20th-century American capitalism—has been shattered. Making and selling their goods abroad, United States multinationals can slash their workforces and wages at home while retaining their revenue and increasing their profits. And that's exactly what they've done.

Is it necessary to move jobs abroad, just because more and more of the customers are abroad? A look at Germany suggests otherwise. Despite the global downturn, the German economy has been booming, exporting so many goods to the expanding markets of the developing world as well as to the rest of Europe that its net trade surplus—the net value of its exports over its imports—comes to 7 percent of its GDP, the highest of any major nation. Germany is anything but a low-wage country: The average hourly compensation—wages plus benefits—of German manufacturing workers is $48, well above the $32 hourly average for their American counterparts. Yet Germany is an export giant while the United States is the colossus of imports.

German multinationals have their own affiliates overseas, but they have also maintained robust, high-quality production at home. Siemens, which is more or less the German equivalent of General Electric, has hundreds of thousands of employees who work abroad, but it recently announced a deal with its major union, IG Metall, that included a pledge not to make any unilateral reductions in its 128,000-employee German workforce. BMW, ThyssenKrupp, and Daimler have gone even further, signing deals with IG Metall to maintain a fixed number of employees in Germany.

These domestic employee-retention pacts are an outgrowth of Germany's more consensual, stakeholder version of capitalism. German workers' organizations have a far greater say than American workers do in the conduct of their employers. By law, employees in large companies get the same number of seats on corporate boards that management does. Unions and management collaborate to ensure that German manufacturing retains and expands its high-quality products and markets. IG Metall has been working with automakers, for instance, to train workers to mass-produce electric cars. "Our goal is to really retain high-value-added manufacturing in Germany," Martin Allspach, the union's policy director, told me when I visited IG Metall headquarters in Frankfurt in November.

The German experience also shows that the structure of finance can have a profound effect on the retention of manufacturing. An entire stratum of German banking, municipally owned savings banks, provides the funds that enable the nation's prosperous, largely family-owned midsized manufacturers, the *Mittelstand,* to upgrade themselves into export dynamos. About two-thirds of Germany's small and midsized businesses get their loans from these banks, which shun capital markets and are restricted to doing business in their own towns. "Over the past decade, banking largely became a self-fulfilling activity," says Patrick Steinpass, the chief economist of the national organization of savings banks. "But our banks are restricted to doing business in their regions; they have to concentrate on the real economy."

The *Mittelstand* is thus able to remain largely immune from many of the pressures that financial markets, with their pressure for ever rising profits and share prices, inflict on American businesses. Klaas Hubner, a former member of Germany's Parliament and the owner of a *Mittelstand* company that sells axle-box housings to Chinese and other nations' high-speed railroads, believes that this freedom from American-style markets is the key to Germany's success. "We don't have short-term strategies, only long-term strategies," he told me. By preserving a vibrant sector of small-scale manufacturing, Germany also has a local capitalism. "I live where my company is located," Hubner said. "I want a good reputation in the town I live in."

No such localism can be found among American business leaders, whose brand of capitalism is keyed solely to their shareholders and top executives. "For a lot of American companies, their actual and psychic energy is focused abroad," says Matthew J. Slaughter, associate dean at Dartmouth's Tuck School of Business and a member of George W. Bush's Council of Economic Advisers from 2005 through 2007. The American way of business is aptly summarized in the McKinsey Global Institute's 2010 report on United States Multinational Corporations: "United States multinationals must pursue new growth opportunities and continually improve operations to remain globally competitive," it says. "They go where the markets are expanding, where the talent lives, and where they can earn superior returns."

J ust how mobile are these rootless corporations in their global chase for profits? It's hard to know, because they're anything but forthcoming about the extent of their employment abroad, much less the number of formerly United States jobs they've actually offshored. Some companies reveal the number of their foreign and domestic employees in their annual 10-K reports to the Securities and Exchange Commission, but many don't, as there's no requirement to do so. The Commerce Department's Bureau of Economic Analysis (BEA) releases its own report annually on the total number of workers employed by United States firms here at home and by their foreign subsidiaries. But there are almost no figures on how many employees work for foreign firms with which American companies contract to make all or part of their products—the Foxconns of the world.

Still, looking at the BEA data on foreign and domestic employment from 1982 through 2008 (the most recent year available) gives us some sense of the shift in the employment patterns of United States-based multinationals. In 1982, 26 percent of the workers at these companies worked for their foreign affiliates. As recently as 2000, that figure had increased only to 28.9 percent, but by 2008, it had risen to 36 percent. The same growing shift toward foreign employment is evident for leading multinationals. In 1992, Ford reported that 53 percent of its employees were in the United States and Canada; by 2009, the share of its workers in North America (including Mexico as well) had shrunk to 37 percent. In 1993, Caterpillar's workforce was 74 percent domestic; by 2008, it was just 46 percent domestic.

The flight of the multinationals to distant climes means the flight of our most advanced employers and of our best jobs. Though less than 1 percent of United States-based companies are multinationals, they account for 74 percent of the nation's private-sector research and development spending since 1990. They also pay better than other American employers—37 percent higher. The employees of their foreign affiliates come considerably cheaper. The BEA 2008 report on multinationals put the average (mean, not median) level of pay and benefits for United States employees at $65,067, while the figure for the employees of their foreign affiliates was $43,236. The figures for employees of unaffiliated contractors are almost never reported by the contractors or by the multinationals whose products they make;

indeed, the very identity of many such contractors and subcontractors is not publicly known. What we do know is that the Bureau of Labor Statistics reports that the average hourly compensation for manufacturing workers is $4.04 in Mexico and $1.36 in China.

As is not the case in Germany, then, America's leading companies are as close to barges as you can get, with the ability and incentive to move their operations abroad and to employ fewer workers, at lower pay, at home. Their failure to resume domestic hiring prolongs the high unemployment that makes it particularly hard for small businesses, which can't go abroad, to increase sales, get loans, and add new workers.

So what are we to do?

P resident Barack Obama, for one, understands the problem. "What is a danger is that we stay stuck in a new normal where unemployment rates stay high," he said in an interview aired on *60 Minutes* the Sunday following the midterm elections. "Businesses make big profits. But they've learned to do more with less." They've also learned to do more elsewhere.

In the absence of private-sector hiring, the recession will just keep rolling along unless the government radically shifts its trade and industrial policies and expands its own role in creating jobs. One approach, as Andy Grove, the former CEO of Intel, termed it in a *BloombergBusinessweek* article this summer, is to "rebuild our industrial commons." Grove proposes we levy a tax on imports from offshored labor and direct the proceeds to the kind of innovative high-tech company that he once led—if and only if such companies mass-produce their inventions here in the United States Tax credits for domestic manufacturing and job creation, tax cuts for corporations that invest and hire at home, and "Buy America" stipulations for government procurement are other ways to bolster domestic manufacturing and the creation of good jobs in the United States. No such provisions, however, were included in the semi-stimulus package of tax-cut extensions that the White House negotiated with congressional Republicans in December—extensions that will provide a modest boost to American consumers but likely not enough to jump-start small-business hiring.

The recession will just keep rolling along unless the government radically shifts its trade and industrial policies.

Another alternative to economic stagnation is a massive dose of investment in America's increasingly decrepit infrastructure, where employment is by its nature tied to place. Much of the funding would have to come from the government, but by no means all. A growing number of pension funds are investing in infrastructure projects alongside governments, though much of it is abroad: Cal PERs, the nation's largest pension fund, owns almost 13 percent of London's Gatwick Airport. What we need to bring such investments home are infrastructure banks, on both the federal and state level, that could leverage public and private funds for infrastructure projects in the United States

In an impressive display of industrial-strength chutzpah, corporate America is now demanding lower tax rates even as it daily disinvests in its home country. Worse yet, the new Congress seems likely to grant its wish—lowering taxes indiscriminately on those rare corporations that invest in America and on those more numerous corporations that abandon it. Is it too much to ask of the government that it discriminate between friend and foe? How about rewarding companies that pledge, as Siemens, Daimler, and BMW have in their own country, to keep or create a specified number of highly skilled jobs here at home? How about mandating, as Germany has, that companies put worker representatives on their boards, as a means of slowing corporate flight? America's economic decline is at bottom institutional, and reversing it requires institutional solutions that change the structure of American corporations.

Absent such reforms, the future trajectory of American corporations is clear. They will drift off, each on their barges, leaving behind them an America receding into penury and squalor.

Critical Thinking

1. How have American businesses been able to have high profits while the American economy is not doing well?

2. What role has the global economy played in this?

3. Where are large American corporations making their profits?

4. To quote the McKinsey Corporation's Global Institute 2010 Report on Global Corporations, "US multinationals must continually pursue new growth opportunities and improve global operations to remain competitive . . . They go where the markets are expanding, where the talent lives, and where they can earn superior returns." Why is this very bad news for the American economy?

Reprinted with permission from *The American Prospect,* by Harold Meyerson, March 2011, pp. 12-16. http://www.prospect.org. *The American Prospect,* 1710 Rhode Island Avenue, NW, 12th Floor, Washington, DC 20036. All rights reserved.

Test-Your-Knowledge Form

We encourage you to photocopy and use this page as a tool to assess how the articles in *Annual Editions* expand on the information in your textbook. By reflecting on the articles you will gain enhanced text information. You can also access this useful form on a product's book support website at www.mhhe.com/cls

NAME: DATE:

_____

TITLE AND NUMBER OF ARTICLE:

_____

BRIEFLY STATE THE MAIN IDEA OF THIS ARTICLE:

_____

LIST THREE IMPORTANT FACTS THAT THE AUTHOR USES TO SUPPORT THE MAIN IDEA:

_____

WHAT INFORMATION OR IDEAS DISCUSSED IN THIS ARTICLE ARE ALSO DISCUSSED IN YOUR TEXTBOOK OR OTHER READINGS THAT YOU HAVE DONE? LIST THE TEXTBOOK CHAPTERS AND PAGE NUMBERS:

_____

LIST ANY EXAMPLES OF BIAS OR FAULTY REASONING THAT YOU FOUND IN THE ARTICLE:

_____

LIST ANY NEW TERMS/CONCEPTS THAT WERE DISCUSSED IN THE ARTICLE, AND WRITE A SHORT DEFINITION:

NOTES

NOTES

NOTES

NOTES